Concurrent and Parallel Computing: Theory, Implementation and Applications

Concurrent and Parallel Computing: Theory, Implementation and Applications

Alexander S. Becker
Editor

Nova Science Publishers, Inc.
New York

Copyright © 2008 by Nova Science Publishers, Inc.

All rights reserved. No part of this book may be reproduced, stored in a retrieval system or transmitted in any form or by any means: electronic, electrostatic, magnetic, tape, mechanical photocopying, recording or otherwise without the written permission of the Publisher.

For permission to use material from this book please contact us:
Telephone 631-231-7269; Fax 631-231-8175
Web Site: http://www.novapublishers.com

NOTICE TO THE READER

The Publisher has taken reasonable care in the preparation of this book, but makes no expressed or implied warranty of any kind and assumes no responsibility for any errors or omissions. No liability is assumed for incidental or consequential damages in connection with or arising out of information contained in this book. The Publisher shall not be liable for any special, consequential, or exemplary damages resulting, in whole or in part, from the readers' use of, or reliance upon, this material. Any parts of this book based on government reports are so indicated and copyright is claimed for those parts to the extent applicable to compilations of such works.

Independent verification should be sought for any data, advice or recommendations contained in this book. In addition, no responsibility is assumed by the publisher for any injury and/or damage to persons or property arising from any methods, products, instructions, ideas or otherwise contained in this publication.

This publication is designed to provide accurate and authoritative information with regard to the subject matter covered herein. It is sold with the clear understanding that the Publisher is not engaged in rendering legal or any other professional services. If legal or any other expert assistance is required, the services of a competent person should be sought. FROM A DECLARATION OF PARTICIPANTS JOINTLY ADOPTED BY A COMMITTEE OF THE AMERICAN BAR ASSOCIATION AND A COMMITTEE OF PUBLISHERS.

LIBRARY OF CONGRESS CATALOGING-IN-PUBLICATION DATA

Concurrent and parallel computing : theory, implementation, and applications / Alexander S. Becker (editor).
   p. cm.
 ISBN 978-1-60456-274-3 (hardcover)
 1. Parallel programming (Computer science) I. Becker, Alexander S.
QA76.642.C67 2008
005.2'75--dc22
                                2007050802

Published by Nova Science Publishers, Inc. ✦ New York

CONTENTS

Preface   vii

Chapter 1   Caravela: A High Performance Stream-Based Concurrent Computing Platform   1
Shinichi Yamagiwa and Leonel Sousa

Chapter 2   Distributed Shared Memory Systems: Principles and Models   39
Azzedine Boukerche and Alba Cristina Magalhaes Alves de Melo

Chapter 3   Performance Analysis of Scheduling Parallel Tasks   67
Keqin Li

Chapter 4   Multi-channel Parallel Adaptation Theory for Rule Discovery   93
Li Min Fu

Chapter 5   An Overview of Parallel and Distributed Java for Heterogeneous Systems: Approaches and Open Issues   113
Jameela Al-Jaroodi, Nader Mohamed, Hong Jiang and David Swanson

Chapter 6   The Performance of Routing Algorithms under Bursty Traffic Loads   133
Timothy Mark Pinkston and Jeonghee Shin

Chapter 7   An Extension of Ambient Calculus for Un-nested Structures   149
Masaki Murakami

Chapter 8   Efficient Exploitation of Grids for Large-Scale Parallel Applications   165
Young Choon Lee, Riky Subrata and Albert Y. Zomaya

Chapter 9   Support and Efficiency of Nested Parallelism in OpenMP Implementations   185
Panagiotis E. Hadjidoukas and Vassilios V. Dimakopoulos

Chapter 10	A Parallel Implementation of an Iterative Reconstruction Algorithm Using a Space-Based Programming Model *P. Knoll and S. Mirzaei*	**205**
Chapter 11	Solving Maximum Concurrent Flow Problems in a Signal-Controlled Road Network *Suh-Wen Chiou*	**213**
Index		**235**

PREFACE

Concurrent computing is the concurrent (simultaneous) execution of multiple interacting computational tasks. These tasks may be implemented as separate programs, or as a set of processes or threads created by a single program. The tasks may also be executing on a single processor, several processors in close proximity, or distributed across a network. Concurrent computing is related to parallel computing, but focuses more on the interactions between tasks. Correct sequencing of the interactions or communications between different tasks, and the coordination of access to resources that are shared between tasks, are key concerns during the design of concurrent computing systems. This new book presents the latest research in the field from around the world.

The usage of computing resources located all over the world is becoming a major trend in distributed computing, since it allows the harnessing of all those idling resources into a massive pool of computational processing power, namely in order to tackle very large scale computational problems. Chapter 1 deals with stream-based computing, in particular the Caravela project and platform. Caravela is a distributed stream-based computing platform, which uses commodity video cards graphics processing units (GPUs) as the main processing units. This chapter presents the concepts and main ideas behind the Caravela platform, describing advanced optimization techniques employed for performing computations on GPUs and a new execution mechanism for distributed pipelined processing, called meta-pipeline. Experimental evaluation is performed by developing and running several different applications on the Caravela platform.

Distributed Shared Memory (DSM) is an abstraction that allows the use of the shared memory programming paradigm on a parallel or distributed environment where no physically shared memory exists. Recently, DSM has received a lot of attention since it provides a good tradeoff between performance and ease of programming. However, in order to design a cost effective DSMsystem, many choices must be made. In Chapter 2, we will cover the following aspects concerning the design of a DSM system: type of the DSMsystem, memory consistency model, memory coherence protocol, implementation level and fault tolerance issues. At the end of the chapter, we discuss five DSM systems in detail and present a comparative table.

We consider the problem of scheduling parallel tasks in parallel systems with identical processors and noncontiguous processor allocation. Chapter 3 contains two parts. In the first part, we are concerned with scheduling independent parallel tasks. We propose and analyze a simple approximation algorithm called H_m, where *m* is a positive integer. Algorithm H_m uses the harmonic system partitioning scheme as the processor allocation strategy. The algorithm has a moderate asymptotic worst-case performance ratio in the range $\left[1\frac{2}{3}..1\frac{13}{18}\right]$ for all m ≥ 6, and a small asymptotic worstcase performance ratio in the range $[1+1/(r+1)..1+1/r]$ when task sizes do not exceed $1/r$ of the total available processors, where $r > 1$ is an integer. Furthermore, we show that if the task sizes are independent and identically distributed (i.i.d.) uniform random variables and task execution times are i.i.d. random variables with finite mean and variance, then the asymptotic average-case performance ratio of algorithm H_m is no larger than 1.2898680..., and for an exponential distribution of task sizes, it does not exceed 1.2898305.... As demonstrated by our analytical as well as numerical results, the asymptotic average-case performance ratio improves significantly when tasks request for smaller numbers of processors. In the second part, we present and analyze an algorithm for scheduling precedence constrained parallel tasks. The algorithm is called LLH_m (Level-by-level and List scheduling using the Harmonic system partitioning scheme), where m ≥ 1 is a positive integer and a parameter of the harmonic system partitioning scheme. There are three basic techniques employed in algorithm LLH_m. First, a task graph is divided into levels and tasks are scheduled level by level to follow the precedence constraints. Second, tasks in the same level are scheduled using algorithm H_m developed earlier for scheduling independent parallel tasks. The list scheduling method is used to implement algorithm H_m. Third, the harmonic system partitioning scheme is used as the processor allocation strategy. It is shown that for wide task graphs and some common task size distributions, as m increases and the task sizes become smaller, the asymptotic average-case performance ratio of algorithm LLH_m approaches one.

In Chapter 4, we introduce a new machine learning theory based on multi-channel parallel adaptation for rule discovery. This theory is distinguished from the familiar parallel-distributed adaptation theory of neural networks in terms of channel-based convergence to the target rules. We show how to realize this theory in a learning system named CFRule. CFRule is a parallel weight-based model, but it departs from traditional neural computing in that its internal knowledge is comprehensible. Furthermore, when the model converges upon training, each channel converges to a target rule. The model adaptation rule is derived by multi-level parallel weight optimization based on gradient descent. Since, however, gradient descent only guarantees local optimization, a multi-channel regression-based optimization strategy is developed to effectively deal with this problem. Formally, we prove that the CFRule model can explicitly and precisely encode any given rule set. Also, we prove a property related to asynchronous parallel convergence, which is a critical element of the multi-channel parallel adaptation theory for rule learning. Thanks to the quantizability nature of the CFRule model, rules can be extracted completely and soundly via a threshold-based mechanism. Finally, the practical application of the theory is demonstrated in DNA promoter recognition and hepatitis prognosis prediction.

Java is gaining considerable recognition as the most suitable language for developing distributed applications in heterogeneous systems due to its portability and machine independence. However, standard Java does not provide easy-to-use features for parallel application development. Therefore, considerable research has been conducted and is underway to provide users with tools and programming models to write parallel applications in Java. This paper reviews a number of representative research projects and outlines the primary approaches used in these projects that enable Java to provide high performance parallel and distributed computing in heterogeneous systems. Chapter 5 shows that most projects fit within one of the following parallel programming models: (1) message (or object-) passing, (2) distributed shared address (or object), (3) multi-threaded, and (4) transparent (or towards seamless) parallelization. Within these categories, the different implementation approaches are discussed. The paper also identifies and discusses a number of related problems and open issues such as benchmarks, porting legacy applications, distributed environment overhead and security.

Routing algorithms are traditionally evaluated under Poisson-like traffic distributions. This type of traffic is smooth over large time intervals and has been shown not necessarily to be representative to that of real network loads in parallel processing and communication environments. Bursty traffic, on the other hand, has been shown to be more representative of the type of load generated by multiprocessor and local area network (LAN) applications, but it has been seldom used in the evaluation of network routing algorithms. Chapter 6 investigates how bursty traffic—specifically, self-similar traffic—affects the performance of well-known interconnection network routing algorithms. Various packet sizes, network resources (i.e., virtual channels) and spatial traffic patterns are used in the analysis. This allows the ability to evaluate performance under load non-uniformities in both time and space which differs from previous research that applies non-uniformity in only the space domain, such as with bit-reversal, matrix transpose, and hot-spot traffic patterns.

One of the important issues on management of data materials such as documents, databases and/or softwares is access control. Chapter 7 presents a formal model of access control of data materials in an organization that consists of a number of user groups. The model presented here is an extension of ambient calculus. As ambient calculus is introduced to model behavior of mobile systems such as agents accessing firewalls, it assumed that target systems have nested structures. We extend the calculus to represent unnested structures of user groups of materials. An example of user authentication protocol is presented.

The grid computing platform has become a promising alternative to high-performance parallel computing systems including supercomputers, mainly due to its affordability, scalability, and capability. Over the past decade, many different types of grids have been constructed to mostly deal with large-scale problems in science and engineering—high-energy physics, bioinformatics, and data-mining. Numerous parallel applications have been developed, and deployed onto grids to solve these problems. Bag-of-tasks (BoT) is a typical application model identified in those parallel applications. An application in this model consists of a large number of independent tasks. Although the scheduling of BoT applications seems to be simple, the heterogeneity and dynamicity of resources on grids much complicate this scheduling. Due to the NP-hardness of the BoT scheduling problem, most previously proposed scheduling algorithms are heuristics. Chapter 8 surveys various BoT scheduling approaches proposing a taxonomy of such algorithms. A set of projects closely related to BoT scheduling on grids are then presented followed by a discussion on the issues, in BoT scheduling, that need further investigation.

Nested parallelism has been a major feature of OpenMP since its very beginnings. As a programming style, it provides an elegant solution for a wide class of parallel applications, with the potential to achieve substantial utilization of the available computational resources, in situations where outer-loop parallelism simply can not. Notwithstanding its significance, nested parallelism support was slow to find its way into OpenMP implementations, commercial and research ones alike. Even nowadays, the level of support is varying greatly among compilers and runtime systems.

In Chapter 9, we take a closer look at OpenMP implementations with respect to their level of support for nested parallelism. We classify them into three broad categories: those that provide full support, those that provide partial support and those that provide no support at all. The systems surveyed include commercial and research ones. Additionally, we proceed to quantify the efficiency of the implementation. With a representative set of compilers that provide adequate support, we perform a comparative performance evaluation. We evaluate both the incurred overheads and their overall behavior, using microbenchmarks and a full-fledged application. The results are interesting because they show that full support of nested parallelism does not necessarily guarantee scalable performance.

Iterative algorithms to reconstruct single photon emission computerized tomography (SPECT) data are based on the mathematical simulation of the acquisition process. The reconstruction times of these methods are much longer than that of routinely used reconstruction methods (such as filtered back projection). Java, a platform independent programming language changed the way of software design by using Jini and JavaSpaces, new technologies that have been introduced recently. By applying JavaSpaces, a *space* is used to store objects persistently which can be used also for effective parallel processing. In Chapter 10, we report a novel approach for iterative reconstruction of SPECT data by means of JavaSpaces, which uses only a standard personal computer equipment and results in significant improvement of reconstruction time due to the fact that several layers of the object are computed in parallel.

An optimal design of concurrent flows in a signal-controlled road network is considered. The input to the problem is a traffic road network with signal-controlled junctions. A set of travel demands needs to be routed where route choices of users are taken into account. In Chapter 11 a mathematical optimization problem is formulated for which the objective is to find a delay-minimizing signal setting such that the largest value of a fraction of every demand can be simultaneously routed without exceeding the available capacities on edges. A fast algorithm globally solving signal settings and maximum concurrent flows is presented together with numerical calculations on example road networks. Improvement on a locally optimal search is achieved by combining the technique of parallel tangents with the gradient projection. As it shows, the proposed algorithm combines the locally optimal search and globally search heuristic achieved substantially promising performance with relatively less computational efforts when compared to traditional methods.

In: Concurrent and Parallel Computing...
Editor: Alexander S. Becker, pp. 1-37

ISBN 978-1-60456-274-3
© 2008 Nova Science Publishers, Inc.

Chapter 1

CARAVELA: A HIGH PERFORMANCE STREAM-BASED CONCURRENT COMPUTING PLATFORM

Shinichi Yamagiwa[*] *and Leonel Sousa*[†]
INESC-ID/IST, TU Lisbon
Rua Alves Redol, 1000-029, Lisboa, Portugal

Abstract

The usage of computing resources located all over the world is becoming a major trend in distributed computing, since it allows the harnessing of all those idling resources into a massive pool of computational processing power, namely in order to tackle very large scale computational problems. This chapter deals with stream-based computing, in particular the Caravela project and platform. Caravela is a distributed stream-based computing platform, which uses commodity video cards graphics processing units (GPUs) as the main processing units. This chapter presents the concepts and main ideas behind the Caravela platform, describing advanced optimization techniques employed for performing computations on GPUs and a new execution mechanism for distributed pipelined processing, called meta-pipeline. Experimental evaluation is performed by developing and running several different applications on the Caravela platform.

1. Introduction

Worldwide distributed computing has become one of the most remarkable application of anonymous computing power, due to the rise and development of distributed execution platforms. These platforms can be based on message passing computing, using a server software such as Globus [18], or a mobile agent-based, migrating among the resources structured as a virtual network [12]. According to published research results [5, 20], worldwide distributed computing is effective in achieving ultra computing power, by the huge

---

[*]E-mail address: yama@inesc-id.pt
[†]E-mail address: las@inesc-id.pt

potential of computing power provided by idling computers spread all over the world. This computing architecture is usually called GRID computing [29]. One of most important issue on GRID computing platform is security, both for users and the peers providing the computing resources.

Stream-based processing is expected to become the most influential a paradigm for the next generation of high performance computing platforms, due to the high extensibility and scalability for concurrent processing [15]. The Cell processor [16] is an example of a recent multi-core processor that is well suited for stream-based processing. Another approach is to take advantage of the Graphics Processing Units (GPUs) that equip the majority of personal computers, for stream-based general purpose processing. Nowadays, the need for realistic graphics scene representations, particularly in the entertainment market, has promoted the growth of GPU performance by leaps and bounds in recent years. This growth-rate has already exceed the ratio defined by the Moore's law [28]. Since GPUs have become commodity components in almost all personal computers, instead of being confined to high-performance computing systems, researchers have been focusing their attention on GPU's potential, as a high performing computational platform. Thus, GPUs are being regarded as new high performance computing platforms, with the ability of speeding up computations and freeing Central Processing Units (CPU) for other tasks.

Contemporary GPUs are fully programmable, which allows their usage in general purpose applications. However, the burden of achieving efficiency rests upon the users/programmers knowledge of graphics processing details, in order to use the GPU resources efficiently. For example, the output of any calculations made on a GPU are performed by rendering to a screen buffer. This mechanism is responsible for one of the main differences in the memory interface and the control of the GPUs, while comparing to CPUs. Therefore, it is up to the programmer to wander between the controlling code for GPU and the one representing the algorithm of the target application. Thus, to allow the programmer to focus on the algorithm without the need of knowing the details of the graphics runtime environment, it is needed to implement a uniform programming interface for GPU-based applications.

The stream-based execution style of programming a GPU has input data streams processed by the core GPU processor in order to generate output data streams. One of the major characteristics of the stream-based processing model is that the GPU does not touch any resource located in the CPU side. Therefore, this execution model can addresses the security issue on GRID referred above. We thus propose a distributed computing platform based on GPUs and on the stream-based computing model. Although it automatically solves the security problem, we need to address the interface disparities when we apply GPUs as the processing units in a distributed computing platform.

A new task unit called *flow-model* is proposed in order to provide a transparent interface to the programmer. Focusing in the flow-model task concept, Caravela project stems many innovative representing extensions and applications centered on the basic flow-model execution mechanism, as shown in Figure 1. The tree is still growing with new leaves, such as optimization techniques for GPU-based applications, a new execution mechanism for stream-based processing environments, and new algorithms that fit to GPU-based computation. In this chapter we report the recent results achieved while researching the Caravela project, which is devoted to the development of models, methods, algorithms and tools for

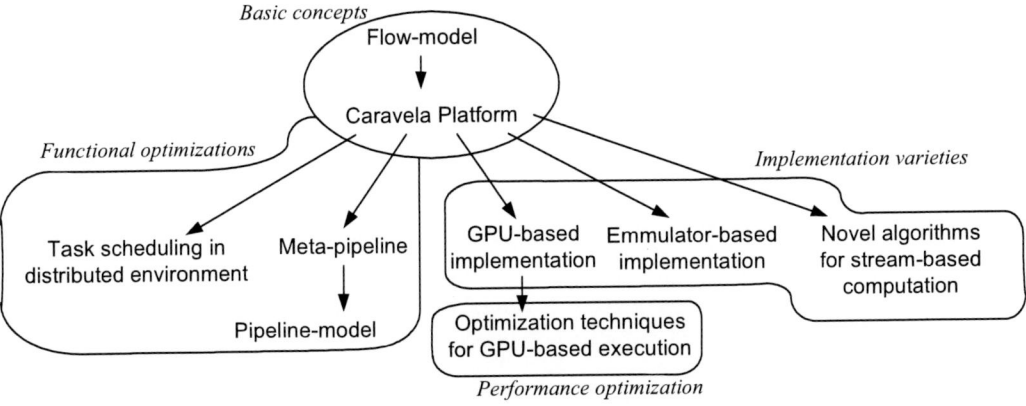

Figure 1. The growing branches of Caravela project.

distributed stream-based computing, namely on GPUs. The next sections present the most significant contributions of the Caravela project and are structured around the following topics.

- **The Caravela platform**, the main target of our research project, is able to setup and form a distributed computing environment for stream-based processing; a first implementation of the Caravela platform is based on GPUs as the processing units.

- **The proposed buffering optimization technique for flow-model execution on GPUs** provides an extension to the Caravela platform for efficiently implementing recursive computations based on the flow-model, which requires feedback from output to input streams. This kind of optimization technique is considered as one of the most important for implementing distributed computing platforms, since the local (GPU) execution must be fast to achieve adequate performance of distributed computing.

- **The Meta-pipeline** implements a new execution mechanism of flow-models using the basic functionality of the Caravela platform. It is also an extension of the Caravela platform that allows to execute multiple flow-models in a pipeline-like manner.

The next section gives a description of the background and motivations of the Caravela project in detail, and points out the long term goals of the Caravela project. Section 3. and section 4. show the design and the implementation of the Caravela platform that, with the referred extensions, is the main product of our research. Section 5. presents a preliminary evaluation of the Caravela Project. Finally, section 6. summarizes this chapter and presents to the following steps of the Caravela project.

2. Backgrounds and Motivations

2.1. GRID Computing

Among the platforms for GRID computing, there are several methods for implementing mechanisms to provide resources for users and to remotely use those resources. One of them is Globus [18], a well known message passing-based platform for GRID computing. The users of the Globus platform can write programs as MPI-based parallel applications [21]. Therefore, applications which have been parallelized by using MPI functions can easily migrated from a local cluster, or a supercomputer-based environment, to the Globus platform. Another example is the agent-based implementation Condor-G [12]. This kind of implementation is mainly used for managing resources in a GRID. The tasks performed in such platforms using remote computing resources are assigned anonymously. It is very difficult for users and peers to trust each other and be sure that the tasks never damage the computing resource and are not damaged by some malicious access. Therefore, in any implementation of GRID platforms the security must be considered as one of the most important issues to be solved.

To achieve trustful communication among users and contributors of computing resources, any GRID platform must address the following main security issues.

- **Data security exchanged among processing resources via network**
  When a program is assigned to a remote processing unit, it must be sent to the resource and, also, the input data must be received by the program. The data transferred via the network can be snooped by a third person using available tools such as tcpdump. This means that the users cannot trust the system. This problem is also a security issue in web-based applications. Therefore, data encryption such as SSL (Secure Socket Layer) is added to the connections between computing resources [11].

- **Program and data security on remote resources**
  On GRID environments, users assign their programs to unknown machines anywhere in the world. Therefore, the users don't want any of the program content or the data be snooped, tampered or stolen by the resource owners. For overcoming this problem, the GRID platforms force the creation of an account for the user that is managed by the administrator.

- **Resource security during program execution**
  This is the most dangerous security problem of the platform. When a program is dispatched by the user to a remote computing resource, it may make use of all the facilities of the resource. This is the typical behavior of a computer *virus*. The GRID environment must have capabilities to restrict the permissions of user programs. Therefore, a GRID platform generally has resource management tools such as GRMS [13].

The first security problem introduced above can be solved by encrypting the data exchanged between resources and users. The second problem can be solved by the administrator of the computing resources, for example by creating user accounts. However, in what respects the third problem, although some solutions can tackle the user program access to resources, such as Java's RMI (Remote Method Invocation) mechanism [14] by restricting the available resources to the program in the virtual machine, it is very hard to configure the restrictions for all the applications. For this reason, in some applications which need to access special resources on a remote host, Java allows the user program to open a potential security hole by using JNI (Java Native Interface) [24]. However, this is inconsistent with the proposed security wall of the virtual machine. Therefore, new mechanisms have to be considered for developing and executing programs in remote systems.

2.2. General Purpose Computation Using GPU

Graphical applications, especially 3D graphics visualization techniques, have dramatically advanced in the last decade. Even in commodity personal computers high performance GPUs are available. The power of GPUs is now growing immensely: for example, hundreds of Giga Floating-point Operations Per Second (GFLOPS) can be achieved by a NVIDIA's Geforce7, which compares quite favorably to the tens of GFLOPS of Intel Core2Duo processors. This is a remarkable and attractive computational resource available for applications that demand huge computation load.

Nowadays, researchers of high performance computing are focusing the research on the performance of GPUs, and researching the possibility for its usage as a replacement for CPUs. The application of the General-Purpose computation on GPU (GPGPU) concept allows to achieve high performance levels [23] [26]. Compiler-oriented support for programming general-purpose applications using GPU resources has already been proposed [6]. Moreover, a cluster-based approach using PCs with high performant GPUs has been reported in [10].

We will now explain the processing steps and architecture that allows GPUs to generate graphics objects in order to display them on a screen. The GPU acts as a co-processor of the CPU via a peripheral bus, such as the AGP or the PCI Express bus, as shown in the Figure 2. A Video RAM (VRAM) is connected to the GPU, which reads/writes graphics objects from/to the VRAM. The CPU controls the GPU operation by sending the object data to the VRAM and a program to the GPU, thus controlling the overall execution of the program.

Figure 3 shows the processing steps performed by the GPU to create a graphical image, and store it in a frame buffer in order to be displayed in a screen. First, the graphics data is prepared as a set of normalized vertices of objects on a referential axis defined by the graphics designer (Figure 3(a)). The vertices will be sent to a vertex processor, in order to change the size or the perspective of the object, which is performed by calculating rotations and transformations of the coordinates. In this step all objects are mapped to a standardized referential axis. In the next step, a rasterizer interpolates the coordinates and defines the planes that form the graphics objects (Figure 3(b)). Finally, a pixel processor receives these planes from the rasterizer, calculates the composed RGB colors from the textures of the objects and sends this color data to the frame buffer (Figure 3(c)). The color data in the frame buffer then can be finally displayed in a screen.

In recent GPUs, the vertex and pixel processors are programmable. The designers of graphics scenes can make programs targeting these specific processors, which must run fast in order to achieve the required number of frames per second. These processors have dedicated floating point processing pipelines that can be also used for GPGPU. However, the output data of the rasterizer, composed by fixed hardware, is exclusively sent to the pixel processor and can not be fetched by the CPU. Thus, in general GPGPU applications only the computing power of the pixel processor is used due to its programmability capabilities and flexibility for I/O data control.

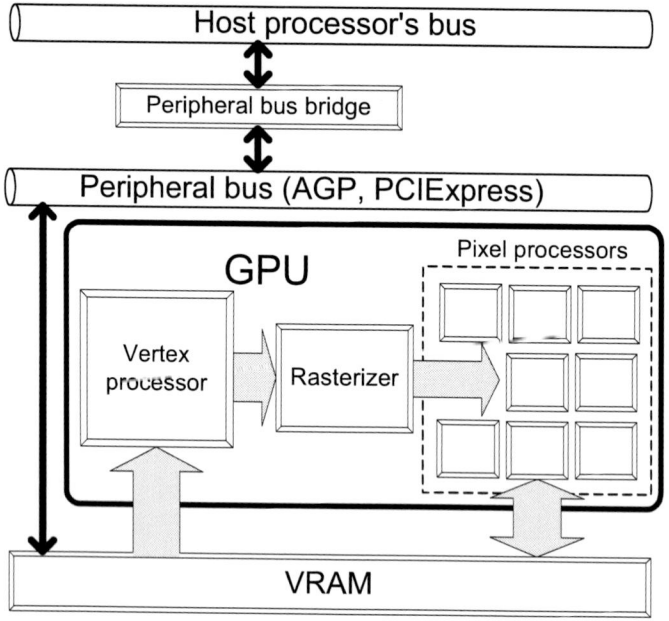

Figure 2. Organization around GPU.

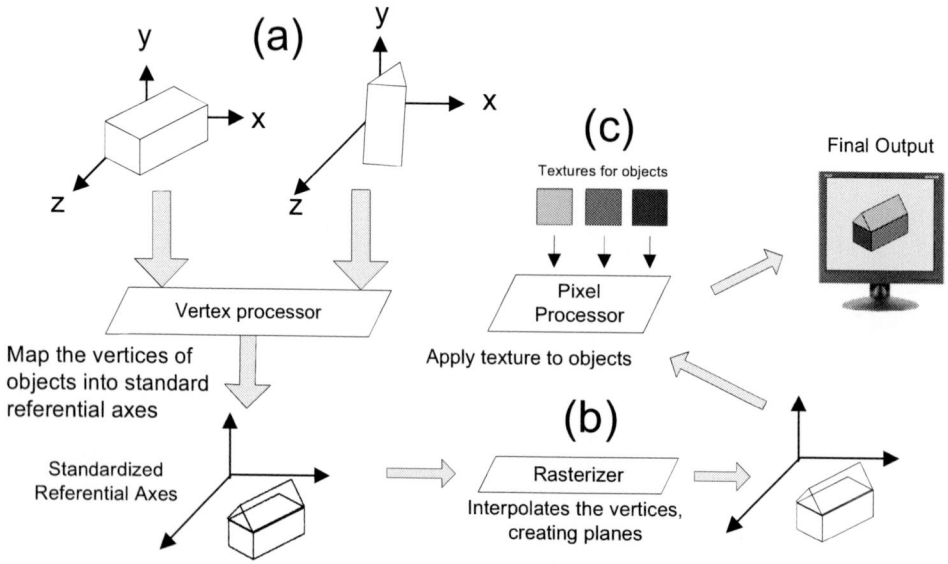

Figure 3. Processing steps for graphics rendering.

The main focus in this chapter is not only the performance of GPUs, but also the execution model on GPUs. As shown above, the pixel processor does not touch any resources and the data sent to it is a stream of massive input data. Then it processes each data unit (pixel color data) and outputs a data stream. This means that the program on the GPU works in a closed environment. Moreover, it is possible to write programs in standard languages, such as the DirectX assembly language, the High Level Shader Language (HLSL) [19], and the OpenGL Shading Language [22]. Thus, the program can be executed on any GPU connected to any computer.

2.3. Functional Comparisons between Graphics Runtimes

To implement GPGPU, programmers need to have practical tools and methodologies to program and to control the execution of the programs. It is worth to note that Operating System (OS) software that runs on CPU is designed to manage general computer resources such as processes, memory and general I/O interfaces. The tools that integrate interfaces for controlling GPU hardware are supported on graphics runtime environments. In recent years, two major graphics runtime environments are available: DirectX [19][1] and OpenGL [27]. To efficiently support multiple graphics runtime environments, care should be taken to understand their differences both in methods and features. For example, if a graphics runtime environment has special functions for tuning performance, the programmer would like to be sure that the application program takes advantage of those functions.

When a GPGPU application is designed, one of the most important issues is the compatibility of graphics runtime environments with different Operating Systems. The DirectX is embedded into Windows. Therefore, its functionality is supported trustfully as long as we are using Windows, but it is not compatible with other OSs such as Linux[2].

On the other hand, OpenGL has been ported to almost all available OS in the market. For Windows, the basic functions are available in the *opengl32* dynamic library. However, for example, an application using vertex or pixel processor needs the functions of OpenGL Extension Specification implemented by GLEW (The OpenGL Extension Wrangler Library) [2] which provides an interface to create program object for the processors. A uniform programming interface for GPGPU not only facilitates GPU programming, but also can automatically take care of the different features of the runtime environments in order to achieve the best performance.

2.3.1. GPU Resource Management

Like multiprocessor systems, GPGPU applications may want take advantage when multiple GPUs are available in a computer, in order to perform concurrently computation. A uniform programming interface for GPGPU should individually manage these GPUs if they are available on the graphics runtime environments.

DirectX is able to manage multiple video adapters separately. It can allow resources, such as input textures, to be allocated separately. Therefore, the applications can be invoked

---

[1] The major DirectX versions currently are 9 and 10. To both versions, the considerations and the observations in this section can be applied.

[2] Although the DirectX9 of WINE [17] emulates the DirectX runtime, Linux itself does not have any native runtime for DirectX.

concurrently on multiple GPUs with accurate controls for the separated resources. On the contrary, OpenGL uses a default video adapter via GLUT [3]. This interface does not allow specifying which video adapter is used. Thus, the application program must accommodate both situations, but automatically switches to a single adapter mode if OpenGL is being used.

2.3.2. Shader Language and Compiler

GPU can execute a dedicated program written in a shader program language. The graphics runtime environments can accept high-level shader language or assembly language. The differences appear at the translation level of the shader code.

DirectX accepts both assembly language and high level languages. The shader code written in the assembly language must follow the *Shader Model* specified by Microsoft. The shader program begins with the shader version instruction, such as `ps_3_0` for Pixel Shader Model 3.0. The assembly-based shader code is assembled by using the `D3DXAssembleShader()` function. The High Level Shader Language (HLSL) is a C language like interface for the shader programming. The compilation is performed by the `D3DXCompileShader()` function. This function takes one of the shader model versions available on the target GPU. The shader version supported by a target GPU is dependent on the GPU architecture. For example, NVIDIA's GeForce7 supports Shader Model 3.0, while GeForce6 only supports versions up to 2.0. This means that even if a shader program is written in HLSL, loop statements are unrolled in GeForce6, because it can not use the loop instruction only supported by the Shader Model 3.0 and above.

DirectX provides a software emulator that supports the Shader Model 3.0 at runtime. This emulator was originally used for the reference design for driver developers. However, a regular user can use this emulator as a substitute of a programmable GPU hardware. Thus, it is possible to validate the shader code behavior even without the corresponding GPU hardware.

OpenGL supports GLSL (OpenGL Shader Language) [22] for writing shader programs. The compilation of a shader program is performed by using the `glCompileShaderARB` function, which uses the compiler functionality of the video driver. Therefore, the syntax checking, restrictions and optimizations are dependent on the driver vendors, even though the basic syntax follows the GLSL specification. In OpenGL, the global variable `GLEW_ARB_fragment_shader` indicates if the GPU is programmable. Because OpenGL does not provide any software emulator, it is impossible to check the behavior of the shader unless programmable GPU hardware is available.

2.3.3. Buffers' Sizes and Memory Management for Graphics

Maximum sizes of input textures and output frame buffers are a constraint that limits the maximum problem size. Since the Video RAM (VRAM) connected to GPU is a limited resource, sizes of texture and frame buffer are defined by the graphics runtime environments. DirectX limits the sizes of texture and frame buffer to the maximum display size, such as 1024x768. OpenGL allows the maximum possible size to be independent of screen size, being possible to create 4096x4096 pixel textures with the recent GPU hardware.

Caravela: A High Performance Stream-Based Concurrent Computing Platform

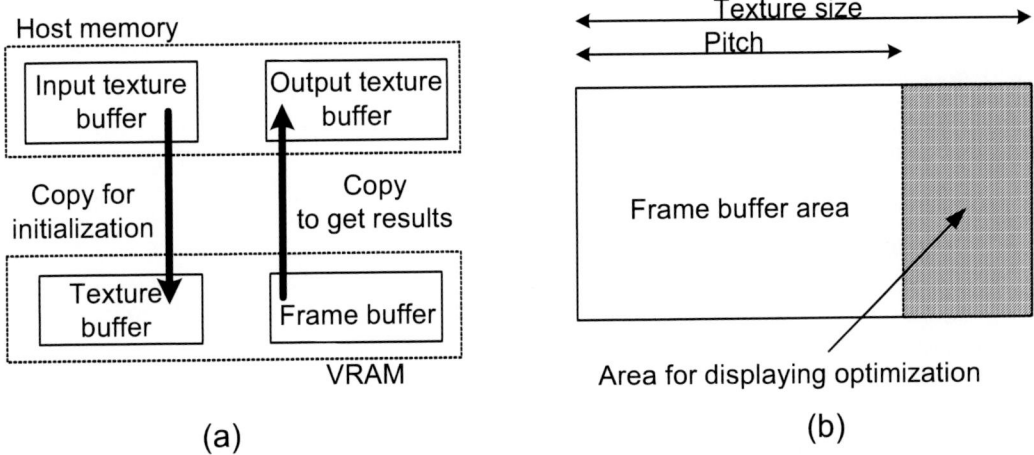

Figure 4. Buffer management for graphics: (a) location of buffers in memory; (b) frame buffer data organization.

The graphics runtime environments provide functions to allocate buffers for input textures and frame buffers. The buffers are allocated on host memory and on VRAM as shown in Figure 4(a). At the execution of a shader program, the input texture buffer allocated on the host memory is copied to the one allocated on the VRAM. Frame output buffers are allocated in the same way and data is copied back from the VRAM to the host memory.

With DirectX, input texture buffer and frame buffer (called *render target*) are created in runtime, namely through the `CreateTexture` method –*Usage* argument specifies the type of the texture, 0 for the input texture and D3DUSAGE_RENDERTARGET for a frame buffer, and have the special memory arrangement shown in Figure 4(b). It includes an optimization area for displaying optimizations, where application is forbidden to touch. Therefore, to initialize input data or to get output data, GPGPU application has to write/read the data considering the *pitch* length. This mechanism prevents dynamically exchange of a texture defined as an input texture with another defined as a frame buffer, because the buffer properties can only be modified by the `CreateTexture` method. Therefore, the data of input texture and the one of frame buffer must be copied to/from the VRAM when the GPGPU application needs to exchange data located in those buffers.

The situation with OpenGL is different, because it manages input textures and frame buffers by defining them just as "textures" which are linked to the target buffers. For example, when a frame buffer is allocated in VRAM by the `glTexImage2D()` function, it will be attached to the frame buffer by the `glFramebufferTexture2DEXT()` function. Applications can change the attachment of the input texture and output frame buffers by using the `glActiveTexture()` and the `glBindTexture()` functions. This means OpenGL is able to dynamically control the pointers to the input texture and the frame buffers in the GPU. Moreover, the data buffer for texture can be provided as a buffer dynamically allocated by application itself, which means that the buffer that holds data to be copied to VRAM is not allocated by the graphics runtime. For example, the `glTexSubImage2D()` function copies the texture data to VRAM and the `glReadBuffer()` function copies the texture data from VRAM. These functions can accept a buffer pointer dynamically allocated on host memory by application. Thus, applications have only to pass the pointer from the frame buffer to the input texture to feedback data for further calculations on GPU. Therefore, OpenGL is now suitable for recursive applications, where previous output data are used in the subsequent computations.

2.4. Discussion

We have focused our research work devising a general and efficient stream-based computing model (flow-model) and developing a distributed/concurrent computing platform based on GPU resources, named *Caravela platform* [7] [30] [32] [33]. The primary aim of the Caravela platform is to implement a high performance and seamless stream-based computing environment based on the proposed flow-model. This model also addresses the security drawback on conventional anonymous world wide distributed computing environment. With the flow-model, no resources around the processing units have to be touched. When GPUs are applied as the processing units, it means no other resources of a computer are used, such as CPU, computer memory and general peripherals, which are all connected to the GPU through a peripheral bus.

To develop an effective distributed computing environment we need to consider mechanisms for executing tasks on remote processing units and to communicate between to those distributed tasks. Moreover, these mechanisms have to be efficiently implemented in order to exploit the capacity of a GPU-based distributed computing platform. Since GPUs have appeared as new type of processing units based on stream-based processing approach, it is also important to research new techniques to extract parallelism and to take advantage of their potentialities for general purpose computing. From this point of view, at least programming interfaces have to be adjusted and disparities of the different graphics runtime environments used to control GPU operation have to be eliminated. For example, with actual Application Programming Interfaces (APIs) when a program for matrix computation produces an NxN matrix the programmer needs to setup a frame buffer where the output matrix is considered to be an NxN pixel plane. Although this is adequated for a graphics application it does not make sense for GPGPU applications. Thus, it is important to define a new API for GPGPU that hides the graphical legacy of GPU. This API should not only hide the graphics runtime details but also to absorb the differences between the different graphics runtimes. Specific programming interfaces for a particular types of graphics cards, e.g. for a given vendor, such as the Compute Unified Device Architecture (CUDA) from NVIDIA [8], are not considered in this work.

Two main aspects are relevant to address the problem of disparity between the graphics environments: the level of complexity to program general purpose applications on GPUs and the achieved performance. To solve the problem of disparities between graphics runtime environments and to adapt the programming to the general purpose processing requirements and characteristics, some solutions have been proposed, such as Sh [1], Scout [25] and Brook [6]. Sh is a graphics processing interface with an object oriented interface for C++. The program for pixel processor is written in Sh language and Sh performs the difficult task of controlling the graphics runtime environments. Scout is another wrapper for graphics that uses a language based on C*. Although details of graphics runtime are hidden

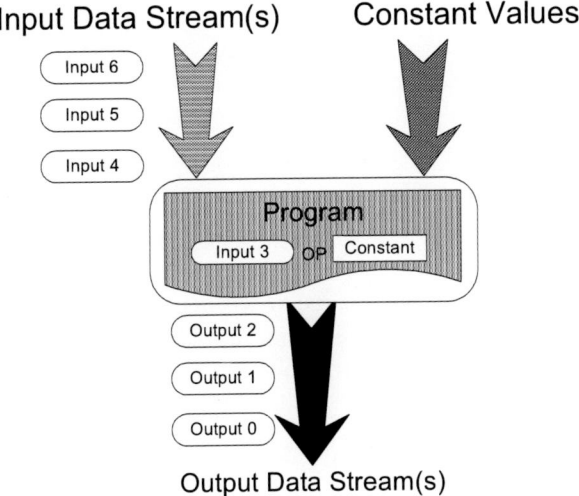

Figure 5. Structure of the flow-model.

in these two cases, they are still targeted for visual applications. Therefore, the programmer can not completely forget graphical dependent environments or issues. Brook is a compiler-oriented interface for GPU-based applications for which programmer just needs to identify functions, with a special keyword (*kernel*), to be transposed to programs on a pixel processor (this program is called *pixel shader*). Although this interface seems to be one of the best solutions for the problem mentioned above, it is hard in practice to tune the performance, namely in what concerns memory access (buffer's management).

Thus, this chapter proceeds by depicting the main aim of the Caravela project, presenting the design and the main implementation aspects of the Caravela platform. It also discusses extensions to the Caravela introduced very recently, namely a new execution mechanism for pipelined processing. In addition, we will show buffering optimization techniques that were implemented to eliminate disparity problems discussed above and to achieve the best performance in memory access.

3. Caravela Platform

3.1. Flow-Model

The execution unit of the Caravela platform is defined as the *flow-model*. As shown in Figure 5, the flow-model is composed of input/output data streams, of constant parameter inputs and of a program which processes the input data streams and generates output data streams, by fetching each input data unit from the input streams. The application program in Caravela is executed as stream-based computation, such as the one of a dataflow processor. However, the input data stream of the flow-model can be accessed randomly because the input data streams are just memory buffers for the program that uses the data. On the other hand, the output data streams are sequences based on the unit of data in the stream. Thus, the program embedded in the flow-model is not able to touch other resources beyond the

I/O data streams.

The ability of a flow-model to represent general purpose computation is one of the issues for the discussion. Although the same type of representation is available for PetriNets, due to the dataflow-like processing style, the flow-model admits loops iterated a finite number of times, which is also supported by the Caravela runtime; the Caravela runtime operates as a resource manager for flow-models. To implement a loop with the flow-model, the output data stream(s) are connected to the input data stream(s), providing data migration among the stream buffers.

The flow-model provides the advantage when applied in distributed environments of encapsulating all the methods to execute a task into a data structure. Therefore, the flow-model can be managed as a task object distributed anywhere, and can be fetched by the Caravela runtime. For example, when a flow-model is placed in a remote machine, an application over Caravela platform can fetch and reproduce the execution mechanism from the remote flow-model.

Regarding the processing unit to be assigned to a flow-model program, any software-based emulator, hardware data-flow processor, dedicated processor hardware, or others, can be applied.

3.2. Runtime Environment

The flow-model execution requires a managing system, which assigns and loads the flow-model program into a processing unit, allocates memory buffers for input/output data streams, copies the input data streams to the allocated buffers and triggers the start of the program. In addition, after program execution, the runtime may need to read back the data from the output stream buffers to forward it to other flow-model or to store it. The Caravela runtime defines two types of functionalities for flow-model execution: the local and the remote execution functions.

For the execution in a local processing unit the runtime checks if the program in the flow-model matches the specification of a local processing unit. To support the remote execution of the flow-model, the Caravela runtime needs a function to respond to requests sent in the Caravela platform by a remote processing resource. The servers placed in the remote resources are categorized into two different types: *worker* and *broker* servers.

- **Worker server**

  The worker server acts as a processing resource that assigns one flow-model to its local processing unit. This server communicates with its client to send/receive output/input data of the flow-model. If an execution request from a client does not include the flow-model itself but an information of the location of the flow-model, the server will fetch it from this location. Then, the server will assign the flow-model to the local processing unit.

- **Broker server**

  The broker server performs as a router to reach the worker servers. The worker servers, after activation, send a request to register its route to one of broker servers. The broker server can have a parent broker server that accepts to register the route to a child broker. This mechanism creates a tree shaped worker network with broker

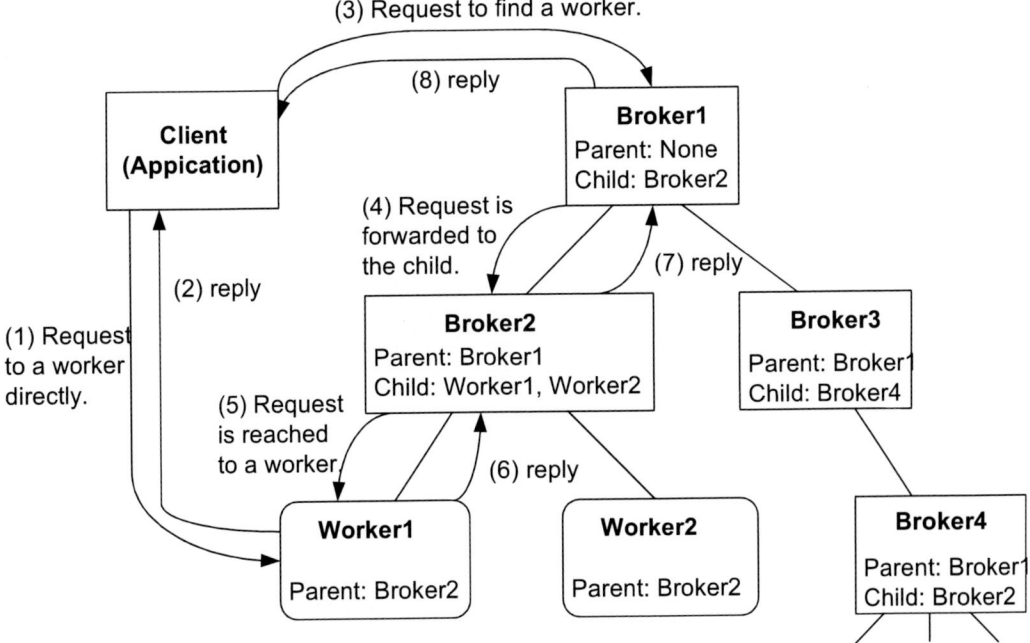

Figure 6. Caravela network example.

servers as trunks of a tree. We call this tree-based virtual network the *Caravela network*.

Figure 6 shows an example of a Caravela network. The workers (Worker1 and Worker2) "belong" to the Broker1 and Broker2. Let us assume that a client tries to find a worker in the Caravela network and sends a request to the Worker1 directly (Figure 6 (1)). In this case, the client must know the route to the Worker1. The reply will be returned to the client directly (Figure 6 (2)). When the client sends the same request to the Broker1 (Figure 6 (3)), the Broker1 will forward the request to the Broker2 according to the routing information about the child (Figure 6(4)). The Broker2 knows that the Worker1 is its children and forwards the request to it (Figure 6 (5)). Finally, the request is processed and an answer returns by the opposite direction of the request and reaches the client (Figure 6(6)(7)(8)).

For security matters, but also to respect resource limitation, the broker and the worker servers may not accept flow-models that specify larger data streams than the limits configured by the servers. This mechanism protects the contributors' environment from the trouble caused by memory overflow. Moreover, the worker servers may specify also a time limitation for the flow-model execution unit: when the time spent by our application exceeds the limit, the worker server may cancel the subsequent flow-model execution. This mechanism allows the resource contributors to configure the percentage of his/her contribution for anonymous computing on Caravela network. Thus, these capabilities of the worker and the broker servers allows to implement a secure environment for GRID computing.

3.3. Application Interface for Executing Flow-Model

The programming interface for the Caravela platform is defined as a set of functions to manage computing resources and to assign flow-models to the available computing resources. To execute applications on the Caravela platform, the steps below have to be followed.

1. **Initialization of the platform**
   In the beginning, the application initializes its context in the Caravela platform. This step creates a local temporal slot for the subsequent management tasks.

2. **Reproduction of flow-model(s)**
   The Application fetches a flow-model, which may be in a remote location.

3. **Acquisition of processing unit(s)**
   To assign the flow-model, the application needs to acquire a processing unit that matches the conditions needed for the flow-model execution. If the application targets execution in a local processing unit, it queries directly the local resource. If the application needs to query the processing units of remote resources, for example when the requirements for the flow-model execution do not match the specification of the local processing unit, it sends a query request to worker or broker servers. If the application queries the worker, the worker will return its availability for flow-model execution. In this case, the application will send the requests directly to it. If the server is a broker, it will tell about all the available processing units it knows. In this case, the application will communicate to the broker server to execute the flow-model. Then the broker server will propagate the requests below to the worker server using its routing information.

4. **Mapping flow-model(s) to processing unit(s)**
   The application needs to map the flow-model to the processing unit reserved in the previous step. In the current step it will assign a program, I/O buffers and constant parameter inputs included in the flow-model. If the targeted processing unit is remote, the application exchanges requests with the worker servers.

5. **Execution of flow-model(s)**
   Before the execution in the processing unit starts, input data streams must be initialized. The procedure to start the execution of the flow-model is called "firing", which corresponds to activating a program in the flow-model and generating output data.

6. **Releasing processing unit(s) and flow-model(s)**
   After the execution of the flow-model it is unmapped from the processing unit. Because the flow-model and the processing unit are not necessary in the next steps, they are released by the application.

7. **Finalization of the platform**
   Finally, the application needs to be terminated to exit from the Caravela environment.

With the design considerations mentioned above we are able to build a distributed processing platform using the flow-model framework. Because the flow-model includes

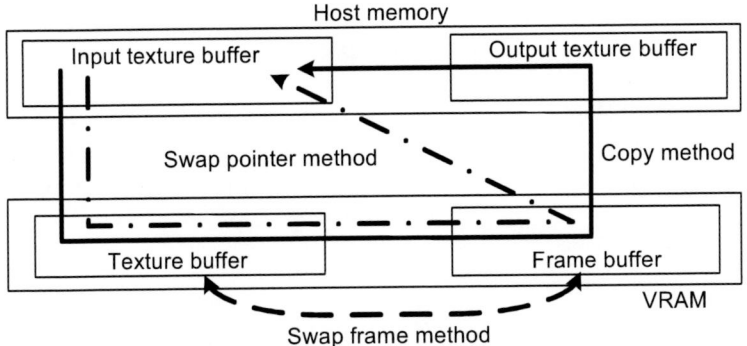

Figure 7. Buffering methods to exchange data between host memory and VRAM.

enough information for independent execution, it performs stream-based processing without touching the resources in the host machine. Therefore, applications in the Caravela platform are able to execute flow-models in a processing unit through secure execution mechanisms.

For the first implementation of Caravela platform, we apply GPUs as the processing units. Therefore, we need to consider a uniformed interfacing technique among the graphics runtimes. In the next section, we will propose a new technique to optimize buffering in the GPU resources (see section 2.3.).

3.4. Buffering Optimization Technique

According to the discussion in section 2.3., herein extensions for the local execution mechanism of the flow-model are proposed. The application interface defined in the previous section specifies a uniformed interface for GPU resources, but there is no discussion how to implement the Caravela platform in order to be efficient in the different graphics runtimes (i.e. between DirectX and OpenGL). Thus the interface is uniform and the implementation has to be tuned to achieve the best performance [34].

The static management for the GPU resources is similar in DirectX and OpenGL, except the inherent differences between the assembly and the high-level languages. Therefore, the interface for the static functionalities is easily defined. However, management of VRAM buffers significantly differs with runtime environments. Since the data I/O operation between host memory and VRAM is a key operation to achieve high performance, the uniform interface must have the capability for tuning the I/O buffering mechanism. For example, considering a recursive application, which has to read previously generated output data as input data for subsequently computation, it is possible to optimize the feedback buffering mechanism. The mechanisms of data exchange found on the runtime environments can be categorized, according to the possible methods to implement feedback (see Figure 7), in the following classes.

- **Copy method**
  This method copies frame buffer data in VRAM to host memory, then copy this data from output to input texture buffer on the host memory and finally copy it back to

the texture buffer in the VRAM. Both DirectX and OpenGL runtime environments provide functions to implement this method.

- **Swap pointer method**
  This method just exchanges pointers between input texture and output texture buffers on host side; only OpenGL provides this method by passing the pointer from `glReadBuffer()` function to `glTexSubImage2D()` function.

- **Swap frame method**
  This is the most efficient method, that directly swaps output buffer and input texture buffer in the VRAM (GPU side). This method is also only available in the OpenGL runtime environment.

These different copy methods have to be considered to implement the uniform interface for GPU-based applications that fully exploit the GPU's potential performance. Moreover, from the user perspective the interface must be unique but it has to implicitly implement the best method depending on the machine and the environment.

3.5. Meta-pipeline

As referred in the previous section, by using the flow-model framework, the Caravela platform can implement a secure and high performance stream-based computing environment, applying GPUs as the processing units. However, the application must manage flow-model execution and data forwarding between the flow-models. Even if flow-models for a target algorithm can be executed in a pipeline manner, there is no direct mechanism to implement it. This section focuses on an extension of the Caravela execution mechanism to support pipelined processing, by directly connecting flow-models assigned to multiple distributed processing units in the Caravela network. The mechanism that executes multiple flow-models whose I/O data streams are directly connected in the Caravela platform is called *meta-pipeline* [35]. The meta-pipeline applies an execution model designated by *pipeline-model*.

3.5.1. Defining Pipeline-Model

As depicted in Figure 8, flow-models whose I/O data streams are directly connected can create a pipeline-model. A pipeline-model may have its own I/O *ports*, which can be seen as its own I/O data streams. Input data streams (1) in Figure 8 are called *ENTRANCE* ports and output data streams (2) in Figure 8 are called *EXIT* ports. Because the pipeline-model is defined to compute programs, it must fulfill the following conditions: 1) one or more EXIT ports must exist; 2) one or more flow-models are included; and 3) any flow-model is connected by at least one I/O data stream. The first condition means that at least an output data stream is provided as the result of the pipeline-model, because otherwise the algorithm would be useless. The second and third conditions mean that a pipeline-model that includes two or more independent processing pipelines is invalid because multiple independent processing pipelines can be separated into different pipeline-models. Note that assumptions about the number of input ports are omitted from the above conditions. This is because the pipeline-model can have a self-generated (feedback) input stream data that results from the

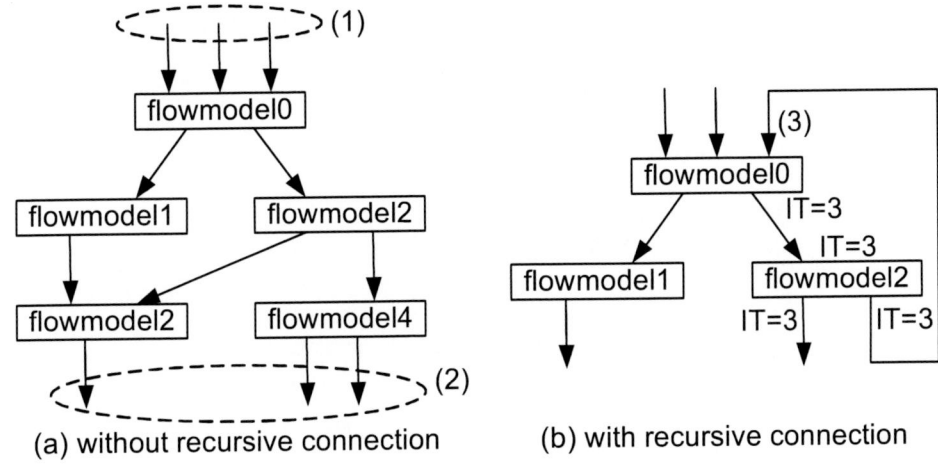

Figure 8. Examples of pipeline-model.

output data stream. This organization can be created for algorithms that generate special data streams, such as the recursive generation of the Fibonacci sequence of numbers.

When all input data streams of a flow-model included in a pipeline-model are available, this flow-model is ready to be executed. After checking this condition for all flow-models, the execution mechanism continues to invoke the pipeline-model. For example, in the pipeline model depicted in Figure 8(a), data for the ENTRANCE ports (1) are prepared. Then, 'flowmodel0' is executed and generates the output data stream needed to 'flowmodel1'. At this time, the input data stream of 'flowmodel1' is available. This execution style will be repeatedly applied in the subsequent flow-models, and thus flow-model execution will be pipelined. In the example of Figure 8(b), at the beginning of the execution the input data streams of 'flowmodel0' never become all ready unless the data stream of the feedback connection is initialized. To avoid a deadlock situation in the pipeline-model's execution, this kind of input data stream, called *INITONCE* port, corresponds to a special port that must be initialized before pipeline execution starts.

To increase flexibility, we also defines a limit number of iterations without initializations of input data for INITONCE port. For example, if the input data stream (3) is defined as an INITONCE port and the *Iteration Limit* (IT) is three, as illustrated in Figure 8(b), the port only has to be initialized every three times the output data is generated by the 'flowmodel2'. In addition to the INITONCE ports, iteration limits are applied to ENTRANCE and EXIT ports. In the case of an ENTRANCE port, an iteration limit restricts input data initialization, an ENTRANCE port is initialized every "number of iteration limit" instances of the flow-model. On the other hand, EXIT port with iteration limit generates output data every "number of iteration limit". Moreover, we call *INTERMEDIATE* port to the I/O streams which are in any one of the categories referred above. The concept of iteration limit is also applied to INTERMEDIATE ports. For instance, as it is illustrated in Figure 8(b), when the iteration limit is set, the output data from 'flowmodel0' is only generated every three executions and the input/output data of 'flowmodel2' are initialized/generated every three iterations of 'flowmodel2'. A merit of the iteration limit is to define an execution set. In this example, 'flowmodel2' can be iterated without initializing the input data stream and with-

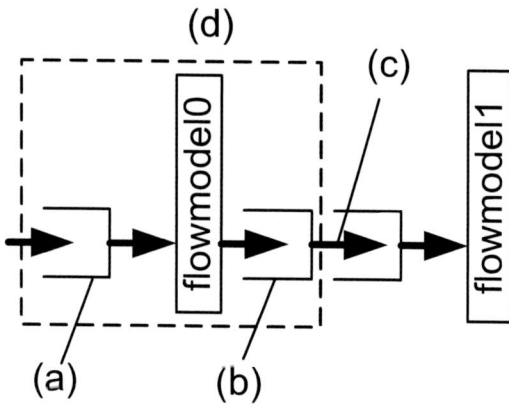

Figure 9. Execution model in pipeline-model.

out generating the output data stream. This removes the obligation of the remote processing unit assigned to a flow-model to send/receive data every execution. Thus, redundant data communication among processing units is avoided.

In summary, flow-model execution in a pipeline-model is repeated while its flow-model's ENTRANCE port(s) or INITONCE port(s) are correctly initialized. Moreover, the executions of flow-models can be parallelized into independent processing units, and the processing being optimized through the iteration limits. Thus, the pipeline-model will behave in a distributed environment as a suitable autonomous stream-based computing unit.

3.5.2. Runtime Environment for Meta-pipeline

The meta-pipeline mechanism has to be implemented in runtime, in order to execute a pipeline-model on GPUs. By checking if all input data streams of a flow-model are ready, the runtime environment provides the maximum number of processing units to execute the flow-models in parallel. Although a connection between flow-models' input and output data streams can be prepared as a shared buffer that receives the output data stream and allows it to be used as the next input data stream, it can cause the execution of flow-models in the pipeline-model to become sequential. A flow-model that is going to be executed can not output its data to the buffer if it is occupied by data for the subsequent flow-model. To avoid this serialization, we define an execution model as depicted in Figure 9: each flow-model has buffers corresponding to its input and output data streams (Figure 9(a)(b)). When the input data streams are initialized and 'flowmodel0' is invoked, its output data streams are stored to the output buffer once (Figure 9(b)). When the subsequent flow-model's input buffer becomes empty, content of the output buffer will be moved to the input buffer (Figure 9(c)). This mechanism avoids serial execution, in the case of Figure 9 between 'flowmodel0' and 'flowmodel1', by using independent buffers for input and output data streams.

Each flow-model group with input/output data stream(s) and its buffers, such as depicted in Figure 9(d), can be invoked as a single flow-model execution using the Caravela library shown later in Table 1. Therefore, when it is mapped to a processing unit in the Caravela platform, the group can be autonomously invoked.

When an output buffer and an input buffer are connected between flow-models and those buffer sizes are different, the data will be copied using the smaller buffer size. For example, if the buffer size of Figure 9(c) is smaller than the one of Figure 9(b), the data in Figure 9(b) is resized to the size of Figure 9(c) and is copied to the destination buffer. Therefore, even if buffers with different sizes are connected in a pipeline-model, the I/O data will be smoothly propagated.

3.5.3. Meta-pipeline Application Interface

An application interface for the meta-pipeline is prepared as additional functions of Caravela library. To invoke a pipeline-model, application follows the eight steps presented below.

1. **Looking for processing units**
   In this step the processing units are acquired by using the conventional Caravela functions shown in Table 1; the processing units can be located locally or remotely.

2. **Creating flow-models**
   In this step, flow-models that are used in a pipeline-model are reproduced from local or remote flow-model; this function is also implemented through the functions associated with the original Caravela platform.

3. **Creating a pipeline-model data structure**
   In this step, a pipeline-model is created as a data structure in the Caravela system.

4. **Registering flow-models and processing units to pipeline-model**
   This step registers in the pipeline-model data structure the flow-models produced in the 2nd step and the processing units queried by the 1st step; a pair (flow-model, processing unit) is named *stage* of the pipeline; application needs to create all the stages in a pipeline-model in this step.

5. **Creating connections among flow-models**
   This step defines connections among I/O data streams of flow-models registered to the different stages of pipeline-model; to fulfill the conditions of being a valid pipeline-model, the application must connect appropriate I/O data streams of flow-models.

6. **Defining INITONCE ports and iteration limits**
   Regarding to the connections defined in the previous step, if a connection creates a loop, it must be marked as an INITONCE port at the corresponding input data stream of the flow-model; iteration limits associated to ports in the pipeline-model must also be specified in this step.

7. **Implementing pipeline-model**
   This step checks if the pipeline-model satisfies the conditions and it is available to be executed; if both conditions are satisfied, all processing units registered to the pipeline-model are reserved; if the resources are located in remote machines, connections to communicate data between stages are established and flow-models associated

to the processing units are sent to them; thereafter, each flow-model becomes ready to be executed waiting for input data via INITONCE/ENTRANCE ports.

8. **Invoking pipeline-model**
   The invocation of the pipeline-model is automatically made by sending input data to its ENTRANCE/INITONCE ports; this operation is performed by the application by providing input data to the first stage of a pipeline-model; the execution mechanism is propagated from the first stage until EXIT ports appear in a stage; the application needs to keep sending input data as long as ENTRANCE/INITONCE ports are waiting for input data and it receives data when it reaches the EXIT ports; due to the pipeline execution mechanism, while the output data is not completely received by the application, the stages associated with the EXIT ports will stall.

Following the steps above, the application sets up a pipeline-model and distributes the registered flow-models through the remote resources. Moreover, the pipeline-model is implicitly executed by the meta-pipeline's runtime when the application provides input data to the ENTRANCE/INITONCE ports. Thus, pipeline-model programmers do not need to explicitly schedule flow-model execution in the application program.

4. Implementation of Caravela Platform

In this section we discuss the main issues related with the implementation of the Caravela platform. The following sections discusses: *i*) implementation issues for the basic flow-model execution mechanisms in local and remote sites; *ii*) buffering optimization techniques that allow to absorb graphics runtime differences and simultaneously to achieve the best performance; and *iii*) a meta-pipeline execution mechanism.

4.1. Packing Flow-Model

A flow-model is described by a data structure. When GPUs are used as processing units of the Caravela platform, the flow-model unit includes a pixel shader program, textures as the input data streams, constant values of the shader program as the input constants and frame buffers as places where the shader program outputs data streams.

The flow-model unit also needs to include other important items related to the requirements of program execution. These requirements include the program's language type, the version and accepted data types. We use the name "pixel" for a unit of the I/O buffer because the pixel processor processes input data for every pixel color. For example, a multiplication is performed with two registers that include ARGB elements as its operands, and outputs a register formed by ARGB elements.

In conclusion, the flow-model defines the number of pixels for the I/O data streams, the number of constant parameters, the data type of the I/O data streams, the pixel shader program and the requirements for the aimed GPU. To give portability to the flow-model, these items are packed into an Extensible Markup Language (XML) file. This mechanism allows the application in a remote computer to fetch the XML file and easily execute the flow-model unit.

Caravela: A High Performance Stream-Based Concurrent Computing Platform

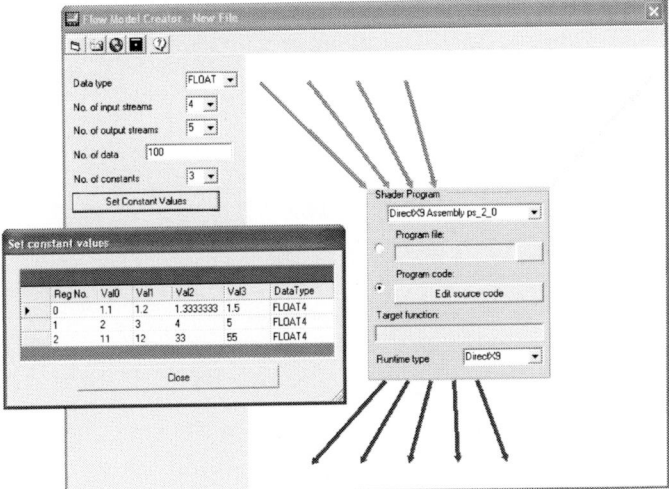

Figure 10. FlowModelCreator application.

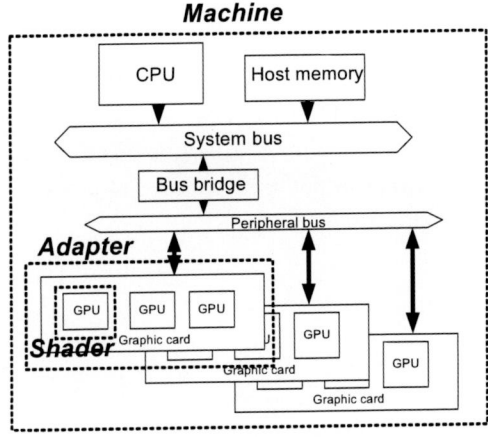

Figure 11. Resource hierarchy in a processing unit.

To help defining the corresponding flow-model, the GUI-based tool, shown in Figure 10, called *FlowModelCreator*, was programmed and is available in the Caravela package.

4.2. Caravela Library

The Caravela platform is mainly composed by a library that supports an API for GPGPU. The Caravela library adopts the definitions for the processing units represented in Figure 11: *Machine* is a host machine of a video adapter, *Adapter* is a video adapter that includes one or multiple GPUs, and *Shader* is a GPU. An application needs to map a flow-model into a shader, to execute the mapped flow-model.

Table 1 shows the basic Caravela functions for a flow-model execution. Using those functions, a programmer can easily implement target applications in the framework of flow-

Table 1. Basic functions of Caravela library

`CARAVELA_CreateMachine(...)`	creates a machine structure
`CARAVELA_QueryShader(...)`	queries a shader on a machine
`CARAVELA_CreateFlowModelFromFile(...)`	creates a flow-model structure from XML file
`CARAVELA_GetInputData(...)`	gets a buffer of an input data stream
`CARAVELA_GetOutputData(...)`	gets a buffer of an output data stream
`CARAVELA_MapFlowModelIntoShader(...)`	maps a flow-model to a shader
`CARAVELA_FireFlowModel(...)`	executes a flow-model mapped to a shader

models, by mapping flow-models to shader(s). Therefore, the programmer does not need to know the graphics runtime environment details: the Caravela library can be one of the solutions to relieve the chief problem of differences between graphical environments mentioned in the previous section.

However, to efficiently support multiple graphics runtime environments in the lower layer of Caravela library, care should be taken to understand their differences in methods and features. If a graphics runtime environment, which a programmer aims to instantiate from the Caravela library, has special performance tuning functions, the programmer would like to be sure that the interface provided by Caravela library takes advantage of that. Therefore, we need to consider extended functions for a uniform interface for GPGPU applications that tunes-up runtime procedures in order to achieve the best performance in different graphics runtime environments.

4.3. Buffer Swapping Function

For fully exploiting the GPU's potential performance in local execution of flow-model, all the different copy methods proposed in section 3.4. have to be considered to design the uniform interface for GPU-based applications. Moreover, from the user perspective the interface must be unique but it has to implicitly perform the best in any machine and environment. In this section, we implement an extended interface in Caravela which hides the differences between runtimes and achieves high performance results.

4.3.1. Static Functionality: Resource Management

Applications using Caravela library tries to acquire a shader for executing a flow-model. The runtime is specified by the argument of `CARAVELA_Initialize()` at the beginning of the application. Then the application calls `CARAVELA_CreateMachine()` to create a definition of host machine. Using the machine structure, it calls `CARAVELA_QueryShader()` trying to find a shader in the machine. Conditions to find the shader, such as the shader model version for DirectX, suitable for the flow-model created by `CARAVELA_CreateFlowmodelFromFile()`, will be passed as arguments. If the conditions match, `CARAVELA_MapFlowmodelIntoShader()` is called to map the flow-model to the shader. This function creates input textures and frame buffers, compiles a program in the flow-model and downloads it into the Shader, by using one of the graphics runtime environments. `CARAVELA_GetInputData()` will create a buffer in host memory and return the buffer. Considering the compatibility for DirectX9, the returned buffer includes a value for the pitch length. The buffer initialization is performed by an access macro named `GETFLOAT32_1D` or `GETFLOAT32_2D` that will calculate an offset to the desired data. After initialization of the input data, `CARAVELA_FireFlowModel()` is called to execute the flow-model, and generates output data from the flow-model; the function implicitly creates the output buffers on the VRAM. Finally, `CARAVELA_GetOutputData()` copies the data from VRAM to a buffer on host memory, and returns the pointer to this buffer to the application. This buffer is also accessed by the `GETFLOAT32_1D` or `GETFLOAT32_2D` macro. Considering the operations above, Caravela library is able to provide the same functionality both for DirectX and OpenGL.

4.3.2. Dynamic Capabilities: Buffer Management

The execution steps of flow-model described in the previous section cover only non-recursive applications; the output streams are never used for further processing. According to section 2.3.3., the buffer management can be optimized in OpenGL, leading to the extensions proposed for the Caravela library.

In the Caravela flow-model, a recursive I/O will be presented as a connection from an output data stream to an input data stream. We define a data structure called *I/O pair* which has an input stream's index number and an output stream's index number of the flow-model. In the uniform programming interface, the I/O pair is created by `CARAVELA_CreateSwapIOPair()` function. To swap the I/O streams, `CARAVELA_SwapFlowmodelIO()` function is called and an I/O pair is passed as an input parameter to the function.

The implementation of `CARAVELA_SwapFlowmodelIO()` differs from DirectX to OpenGL due to the availability of different buffer management mechanisms. The DirectX version performs the copy method presented above while the OpenGL version implements the swap pointer method or the swap frame method. The implementation of the swap pointer method is straightforward, by passing a pointer from the `glReadBuffer()` function to the `glTexSubImage2D()` function it avoids copy operations, such as `memcpy()`. The implementation of the swap frame method is more tricky: OpenGL allows only a frame buffer that is already assigned to be used as the input texture buffer on GPU. Therefore, before exchanging the I/O pair, the input buffer must be considered as an additional frame buffer by using the `glFramebufferTexture2DEXT()` function. After assigning the frame buffer, the I/O pair will be exchanged at every call of `CARAVELA_SwapFlowmodelIO()`. Performance tuning is performed by automatically adopting the fastest method.

Summarizing, applications with a recursive algorithm initializes an input buffer of a flow-model registered to an I/O pair at the first iteration. After the execution of the flow-model, `CARAVELA_SwapFlowmodelIO()` is called to exchange the data of the I/O pair. After the first iteration, the application does not need to use `CARAVELA_GetInputData()`. Therefore, with reduction of data copy operations it is expected an improvement in the processing performance.

Table 2. Extension of the Caravela library for the meta-pipeline model

`CARAVELA_CreatePipeline(...)`	creates data structure for pipeline-model
`CARAVELA_AddShaderToPipeline(...)`	adds a shader to a pipeline-model
`CARAVELA_AttachFlowmodelToShader(...)`	associates a shader to a pipeline-model
`CARAVELA_ConnectIO(,.)`	defines connections between stages
`CARAVELA_ImplementPipelineModel(...)`	assigns flow-model to machines
`CARAVELA_SendInputDataToPipeline(...)`	sends data to ENTRANCE/INITONCE ports
`CARAVELA_ReceiveOutputDataFromPipeline(...)`	receives output data from EXIT ports

4.4. Meta-plpeline Functions

4.4.1. Library Functions for Meta-pipeline

The meta-pipeline is implemented as a set of C-based functions listed in table 2. These library functions are included in the Caravela library as an extension to the original set of functions presented in Table 1. For example, machine creation and shader acquisition are performed by the original Caravela functions.

After an application has acquired shaders, the specific functions to implement the meta-pipeline model are invoked. First, `CARAVELA_CreatePipeline()` function is called to create a data structure for the pipeline-model. In the next step, `CARAVELA_AddShaderToPipeline()` function adds a shader acquired by `CARAVELA_QueryShader()`, through the conventional Caravela library to the pipeline-model data structure. The `CARAVELA_AttachFlowmodelToShader()` function is used for associating a shader to a flow-model previously created by the `CARAVELA_CreateFlowModelFromFile()`. Here, a pair of a shader and a flow-model has been registered in the pipeline-model. Thus, the stages in the pipeline-model have been defined.

To define connections between stages, `CARAVELA_ConnectIO()` function is used. Its arguments are an identification of a flow-model already registered in a pipeline-model and input/output data streams' indices for the flow-model. After successfully defining the connections, the I/O data streams are marked as INTERMEDIATE ports. If needed, `CARAVELA_SpecifyInitOncePort()` is called after making a connection to specify that an INTERMEDIATE port is an INITONCE port. Regarding to the iteration limit, as mentioned in the previous section, after creating connections among stages, `CARAVELA_SpecifyEntrancePort()`, `CARAVELA_SpecifyExitPort()` and `CARAVELA_SpecifyIntermediateInput/Output()` functions can be called to specify iteration limits at some ports. From now on the pipeline-model is configured and application can start implementing the pipeline of flow-models.

The function `CARAVELA_ImplementPipelineModel()` assigns flow-model/shader pairs (i.e. stages) to machines and returns arrays of ENTRANCE and EXIT ports; it does not execute any stages in the pipeline-model. Those executions are performed by the `CARAVELA_SendInputDataToPipeline()` function, that sends input data to ENTRANCE ports, and `CARAVELA_ReceiveOutputDataFromPipeline()` function that receives output data from the EXIT ports. These functions internally have the

```
// Preparing input data
Input_data = ...;
While(1){
        // Sending input data to pipeline-model.
        if(CARAVELA_SendInputDataToPipeline(
            pipelinemodel,  // a pipeline-model
            port,           // an ENTRANCE port to be initialized.
            input_data,
            number_of_data) == CARAVELA_SUCCESS){
                    // Preparing the next input data
                    Input_data = ...;
        }
        // Getting output data from pipeline-model.
        if(CARAVELA_ReceiveOutputDataFromPipeline(
            pipelinemodel,  // a pipeline-model
            port,           // an EXIT port to be initialized.
            &flowmodel,     // a flow-model of the port (output from function)
            &index,         // an index of output stream of flow-model
                                                    (output from function)
            &output_data,   // (output from function)
            &number_of_data // (output from function)
            ) == CARAVELA_SUCCESS){
                    // Processing output data
        }
}
```

Figure 12. Code for pipeline-model execution.

procedure for executing the stages. If the condition for executing a stage is satisfied, the execution is propagated from one stage to the next. This execution mechanism can be local or remote.

4.4.2. Execution Mechanism of Meta-pipeline

Execution of a pipeline-model is fired by input data in ENTRANCE ports. Therefore input data must be provided to the ports repeatedly after they have consumed the data. Moreover, results generated from EXIT ports must be read by the application to avoid stalls. The coding style of pipeline-model execution is illustrated in Figure 12, with an iteration trying to input new data to ENTRANCE ports and to get new results from EXIT ports.

For executing stages in local shaders, `CARAVELA_SendInputDataToPipeline()` and `CARAVELA_ReceiveOutputDataFromPipeline()` functions have the chances to execute the stages by repeatedly utilizing the executions shown in Figure 12. Thus, these functions execute available stages while any ENTRANCE port is not empty and any EXIT port can output data.

For executing stages on remote shaders, `CARAVELA_ImplementPipelineModel()` function distributes flow-models associated to stages in a pipeline-model to worker servers. Worker servers prepare its shader resources for receiving flow-models and wait for data input in the respective ENTRANCE ports. When the worker servers receive input data for flow-models and execute it, they forward the output data to the other worker servers that have the subsequent flow-models in the pipeline-model. The execution of a flow-model in a worker server is fired by input data. Therefore, application does not need explicitly to activate each flow-model distributed in remote shaders, as it for the case of local execution.

Table 3. Experimental setup

	Machine1	Machine2
Chipset	nForce4 Ultra	945GM Express
CPU	AMD Opteron 170@2GHz	Intel CoreDuo T2300@1.66GHz
Main memory	2x1GB DDR 400	2x512MB DDR2 533
Graphics board	MSI NX7300GS 256MB DDR	NVIDIA GeForce Go 7400 128MB DDR2
Display size	1280x1024	1280x800
OS	WindowsXP Pro	WindowsXP Home

To conclude this part, it can be said that the meta-pipeline mechanism allows a application program to define execution stages, which are implicitly executed in local or in remote machines.

5. Preliminary Experimental Evaluation

After presenting the Caravela plaform, let us now show preliminary experimental evaluation that has been performed in Caravela project. This evaluation has three main targets: *i*) the programmability of applications based on flow-model and its performance, *ii*) the effectiveness of the buffer swapping optimization for local execution, and finally *iii*) the programmability of applications using the meta-pipeline model.

5.1. Application Examples Using Flow-Models

A first evaluation have shown the programmability of flow-model based applications and the performance impact of the buffer swapping optimization technique. Other three experimental evaluations were made and are considered in this section: *i*) analysis of copy operation on GPU-based application, *ii*) performance of different buffering methods, and *iii*) overall performance analysis for real applications. For these evaluations, a Finite Impulse Response (FIR) filter and an Infinite Impulse Response (IIR) filter, that performs recursive computation, are considered. The execution times presented in this section have been obtained with the machines presented in Table 3.

5.1.1. FIR and IIR Filter Kernels

FIR and IIR filters are well-known kernels applied to 1D signal processing and image processing (2D). These linear filters apply the following computation– $y = f(x)$:

$$FIR: y_n = \sum_{i=0}^{15} b_i * x_{n-i} \qquad (1)$$

$$IIR: y_n = \sum_{i=0}^{7} b_i * x_{n-i} + \sum_{k=1}^{8} b_k * y_{n-k} \qquad (2)$$

Caravela: A High Performance Stream-Based Concurrent Computing Platform

```
void main(){
  int i,j;
  float inv = 1.0/Const4.x;
  vec4 res = vec4(0.0,0.0,0.0,0.0);
  vec2 coord = gl_TexCoord[0].xy;
  vec4 data0 = texture2D(CaravelaTex0, coord);
  coord.x+=inv;
  vec4 data1 = texture2D(CaravelaTex0, coord);
  coord.x+=inv;
  vec4 data2 = texture2D(CaravelaTex0, coord);
  for( j=0; j<4;j++)
    res.x += data0[j] * Const0[j];
  for( j=0; j<4;j++)
    res.x += data1[j] * Const1[j];
  // for y value
  for(j=1;j<4;j++)
    res.y += data0[j] * Const0[j-1];
  res.y += data1[0] * Const0[3];
  for( j=1; j<4; j++ )
    res.y += data1[j] * Const1[j-1];
  res.y += data2[0] * Const1[3];
  // for z value
  for(j=2;j<4;j++)
    res.z += data0[j] * Const0[j-2];
  for(j=0;j<2;j++)
    res.z += data1[j] * Const0[j+2];
  for( j=2; j<4; j++ )
    res.z += data1[j] * Const1[j-2];
  for(j=0;j<2;j++)
    res.z += data2[j] * Const1[j+2];
  // for w value
  res.w += data0[3] * Const0[0];
  for(j=0; j<3; j++ )
    res.w += data1[j] * Const0[j+1];
  res.w += data1[3] * Const1[0];
  for(j=0; j<3; j++ )
    res.w += data2[j] * Const1[j+1];
  // fetch output data
  coord = gl_TexCoord[0].xy;
  data0 = texture2D(CaravelaTex1, coord);
  coord.x+=inv;
  data1 = texture2D(CaravelaTex1, coord);
  coord.x+=inv;
  data2 = texture2D(CaravelaTex1, coord);
  Repeat the same accumulations
  gl_FragData[0] = res;
}
```

(a) IIR program embedded in flow-model

(b) Organization of IIR flow-model

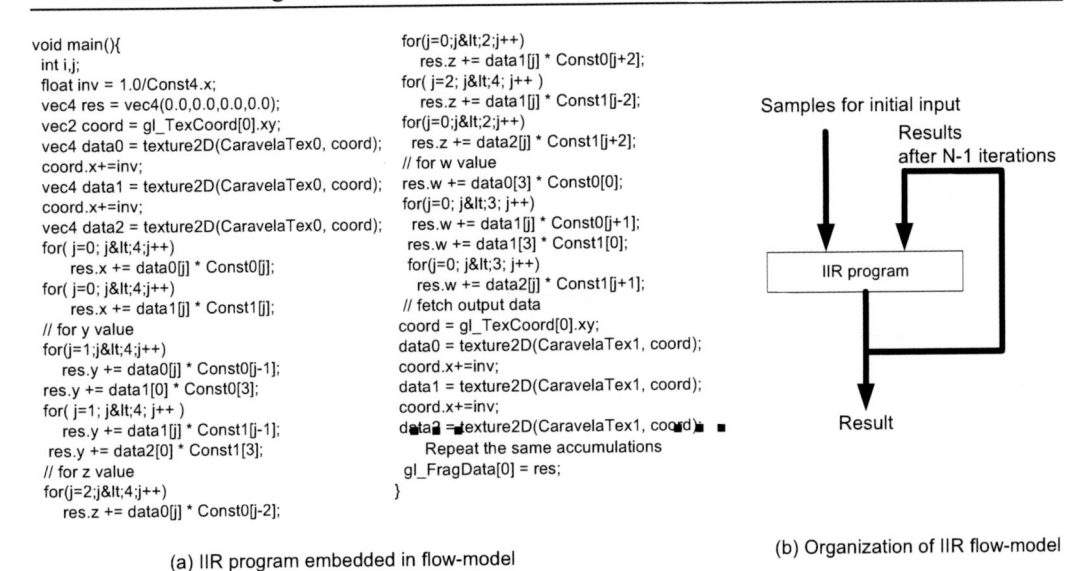

Figure 13. Flow-model for IIR filter kernel.

In both cases the filter coefficients (16 taps) are constant values available at the input of the flow-model. The flow-model for the FIR filter only consists of an input stream for the input signal while the flow-model for IIR filter consists of two input streams, one for the input samples and another for the feedback path (y_{n-k} in eq. 2).

The programs in the flow-models were written in the HLSL and compiled to the Pixel Shader Model 3.0 profile of DirectX, and in GLSL for OpenGL. The program fetches the input data stream controlling the sampler register that obtains the address information for the input data. Then, the computation corresponding to equations (1) and (2) is performed. Note that a register computes in parallel four single precision floating point values. Therefore, each output from the program corresponds to four results.

Figure 13(a) shows the program, written in GLSL and embedded into the IIR filter's flow-model. The organization of the flow-model is illustrated in Figure 13(b), which is managed by the FlowModelCreator application and is packed into an XML file. As illustrated in the figure, this flow-model is targeted to recursive execution. Therefore, the program presents the accumulation of the results from the multiply and add operations with coefficients provided by the constant inputs. In addition, the program uses the recursive input provided by the results after the $(N-1)$th iteration. Thus, the flow-model will provide results recursively processed by each execution by CARAVELA_FireFlowModel() function.

On both applications, the steps from the creation of the flow-model to its mapping to a shader are performed in exactly the same way. However, in IIR filter case, the feedback of output values is performed by an I/O pair, allowing the reuse of the output results. From the second execution of the CARAVELA_FireFlowModel() function, the CARAVELA_SwapFlowmodelIO() function is called to exchange a I/O pair. In the flow-model depicted in Figure 13(b), the I/O pair is defined with the second input of the input data streams and the output data stream.

```
CARAVELA_Initialize(RUNTIME_DIRECTX9);
CARAVELA_CreateMachine(LOCAL_MACHINE,NULL,&machine);            (1)
CARAVELA_CreateFlowModelFromFile(FLOWMODEL_FILE,NULL,&flowmodel,&flowmodel_err);   (2)
CARAVELA_QueryShader(machine,&flowmodel->ShaderCondition, &shader);   (3)
CARAVELA_MapFlowModelIntoShader(shader,flowmodel,&compile_err,&fuse);   (4)
CARAVELA_GetInputData(flowmodel,0,&input_matrix);
for(i=0;i<NUMDATA;i++)
    for(j=0;j<NUMDATA*4;j++)
        GETFLOAT32_2D(input_matrix,NUMDATA,i,j) = input_martix_orig[i][j];   (5)
CARAVELA_FireFlowModel(fuse);                                   (6)
CARAVELA_GetOutputData(flowmodel,0,&output_matrix);
printf("output[%u][%u]=%f\n", NUMDATA-3,NUMDATA*4-3,
        GETFLOAT32_2D(output_matrix,NUMDATA,NUMDATA-3,NUMDATA*4-3));   (7)
CARAVELA_UnmapFlowModelFromShader(flowmodel);
CARAVELA_ReleaseFlowModel(flowmodel);
CARAVELA_ReleaseMachine(machine);                               (8)
CARAVELA_Finalize(RUNTIME_DIRECTX9);
```

(a) Caravela runtime code for local execution

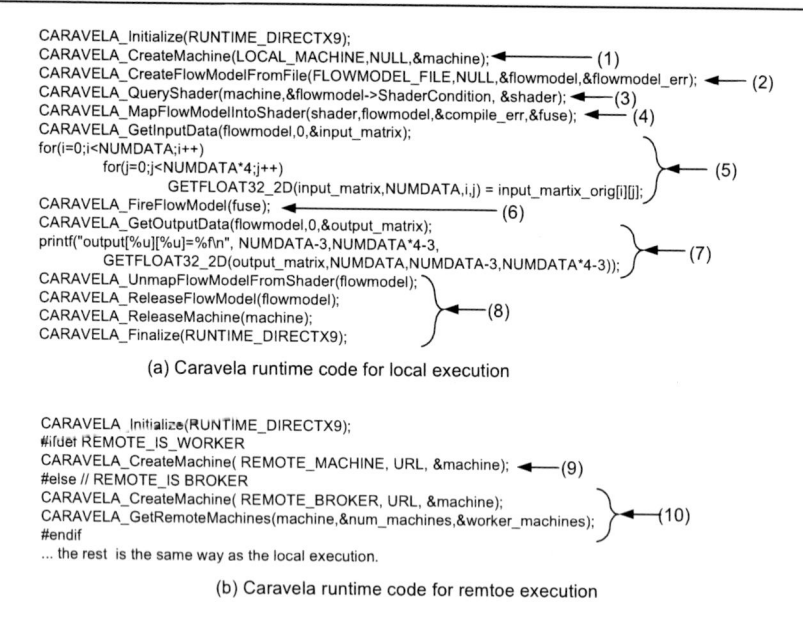

```
CARAVELA_Initialize(RUNTIME_DIRECTX9);
#ifdef REMOTE_IS_WORKER
CARAVELA_CreateMachine( REMOTE_MACHINE, URL, &machine);         (9)
#else // REMOTE_IS_BROKER
CARAVELA_CreateMachine( REMOTE_BROKER, URL, &machine);
CARAVELA_GetRemoteMachines(machine,&num_machines,&worker_machines);   (10)
#endif
... the rest is the same way as the local execution.
```

(b) Caravela runtime code for remtoe execution

Figure 14. An example of application code on the Caravela platform for performing local and remote flow-model execution.

The evaluation results that will be presented consider the execution time of 30 iterations per application, varying the input signals between 1M (Mega=2^{20}), 4M and 16M samples.

5.1.2. A Local Execution Example

Code for local execution of the flow-model using Caravela library functions is shown in Figure 14(a). The machine is created in step (1) and the flow-model is reproduced in step (2) from an XML file defined in the FLOWMODEL_FILE macro. Using the machine data structure, step (3) queries a shader from the local machine. If it is successful, the flow-model will be mapped to the shader in step (4). Here, the input data stream is initialized as shown in step (5). After initialization, the flow-model will be fired in step (6). This function will block the subsequent execution until its execution has been finished. Therefore, the code for getting the output in step (7) is executed right after the firing. Finally, the flow-model and the shader are released in step (8).

Thus, the interface for executing the flow-model execution in the local machine is simple and transparent. A programmer can perform general-purpose computation on the Caravela platform without taking care of the details of the processing units that are used.

5.1.3. A Remote Execution Example

There are two different ways to perform remote execution of a flow-model. A first option consists in requesting a processing unit to a specific worker server as shown in step (9) of Figure 14(b). In this case, a remote machine is created as REMOTE_MACHINE with the URL for the remote worker. All the subsequent steps, such as querying shaders and mapping the flow-model, are performed by using the machine structure returned by

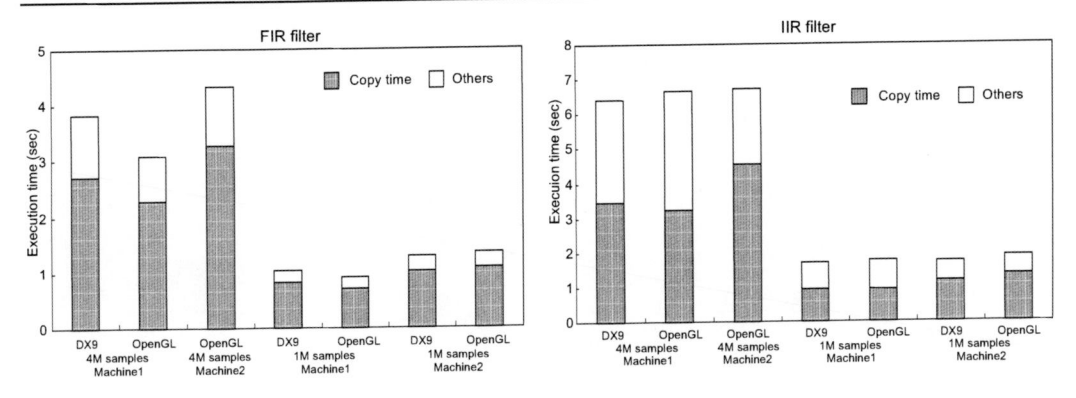

Caravela: A High Performance Stream-Based Concurrent Computing Platform 29

Figure 15. Overhead analysis for copy operation.

CARAVELA_CreateMachine(). The other option is to request the acquisition of a processing unit via a broker server. As shown in step (10) of Figure 14(b), the machine structure will be created by passing REMOTE_BROKER to the CARAVELA_CreateMachine() function with the URL for a remote broker server, and the machine structure returned by the function will be passed to the CARAVELA_GetRemoteMachines() function. Finally, the available machines returned by the function will be used by the application. The communication itself will be performed via the broker server. In both cases, the processing steps after machine creation are the same as those presented in the description of local execution in Figure 14(a). Thus, it is easy for the application designer to migrate it from local to remote execution, by changing only a small part of the code for machine creation.

As explained above, by using flow-model framework, the application design is transparent, and can be assisted by the FlowModelCreator graphical interface. After designing flow-model, the functions of Caravela library can be called in a straight way to execute the flow-model. Thus it can be concluded that Caravela platform provides a transparent interface for stream-based computing and that it allows local or remote task execution on GPUs. The programmer can manage the processing resources and tune the performance by identifying the most efficient machines in the computing platform.

5.1.4. Performance Impact of Buffer Swapping Function

Herein it is evaluated the buffer swapping optimization mechanism by using the I/O pair. Before analyzing the performance of buffering methods, it is important to know how much time takes the copy operations between host memory and VRAM. Figure 15 shows the copy times for the FIR and the IIR filter applications executed on DirectX and OpenGL, with the Caravela library using the copy method used to perform the recursive feedback operation. The texture size limits imposed by the maximum screen size in DirectX does not allow to comsider 4M input samples in Machine2 (no time is presented for these cases in Figure 15).

Figure 15 also shows the total execution times on Machine1 and Machine2 and isolates the time for copy operations (shown as Copy time) from the remaining time. The remaining time includes the time for copy operation between buffers allocated on host memory, calculation time on GPU and setup time for GPU execution. The execution times on both runtime environments are similar, requiring 70% to 80% to copy between host memory and

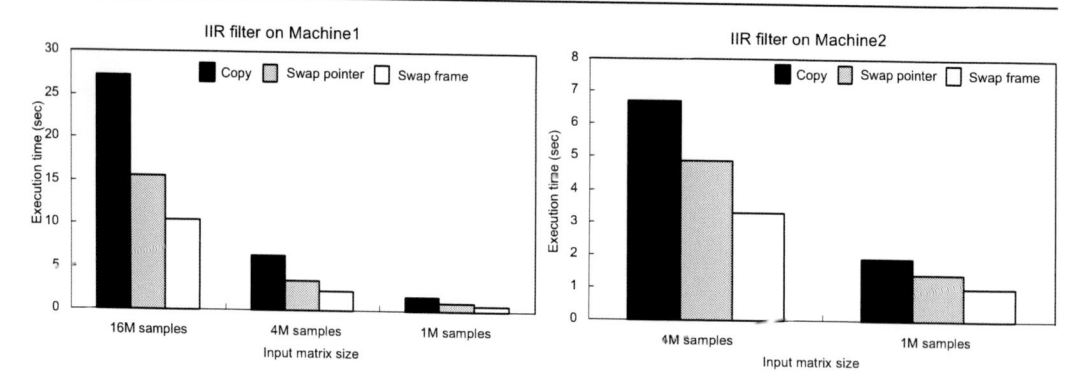

Figure 16. Buffering method comparison.

VRAM. Since the FIR filter does not need to feedback the output data to the input in host memory, the relative time for the copy operation is larger than the one of the IIR filter. The IIR filter requires additional copy operations on host memory to move the result of calculation at every iteration from the output buffer to the input buffer, but this time is included in Figure 15 in "others". According to the result shown in Figure 15, it can be concluded that it is essential to optimize the buffering operation in order to reduce the time spent in copy operations on GPGPU applications.

Let us now compare the performance between the copy method, the swap pointer method and the swap frame method for recursive applications, using as case study the IIR filter. The swap pointer and the swap frame methods are implemented on the CARAVELA_SwapFlowmodelIO() function. The results on the Machine2 with 16M samples are not available because the memory capacity in this machine is limited, so it is required to swap the content of the main memory to the hard disk.

Figure 16 shows the elapsed time of the IIR filter using the different methods and varying the number of input samples. The swap pointer method shows better performance than the copy method because the copy operations performed on the host memory are reduced. A performance improvement from 20% to 40% is achieved by the swap pointer method regarding to the copy method; this improvement is caused by the removal of the copy operations on the host memory. Moreover, a performance improvement about 30% is achieved with the swap frame method regarding to the swap pointer method. Therefore, the performance achieved by the swap frame method corresponds to an overall improvement about 55% to 60%. This is a remarkable performance improvement which has a profound impact in the processing time of recursive applications in GPUs.

5.1.5. Comparing to CPU Performance

This section compares the performance of graphics runtime environments with CPU-based approaches for filtering application. For DirectX only the copy method is available, while for OpenGL the swap frame method is applied, in order to achieve the best performance.

Figures 17 and 18 compare the GPU-based implementation with the CPU-based one. Regarding the FIR filter, DirectX shows a little bit more overhead comparing to OpenGL. The performance of GPU-based implementation using the Caravela library is 7 to 13 times,

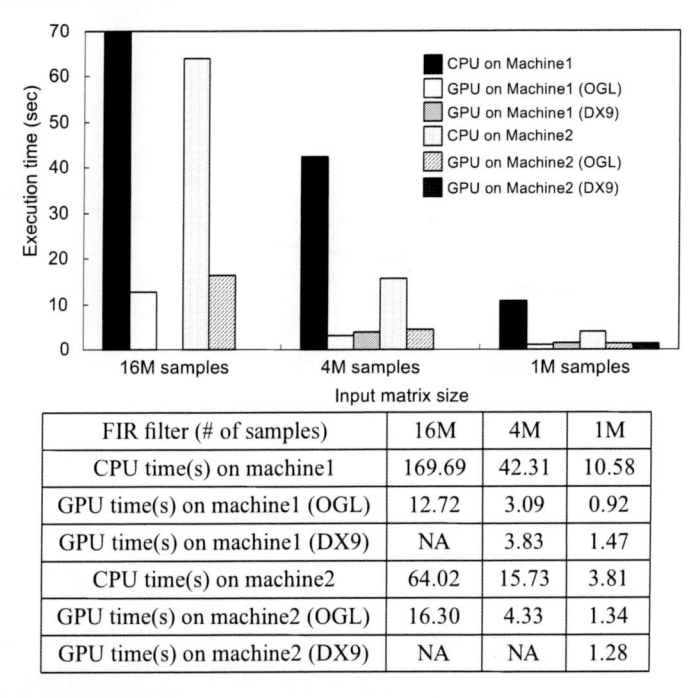

Caravela: A High Performance Stream-Based Concurrent Computing Platform

FIR filter (# of samples)	16M	4M	1M
CPU time(s) on machine1	169.69	42.31	10.58
GPU time(s) on machine1 (OGL)	12.72	3.09	0.92
GPU time(s) on machine1 (DX9)	NA	3.83	1.47
CPU time(s) on machine2	64.02	15.73	3.81
GPU time(s) on machine2 (OGL)	16.30	4.33	1.34
GPU time(s) on machine2 (DX9)	NA	NA	1.28

Figure 17. Overall performance comparison of GPU versus CPU performance to FIR filtering (NA: Not Available).

and 3 to 4 times, faster than the CPU-based implementation on the Machine1, and the Machine2, respectively. Regarding IIR filtering, the DirectX shows worse performance than OpenGL due to the overhead caused by the copy method. Considering the performance on both runtime environments, the GPU-based implementation for the IIR filter using Caravela library is 6 to 18 times, and 2 to 5 times, faster than the CPU-based implementation on the Machine1, and the Machine2, respectively.

5.2. Application Example of Meta-pipeline

To evaluate the meta-pipeline mechanism, this section discusses a simple but realistic application example, the computation of a 2D Discrete Wavelet Transform (DWT).

5.2.1. 2D Discrete Wavelet Transform

The DWT [9] is one of the powerful transforms for image processing used in several applications, such as compression (JPEG2000 standard), denoising, edge detection and feature extraction. The DWT decomposes an input signal $S(i)$ into two sub-band coefficient sets: a set of low frequency coefficients $L(i)$ and a set of high frequency ones $H(i)$. To perform the wavelet decomposition, using a low-pass and a high-pass filter, linear filtering is applied to the input signal $S(i)$, followed by decimation. Representing a k-th low-pass filter coefficient by $l(k)$ and a high-pass filter one by $h(k)$, the i-th DWT coefficient at the

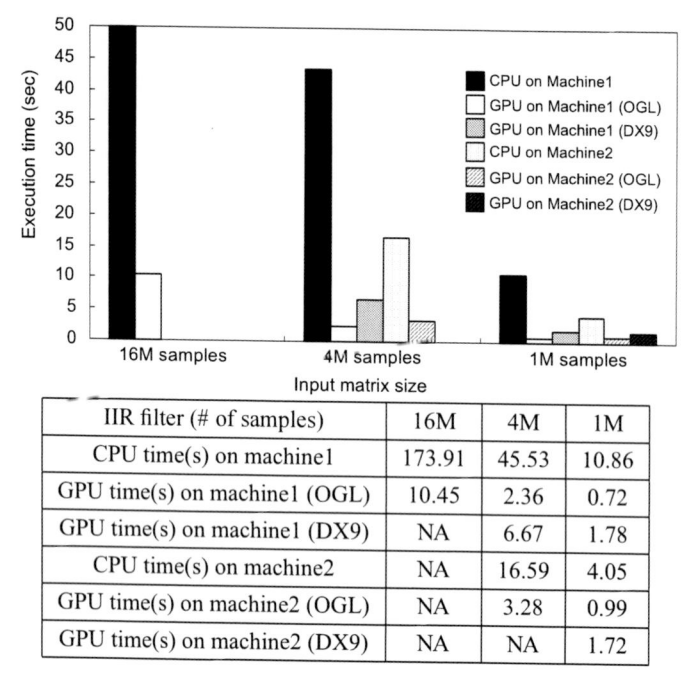

Figure 18. Overall performance comparison of GPU versus CPU performance to IIR filtering (NA: Not Available).

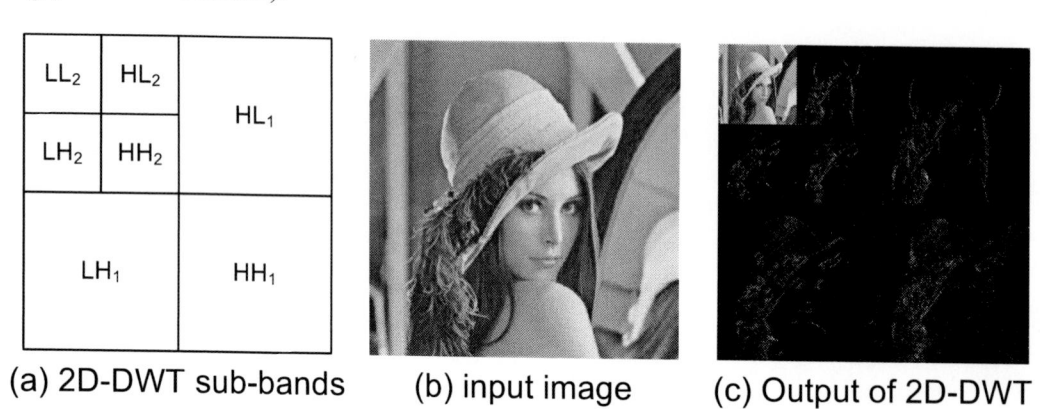

IIR filter (# of samples)	16M	4M	1M
CPU time(s) on machine1	173.91	45.53	10.86
GPU time(s) on machine1 (OGL)	10.45	2.36	0.72
GPU time(s) on machine1 (DX9)	NA	6.67	1.78
CPU time(s) on machine2	NA	16.59	4.05
GPU time(s) on machine2 (OGL)	NA	3.28	0.99
GPU time(s) on machine2 (DX9)	NA	NA	1.72

(a) 2D-DWT sub-bands (b) input image (c) Output of 2D-DWT

Figure 19. 2D-DWT example with 2 decomposition levels

corresponding sub-band is computed by:

$$L(i) = \sum_{k=0}^{K-1} S(2i + k)l(k) \quad (3)$$

$$H(i) = \sum_{k=0}^{K-1} S(2i + k)h(k) \quad (4)$$

where K is the number of filter coefficients. Here, the decimation is already performed by the equations 3 and 4, thus the number of coefficients per sub-band becomes half the number of samples of the input signal.

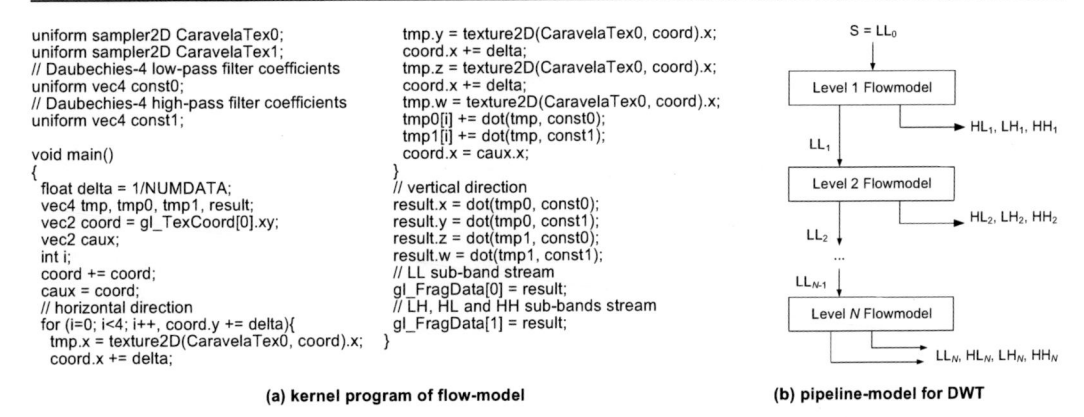

```
uniform sampler2D CaravelaTex0;          tmp.y = texture2D(CaravelaTex0, coord).x;
uniform sampler2D CaravelaTex1;          coord.x += delta;
// Daubechies-4 low-pass filter coefficients   tmp.z = texture2D(CaravelaTex0, coord).x;
uniform vec4 const0;                     coord.x += delta;
// Daubechies-4 high-pass filter coefficients  tmp.w = texture2D(CaravelaTex0, coord).x;
uniform vec4 const1;                     tmp0[i] += dot(tmp, const0);
                                         tmp1[i] += dot(tmp, const1);
void main()                              coord.x = caux.x;
{                                        }
  float delta = 1/NUMDATA;               // vertical direction
  vec4 tmp, tmp0, tmp1, result;          result.x = dot(tmp0, const0);
  vec2 coord = gl_TexCoord[0].xy;        result.y = dot(tmp0, const1);
  vec2 caux;                             result.z = dot(tmp1, const0);
  int i;                                 result.w = dot(tmp1, const1);
  coord += coord;                        // LL sub-band stream
  caux = coord;                          gl_FragData[0] = result;
  // horizontal direction                // LH, HL and HH sub-bands stream
  for (i=0; i<4; i++, coord.y += delta){ gl_FragData[1] = result;
    tmp.x = texture2D(CaravelaTex0, coord).x;  }
    coord.x += delta;
```

(a) kernel program of flow-model   (b) pipeline-model for DWT

Figure 20. Flow-model and pipeline-model of 2D-DWT

Due to the separable property of DWT, two dimensional DWT (2D-DWT) can be performed by sequentially applying the above equations through the horizontal and vertical image directions. It generates 4 sub-bands (i.e. LL, HL, LH and HH as shown in Figure 19(a)). Each sub-band corresponds to a possible combination of direction (horizontal/vertical) and filter response (low/high-pass). To generate four new sub-bands, the same calculation is applied to the new LL sub-band representation. This recursive calculation is iterated until the given number of decomposition levels (typically 3 to 5 levels) is achieved. Figure 19(c) shows a result of 2D-DWT with 2 decomposition levels calculated from the input image in Figure 19(b).

5.2.2. Pipeline-model for 2D DWT

Let us think about the organization of pipeline-model of 2D-DWT. The recursive nature of N-level DWT decomposition suggests a pipeline organization where each pipeline stage corresponds to one decomposition level. Each stage in this pipeline can be a single kernel program that generates LL_n sub-band used in the next stage. It also needs to generate the remaining sub-bands. Therefore, a flow-model with an input stream and two output streams is applied to each stage in the pipeline, which calculates the following equations (LL_n corresponds to one of the output streams and HL_n, LH_n and HH_n to the other):

$$LL_n(i,j) = \sum_{k=0}^{K-1}\sum_{m=0}^{M-1} LL_{n-1}(2i+k, 2j+m)l(m)l(k);$$

$$HL_n(i,j) = \sum_{k=0}^{K-1}\sum_{m=0}^{M-1} LL_{n-1}(2i+k, 2j+m)h(m)l(k);$$

$$LH_n(i,j) = \sum_{k=0}^{K-1}\sum_{m=0}^{M-1} LL_{n-1}(2i+k, 2j+m)l(m)h(k);$$

$$HH_n(i,j) = \sum_{k=0}^{K-1}\sum_{m=0}^{M-1} LL_{n-1}(2i+k, 2j+m)h(m)h(k).$$

The program included in the flow-model is written in OpenGL and shown in Figure 20(a). It receives an input data stream that includes the previous LL sub-band and generates two output data streams.

Using this flow-model, a pipeline-model illustrated in Figure 20(b) can be defined; each stage in the pipeline-model consists of the flow-model in Figure 20(a). As the number of level increases, the input and output data stream sizes becomes 1/4 of the previous level. At the flow-model for level1, the input data stream becomes an ENTRANCE port of the pipeline-model. One of the output data streams of the flow-model is connected to the next stage (i.e. INTERMEDIATE port). The other, which is marked as EXIT port, generates the sub-bands at the corresponding decomposition level.

The pipeline-model is created by the meta-pipeline function defined in section 4.4.. After implementing the pipeline-model and providing the image data to the ENTRANCE port, the Caravela runtime executes each stage whenever the input data is prepared. If it is performed in a local shader, each stage is assigned to the shader and is replaced to the other stage automatically. When it is executed on remote worker servers, each flow-model is assigned to a worker and it waits for the input data that is propagated from the previous pipeline stage.

6. Summary and Future Directions

The massive computational power available in off-the-shelf Graphics Processing Units (GPUs) can pave the way for its usage for general purpose processing (GPGPU). However, current interfaces to program GPU operation are still oriented towards graphics processing. This chapter presents the Caravela reserch project, devoted to the research of stream-based computation models, the development of programming interfaces and the implementation of distributed computing platforms based on the devised models.

The chapter presents the proposed flow-model and describes the design and the implementation of the distributed Caravela platform based on GPUs, available in commodity personal computers. The application interface to the Caravela platform is transparent to program the execution steps for the local and the remote execution mechanisms. The provided uniform interface hides differences in graphics runtime environments (e.g. DirecX and the OpenGL) and allows programmer of GPGPU to concentrate on the programming of algorithms instead of wasting time with details of graphical programming environments. Moreover, for recursive applications implemented on local resources, an optimization technique called the swap frame has been developed for exchanging data between output and input in a very efficient way. This technique was implemented as an extension of the Caravela library for the OpenGL runtime environment, using the functions handling the I/O pair, which implements recursive feedback in a flow-model.

For distributed computing, it has been developed a pipelined execution mechanism of the flow-models, called meta-pipeline, which distributes the flow-models in the Caravela network. This mechanism, implemented as an extension of the original Caravela platform, creates a virtual meta network of flow-model units and execute them with data received at the input of the virtual network.

Experimental results show that the Caravela platform, namely under local execution, is able to significantly improve the performance of stream-based computation, when compared to CPU-based execution. The implemented optimization technique for data exchanging allows to improve the performance of GPU based applications by more than 50%.

Future directions of the Caravela project include the evaluation of the GPU based distributed computing platform. Regarding to meta-pipeline, we consider to implement a graphics user interface to describe the pipeline-model. This is an important aspect, because the process of configuring the pipeline and defining the attributes of ports are tedious and propitious to introduce mistakes. In what regarding high performance concurrent computing, we are developing a GPU based cluster [10]. In such a cluster, the Message Passing Interface (MPI) [31] is used to communicate between computers. We are considering the combination of both MPI and Caravela interfaces, by putting together the functions in a library to compute, according to the flow-model, and to communicate. Finally, we also consider to implement a library for scientific computation such as BLAS [4], to show the effectiveness of the Caravela platform.

Acknowledgment

This work is partially supported by the Portuguese Foundation for Science and Technology (FCT) through the FEDER program.

References

[1] Sh: A high-level metaprogramming language for modern GPUs (http://libsh.org/).

[2] The OpenGL Extension Wrangler Library (http://glew.sourceforge.net/).

[3] The OpenGL Utility Toolkit (GLUT) Programming Interface API Version 3 (http://www.opengl.org/documentation/specs/glut/).

[4] Basic Linear Algebra Subprograms (http://www.netlib.org/blas/).

[5] D. Bernholdt, S. Bharathi, and et al. The earth system grid: Supporting the next generation of climate modeling research. *Proceedings of the IEEE*, **93**:485–495, 2005.

[6] I. Buck, T. Foley, D. Horn, J. Sugerman, K. Fatahalian, M. Houston, and P. Hanrahan. Brook for GPUs: stream computing on graphics hardware. *ACM Transactions on Graphics*, **23**(3):777–786, 2004.

[7] Caravela webpage – http://www.caravela-gpu.org/.

[8] CUDA webpage – http://developer.nvidia.com/object/cuda.html.

[9] I. Daubechies. *Ten Lectures on Wavelets*. Number 61 in CBMS/NSF Series in Applied Math. 1992.

[10] Z. Fan, F. Qiu, A. Kaufman, and S. Yoakum-Stover. GPU Cluster for High Performance Computing. In *Proceedings of the ACM/IEEE Conference on Supercomputing*, page 47. IEEE Computer Society, 2004.

[11] A. Freier, P. Karlton, and P. Kocher. *The SSL Protocol Version 3.0*. Netscape communications corporation, 1996.

[12] J. Frey, T. Tannenbaum, I. Foster, M. Livny, and S. Tuecke. Condor-G: A Computation Management Agent for Multi-Institutional Grids. In *Proceedings of the 10th IEEE Symposium on High Performance Distributed Computing (HPDC)*, pages 55–63, 2001.

[13] GridLab Resource Management System – http://www.gridlab.org/WorkPackages/wp-9/.

[14] W. Grosso. *Java RMI*. Oreilly Media, first edition, 2001.

[15] J. Gummaraju and M. Rosenblum. Stream programming on general-purpose processors. In *Proceedings of the 38th annual IEEE/ACM International Symposium on Microarchitecture (MICRO)*, pages 343–354. IEEE Computer Society, 2005.

[16] H. Hofstee. Power efficient processor architecture and the cell processor. In *Proceedings of the 11th International Symposium on High-Performance Computer Architecture (HPCA)*, pages 258–262. IEEE Computer Society, 2005.

[17] DirectX for WINE homepage. http://directxwine.sourceforge.net/.

[18] Globus Alliance (http://www.globus.org/).

[19] DirectX webpage (http://www.microsoft.com/directx).

[20] R. Jacob, C. Schafer, I. Foster, M. Tobis, and J. Anderson. Computational design and performance of the fast ocean atmosphere model, version one. In *International Conference on Computational Science*, pages 175–184, 2001.

[21] N. Karonis, B. Toonen, and I. Foster. MPICH-G2: A grid-enabled implementation of the message passing interface. *Journal of Parallel and Distributed Computing*, **63**(5):551–563, 2003.

[22] J. Kessenich, D. Baldwin, and R. Rost. The OpenGL Shading Language. *3Dlabs, Inc. Ltd.*, 2006.

[23] P. Kondratieva, J. Krüger, and R. Westermann. The Application of GPU Particle Tracing to Diffusion Tensor Field Visualization. In *IEEE Visualization*, pages 73–78, 2005.

[24] Sheng Liang. *Java Native Interface: Programmer's Guide and Specification*. Addison-Wesley Professional, first edition, 2001.

[25] P. McCormick, J. Inman, J. P. Ahrens, C. Hansen, and G. Roth. Scout: A Hardware-Accelerated System for Quantitatively Driven Visualization and Analysis. In *Proceedings of the conference on Visualization*, pages 171–178, Austin, 2004. IEEE Computer Society.

[26] K. Moreland and E. Angel. The FFT on a GPU. In *Proceedings of the ACM SIGGRAPH/EUROGRAPHICS conference on Graphics hardware*, pages 112–119, Aire-la-Ville, Switzerland, 2003. Eurographics Association.

[27] OpenGL Architecture Review Board, D. Shreiner, M. Woo, J. Neider, and T. Davis. *OpenGL Programming Guide: The Official Guide to Learning OpenGL, Version 2*. Addison Wesley, 2005.

[28] J. Owens, D. Luebke, N. Govindaraju, M. Harris, J. Kruger, A. Lefohn, and T. Purcell. A survey of general-purpose computation on graphics hardware. In *Eurographics 2005, State of the Art Reports*, pages 21–51, August 2005.

[29] D. Reed, C. Mendes, C. Lu, I. Foster, and C. Kesselman. *The Grid 2: Blueprint for a New Computing Infrastructure - Application Tuning and Adaptation*. Morgan Kaufman, San Francisco, second edition, 2003.

[30] L. Sousa and S. Yamagiwa. Caravela: A distributed stream-based computing platform. In *3rd HiPEAC Industrial Workshop, IBM Haifa Labs, Israel*, April 2007.

[31] N. Doss W. Gropp, E. Lusk and A. Skjellum. A high-performance, portable implementation of the MPI message passing interface standard. *Parallel Computing*, **22**(6):789–792, 1996.

[32] S. Yamagiwa and L. Sousa. Caravela: A novel stream-based distributed computing environment. *IEEE Computer Magazine*, **40**(5):70–77, 2007.

[33] S. Yamagiwa and L. Sousa. Design and implementation of a stream-based distributedcomputing platform using graphics processing units. In *Proceedings of the 4th International Conference on Computing Frontiers*, pages 197–204. ACM Press, 2007.

[34] S. Yamagiwa, L. Sousa, and D. Antao. Data buffering optimization methods toward a uniform programming interface for gpu-based applications. In *Proceedings of the 4th International Conference on Computing Frontiers*, pages 205–212. ACM Press, 2007.

[35] S. Yamagiwa, L. Sousa, and T. Brandao. Meta-pipeline: A new execution mechanism for distributed pipeline processing. In *Proceedings of the Sixth International Symposium on Parallel and Distributed Computing (ISPDC)*, page 5. IEEE Computer Society, 2007.

Chapter 2

DISTRIBUTED SHARED MEMORY SYSTEMS: PRINCIPLES AND MODELS

Azzedine Boukerche[1]*and Alba Cristina Magalhaes Alves de Melo*[2][†]
[1]PARADISE Research Laboratory, SITE, University of Ottawa, Canada
[2]Department of Computer Science,
University of Brasilia (UnB), Brazil

Abstract

Distributed Shared Memory (DSM) is an abstraction that allows the use of the shared memory programming paradigm on a parallel or distributed environment where no physically shared memory exists. Recently, DSM has received a lot of attention since it provides a good tradeoff between performance and ease of programming. However, in order to design a cost effective DSM system, many choices must be made. In this chapter, we will cover the following aspects concerning the design of a DSM system: type of the DSM system, memory consistency model, memory coherence protocol, implementation level and fault tolerance issues. At the end of the chapter, we discuss five DSM systems in detail and present a comparative table.

Keywords: distributed shared memory, parallel programming paradigm, memory consistency model

AMS Subject Classifications: 68M14, 68M19, 68Q85

1. Introduction

In the last years, the use of the shared memory programming paradigm in distributed architectures where no physically shared memory exists has received a lot of attention. This is basically for two reasons. First, the shared memory programming paradigm is often considered easier than the message passing counterpart, since communication is implicit and the programmer does not have to deal with aspects such as marshalling and unmarshalling,

---

[*]E-mail address: boukerch@site.uottawa.ca
[†]E-mail address: albamm@cic.unb.br

among others. Second, having a unique parallel programming model can help to make portable parallel programs.

In order to make shared memory programming possible in distributed architectures, we must create a shared memory abstraction that parallel processes can access. This abstraction is called Distributed Shared Memory (DSM) and can be implemented in software basically by two different approaches: shared objects and shared virtual memory (SVM). In the first approach, the DSM is seen as an object or a set of objects. Operations on the DSM are methods that access the memory object(s). The second approach was proposed by K. Li [34]. In this case, the conventional virtual memory mechanism is used to map the DSM into the virtual address space of each parallel process. Operations in the shared memory abstraction are memory addressing operations. Thus, SVM is implemented as a single paged, virtual address space over a set of computers that is managed by the virtual memory system [34].

Although most of the implementations of DSM systems are exclusively in software, many hardware implementations do exist. These later ones usually have high performance and are completely transparent to the programmer. However, the cost of hardware DSM implementations is also high and the time needed to develop such systems is still considerable. In section 2., these three types of DSM systems are presented as well as their basic mechanisms. In order to improve performance, DSM systems usually replicate data thus creating a potential consistency problem. The first DSM systems tried to give parallel programmers the same guarantees they had when programming uniprocessors. It has been observed that providing such a strong memory consistency model creates a huge coherence overhead, slowing down the parallel application and bringing frequently the system into a thrashing state [43]. To alleviate this problem, researchers have proposed to relax some consistency conditions, thus creating new shared memory behaviours that are different from the traditional uniprocessor one. Relaxed memory models aim to reduce this overhead by allowing replicas of the same data to have, for some period of time, different values [3]. By doing this, relaxed models provide a programming model that is complex since, at some moments, the programmer is conscious of replication.

In the shared memory programming paradigm, synchronization operations must be used every time processes want to restrict the order in which memory operations should be performed. Using this fact, hybrid Memory Consistency Models guarantee that processors only have a consistent view of the shared memory at synchronization time. This allows a great overlapping of basic read and write memory accesses that can potentially lead to considerable performance gains.

Choosing a memory consistency model is a tradeoff between performance and ease of programming [45]. Usually, models that provide a good performance are difficult to program and vice-versa. Also, the choice of the best memory consistency model for a given application depends on the application's own shared memory access pattern. Section 3. discusses memory consistency models in detail. First, a system model is presented and then the following memory consistency models are introduced: atomic consistency, sequential consistency, causal consistency, PipelinedRAM consistency, release consistency and scope consistency. Also, we present some efforts made in order to formalize memory consistency models.

While the memory consistency model defines when consistency should be ensured, coherence protocols define how it should be done. Indeed, there are many coherence protocols that can be used to implement the same memory consistency model. When desinging a coherence protocol for DSM systems, there are many choices to be made: write-invalidate or write-update, Multiple Readers/Single Writer (MRSW) or Multiple Readers/Multiple Writers (MRMW), homeless or home-based protocols. It has also been observed that the choice of the best coherence protocol depends on the reference pattern exhibited by an application at a particular moment. Many adaptive coherence protocols were proposed that analyze the access patterns of a parallel application and dynamically choose the protocol that is best suited. Section 4. discusses these design choices in detail.

For any system running on a parallel or distributed platform that aims to be used in large scale, fault tolerance mechanisms must be considered. Usually, fault tolerance is achieved by periodically checkpointing each process that compose the system and, in the case of a failure, recovering the system to a previous consistent system state by activating the saved checkpoints [14]. Many coordinated and uncoordinated checkpointing strategies were proposed for DSM systems. Section 5. presents some basic concepts of rollback/recovery and checkpointing strategies and how their are adapted to DSM systems.

Many DSM systems have been proposed in the literature. In the site called "DSM home pages" (*www.cs.umd.edu/ keleher/dsmx.html*), there are 51 DSM systems listed. In section 6., we will discuss five of them: Ivy, TreadMarks, JIAJIA, Orca and DASH. Also, we present a comparative table containing resumed information about 12 DSM systems.

2. Basic Design Issues

The Distributed Shared Memory is an abstraction created to allow programmers of a distributed memory architecture to use the shared memory programming paradigm. At the lowest level, the mechanisms that simulate the shared memory communicate by message exchange. At the programmers interface level, however, the DSM creates the illusion of a global memory which is directly accessible by all processors. Figure 1 illustrates the DSM.

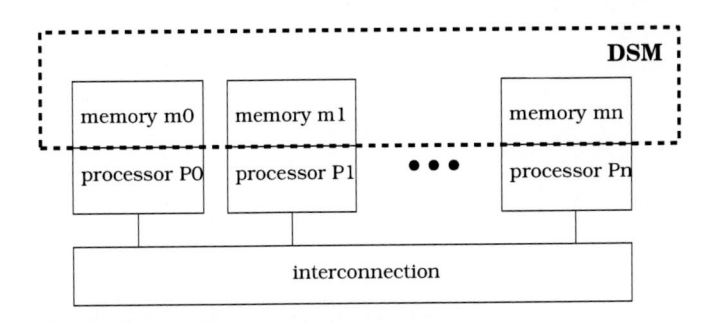

Figure 1. DSM abstraction.

2.1. DSM Types

There are three types of DSM systems: page-based, object-based and hardware-based. The first two belong to the class of software DSM systems. The difference between them is that the first one treats the DSM as an unstructured memory space and the second one imposes some structure to the DSM. Hardware DSM systems use specialized hardware to create the DSM. In this section, we will discuss these three types of DSM systems, as well as mechanisms to locate data in them.

2.1.1. Page-based DSM Systems

Page-based DSM systems use a technique known as Shared Virtual Memory (SVM), proposed by K. Li [34]. In this approach, the shared data compose a unique and global address space, which is mapped into the address space of each parallel process that composes the DSM application by the standard virtual memory management system.

The data that compose the DSM are accessed through *LOAD* and *STORE* machine instructions. If the data are local and there is no violation on access permissions, DSM data are accessed in a way that is completely transparent to the DSM system. However, when data are not mapped to local page frames or there is an access type violation, a *page fault* exception is generated. The operating system receives this exception and forwards it to the DSM system, which retrieves the page that caused the *page fault* from a remote node, places it in the local memory and instructs the OS to re-execute the instruction that caused the exception. As can be noticed, this is very similar to the traditional virtual memory system behavior. However, in the DSM case, pages are retrieved from remote nodes, instead of the local disk.

Page-based DSM systems can be completely transparent to the programmers by mapping the entire data segment of the processes into the DSM. This was the approach used in Ivy [35]. Nevertheless, most of the recent DSM systems (e.g. TreadMarks [26], JIAJIA [21]) offer primitives for mapping and unmapping memory regions into the DSM space. Although incurring in some transparency loss, this approach permits the programmer to choose the exact size of the region that will be mapped into the DSM, which generally reduces the size of the DSM, when compared with the first approach. Most of the page-based DSM systems in the literature are implemented as user-level runtime systems that map and control the DSM regions through Unix-like system calls such as *mmap* and *mprotect*, respectively. The *page fault* exceptions are treated by a *SIGSEGV* signal handler.

2.1.2. Object-based DSM Systems

In this approach, the DSM is structured as a collection of objects that can be accessed through high-level operations. In this section, we will use a broad definition of object-based DSM system which includes object-oriented, shared-variable and immutable data approaches. In the literature, the semantic of object-based systems that we will use here is sometimes called *middleware* approach [12]. In object-based DSM systems, the objects that compose the DSM are accessed through high-level operations that, among others, allow the programmer to read and write values from/to the DSM respectively. Orca [7], Linda [10] and Bayou [54] are examples of object-based DSM systems. By imposing an structure to the DSM, object-based systems are usually less error prone. However, in this case, the support of a programming language is required. Also, the performance of this kind of system is usually worse than the page-based systems, since a more abstract programming model must be created and managed.

2.1.3. Hardware-based DSM Systems

Hardware-based DSM systems aim to improve performance by implementing the DSM (or some DSM mechanisms) in hardware. These systems have complex and specialized hardware components that handle DSM requests in a way that is often transparent to the software. This approach usually achieves high performance and a high degree of transparency. However, the implementation cost and the time needed to deploy such systems is also high [12]. DASH [33], Alewife [4] and DDM [18] are examples of hardware-based DSM systems.

2.2. Locating Data in a DSM System

In a DSM system, the physical location of a data item changes frequently and, when a reference to non-local data is generated, the DSM system must able to find it. In a system with n nodes, the data item can be in any one of these nodes or even in many of them, since DSM systems usually replicate data. Thus, the DSM system must keep track of the location of each data item in the system and locate it fast. In this section, we will focus on page-based DSM systems and so, the problem to be solved is to locate a page. However, the techniques explained here are easily adapted to object-based and hardware-based systems.

Page managers are the entities which are responsible to keep the following information about the page: copy set, owner, access rights, utilization statistics, among others. Since DSM systems usually replicate data, each page can be in many nodes simultaneously. The set of nodes where a page resides at a given moment is called *copy set*. The *owner* of the page is the node that has most access rights over the page. Often, before writing on a page, a node must obtain ownership over it. Also, we need to keep track of the current access right to the page (*none, read-only, read-write*) and also maintain some statistics. In general, each page p has its manager that is contacted each time a non-local access on p is generated. Li and Hudak [36] proposed three strategies to structure the page manager: centralized, fixed distributed and dynamic distributed.

In the centralized approach, there is only one page manager in the whole system. Each time a node needs to know the location of a page, it sends a message to the centralized page manager, which keeps track of the location of all pages in the system. This approach, although simple, is rarely used since the centralized page manager becomes quickly saturated. In the fixed distributed approach, each node is responsible to manage a subset of the pages of the DSM system. The mapping between a page and its page manager is usually done through a mathematical function that receives the page number and obtains the number of its manager node. The mathematical function $pm(i)$ returns the page manager of page i and can be as simple as $i \bmod n$, where n is the number of nodes, or can involve complex hash techniques [36]. When a *page fault* on p is generated, the faulting node sends a message to $pm(p)$. Having received the message, the node $pm(p)$ sends back the page location to the requesting node.

In the dynamic distributed approach, the page manager is one of the nodes that have (or had) the page in its local memory. The location of each page manager is contained in local tables placed in each node. These tables contain the field *ProbOwner* which indicates which node is the probable owner of the page. In the case of a *page fault*, the faulting node sends the request to the *ProbOwner*. If the *ProbOwner* is still the page manager, it replies to the faulting node. If it is no more the owner, it forwards the request to the node contained in its *ProbOwner* field. At the end of the *ProbOnwer* chain, the actual page manager is found [36]. Most DSM systems use the fixed distributed approach to find information about the page since it has good performance and simple implementation.

3. Memory Consistency Models

Intuitively, the programmer assumes that the instructions that compose his or her program are executed one after the other (in a serial way) and memory operations are executed atomically. This informal model is used to reason about the results a program can produce. A Memory Consistency Model formalizes this concept by defining the order in which the memory operations must be perceived by the programmer [3]. Since the Memory Consistency Model defines the apparent order and not the real order of memory operations execution, many optimizations can be made in a uniprocessor machine while still respecting the intuitive model. Unfortunately, when we try to apply the same optimizations to a distributed or parallel environment, the intuitive model is violated and programming becomes more complex since the programmer must be conscious of the distributed nature of the physical memory.

3.1. System Model

To study memory consistency models, a system model must be defined [45] [3]. In the model that we will use in this section, a *parallel program* is executed by a *system*. A *system* is a finite set of *processors*. Each *processor* executes a process that issues a set of operations on the shared global memory M. The shared global memory M is an abstract entity composed by all addresses that can be accessed by a program. Each processor p_i has its own local memory m_i that caches all memory addresses of M (figure 2).

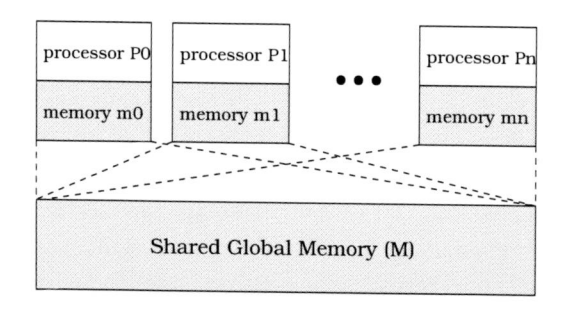

Figure 2. System Model.

Each memory operation is first *issued* and then *performed*, i. e., memory operations are non-atomic. A memory operation $o_{pi}(x)v$ is issued when processor p_i executes the instruction $o_{pi}(x)v$. A read operation $r_{pi}(x)v$ is performed when a write operation on the same location x cannot modify the value v returned to p_i. Read operations of p_i are always done on the local memory m_i.

A write operation $w_{pi}(x)v$ is in fact a set of memory operations $\sum_{i=0}^{n-1} w_{pi}x(v)$ where n is the number of processors. A write operation $w_{pi}(x)v$ is *performed with respect to processor* p_j when the value v is written to the address x on the local memory m_j of p_j. A write operation $w_{pi}(x)v$ is *performed* when it is performed with respect to all processors that compose the system.

Acquire and *release* memory accesses are seen as special read and write accesses, respectively.

At the beginning of the execution, it is assumed that all memory locations are initialized to 0. At the end of the execution, all memory operations must be performed. Each process running on a processor p_i is described by a local execution history H_{pi}, that is an ordered sequence of memory operations issued by p_i. The execution history H is the union of all H_{pi}. A graphical representation of H is shown in Figure 3. In this particular history, there are 3 processors, p_0, p_1 and p_2. Time corresponds to the horizontal axis and flows from left to right. The graphical notation $w(x)v$ represents the instant when the write operation is issued and $r(x)v$ the moment the read operation is performed.

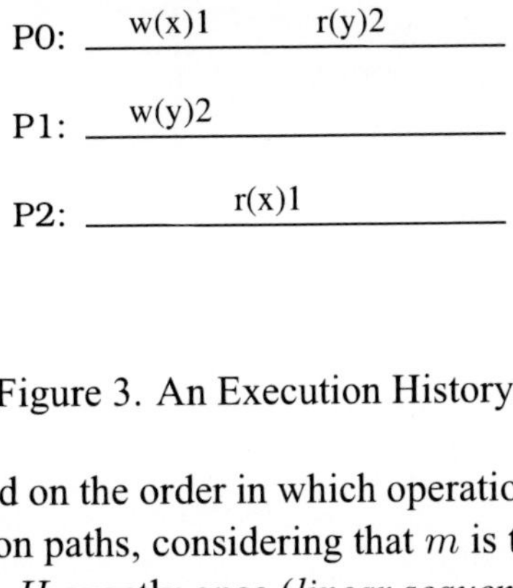

```
P0: _____w(x)1_____r(y)2_____

P1: _____w(y)2_____

P2: _____r(x)1_____
```

Figure 3. An Execution History.

If no restriction is imposed on the order in which operations are seen by the processors, there are $m!$ possible execution paths, considering that m is the total number of operations and each operation appears in H exactly once (*linear sequence*). For instance, $w_{p0}(x)1 \rightarrow w_{p1}(y)2 \rightarrow r_{p0}(x)1 \rightarrow r_{p2}(y)2$ is a linear sequence of H.

Most of the memory consistency models proposed in the literature respect at least two orders [39]: *legal sequence* and *program order*. A linear sequence is legal if all read operations $r_{pi}(x)v$ return the value written by the immediatelly precedent write operation on memory position v. The program order states that [43] if $o1$ and $o2$ are operations issued by the same processor p_i and $o1$ is issued before $o2$ then $o1 \overrightarrow{po} o2$. There are basically two classes of memory models: uniform and hybrid models[43]. A uniform model considers only read and write memory operations to define consistency conditions whereas a hybrid model considers also synchronization operations in this definition.

In execution histories, some operation orderings are allowed and some orderings are forbidden. The decision of which orderings are valid is made by the memory consistency model. Thus, the memory consistency model de defines an order relation on a set of shared memory accesses (H_x) [3]. One execution history is valid on a memory consistency model if it respects the order relation defined by the model. In other words, a history Q is valid on a memory consistency model if there is at least one linear legal sequence on Q that respects this order.

3.2. Strong Memory Consistency Models

3.2.1. Atomic Consistency

Atomic Consistency is the strongest and the oldest memory consistency model [43]. It defines a total order on all shared memory accesses (H) and, besides, imposes that physical time order must be preserved. In order to define what orderings are valid when more than one access occur at the same physical time, many variations of Atomic Consistency have been proposed, such as static atomic consistency and dynamic atomic consistency [19].

In atomic consistency, physical time is divided in non-overlapping time intervals. All memory operations issued in time interval t_i must be perfomed at the end of t_i. In other words, a memory operation $o_{pi}(x)v$ must be performed before p_i issues the next operation. Also, the order imposed by physical time must be respected. Figure 4 illustrates an atomic consistent execution history.

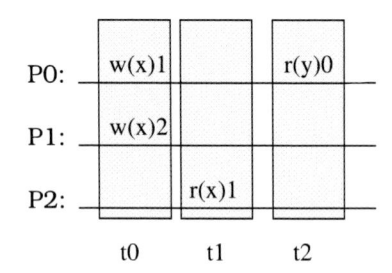

Figure 4. An Atomic Consistent Execution History.

In this particular history, there are 3 processors, p_0, p_1 and p_2 and 3 time intervals t_0, t_1 and t_2. Operations $w_{p0}(x)1$ and $w_{p1}(x)2$ occur in the same time interval. One valid execution order for H in atomic consistency is $w_{p1}(x)2 \rightarrow w_{p0}(x)1 \rightarrow r_{p2}(x)1 \rightarrow r_{p0}(y)0$. Thus, this history is valid on atomic consistency. There are no examples of DSM systems that implement Atomic Consistency. Preserving physical time order for every shared memory access is very time-consuming in systems where no global physical clocks exists.

3.2.2. Sequential Consistency

Sequential Consistency (SC) was proposed by Lamport [31] as a correctness criterion for shared memory multiprocessors. In SC, "the result of any execution is the same as if the operations of all processors were executed in some sequential order, and the operations of each individual processor appear in this sequence in the order specified by its program". In other words, the result of a sequential consistent execution must be equivalent to some sequential execution of the operations of all processors, in which the program order between operations is preserved. Thus, Sequential Consistency imposes a total order on shared memory accesses where program order must be respected.

Figure 5 shows a sequentially consistent execution history.

```
P0: _____w(x)1_____

P1: _____w(y)2  w(x)2_____

P2: _____r(y)2  r(x)0_____
```

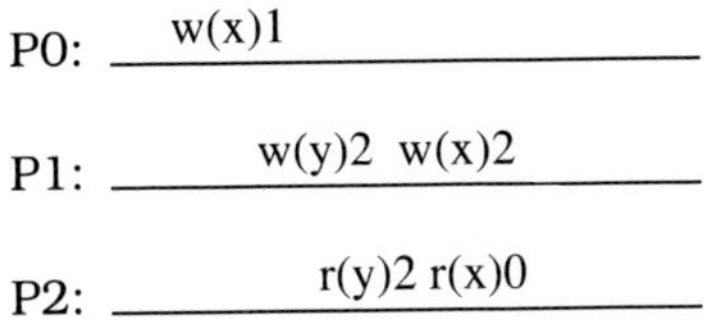

Figure 5. A Sequentially Consistent Execution History.

In this particular history, there are 3 processors, p_0, p_1 and p_2. It is a sequentially consistent execution history since it is possible to derive at least one sequence of all memory operations (H) where all processors agree. The following execution order is a valid execution under SC: $w_{p1}(y)2 \to r_{p2}(y)2 \to r_{p2}(x)0 \to w_{p0}(x)1 \to w_{p1}(x)2$. Note, however, that it is not the only valid sequence that can be derived. The sequence $w_{p1}(y)2 \to r_{p2}(y)2 \to r_{p2}(x)0 \to w_{p1}(x)2 \to w_{p0}(x)1$ is also a valid execution sequence on SC. This execution history is not valid on atomic consistency since the physical time order is not respected. Most of the first DSM systems implement sequential consistency. Ivy [35] and Mirage [16] are examples of sequentially consistent DSM systems.

3.3. Relaxed Uniform Memory Consistency Models

Since sequential consistency ensures that all processors will see the same order of all memory operations, most of the applications programmed for monoprocessors run correctly on sequential consistency. However, the overhead introduced to guarantee this strong condition is usually very huge and that was the motivation to create relaxed memory models. In relaxed memory models, it is no longer necessary for all processors to agree on the order of all shared memory accesses. Thus, a total order in H is not required [3]. Also, each processor sees only the operations it issues and the write operations of the other processors (H_{pi+w}).

3.3.1. Causal Consistency

Causal consistency is a relaxed memory model that is based on a variation of the potential causal order relation defined by Lamport[30]. In causal consistency, it is only necessary for all processors to agree on the order of the operations that respect causal order. The operations that are causally independent (concurrents) can be seen in different orders by different processors. Informally, causal order is based on two order relations: ready-by and program order. The read-by order states that, if a processor p_i reads a value v on memory position x that was written by the operation $w_{pj}(x)v$ then $w_{pj}(x)v \overrightarrow{rb} r_{pi}(x)v$. In other words, $w_{pj}(x)v$ is read by $r_{pi}(x)v$. The program order used here was defined in section 3.1.. The potential causal order relation is defined to be the irreflexive transitive closure of two order relations (program order and read-by order) [30].

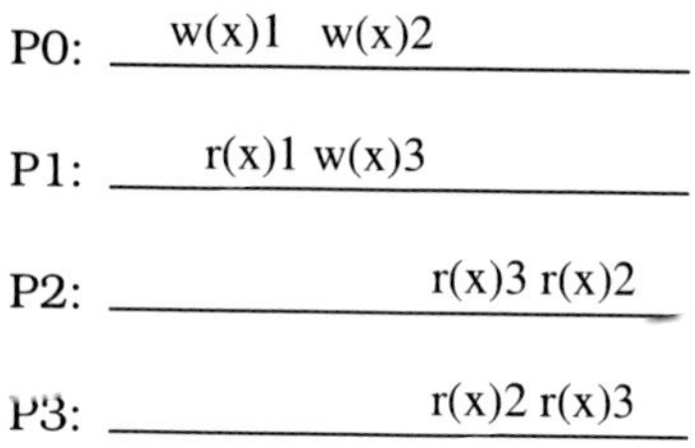

```
P0:    w(x)1  w(x)2

P1:    r(x)1  w(x)3

P2:                  r(x)3  r(x)2

P3:                  r(x)2  r(x)3
```

Figure 6. A Causally Consistent Execution History.

The history presented in figure 6 is causally consistent since it is possible to derive at least one possible order that respects Causal Consistency for each processor. Note that each processor must only see its own operations and the write operations of the other processors (H_{pi+w}). As said before, the restrictions imposed by causal consistency are program order and read-by order. By transitivity, all orders in H_{pi+w} must then include $w_{p0}(x)1 \rightarrow w_{p1}(x)3$ (derived from $w_{p0}(x)1 \rightarrow r_{p1}(x)1 \rightarrow w_{p1}(x)3$). Thus, possible orderings are:

$H_{p0+w} : w_{p0}(x)1 \rightarrow w_{p0}(x)2 \rightarrow w_{p1}(x)3$
$H_{p1+w} : w_{p0}(x)1 \rightarrow r_{p1}(x)1 \rightarrow w_{p1}(x)3 \rightarrow w_{p0}x(2)$
$H_{p2+w} : w_{p0}(x)1 \rightarrow w_{p1}(x)3 \rightarrow r_{p2}(x)3 \rightarrow w_{p0}(x)2 \rightarrow r_{p2}(x)2$
$H_{p3+w} : w_{p0}(x)1 \rightarrow w_{p0}(x)2 \rightarrow r_{p3}(x)2 \rightarrow w_{p1}(x)3 \rightarrow r_{p3}(x)3$

Although the history in figure 6 is valid in Causal Consistency, it is not valid in Sequential Consistency, since it is impossible to derive a total order on H that respects program order.

Causal consistency was proposed by John and Ahamad [25] and implemented in the system Clouds.

3.3.2. PipelinedRAM Consistency

PipelinedRAM Consistency was defined by Lipton and Sandberg [38] and belongs to a family of memory consistency models usually called as processor consistency. PipelinedRAM relaxes some conditions imposed by causal consistency, requiring only that writes issued by the same processor must be observed by all processors in the order they where issued. In other words, among the operations issued by other processors, only write operations must obey the program order.

Considering the history presented in figure 7, the following H_{pi+w} can be derived:
$H_{p0+w} : w_{p0}(x)1 \rightarrow w_{p1}(x)2$
$H_{p1+w} : w_{p0}(x)1 \rightarrow r_{p1}(x)1 \rightarrow w_{p1}(x)2$
$H_{p2+w} : w_{p0}(x)1 \rightarrow r_{p2}(x)1 \rightarrow w_{p1}(x)2 \rightarrow r_{p2}(x)2$
$H_{p3+w} : w_{p1}(x)2 \rightarrow r_{p3}(x)2 \rightarrow w_{p0}(x)1 \rightarrow r_{p3}(x)1$

As it was possible to derive valid H_{pi+w} for every p_i, this execution history is valid on PipelinedRAM consistency. Note, however, that the same history is not a valid history on Causal Consistency since the order read-by is violated in H_{p3+w}.

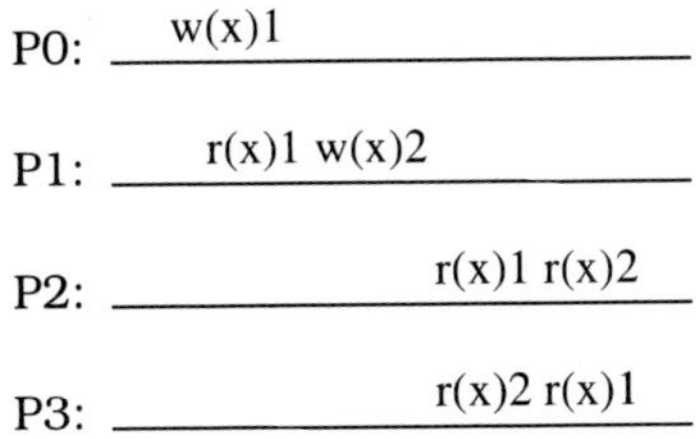

```
P0:  ____w(x)1_____

P1:  ____r(x)1 w(x)2_____

P2:  _____r(x)1 r(x)2_____

P3:  _____r(x)2 r(x)1_____
```

Figure 7. A PipelinedRAM Consistent Execution History.

Many processor architectures implement memory consistency models that belong to the processor consistency family. Examples of processor consistent machines are the VAX8800 and the DEC Alpha [47].

3.4. Relaxed Hybrid Memory Consistency Models

Even on uniprocessor systems, processes that use only the basic read and write shared memory operations to communicate can produce unexpected results. For this reason, synchronization operations must be used every time processes want to restrict the order on which memory operations should be performed. Using this fact, hybrid Memory Consistency Models guarantee that processors only have a consistent view of the shared memory at synchronization time [43]. This allows a great overlapping of basic memory accesses that can potentially lead to considerable performance gains.

Defining hybrid Memory Models is more complex than defining uniform ones. This is basically for two reasons. First, there are more types of operations that must be considered. There is at least one more type of memory operation: $sync$ (synchronization type). Second, there are at least two different orders: one order that relates basic operations to synchronization operations and one order that relates synchronization operations exclusively [39]. Basically, the definition of a hybrid Memory Consistency Model must answer three questions: (1) which modifications must be propagated; (2) which processes must receive the modifications; and (3) which event will ensure that modifications preceding it are surely performed.

The most widely used hybrid memory consistency models are Release Consistency (RC) and Scope Consistency (ScC). Both answer these three questions distinctly. RC specifies that (1) all previous modifications must be propagated to (2) all processes on (3) a release synchronization access whereas ScC guarantees that (1) all previous modifications that belong to the consistency scope defined by lock l must be propagated to (2) the next process that opens consistency scope l at the moment of (3) an acquire synchronization access on lock l. The analysis of execution histories on hybrid memory consistency models is far more complex than on uniform memory models and it is beyond the scope of this chapter. For detailed information on this subject, please refer to [39] [19] [45].

In the rest of this section, Release Consistency and Scope Consistency are discussed.

3.4.1. Release Consistency

Release Consistency (RC) was defined by Gharachorloo et al. in [17] and is one of the most popular Hybrid Memory Models. In Release Consistency, competing accesses are called special accesses. Special accesses are divided into synchronization operations and non-synchronization operations. There are two subtypes of synchronization operations: *acquire* accesses and *release* accesses. Read and write memory operations are called ordinary accesses.

Informally, in Release Consistent systems, it must be guaranteed that [17]: before an ordinary access performs, all previous acquire accesses must be performed; and before a release performs with respect to any other processor, all previous ordinary accesses must be performed. There is also a third condition that requires special accesses to be processor consistent (RC_{pc}) or sequentially consistent (RC_{sc}) [3].

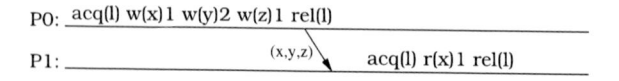

```
P0: acq(l) w(x)1 w(y)2 w(z)1 rel(l)
                        (x,y,z)
P1:                             acq(l) r(x)1 rel(l)
```

Figure 8. A Release Consistent Execution History.

Figure 8 presents a release consistent execution history. The operations *acq(l)* and *rel(l)* correspond both to the acquire and release of lock l. Assuming that the order on which the synchronization operations occured was $acq_{p0}(l) \rightarrow rel_{p0}(l) \rightarrow acq_{p1}(l) \rightarrow rel_{p1}(l)$, when p_1 acquires lock l, it is guaranteed that the operations $w_{p0}(x)1$, $w_{p0}(y)2$ and $w_{p0}(z)1$ are performed when considering RC_{sc}. The arrows represent the moment when the values are updated. In this case, three updates are merged in a single message at release time.

Release consistency is very successful since it provides potential improvements in performance while still providing a relatively simple programming model. This is basically due to a theoretical result that states that programs known as *properly labeled*, produce in RC_{sc} the same results they would produce when executing on sequential consistency [17].

Lazy release consistency (LRC) was first proposed as a protocol to implement release consistency [15] but some researchers consider it as a distinct memory consistency model. LRC postpones the propagation of the modifications until the moment of the next acquire. At this moment, all preceeding accesses are performed with respect to the processor that acquires the lock [15]. Figure 9 shows the moment when the modifications are propagated in LRC.

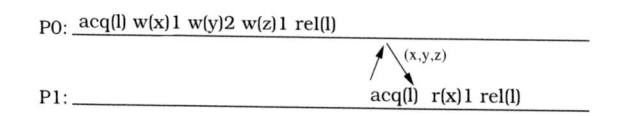

```
P0: acq(l) w(x)1 w(y)2 w(z)1 rel(l)
                              (x,y,z)
P1:                           acq(l) r(x)1 rel(l)
```

Figure 9. Propagation of the modifications in LRC.

Munin [11] and TreadMarks [26] are examples of Release Consistent Software DSM systems. DASH [33] is a Release Consistent hardware DSM.

3.4.2. Scope Consistency

The goal of Scope Consistency (ScC) is to take advantage of the association between synchronization variables and ordinary shared variables they protect. It was proposed by Iftode, Singh and Li [23]. In Scope Consistency, executions are divided into consistency scopes that are defined in a per lock basis. Scope Consistency orders only synchronization and data accesses that are related to the same synchronization variable. The association between shared data and the synchronization variable that guards them is implicit and depends on program order. Informally, a system is scope consistent if (1) before a new section of a consistency scope is allowed to open at process p, any write previously performed with respect to that consistency scope must be performed with respect to p; and (2) a memory access is allowed to perform with respect to a process p only after all consistency scope sessions previously entered by p (in program order) have been successfully opened [23].

Scope Consistency is a memory model that requires that consistency must be guaranteed when a process acquires a lock or when it reaches a synchronization barrier. In the first case, consistency is maintained in a per-lock basis, i.e., only the shared variables that were modified on the critical section guarded by lock l are guaranteed to be updated when a process acquires lock l. On a synchronization barrier, however, consistency is globally maintained and all processes are guaranteed to see all past modifications to the shared data. As Scope Consistency aims to reduce the coherence overhead while still providing a programming model that is close to the one offered by Release Consistency, several Scope Consistent DSM systems were proposed recently. JIAJIA [21] and Brazos [52] are examples of scope consistent software DSMs.

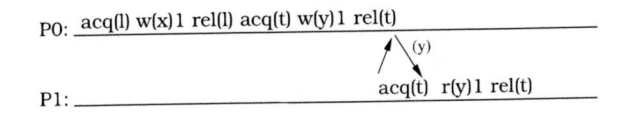

```
P0: ___acq(l) w(x)1 rel(l) acq(t) w(y)1 rel(t)_____
                                    ↗ ↘ (y)
P1: _____acq(t)  r(y)1 rel(t)___
```

Figure 10. A Scope Consistent Execution History.

Figure 10 presents the progragations of modifications on a scope consistent execution history. When processor p_1 acquires lock t, it only receives the modification $y = 1$ made inside the scope defined by t. Note that, in release consistency, p_1 would receive both $x = 1$ and $y = 1$, when acquiring lock t.

3.5. Formal Definitions of Memory Consistency Models

As can be seen, many memory consistency models have been proposed in the literature. Originally, the consistency requirements have not been defined in a formal way. In some cases, this led to different interpretations of the same memory model. To avoid this kind of problem, researchers proposed formal frameworks where many memory consistency models can be defined and compared.

Adve [3] proposed a quite complete methodology to specify memory models. A great number of memory models were considered. The aim of her work was to define relaxed models in terms of Sequential Consistency. The central hypothesis of this study is that all parallel programmers would prefer to reason as if they were programming a time-sharing uniprocessor.

A set of formal definitions was also proposed by Raynal and Schiper [48]. The objective of this study was to understand memory models and compare them. The following Memory Models were defined using the proposed notation: Atomic Consistency, Sequential Consistency, Causal Consistency and PipelinedRAM Consistency. Kohli, Neiger and Ahamad [45] also proposed a formal framework to relate memory models where Sequential Consistency, Total Store Order (TSO), Processor Consistency and Release Consistency were defined. Heddaya and Sinha[19] proposed a formalism and a system - Mermera - that permits multiple memory models in a single execution. The following memory models were formally defined: Sequential Consistency, PRAM Consistency, Slow Memory and Local Consistency. Higham, Kawash and Verwaal[20] proposed a framework to describe Memory Consistency Models. The authors defined Atomic Consistency, Sequential Consistency, Data Coherence, PipelinedRAM Consistency, Processor Consistency, Weak Ordering, TSO and Partial Store Order (PSO). Also, Weiwu, Weisong and Zhimin[55] proposed a framework where memory consistency models are defined in terms of synchronization mechanisms used to order conflicting accesses. The following memory models were defined: Sequential Consistency, Release Consistency and Scope Consistency. Melo [39] proposed function-based definitions that permit very relaxed models to be described in a relatively simple way. The following memory models were defined: Atomic Consistency, Sequencial Consistency, Causal Consistency, PipelinedRAM Consistency, Slow Memory, Weak Ordering, Release Consistency and Scope Consistency.

Even with formal definitions, the most widely used relaxed memory consistency models are so complex that it still difficult to say if some undesirable interleavings can be produced. Besides, the problem of computing the possible orderings for execution histories is shown to be co-NP-hard [44]. The works of [46], [40] and [41] analyze execution histories on multiple memory consistency models, showing the possible orderings, if they do exist.

4. Memory Coherence Protocols

In this section, we discuss the most important decisions that must be taken when designing a memory coherence protocol: propagation of modifications, number of simultaneous writers and modification management.

4.1. Propagation of Modifications

There are two basic coherence protocols which are traditionally used to solve the cache coherence problem: write-invalidate and write-update protocols [13]. These two protocols are usually adapted to fit DSM requirements.

In general, at consistency time, a write-invalidate protocol guarantees that there is only one copy of the data in the system. If these data are further needed, they are fetched from the only node that has a valid copy. On the other hand, a write-update protocol allows many copies of the same data to be valid at consistency time and generally guarantees that updates will be done atomically and totally ordered.

It is well-known that write-invalidate protocols should be used when accesses to shared data will not be issued in a near future by the other processors. On the contrary, write-update protocols are often preferred when many processors simultaneously read and write the same data. Although most of DSM systems use write-invalidate based protocols (TreadMarks [26], JIAJIA [21], ATMK [5]), some recent DSM systems offer also write-update protocols (ADSM [42], Brazos [52]).

4.2. Number of Simultaneous Writers

Another characteristic that is important in a coherence protocol for DSM systems is the number of simultaneous writers allowed. The most intuitive approach allows only one processor to write data at a given moment (single-writer protocol). However, as the unity of consistency in DSM is often a page, false sharing can occur when two or more processors want to access independent variables that belong to the same page. To reduce the effects of false sharing, many DSM systems use multiple-writer protocols, allowing many processors to have write access to the same page simultaneously and then merging the multiple versions of the page when a consistent view is required.

Multiple-writers protocols were first proposed in Munin [11] and are generally implemented for LRC and Scope Consistent DSM systems as follows. If a write fault occurs inside a critical section, the original page is copied to a *twin* before write access is granted. When the lock is released, the pages are compared to their twins and the differences between them (*diffs*) are generated. At acquire time, the lock manager sends to the acquiring process an acquire message containing the identifications of the pages that are no longer valid (*write notices*). These pages are invalidated or updated before the application continues its execution.

4.3. Modification Management

There are two basic approaches used to manage the information needed to execute coherence protocols in page-based DSM systems: home-based and homeless. In home-based systems, each page is assigned to a node (*home node*) that concentrates all modifications made to the page. Every time an updated version of the page is needed, it is sufficient to contact the home node in order to fetch the page.

In the homeless approach, each processor that modifies a page maintains such modifications locally. In order to obtain an updated version of the page, a node must collect the modifications that are distributed all over the system. Modifications are kept by each node and garbage collection is required. Home-based protocols do have some advantages. First, each access fault requires only communication with the home node. Second, since modifications are eagerly applied at the home node, there is no need to keep additional control structures such as *twin pages* or *diffs*. However, as modifications are eagerly sent to the home node, such protocols generally require additional messages. Also, on an access fault, homeless protocols fetch only the modifications made to the page (*diffs*) while home-based protocols fetch the whole page [21].

5. Checkpointing/Recovery Mechanisms for DSM Systems

For long run applications, fault tolerance mechanisms are very useful since, in the case of a failure, they avoid computation to be restarted from the beginning. Usually, fault tolerance is achieved by saving periodically the system state to a non-volatile memory. In the case of a failure, the system state is read and computation can be restarted from it. The act of saving the state of a process is known as *checkpointing* and the act of restarting the computation from a checkpoint is *recovery*. In this section, we will discuss checkpointing/recovery protocols for DSM systems.

5.1. Checkpointing Strategies

Checkpointing has been extensively studied in the research area of distributed systems [14]. In a generic way, three types of strategies exist for checkpointing an application: coordinated, uncoordinated or communication-induced. Coordinated checkpointing is achieved by establishing a checkpointing session that captures a global consistent state of the execution and saves it to stable storage. Usually, all processes stop regular message activity to take their checkpoints, in a coordinated way. Rollback/recovey is quite simple and is done by activating the last set of checkpoints. However, in uncoordinated (or independent) checkpointing, there is no need to establish checkpointing sessions and all processes can take their checkpoints whenever they want. However, rollback/recovery in this case is unbounded and garbage collection is complex [14]. To overcome this problem, message logging is often associated with uncoordinated checkpointing.

Communication-induced checkpointing piggybacks dependency related information on the regular messages exchanged by the processes [14]. Doing that, checkpointing does not need special "checkpoint session" messages but, in some cases, more chekpoints than the necessary are taken. In a generic way, when a process receives a message, it analyzes the dependency related information contained in it and, in some cases, takes a forced checkpointing before processing the message.

5.2. Strategies for DSM Systems

In DSM systems, research in rollback/recovery is concentrated in adapting either coordinated or uncoordinated checkpointing strategies from message-passing systems to the DSM environment. Most of the strategies proposed in the literature take advantage of some characteristics of the DSM memory coherence protocol in order to reduce the checkpoint file size. By doing this, a reduction on the failure-free overhead is usually achieved but, since very specific characteristics are taken into account, portability is compromised.

In [24], a coordinated checkpointing mechanism is proposed that keeps track of the DSM processes interactions by building a communication tree in order to reduce the number of processes involved in a checkpointing session. Incremental checkpoints are taken only for this subset of processes and stored to disk.

A coordinated checkpointing strategy for TreadMarks [26] is presented in [28]. Coherence-related information contained in *write notices* are used to decide which data really need to be saved in the checkpoint.

An uncoordinated checkpointing strategy for home-based release consistent DSM systems is presented in [53]. Logs of DSM operations are maintained in remote memories for further use in the recovery mechanism. Only one failure is supported.

A logging strategy for ADSM [42] is proposed in [29]. Coherence-related information is logged according to the coherence protocol which is in use. The protocols considered are multiple-writer/write-invalidate and single-writer/write-update. Coordinateed and uncoordinated checkpointing can be used. The use of coordinated checkpointing with logging is justified since, with this proposed technique, the size of the logs can be reduced.

In [6], the impact of locks and barriers in sequential consistent DSM systems is analyzed. Kernel-level support is used to keep track of data dependencies in either coordinated and uncoordinated checkpointing.

A checkpointing/recovery mechanism is described in [51] for the Plurix Operating System, which implements page-based DSM operations and uses transactional consistency. In [1, 2, 27], a more generic approach is proposed that does not use coherence related information and can be integrated to scope consistent or release consistent DSM systems that use synchronization barriers. Coordinated checkpointing is taken by a checkpointing library when all processes arrive in a barrier. In the case of a failure, all processes activate from their previously taken checkpoints, restarting execution from the last synchronization barrier.

In most of these systems, coherence related information is used to decide which information will be included in the checkpoint. Also, most of these works deployed their own checkpoint libraries and modifications made to the operating system kernel must be often taken into account by the checkpoint library. Modifications into the kernel itself are made in [6] and [51].

6. Examples of DSM Systems

6.1. Ivy

Ivy was proposed by K. Li in [35]. It is the first DSM system that implements the shared virtual memory. An Ivy program is a set of lightweight processes that can be placed on multiple processors and share a unique paged address space. The local memories of each process are seen as caches of the shared address space. When a reference to a remote page is produced, a *page fault* is generated. At this moment, a write-invalidate multiple readers/single write(MRSR) coherence protocol (section 4.) is executed to guarantee sequential consistency (section 3.). After that, the page is retrieved from the remote node and the faulting instruction is re-executed. In order to locate the page, Ivy implemented three algorithms: centralized manager, fixed distributed manager and dynamic distributed manager (section 2.2.). Ivy was implemented at user-level, but the kernel of the Aegis operating system was modified in order to support it. Each processor executes an Ivy server which is composed by five modules: process manager, memory allocator, initializer, remote operations, memory mapping (figure 11).

The process manager module is responsible for process synchronization and migration. The migration maechanism in Ivy is very simple and consists of migrating the process status and the page that contains the instruction it is executing at the moment. The other pages

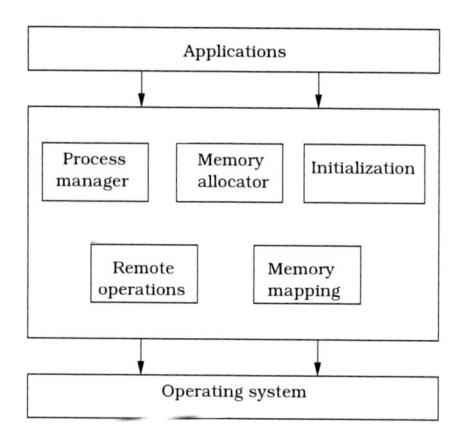

Figure 11. Ivy's structure.

will remain in the source node and will be migrated on reference. The synchronization mechanism offered by Ivy is the event counter, which is itself implemented in the DSM.

A prototype of Ivy was implemented at an Apollo DOMAIN computer system [35]. Under the name of Shiva [37], Ivy was ported to an Intel iPSC/2 hypercube with 128 nodes. The main difference between Ivy and Shiva is that the latter provides semaphores as synchronization mechanisms, instead of event counters. The P and V semaphore primitives are implemented by message passing and are managed by a dynamic distributed strategy.

6.2. TreadMarks

TreadMarks was proposed by Keleher, Cox, Dwarkadas and Zwaenenpoel in [26]. It is a page-based DSM system that implements Lazy Release Consistency (section 3.) using a homeless write-invalidate multiple-readers/multiple-writers protocol (MRMW) that uses *diffs*, *twin pages* and *write notices* (section 4.).

Each page is assigned a fixed distributed manager and can be in four different states: *unmapped*, *invalid*, *read-only* and *read-write*. Three types of *page fault* can occur: cold miss, coherence miss and protection fault. A cold miss occurs when the page is first accessed by a processor which is not its manager. The manager sends a copy to the faulting node and the page state is set to *read-only*. A coherence miss occurs when a page is accessed after being invalidated by the coherence protocol and a protection fault occurs when the page has *read-only* access right and a write access to it is generated. A *twin* page is created and the page is granted the *read-write* access.

The implementation of LRC relies on the notion of intervals. An interval is created each time an *acquire* or *release* is executed by a process. Since intervals of different processes are partially ordered, a vector timestamp [12] is used to represent each interval. By comparing vector timestamps, it is guaranteed that a process that is acquiring a lock will be notified about all modifications that have occurred before its current interval [26]. This notification is made by the previous lock releaser, that sends to the lock acquirer *write notices* containing the pages that were modified and, thus, are no longer valid. Upon receiving the write notices, the pages are invalidated.

When an access is generated to an invalidated page, *diffs* are collected from remote processors according with the vector timestamps and applied to the local copy. Note that the *diffs* must be kept until all processors have applied them in their local pages. In order to discard *diffs*, a garbage collector is used. A lazy diffing protocol is used to postpone the moment of diff generation [26].

TreadMarks provides the following synchronization mechanisms: locks, barriers and condition variables. Lock managers are assigned by a fixed distributed strategy and barriers have a centralized manager.

It is a very successful DSM system that runs at many different platforms in 45 sites around the world (see *www.cs.rice.edu/willy/TreadMarks/users.html*).

6.3. JIAJIA

JIAJIA is a software DSM system proposed by Hu, Shi and Tang [21]. It is a page-based DSM system that implements the Scope Consistency memory model (section 3.) with a home-based write-invalidate multiple-writer protocol (section 4.). In JIAJIA, the shared memory is distributed among the nodes in a NUMA-architecture basis. Each shared page has a home node. A page is always present in its home node and it is also copied to remote nodes on an access fault. There is a fixed number of remote pages that can be placed at the memory of a remote node. When this part of memory is full, a replacement algorithm is executed.

Each lock is assigned to a lock manager. The functions that implement lock acquire, lock release and synchronization barrier in JIAJIA are jia_lock, jia_unlock and jia_barrier, respectively [22]. Additionally, JIAJIA provides condition variables that are accessed by jia_setcv and jia_waitcv, to signal and wait on conditions, respectively. The programming style provided is SPMD (Single Program Multiple Data) and each node is distinguished from the others by a global variable jiapid [22].

On a release access, the releaser sends all modifications made inside the critical section to the home node of each modified page. The home node applies all modifications to its own copy and sends an acknowledgment back to the releaser. When all acknowledgements arrive, the lock releaser sends a message containing the numbers of the pages modified inside the critical section (write notices) to the lock manager [21].

On an acquire access, the acquirer sends an ACQ message to the lock manager. When the lock manager decides that the lock can be granted to the acquirer, it responds with a lock granting message that contains all write notices associated with that lock. Upon receiving this message, the acquirer invalidates all pages that have write notices associated, since their contents are no longer valid (figure 12).

On a barrier access, the arriving process generates the diffs of all pages that were modified since the last barrier. Then, it sends the diffs to the respective home nodes. The home nodes receive the diffs, apply them and send an acknowledgement to the arriving process. Then, the arriving process sends a BARR message containing the write notices of all modified pages to the owner of the barrier. When all processes arrive at the barrier, the owner of the barrier sends back a message BARRGRANT containing the write notices of all pages modified since the last barrier. Upon receiving this message, the processes invalidate the

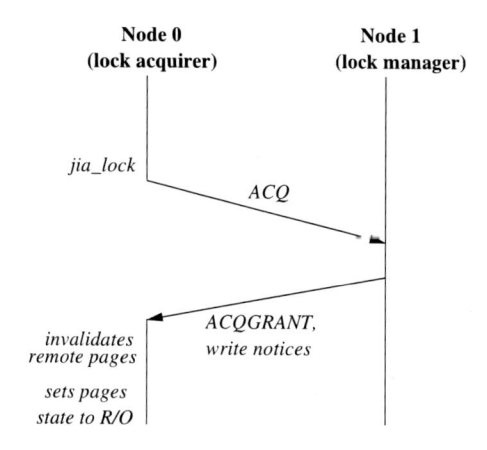

Figure 12. Lock aquire operation in JIAJIA.

pages contained in the write notices and continue execution. Figure 13 illustrates the behavior of jia_barrier. For the sake of simplicity, it represents only operations made from the point of view of node 1.

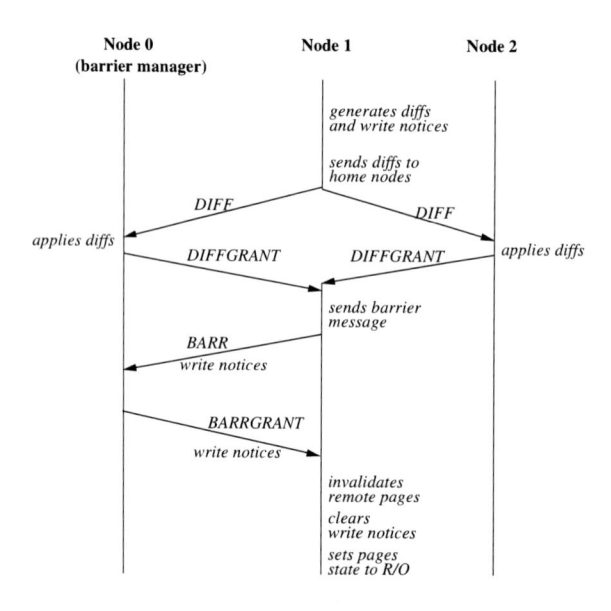

Figure 13. Barrier Synchronization in JIAJIA.

JIAJIA also offers some optional features such as home migration and load balancing, among others. These features can be activated and de-activated by the function *jia_config (option, value)*, where option is the feature and value can be either ON or OFF. At the beginning of the execution, all features are set to OFF [22].

6.4. ORCA

Orca is in fact an object-based parallel programming system that provide access to an object-based DSM [7]. It is composed by a language, a compiler and a runtime system.

In Orca, processes communicate through shared data objects, which are instances of shared data types [8]. An operation an object can consist of a set of guarded statements where an invocation to an operation blocks until one of the statements become true. If two or more statements are true, one of them is chosen non-deterministically.

Each Orca object can be in two states: *single copy* or *replicated*. When an object is not replicated, all operations are handled by a centralized node, that executes the operation and returns the result to the requester. If the object is replicated, Orca enforces sequential consistency (section 3.) either by a reliable totally ordered multicast offered by hardware or the underlying system or by a two-phase, write-update primary copy algorithm [7].

The two-phase algorithm works as follows. If a process wants to update an object, it sends a message to the primary copy of the object. The primary copy object sends lock messages to the nodes holding copies of it. After receiving all acknowledgments, it is guaranteed that all copies of the object are locked. The second phase begins when the primary copy sends a message to all nodes to update the object and unlock it.

An interesting characteristic of Orca is that it provides selective replication of objects. In this approach, the runtime analyzes the objects' access patterns adjusting dynamically the number of copies [8].

6.5. DASH

DASH (Directory Architecture for SHared Memory) is a release consistent NUMA-like hardware DSM system proposed by Lenosky et al [32]. In DASH, each node is composed by a set of processors with their caches, a local shared memory, a shared cache for pending remote accesses and a directory controller, which is the interface between the node and the interconnection network and also maintains coherence inter-node. Figure 14 illustrates the DASH architecture.

A snoopy cache coherence protocol is used to maintain coherence among the processors that belong to the same node and a directory based cache coherence protocol maintains coherence outside the node.

DASH implements release consistency using an eager coherence protocol that works as follows. Write operations are issued to write buffers and processors are allowed to proceed, issuing the next operations. As stated in release consistency (section 3.), all read and write operations preceeding the release must be performed before the release performs. DASH guarantees this condition by offering a *fence* primitive, that stalls the processor until the write buffer is empty. It is an eager protocol since write operations are sent to other processors as soon as they are issued. At release time, the processors only wait for the operations to complete [32].

A DASH prototype was built were each node is a Silicon Graphics 4D/240, which is composed by four processors with first and second level caches. The nodes are interconnected by a mesh interconnection network.

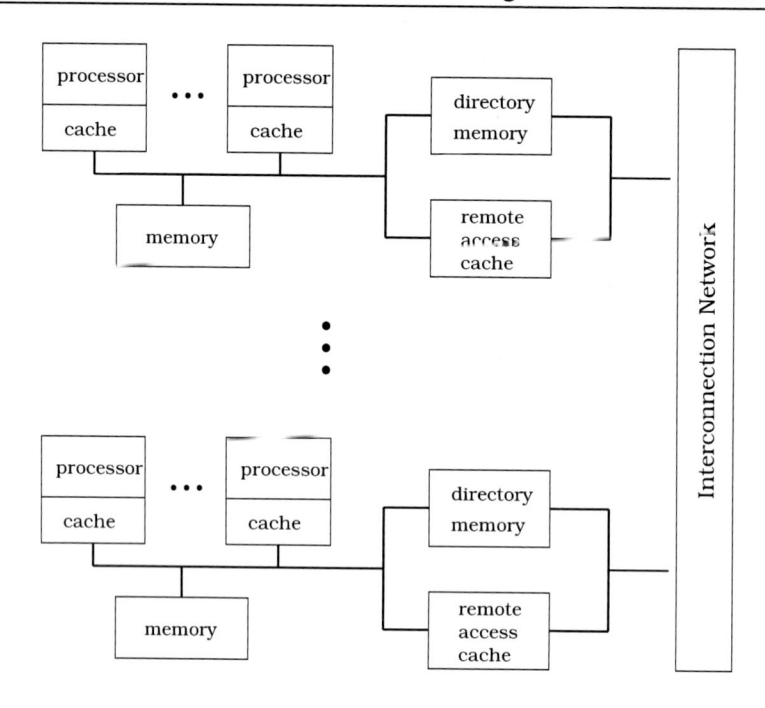

Figure 14. Architecture of DASH.

6.6. Comparative Table

In this subsection, we present a comparative table containing some of the characteristics of 12 DSM systems proposed in the literature.

7. Conclusion

Distributed Shared Memory is a quite mature research field that received its first impulse with the work of K. Li [34] in 1986. Since then, several research teams have been working on several aspects of this subject that mainly concerns memory consistency models, memory coherence protocols and, more recently, fault tolerance related issues. The results of these efforts can be seen on 51 DSM systems that are listed in the literature. Many of these systems are used in many research institutions all around the world.

In this chapter, we presented a detailed overview of the most important aspects and design issues concerning Distributed Shared Memory Systems. First, we presented the types of DSM systems and basic mechanisms used to retrieved data in them. One of the most important and complex aspects of any DSM system is the memory consistency model, since it determines in which order memory operations will be perceived by the programmer. We have also presented several memory consistency models using a unified system model. Also, the problem of formalizing these model and deciding which results can be produced on them was discussed. The orders imposed by the memory consistency model must be guaranteed by memory coherence protocols that implement them. We also discussed the

Table 1. Comparative table with 12 DSM systems

Name	Type	Consistency Model	Coherence Protocol
Alewife [4]	Hardware	Sequential	MRSW,invalidate
Brazos [52]	Page	Scope	MRMW,update,homeless
DASH [32]	Hardware	Release	MRSW,invalidate
Ivy [35]	Page	Sequential	MRSW, invalidate
JIAJIA [21]	Page	Scope	MRMW,home,invalidate
Orca [7]	Object	Sequential	MRSW,update
Midway [9]	Object	Multiple	Multiple
Mirage [16]	Page	Sequential	MRSW,invalidate
Munin [11]	Page	Release	Multiple
Shasta [50]	Object	Release	home-based,invalidate
Typhoon [49]	Hardware	Multiple	invalidate
TreadMarks [26]	Page	Release	MRMW,homeless,invalidate

main aspects that should be considered when designing a coherence protocol for DSM systems.

More recently, a growing interest has been evolving towards providing some kinds of fault tolerance to DSM applications. In this chapter, we have presented several well-known coordinated and uncoordinated checkpointing strategies as well as their respective recovery policies. Finally, we have described five DSM systems focusing mainly on their general architectures, memory consistency models and memory coherence protocols.

References

[1] A. Boukerche, A. De Melo, J. Koch and C. Galdino, "Multiple and Coordinated Checkpointing Protocol for DSM Systems", *IEEE Proceedings of Int'l Conference on Parallel Processing and PEN-PCGCS,* Oslo, Norway, June, 2005.

[2] A. Boukerche, J. Koch and A. Melo, "Integrating Coordinated Checkpointing and Recovery Mechanisms into DSM Synchronization Barriers", *the 4th International Workshop on Efficient and Experimental Algorithms (WEA 2005)*, Greece, LNCS

[3] S. Adve. *Designing Memory Consistency Models for Shared-Memory Multiprocessors.* PhD thesis, University of Wisconsin-Madison, 1993.

[4] A. Agarwal, R. Bianchini, D. Chaiken, F. Chong, K. Johnson, D. Kranz, J. Kubiatowicz, B. Lim, K. Mackenzie, and D. Yeung. The mit alewife project. *IEEE Proceedings,* 1999.

[5] C. Amza, A. Cox, S. Dwarkakas, and W. Zwaenenpoel. Software dsm protocols that adapt between single writer and multiple writer. In *Proc. of the HPCA,* pages 261–171. IEEE, February 1997.

[6] R. Badrinath and C. Morin. Locks and barriers in checkpointing and recovery. In *Proc. of the IEEE/ACM Conf. on Cluster Computing and the Grid (CCGrid)*, 2004.

[7] H. E. Bal, M. F. Kaashoek, and A. S. Tanenbaum. Experience with distributed programming in orca. *IEEE Transactions on Software Engineering*, 18:190–205, 1992.

[8] H. E. Bal, J. G. Steiner, and A. S. Tanenbaum. Programming languages for distributed computing systems. *ACM Computing Surveys*, 21(3):261–321, 1989.

[9] B. N. Bershad, M. J. Zekauskas, and W. A. Sawdon. The midway distributed shared memory system. In *Proc. of the COMPCOM*, 1993.

[10] N. Carriero and D. Gelernter. Linda in context. *Communications of the ACM*, 32:444–458, 1989.

[11] J. Carter. *Efficient Distributed Shared Memory Based on Multi-Protocol Release Consistency*. PhD thesis, Rice University, 1994.

[12] G. Coulouris, J. Dollimore, and T. Kindberg. *Distributed Systems: Concepts and Design*. Addison-Wesley, 2001.

[13] D. Culler, J. Singh, and A. Gupta. *Parallel Computer Architecture: A Hardware/Software Approach*. Morgan Kauffman, 1998.

[14] M. Elnozahy, L. Alvisi, and L. Wang. A survey of rollback/recovery protocols for message-passing systems. Technical Report TR-CMU-CS-96-181, Carnegie-Mellon University, 1996.

[15] P. Keleher et al. Lazy release consistency for software distributed shared memory. In *Proc. of the 19th Symposium on Computer Architecture (ISCA)*, pages 13–21, 1992.

[16] B. D Fleish and G. J. Popek. Mirage: a coherent distributed shared memory design. In *Proc. of the 14th ACM Symposium on Operating Systems*, pages 221–231. Stanford University, 1989.

[17] K. Gharachorloo. Memory consistency and event ordering in scalable shared-memory multiprocessors. In *Int. Symp. On Computer Architecture (ISCA)*, pages 15–24. ACM, May 1990.

[18] E. Hagerstein, A. Landin, and S. Haridi. Ddm - a cache-only memory architecture. *IEEE Computer*, pages 44–54, 1992.

[19] A. Heddaya and H. Sinha. An implementation of mermera: a shared memory system that mixes coherence with non-coherence. Technical Report BU-CS-93-006, Boston University, 1989.

[20] L. Higham, J. Kawash, and N. Verwaal. Defining and comparing memory consistency models. In *Proc. of the Int. Conference on Parallel and Distributed Computing Systems (PDCS)*. ACM, October 1997.

[21] S. Hu, W. Shi, and Z. Tang. Jiajia: An svm system based on a new cache coherence protocol. In *High Performance Computing and Networking (HPCN)*, pages 463–472. Springer-Verlag, April 1999.

[22] W. Hu and W. Shi. Jiajia users manual. Technical report, Chinese Academy of Sciences, 1999.

[23] L. Iftode, J. Singh, and K. Li. Scope consistency: Bridging the gap between release consistency and entry consistency. In *8th ACM SPAA '96*, pages 277–287. ACM, June 1996.

[24] G. Janakiraman and Y. Tamir. Coordinated checkpointing-rollback error recovery for dsm multicomputers. In *Proc. the 13th Symposium on Reliable Distributes Systems*, 1994.

[25] R. John and M. Ahamad. Causal memory: Implementation, programming support and experiences. Technical Report GIT-CC-93/10, Georgia Institute of Technology, 1993.

[26] P. Keleher, A. Cox, S. Dwarkakas, and W. Zwaenenpoel. Treadmarks: Distributed shared memory on standard workstations and operating systems. In *Usenix*, pages 115–132, 1994.

[27] J. G. Koch and A. C. M. A. Melo. Coordinated checkpointing and recovery mechanisms for dsm systems. In *Proc. of the 3rd Int. Information and Telecommunication Technologies Symposium*. IEEE R9, 2004.

[28] A. Kongmunvattana, S. Tanchatchawal, and N. Tzeng. Coherence-based coordinated checkpointing for software distributed shared memory systems. In *Proc. of Int. Conf. on Distributed Computing Systems (ICDCS)*, 2000.

[29] A. Kongmunvattana and N. Tzeng. Logging and recovery in adaptative software distributed shared memory systems. In *Proc. of the 18th Symposium on Reliable Distributed Systems*, 1999.

[30] L. Lamport. Time, clocks and ordering of events in a distributed system. *Communications of the ACM*, pages 558–565, 1978.

[31] L. Lamport. How to make a multiprocessor computer that correctly executes multiprocess programs. *IEEE Transactions on Computers*, pages 690–691, 1979.

[32] D. Lenosky, J. Laudon, K. Gharachorloo, A. Gupta, and J. Hennessy. The directory-based cache coherence protocol for the dash multiprocessor. In *Int. Symposium on Computer Architecture*, pages 148–158, 1990.

[33] D. Lenosky, J. Laudon, T. Joe, D. Nakahira, L. Stevens, and A. Gupta. The dash prototype: Logic overhead and performance. *IEEE Transactions on Parallel and Distributed Systems*, 4(1):41–61, 1993.

[34] K. Li. *Shared Virtual Memory on Loosely Coupled Architectures*. PhD thesis, Yale University, 1986.

[35] K. Li. Ivy: A shared virtual memory system for parallel processing. In *Int. Conference on Parallel Processing*, pages 94–101, 1988.

[36] K. Li and P. Hudak. Memory coherence in shared virtual memory systems. *ACM Transactions on Computer Systems*, **4**(7):321–359, 1989.

[37] K. Li and R. Schaefer. A hypercube shared virtual memory system. In *Int. Conference on Parallel Processing*, pages 125–132, 1989.

[38] R. Lipton and J. Sandberg. Pram: A scalable shared memory. Technical Report TR-180-88, Princeton University, 1988.

[39] A. C. M. A. Melo. Defining uniform and hybrid memory consistency models on a unified framework. In *Proc. of the 32nd Hawaiian Int. Conference on System Sciences (HICSS)*. IEEE Computer Society, 1999.

[40] A. C. M. A. Melo and S. C. Chagas. Visual-mcm: Visualising execution histories on multiple memory consistency models. In *Parallel Computation: Proc. of the 4th Int. ACPC Conference*, pages 500–509. *Lecture Notes in Computer Science* **1557**, 1999.

[41] A. C. M. A. Melo and N. S. B. Silva. Visualizing execution histories on release consistency and scope consistency memory models. In *Proc. of the 2nd Workshop on Software Distributed Shared Memory (WSDSM)*, 2000.

[42] L. Monnerat and R. Bianchinni. Efficiently adapting to sharing patterns in software dsms. In *Proc. of the HPCA 98*. IEEE Computer Society, 1998.

[43] D. Mosberger. Memory consistency models. *Operating Systems Review*, pages 18–26, 1993.

[44] R. Netzer and B. Miller. On the complexity of event ordering for shared memory parallel program executions. Technical Report TR-908, University of Wisconsin-Maddison, 1990.

[45] G. Neiger P. Kohli and M. Ahamad. A characterization of scalable shared memories. Technical Report GIT-CC-93/04, Georgia Institute of Technology, 1993.

[46] S. Park and D. Dill. An executable specification and verifier for relaxed memory order. *IEEE Transactions on Computers*, **48**(2):227–235, 1999.

[47] D. Patterson and J. Hennessy. *Computer Architecture: a Quantitative Approach*. Morgan Kauffmann Publishers Inc., 1996.

[48] M. Raynal and A. Schiper. A suite of formal definitions for consistency criteria in distributed shared memories. Technical Report TR-PI-968, IRISA, France, 1995.

[49] S. K. Reinhard, J. T. Laurus, and D. A. Wood. Tempest and typhoon: User-level shared memory. In *Proc. of the 21st Int. Conf. on Computer Architecture (ISCA)*, 1994.

[50] D. Scales, K. Gharachorloo, and C. A. Thekkath. Shasta: A low overhead software-only approach for supporting fine-grain shared memory. In *Proc. of the Int. conf. on Architectural Support for Programming Languages and Operating Systems (ASPLOS)*, 1996.

[51] M. Schoettner, S. Frenz, R. Goeckelmann, and P. Schultess. Checkpointing and recovery in a transaction-based dsm operating system. In *Proc. of the IASTED Int. conf. on Parallel and Distributed Computing and Networks*, 2004.

[52] E. Speight and J. Bennet. Brazos: a third generation dsm system. In *USENIX/WindowsNT Workshop*, pages 95–106, 1997.

[53] F. Sultan, T. Nguyen, and L. Iftode. Scalable fault tolerant distributed shared memory. In *Pro. of the Int. Conf. on High Performance Networking and Computing (HPCN)*, 2000.

[54] D. B. Terry, K. Petersen, M. J. Spreitzer, and M. M. Theimer. The case for non-transparent replication: Examples from bayou. *IEEE Data Engineering*, pages 12–20, 1998.

[55] H. Weiwu, S. Weisong, and T. Zhimin. A framework of memory consistency models. *Journal of Computer Science and Technology*, **13**(2):110–124, 1998.

Chapter 3

PERFORMANCE ANALYSIS OF SCHEDULING PARALLEL TASKS

Keqin Li[*]

Department of Computer Science,
State University of New York, New Paltz, New York 12561

Abstract

We consider the problem of scheduling parallel tasks in parallel systems with identical processors and noncontiguous processor allocation. The chapter contains two parts. In the first part, we are concerned with scheduling independent parallel tasks. We propose and analyze a simple approximation algorithm called H_m, where m is a positive integer. Algorithm H_m uses the harmonic system partitioning scheme as the processor allocation strategy. The algorithm has a moderate asymptotic worst-case performance ratio in the range $[1\frac{2}{3}..1\frac{13}{18}]$ for all $m \geq 6$, and a small asymptotic worst-case performance ratio in the range $[1 + 1/(r+1)..1 + 1/r]$ when task sizes do not exceed $1/r$ of the total available processors, where $r > 1$ is an integer. Furthermore, we show that if the task sizes are independent and identically distributed (i.i.d.) uniform random variables and task execution times are i.i.d. random variables with finite mean and variance, then the asymptotic average-case performance ratio of algorithm H_m is no larger than 1.2898680..., and for an exponential distribution of task sizes, it does not exceed 1.2898305.... As demonstrated by our analytical as well as numerical results, the asymptotic average-case performance ratio improves significantly when tasks request for smaller numbers of processors. In the second part, we present and analyze an algorithm for scheduling precedence constrained parallel tasks. The algorithm is called LLH_m (Level-by-level and List scheduling using the Harmonic system partitioning scheme), where $m \geq 1$ is a positive integer and a parameter of the harmonic system partitioning scheme. There are three basic techniques employed in algorithm LLH_m. First, a task graph is divided into levels and tasks are scheduled level by level to follow the precedence constraints. Second, tasks in the same level are scheduled using algorithm H_m developed earlier for scheduling independent parallel tasks. The list scheduling method is used to implement algorithm H_m. Third, the harmonic system partitioning scheme is used as the processor allocation strategy. It is shown that for wide task graphs and some common task size distributions, as m

---

[*]E-mail address: lik@newpaltz.edu

increases and the task sizes become smaller, the asymptotic average-case performance ratio of algorithm LLH$_m$ approaches one.

Keywords: Approximation algorithm, average-case performance ratio, harmonic system partitioning scheme, parallel task, precedence constraint, task scheduling, wide task graph, worst-case performance ratio.

1. Introduction

1.1. Motivation

A parallel computation that consists of precedence constrained parallel tasks can be specified as a quintuple $C = \langle P, T, \prec, \pi, \tau \rangle$. P is the number of processors available, that is, there are P identical processors allocated to the parallel computation C. $T = \{T_1, T_2, ..., T_n\}$ is a set of parallel tasks. $\prec$ is a partial order (or, a set of precedence constraints) on T, i.e., if $T_i \prec T_j$, then task T_j cannot start its execution until task T_i finishes. $\pi : T \to [1..P]$ gives the processor requirements of the tasks, i.e., $\pi(T_i)$ is the number of processors needed to execute task T_i, where $\pi(T_i)$ is also called the size of T_i. $\tau : T \to (0, +\infty)$ describes the execution times of the tasks, i.e., $\tau(T_i)$ is the execution time of task T_i. Given a specification of a parallel computation $C = \langle P, T, \prec, \pi, \tau \rangle$, the problem of *scheduling precedence constrained parallel tasks* is to find a nonpreemptive schedule of the tasks in T in a parallel system with P processors, such that the schedule length (i.e., the completion time of the n tasks) is minimized. Notice that to execute task T_i, any $\pi(T_i)$ of the P processors can be allocated to T_i. This scheduling problem has applications in parallel computing systems such as symmetric shared memory multiprocessors and multicomputers with completely connected networks and even in distributed computing systems such as bus-connected networks of workstations. In these systems, a processor allocation mechanism is independent of the topology of an interconnection network. To make our scheduling model simple and manageable, we assume that intertask communication times, synchronization costs, and the effect of shared resource contention are already included in task execution times.

The above scheduling problem includes many well known problems in operations research and computer science as special cases. When each task requires only one processor and executes in unit time, i.e., $\pi(T_i) = 1$ and $\tau(T_i) = 1$ for all $1 \le i \le n$, the problem becomes the *precedence constrained scheduling* problem [20, 29]. When there is no precedence constraint, i.e., $\prec$ is empty, and each task requires only one processor, the problem reduces to the classic *multiprocessor scheduling* problem for sequential tasks [13, 16]. When there is no precedence constraint and all tasks execute in unit time, the problem reduces to the *one dimensional bin packing* problem [18, 19]. All these problems are NP-hard [11] and have been studied extensively in the literature (see [7, 14, 15] for surveys and more references on these and related problems). These three problems imply that our scheduling problem is substantially more difficult than other similar scheduling problems. The reason is three-fold, namely, precedence constraints among tasks, inherent difficulty in scheduling (even independent) tasks, and processor allocation in parallel systems. Any one of the three issues alone makes our problem NP-hard. In other words, we are facing a scheduling problem with both precedence and processor constraints. An efficient heuristic algorithm should have good strategies to handle all the three difficult issues.

Notice that our problem is different from the ones studied in [28, 30], where tasks are malleable, i.e., each task may be executed with variable numbers of processors, and execution times are adjusted accordingly to reflect various speedup assumptions. The problems of scheduling malleable parallel tasks have been investigated by many researchers in recent years, and a large body of literature exists. Our problem is also different from the one studied in [25], where it is required that $\pi(T_i)$ contiguous processors should be allocated to task T_i. Such a requirement makes the problem even more difficult to solve. The special case for scheduling precedence constrained sequential tasks has been studied extensively [13, 16, 17, 21]. The special case for scheduling independent parallel tasks has recently been investigated in [23].

A feasible and effective way to solve NP-hard problems is to use heuristic (or, approximation) algorithms that produce near-optimal solutions. Let $A(C)$ be the makespan of the schedule generated by an algorithm A for a parallel computation C, and $\text{OPT}(C)$ be the makespan of an optimal schedule of C. The quantity $R_A = \sup_C (A(C)/\text{OPT}(C))$ is called the *absolute worst-case performance ratio* of algorithm A. The quantity

$$R_A^\infty = \lim_{Z \to \infty} \left(\sup_{\text{OPT}(C)/\tau^* = Z} \left(\frac{A(C)}{\text{OPT}(C)} \right) \right)$$

is called the *asymptotic worst-case performance ratio* of algorithm A, where τ^* is the longest execution time of the n tasks. Our definition implies that we are interested in the asymptotic behavior of an algorithm when the individual task execution times are less and less significant compared to the overall execution time of a parallel computation as the size of the parallel computation increases. If there exist two constants α and β such that for all C, $A(C) \leq \alpha \cdot \text{OPT}(C) + \beta\tau^*$, then $R_A^\infty \leq \alpha$, and α is called an *asymptotic worst-case performance bound* of algorithm A. Moreover, if for any small $\epsilon > 0$ and all large $Z > 0$, there exists C, such that $\text{OPT}(C)/\tau^* \geq Z$ and $A(C) \geq (\alpha - \epsilon)\text{OPT}(C)$, then the bound α is called tight, i.e., $R_A^\infty = \alpha$. When task sizes and execution times are random variables, both $A(C)$ and $\text{OPT}(C)$ become random variables, and $\bar{R}_A^n = E(A(C))/E(\text{OPT}(C))$ is called the *average-case performance ratio* of algorithm A for n tasks, where $E(\cdot)$ stands for the expectation of a random variable. The quantity

$$\bar{R}_A^\infty = \lim_{n \to \infty} \left(\frac{E(A(C))}{E(\text{OPT}(C))} \right)$$

is called the *asymptotic average-case performance ratio* of algorithm A. Of course, $\bar{R}_A^\infty$ depends on the probability distributions of task sizes and execution times. If there exists a constant γ such that for all C, $E(A(C)) \leq \gamma \cdot E(\text{OPT}(C))$ as $n \to \infty$, then $\bar{R}_A^\infty \leq \gamma$, and γ is called an *asymptotic average-case performance bound* of algorithm A.

1.2. Scheduling Independent Parallel Tasks

The chapter contains two parts. In the first part, we consider the problem of scheduling independent parallel tasks (i.e., a parallel computation with empty $\prec$) in parallel systems with identical processors [23]. The problem is NP-hard, since it includes the bin packing problem as a special case when all tasks have unit execution time. We notice that the problem of scheduling independent parallel tasks looks similar to but is quite different from the two dimensional rectangle packing problem [1, 2, 12, 27], where each task T_i is treated as a rectangle with width $\pi(T_i)$ and height $\tau(T_i)$. The rectangle packing model implies that processors should be allocated in contiguous groups. However, contiguous processor allocation is not required in our model, where any $\pi(T_i)$ processors can be allocated to T_i. Our problem could be regarded as a resource constraint scheduling problem [4, 9], where the resource is a set of processors.

The rectangle packing problem has been extensively studied, where a complicated algorithm with asymptotic worst-case performance ratio as low as 1.25 has been found [1]. Even though the algorithm in [1] for rectangle packing can also be applied to solve our problem, we propose and analyze a simple approximation algorithm called H_m, where m is a positive integer. Algorithm H_m uses the harmonic system partitioning scheme as the processor allocation strategy. The algorithm has a moderate asymptotic worst-case performance ratio $1.666... \leq R_{H_m}^\infty \leq 1.722...$ for all $m \geq 6$; but the algorithm has a small asymptotic worst-case performance ratio $1 + 1/(r+1) \leq R_{H_m}^\infty \leq 1 + 1/r$ when task sizes do not exceed P/r, where $r > 1$ is an integer. We notice that the capability to deal with small tasks is important in real applications since many task sizes are relatively small as compared with the system size so that a large scale parallel system can be shared by many users simultaneously. However, it is not clear whether the algorithm in [1] has such capability. Furthermore, the simplicity of our algorithm allows us to conduct average-case performance analysis. In particular, we show that if the numbers of processors requested by the tasks are independent and identically distributed (i.i.d.) random variables uniformly distributed in the range $[1..P]$, and task execution times are i.i.d. random variables with finite mean and variance, then $\bar{R}_{H_m}^\infty \leq 1.2898680....$ For an exponential distribution of task sizes, we have $\bar{R}_{H_m}^\infty \leq 1.2898305....$ As demonstrated by our analytical as well as numerical results, the asymptotic average-case performance ratio improves significantly when tasks request for smaller numbers of processors. We notice that there is lack of such results on probabilistic algorithm analysis, especially in multi-dimensional cases [5]. The average-case performance of the algorithm in [1] is unknown.

1.3. Scheduling Precedence Constrained Parallel Tasks

It is still not clear whether there exists an approximation algorithm A which has finite asymptotic worst-case performance ratio R_A^∞ or finite asymptotic average-case performance ratio $\bar{R}_A^\infty$ for scheduling precedence constrained parallel tasks. In [22], the author showed that for many heuristic choices of the initial priority list, the list scheduling (LS) algorithm has unbounded R_{LS}. However, it was also shown that when task sizes are bounded from above by a fraction of P, the list scheduling algorithm has finite R_{LS}. In particular, if $\pi(T_i) \leq qP$ for all $1 \leq i \leq n$, where $1/P \leq q \leq 1$ is a constant, then we have

$$R_{LS} \leq \frac{(2-q)P}{(1-q)P + 1}.$$

A similar bound of $(2-q)/(1-q)$ was also obtained in [8]. Nevertheless, list scheduling algorithms are fundamentally limited due to their inability to handle precedence constraints, task execution times, and task sizes simultaneously.

It is interesting to point out that the problem of *scheduling precedence constrained parallel tasks on multicomputers with contiguous processor allocation* has recently been considered in [25]. In this problem, there are P identical processors, say, $M_1, M_2, ..., M_P$, allocated to a parallel computation C. It is required that $\pi(T_i)$ contiguous processors, i.e., $M_k, M_{k+1}, M_{k+2}, ..., M_{k+\pi(T_i)-1}$, for some k, are allocated to a task T_i. The contiguous processor allocation requirement is based on the fact that processors in a multicomputer system is connected by a certain network, e.g., a linear array, which is the simplest topology. Therefore, the processors allocated to a task should be able to form a subsystem that has the same topology as the original system. In [25], an algorithm called LLB (*L*evel-by-level and *L*argest-task-first scheduling with a *B*inary system partitioning scheme) was proposed. There are three basic techniques employed in algorithm LLB, namely, level by level scheduling for handling the precedence constraints, the largest-task-first strategy for scheduling independent parallel tasks on each level, and the binary system partitioning scheme for processor allocation and for supporting the implementation of the largest-task-first scheduling algorithm.

While algorithm LLB can certainly be used to solve the problem considered in this chapter, that is, scheduling precedence constrained parallel tasks in parallel systems with noncontiguous processor allocation, we notice that algorithm LLB has several limitations. For example, the binary system partitioning scheme requires the system size P to be a power of 2. Strictly speaking, algorithm LLB only solves a special case of our scheduling problem. Since the binary system partitioning scheme is mainly designed for contiguous processor allocation and since we only consider noncontiguous processor allocation, there are chances to improve the performance by using more efficient system partitioning and processor allocation schemes. The main limitation of algorithm LLB is that its average-case performance does not improve when task sizes are small, since the amount of internal fragmentation caused by the binary system partitioning scheme does not reduce as tasks become small. Intuitively, better heuristics exist that are able to produce better schedules for small tasks.

In the second part of the chapter, we present and analyze an algorithm for scheduling precedence constrained parallel tasks in parallel systems with noncontiguous processor allocation [24]. The algorithm is called LLH_m (*L*evel-by-level and *L*ist scheduling using the *H*armonic system partitioning scheme), where $m \geq 1$ is a positive integer and a parameter of the harmonic system partitioning scheme. There are three basic techniques employed in algorithm LLH_m to handle the three difficult issues in our scheduling problem. First, similar to algorithm LLB, a task graph is divided into levels and tasks are scheduled level by level to follow the precedence constraints. Second, tasks in the same level are scheduled using algorithm H_m developed earlier for scheduling independent parallel tasks. The list scheduling method is used to implement algorithm H_m. Third, the harmonic system partitioning scheme is used as the processor allocation strategy, which is more efficient than the binary system partitioning scheme. It is shown that for wide task graphs and some common task size distributions, as the size of a computation n and m increase and the task sizes become smaller, the average-case performance ratio $\bar{R}^n_{\text{LLH}_m}$ of algorithm LLH_m approaches one. That is, if $\pi(T_i) \leq P/r$ for all $1 \leq i \leq n$, where $r \geq 1$ is an integer, then we have $\lim_{r \to \infty} \lim_{m \to \infty} \bar{R}^\infty_{\text{LLH}_m} = 1$.

It is worth to mention that for unit-time tasks, an asymptotic worst-case performance bound of 2.7 can be achieved [10]. We also notice that the level-by-level scheduling method was also used in [3] to schedule parallel tasks with identical execution times.

2. Part I: Independent Parallel Tasks

2.1. Algorithm H_m

To schedule a list $L = (T_1, T_2, ..., T_n)$ of n independent parallel tasks, algorithm H_m divides L into m sublists $L_1, L_2, ..., L_m$ according to task sizes (i.e., numbers of processors requested by tasks), where $m \geq 1$ is a positive integer. For $1 \leq k \leq m-1$, define $L_k = \{T_i \in L \mid P/(k+1) < \pi(T_i) \leq P/k\}$, i.e., L_k contains all tasks in L that have sizes in the interval $I_k = (P/(k+1), P/k]$. Define $L_m = \{T_i \in L \mid 0 < \pi(T_i) \leq P/m\}$, i.e., L_m contains all tasks whose sizes are in the range $I_m = (0, P/m]$. The partition of $(0, 1]$ into intervals $I_1, I_2, ..., I_k, ..., I_m$ is called *the harmonic system partitioning scheme* whose idea is to schedule tasks of similar sizes together. The similarity is defined by the intervals $I_1, I_2, ..., I_k, ..., I_m$. For tasks in L_k, processor utilization is higher than $k/(k+1)$. As k increases, the similarity among tasks in L_k increases, and processor utilization also increases. Hence, the harmonic system partitioning scheme is very good at handling small tasks.

Algorithm H_m produces schedules of the L_k's sequentially and separately. To process tasks in L_k, where $1 \leq k \leq m-1$, the P processors are partitioned into k groups, $G_1, G_2, ..., G_k$, each contains P/k processors. Each group G_j of processors is treated as a unit, and is assigned to a task in L_k. This is basically the harmonic system partitioning and processor allocation scheme. Such an allocation can be implemented using, for example, the list scheduling algorithm [13]. Suppose $L_k = (T_1^k, T_2^k, ..., T_{n_k}^k)$, where n_k is the number of tasks in L_k. Initially, group G_j is assigned to T_j^k, where $1 \leq j \leq k$, and $T_1^k, T_2^k, ..., T_k^k$ are removed from L_k. Upon the completion of a task T_j^k, the first unscheduled task in L_k, i.e., T_{k+1}^k, is removed from L_k and scheduled to execute on G_j. This process repeats until all tasks in L_k are finished. Then algorithm H_m begins the scheduling of the next sublist L_{k+1}.

For L_m, there is no need to divide the P processors. The list scheduling algorithm is again employed here. Let $L_m = (T_1^m, T_2^m, ..., T_{n_m}^m)$. Initially, as many tasks in L_m are scheduled as possible, i.e., tasks $T_1^m, T_2^m, ..., T_s^m$ start their execution, where s is defined in such a way that the total size of $T_1^m, T_2^m, ..., T_s^m$ is no larger than P, but the total size of $T_1^m, T_2^m, ..., T_{s+1}^m$ exceeds P. When a task finishes, the next task in L_m begins its execution, provided that there are enough idle processors. Notice that it is the scheduling of tasks in L_m that takes advantage of noncontiguous processor allocation.

2.2. Worst-Case Performance Analysis

Let $\mathrm{H}_m(L)$ be the makespan of the schedule produced by algorithm H_m for L, and $\mathrm{OPT}(L)$ be the makespan of an optimal schedule of L. The worst-case performance of H_m is given by the following theorem.

Theorem 1 *For any list L of n tasks and $m \geq 3$, we have*

$$H_m(L) \leq 1\frac{13}{18}\text{OPT}(L) + (m-1)\tau^*,$$

where τ^* is the longest execution time of the n tasks. Furthermore, for $m \geq 6$ and any large $Z > 0$, there exists L, such that $\text{OPT}(L)/\tau^* \geq Z$ and $H_m(L)/\text{OPT}(L) = 1\frac{2}{3}$. Therefore, for all $m \geq 6$, we have $1.666... \leq R_{H_m}^\infty \leq 1.722....$

Proof. Assume that all tasks in L are executed in the time interval $[0, H_m(L)]$, and that tasks in L_k are scheduled in $[t_k, t_{k+1}]$, where $1 \leq k \leq m$, i.e., the first task in L_k starts at time t_k, and the last completion time of the tasks in L_k is t_{k+1}. Let s_k be the starting time of the last task $T_{n_k}^k$ in L_k. Define $z_1 = t_2 - t_1$, and for all $2 \leq k \leq m$, define $z_k = s_k - t_k$, and $r_k = t_{k+1} - s_k$ be the remaining execution time of L_k once $T_{n_k}^k$ starts. Clearly, $r_k \leq \tau^*$, and

$$\begin{aligned} H_m(L) &= z_1 + z_2 + z_3 + \cdots + z_m + r_2 + r_3 + \cdots + r_m \\ &\leq z_1 + z_2 + z_3 + \cdots + z_m + (m-1)\tau^*. \end{aligned} \quad (1)$$

We give several lower bounds for $\text{OPT}(L)$. First, tasks in L_1 have large sizes such that no two of them can execute in parallel. Therefore, we have

$$\text{OPT}(L) \geq z_1. \quad (2)$$

Second, there can be at most two tasks from L_2 that can execute at the same time, and there can be at most one task from L_2 that can execute simultaneously with a task in L_1. Thus,

$$\text{OPT}(L) \geq z_1 + \frac{2z_2 - z_1}{2} = \frac{z_1}{2} + z_2. \quad (3)$$

Third, define the area of a task T_i to be $\pi(T_i)\tau(T_i)$, and the total area of L_k to be $A_k = \sum_{T_i \in L_k} \pi(T_i)\tau(T_i)$ for $1 \leq k \leq m$, and $A = A_1 + A_2 + \cdots + A_m$. For convenience, we assume that processor requirements are normalized such that $0 < \pi(T_i) \leq 1$ for all $1 \leq i \leq n$. Clearly, $\text{OPT}(L) \geq A$. We give a lower bound for A as follows. For $1 \leq k \leq m-1$, we notice that all the k groups $G_1, G_2, ..., G_k$ are busy until $T_{n_k}^k$ starts its execution. That is, during time interval $[t_k, s_k]$, at least $k/(k+1)$ of the processors are busy, i.e., we have $A_k > (k/(k+1))z_k$. For L_m, we note that during time interval $[t_m, s_m]$, the percentage of busy processors is at least $(m-1)/m$, i.e., $A_m > ((m-1)/m)z_m$; otherwise, some tasks should start earlier. Hence,

$$\text{OPT}(L) \geq \frac{1}{2}z_1 + \frac{2}{3}z_2 + \frac{3}{4}z_3 + \cdots + \frac{m-1}{m}z_{m-1} + \frac{m-1}{m}z_m. \quad (4)$$

Now let us consider the ratio

$$Q = \frac{z_1 + z_2 + z_3 + \cdots + z_{m-1} + z_m}{\max\left(z_1, \frac{1}{2}z_1 + z_2, \frac{1}{2}z_1 + \frac{2}{3}z_2 + \cdots + \frac{m-1}{m}z_{m-1} + \frac{m-1}{m}z_m\right)}. \quad (5)$$

Let $x = z_3 + \cdots + z_m$. Apparently,

$$Q \leq \frac{z_1 + z_2 + x}{\max\left(z_1,\ \frac{1}{2}z_1 + z_2,\ \frac{1}{2}z_1 + \frac{2}{3}z_2 + \frac{3}{4}x\right)}. \quad (6)$$

We leave the proof of the following result to the interested reader:

$$\frac{z_1 + z_2 + x}{\max\left(z_1,\ \frac{1}{2}z_1 + z_2,\ \frac{1}{2}z_1 + \frac{2}{3}z_2 + \frac{3}{4}x\right)} \leq 1\frac{13}{18}, \quad \text{where } z_1, z_2, x \geq 0. \quad (7)$$

Combining Equations (1)–(7), we get $\mathrm{H}_m(L) \leq 1\frac{13}{18}\mathrm{OPT}(L) + (m-1)\tau^*$.

To show the lower bound for $R^\infty_{\mathrm{H}_m}$, let us consider a list L of tasks which contains n tasks of size $\frac{1}{2}+\epsilon$, n tasks of size $\frac{1}{3}+\epsilon$, and n tasks of size $\frac{1}{6}-2\epsilon$, where n is a multiple of 6, and $\epsilon > 0$ is a very small quantity. All tasks have unit execution time. Clearly, $\mathrm{OPT}(L) = n$. Algorithm H_m divides L into L_1, L_2, and L_6, and $\mathrm{H}_m(L) = n + n/2 + n/6 = 1\frac{2}{3}n$. Thus, we can choose n a sufficiently large number while keeping $\mathrm{H}_m(L)/\mathrm{OPT}(L) = 1\frac{2}{3}$. This completes the proof of the theorem. ∎

For tasks with small sizes, algorithm H_m exhibits much better performance due to increased processor utilization in the harmonic system partitioning scheme, as claimed by the following theorem.

Theorem 2 *For any list L of n tasks, such that $\pi(T_i) \leq P/r$ for all $1 \leq i \leq n$, where $r > 1$ is an integer, we have*

$$\mathrm{H}_m(L) \leq \left(1 + \frac{1}{r}\right)\mathrm{OPT}(L) + (m - r + 1)\tau^*.$$

Furthermore, for $m \geq r+1$ and any large $Z > 0$, there exists L, such that $\mathrm{OPT}(L)/\tau^* \geq Z$ and $\mathrm{H}_m(L)/\mathrm{OPT}(L) = 1 + 1/(r+1)$. Therefore, we have $1 + 1/(r+1) \leq R^\infty_{\mathrm{H}_m} \leq 1 + 1/r$.

Proof. The proof is similar to that of Theorem 1. Since $r \geq 2$ and sublists $L_1, L_2, ..., L_{r-1}$ are empty, Equation (1) becomes

$$\mathrm{H}_m(L) \leq z_r + z_{r+1} + \cdots + z_m + (m - r + 1)\tau^*.$$

By using the area lower bound for $\mathrm{OPT}(L)$, we have

$$\begin{aligned}
\mathrm{OPT}(L) &\geq \left(\frac{r}{r+1}\right)z_r + \left(\frac{r+1}{r+2}\right)z_{r+1} + \cdots + \left(\frac{m-1}{m}\right)z_{m-1} + \left(\frac{m-1}{m}\right)z_m \\
&\geq \frac{r}{r+1}(z_r + z_{r+1} + \cdots + z_m).
\end{aligned}$$

The above two inequalities give the asymptotic worst-case performance bound $1 + 1/r$ in the theorem. To show the lower bound $1 + 1/(r+1)$ for $R^\infty_{\mathrm{H}_m}$, let us consider a list L which contains nr tasks of size $1/(r+1)+\epsilon$, and n tasks of size $1/(r+1)-r\epsilon$, where n is a multiple of $r+1$, and ϵ is a sufficiently small value. All tasks have unit execution time. Clearly,

$\mathrm{OPT}(L) = n$. Algorithm H_m divides L into L_r and L_{r+1}, and $\mathrm{H}_m(L) = n + n/(r+1)$. Thus, we can choose n sufficiently large while keeping $\mathrm{H}_m(L)/\mathrm{OPT}(L) = 1 + 1/(r+1)$. ∎

When $r \geq 5$, algorithm H_m has better asymptotic worst-case performance ratio than the algorithm in [1].

The asymptotic worst-case performance ratio of algorithm H_m is better than that of the largest-task-first (LTF) scheduling algorithm supported by the binary system partitioning scheme [25] in scheduling independent parallel tasks. Due to internal fragmentation in the binary system partitioning scheme, about half of the allocated processors are wasted in the worst case. Hence, the asymptotic worst-case performance ratio of algorithm LTF is $R_{\mathrm{LTF}}^\infty = 2$, which does not improve when task sizes are small. However, as task sizes become smaller, the asymptotic worst-case performance ratio of algorithm H_m gets better, and eventually, approaches one.

2.3. Average-Case Performance Analysis

For the purpose of the average-case performance analysis, we make the following assumptions.

(A1) The task sizes are normalized such that $0 < \pi(T_i) \leq 1$, and that the $\pi(T_i)$'s are independent and identically distributed (i.i.d.) random variables with a common probability density function $f(x)$ in the range $(0, 1]$.

(A2) The $\tau(T_i)$'s are i.i.d. random variables with mean μ and variance σ^2, where μ and σ are any finite numbers independent of n. Let $c = \sigma/\mu$ denote the coefficient of variation.

(A3) The probability distributions of task sizes and execution times are independent of each other.

Theorem 3 *Under the assumptions (A1)-(A3) on task sizes and execution times, we have the following asymptotic average-case performance bound for algorithm H_m:*

$$\bar{R}_{\mathrm{H}_m}^\infty = \lim_{n \to \infty} \left(\frac{E(\mathrm{H}_m(L))}{E(\mathrm{OPT}(L))} \right) \leq \frac{\sum_{k=1}^{m-1} \frac{1}{k} \int_{\frac{1}{k+1}}^{\frac{1}{k}} f(x)dx + \frac{m}{m-1} \int_0^{\frac{1}{m}} xf(x)dx}{\max \left(\int_0^1 xf(x)dx, \int_{\frac{1}{2}}^1 f(x)dx \right)}.$$

(Remark. Note that the bound only depends on $f(x)$.)

Proof. It is clear that the mean task size is

$$\bar{\pi} = \int_0^1 xf(x)dx.$$

Since a task size falls into I_k with probability $\int_{I_k} f(x)dx$, where $I_k = (1/(k+1), 1/k]$ for all $1 \leq k \leq m-1$, and $I_m = (0, 1/m]$, the expected number of tasks in L_k is

$$E(n_k) = \left(\int_{I_k} f(x)dx\right)n,$$

for all $1 \leq k \leq m$. Also, the expected size of tasks in L_k is

$$\bar{\pi}_k = \frac{\int_{I_k} xf(x)dx}{\int_{I_k} f(x)dx}.$$

Since the area of a task T_i has expectation $\bar{\pi}\mu$, and tasks in L_1 have to be executed sequentially, we have

$$E(\mathrm{OPT}(L)) \geq \max\left(n\bar{\pi}\mu, E(n_1)\mu\right) = Dn\mu, \tag{8}$$

where

$$D = \max\left(\bar{\pi}, E(n_1)/n\right) = \max\left(\int_0^1 xf(x)dx, \int_{\frac{1}{2}}^1 f(x)dx\right).$$

Let H_k be the makespan of the schedule for L_k. Then, $E(\mathrm{H}_m(L)) = E(H_1) + E(H_2) + \cdots + E(H_m)$. Clearly,

$$E(H_1) = E(n_1)\mu = \left(\int_{\frac{1}{2}}^1 f(x)dx\right)n\mu. \tag{9}$$

For $2 \leq k \leq m-1$, we have $E(H_k) = E(z_k) + E(r_k)$, and

$$E(z_k) \leq \frac{E(n_k)}{k}\mu.$$

Furthermore, r_k is no more than the maximum of k random execution times. It is well known from order statistics [6] that the mean of the maximum of q i.i.d. random variables $X_1, X_2, ..., X_q$ with mean μ and variance σ^2 is

$$E(\max(X_1, X_2, ..., X_p)) \leq \mu + \frac{q-1}{\sqrt{2q-1}}\sigma.$$

Therefore,

$$\begin{aligned} E(H_k) &\leq \frac{E(n_k)}{k}\mu + \mu + \frac{k-1}{\sqrt{2k-1}}\sigma \\ &= \left(\frac{1}{k}\left(\int_{I_k} f(x)dx\right)n + 1\right)\mu + \frac{k-1}{\sqrt{2k-1}}\sigma. \end{aligned} \tag{10}$$

Finally, we consider H_m. Since

$$E(A_m) = E(n_m)\bar{\pi}_m\mu = \left(\int_{I_m} xf(x)dx\right)n\mu,$$

and the processor utilization is at least $1 - 1/m$ in the time interval $[t_m, s_m]$, we get

$$E(H_m) \leq \frac{E(A_m)}{1 - 1/m} + E(r_m) = \frac{m}{m-1}\left(\int_{I_m} xf(x)dx\right)n\mu + E(r_m).$$

For $E(r_m)$, the main difficulty is that when task $T_{n_m}^m$ starts execution, the number of active tasks still in execution is unknown, which could be as large as n_m, the total number of tasks in L_m. Since $E(n_m)$ could be $\Theta(n)$, we use the following quite loose upper bound for $E(r_m)$, that is, r_m is no more than the maximum of n random execution times,

$$E(r_m) \leq \mu + \frac{n-1}{\sqrt{2n-1}}\sigma < \mu + \sqrt{\frac{n}{2}}\sigma.$$

Therefore, we get

$$E(H_m) \leq \left(\frac{m}{m-1}\left(\int_{I_m} xf(x)dx\right)n + 1\right)\mu + \sqrt{\frac{n}{2}}\sigma. \tag{11}$$

Combining Equations (9)–(11), we obtain

$$E(\mathrm{H}_m(L)) \leq \left(\int_{\frac{1}{2}}^{1} f(x)dx + \sum_{k=2}^{m-1} \frac{1}{k}\int_{\frac{1}{k+1}}^{\frac{1}{k}} f(x)dx \right.$$
$$\left. + \frac{m}{m-1}\int_0^{\frac{1}{m}} xf(x)dx + \frac{m-1}{n}\right)n\mu + \left(\sum_{k=2}^{m-1} \frac{k-1}{\sqrt{2k-1}} + \sqrt{\frac{n}{2}}\right)\sigma.$$

Notice that

$$\frac{k-1}{\sqrt{2k-1}} < \sqrt{\frac{k}{2}}$$

for all $k \geq 1$. Consequently,

$$\sum_{k=2}^{m-1} \frac{k-1}{\sqrt{2k-1}} < \sum_{k=2}^{m-1} \sqrt{\frac{k}{2}} < \int_2^m \sqrt{\frac{x}{2}}dx < \frac{\sqrt{2}}{3}m^{1.5}.$$

The above calculations give rises to

$$E(\mathrm{H}_m(L)) \leq \left(\sum_{k=1}^{m-1} \frac{1}{k}\int_{\frac{1}{k+1}}^{\frac{1}{k}} f(x)dx + \frac{m}{m-1}\int_0^{\frac{1}{m}} xf(x)dx + \frac{m-1}{n}\right)n\mu$$
$$+ \left(\frac{\sqrt{2}}{3}m^{1.5} + \sqrt{\frac{n}{2}}\right)\sigma. \tag{12}$$

Using Equations (8) and (12), we obtain

$$\frac{E(\mathrm{H}_m(L))}{E(\mathrm{OPT}(L))} \leq \frac{1}{D}\left(\sum_{k=1}^{m-1} \frac{1}{k}\int_{\frac{1}{k+1}}^{\frac{1}{k}} f(x)dx + \frac{m}{m-1}\int_0^{\frac{1}{m}} xf(x)dx + \frac{m-1}{n}\right)$$
$$+ \frac{1}{D}\left(\frac{\sqrt{2}}{3}\cdot\frac{m^{1.5}}{n} + \sqrt{\frac{1}{2n}}\right)\frac{\sigma}{\mu}$$
$$= \frac{1}{D}\left(\sum_{k=1}^{m-1} \frac{1}{k}\int_{\frac{1}{k+1}}^{\frac{1}{k}} f(x)dx + \frac{m}{m-1}\int_0^{\frac{1}{m}} xf(x)dx\right) + O\left(\frac{m^{1.5}}{n} + \frac{1}{\sqrt{n}}\right).$$

It is clear that as $n \to \infty$, we get the asymptotic average-case performance bound in the theorem. ∎

2.4. Example Distributions

We give two task size distributions to exemplify the asymptotic average-case performance bound in Theorem 3.

Uniform Distributions. Let us consider the uniform distributions, that is, the $\pi(T_i)$'s are i.i.d. random variables uniformly distributed in the range $(0, 1/r]$, where $r \geq 1$ is a positive integer. That is, $f(x) = r$ for $0 < x \leq 1/r$. (Notice that when P is sufficiently large, a discrete uniform distribution on $\{1, 2, ..., P/r\}$ can be treated as a continuous uniform distribution on $(0, 1/r]$.)

Theorem 4 *If the $\pi(T_i)$'s are i.i.d. random variables uniformly distributed in the range $(0, 1/r]$, we have $\bar{R}_{H_m}^\infty \leq B_r$, that is,*

$$E(\mathrm{H}_m(L)) \leq B_r E(\mathrm{OPT}(L)),$$

as $n \to \infty$, where

$$B_r = 2r^2 \left(\frac{\pi^2}{6} - \frac{1}{r} - \left(1 + \frac{1}{2^2} + \cdots + \frac{1}{(r-1)^2} \right) \right),$$

as $m \to \infty$.

Proof. We examine the numerator and denominator of the bound in Theorem 3. The denominator is simply

$$D = \max\left(\int_0^1 x f(x) dx, \int_{\frac{1}{2}}^1 f(x) dx \right) = \frac{1}{2r},$$

and the numerator is

$$N = r \left(\sum_{k=r}^{m-1} \frac{1}{k^2(k+1)} + \frac{1}{2m(m-1)} \right).$$

Since

$$\frac{1}{k^2(k+1)} = \frac{1}{k^2} - \frac{1}{k} + \frac{1}{k+1},$$

we have

$$\sum_{k=r}^{m-1} \frac{1}{k^2(k+1)} = \left(\sum_{k=r}^{m-1} \frac{1}{k^2} \right) - \frac{1}{r} + \frac{1}{m}.$$

Note that

$$\sum_{k=r}^{m-1} \frac{1}{k^2} = \sum_{k=1}^{\infty} \frac{1}{k^2} - \sum_{k=1}^{r-1} \frac{1}{k^2} - \sum_{k=m}^{\infty} \frac{1}{k^2} \leq \frac{\pi^2}{6} - \sum_{k=1}^{r-1} \frac{1}{k^2} - \frac{1}{m}.$$

Thus, we have
$$\sum_{k=r}^{m-1} \frac{1}{k^2(k+1)} \le \frac{\pi^2}{6} - \frac{1}{r} - \left(1 + \frac{1}{2^2} + \cdots + \frac{1}{(r-1)^2}\right),$$
and
$$N \le r\left(\frac{\pi^2}{6} - \frac{1}{r} - \left(1 + \frac{1}{2^2} + \cdots + \frac{1}{(r-1)^2}\right) + \frac{1}{2m(m-1)}\right).$$

By choosing m sufficiently large, the average-case performance bound N/D can be made arbitrarily close to B_r. ∎

When $r = 1$, the asymptotic average-case performance bound given in Theorem 4 is $B_1 = \pi^2/3 - 2 = 1.2898680...$. To show the quality of the average-case performance bound B_r in Theorem 4, we give the following numerical data.

$$\begin{aligned}
B_1 &= 1.2898680... \\
B_2 &= 1.1594720... \\
B_3 &= 1.1088121... \\
B_4 &= 1.0823327... \\
B_5 &= 1.0661449... \\
B_6 &= 1.0552487... \\
B_7 &= 1.0474219... \\
B_8 &= 1.0415306... \\
B_9 &= 1.0369372... \\
B_{10} &= 1.0332559...
\end{aligned}$$

It is clear that $B_r < 1 + 1/r$ for all $r > 1$, i.e., B_r is less than the asymptotic worst-case performance bound in Theorem 2.

Exponential Distributions. Though closed form solutions are not available, the average-case performance bounds of algorithm H_m could be calculated using Theorem 3 numerically for arbitrary probability distribution of task sizes. For instance, let us consider a truncated exponential distribution, i.e.,
$$f(x) = \frac{\lambda e^{-\lambda x}}{1 - e^{-\lambda}}, \qquad 0 < x \le 1.$$

Theorem 5 *If the $\pi(T_i)$'s are i.i.d. random variables exponentially distributed in the range $(0, 1]$, we have $\bar{R}_{H_m}^\infty \le B_\lambda$, that is,*
$$E(H_m(L)) \le B_\lambda E(\text{OPT}(L)),$$
as $n \to \infty$, where
$$B_\lambda = \frac{\displaystyle\sum_{k=1}^\infty \frac{1}{k} \cdot \frac{e^{-\lambda/(k+1)} - e^{-\lambda/k}}{1 - e^{-\lambda}}}{\dfrac{1}{\lambda} - \dfrac{e^{-\lambda}}{1 - e^{-\lambda}}},$$
as $m \to \infty$.

Proof. It can be easily verified by straightforward calculation that the numerator and denominator in Theorem 3 are

$$N = \sum_{k=1}^{m-1} \frac{1}{k} \cdot \frac{e^{-\lambda/(k+1)} - e^{-\lambda/k}}{1 - e^{-\lambda}} + \frac{m}{m-1} \cdot \frac{1}{1 - e^{-\lambda}} \left(\frac{1 - e^{-\lambda/m}}{\lambda} - \frac{e^{-\lambda/m}}{m} \right),$$

and

$$D = \max\left(\frac{1}{\lambda} - \frac{e^{-\lambda}}{1 - e^{-\lambda}}, \frac{e^{-\lambda/2} - e^{-\lambda}}{1 - e^{-\lambda}} \right) = \frac{1}{\lambda} - \frac{e^{-\lambda}}{1 - e^{-\lambda}},$$

respectively. By letting $m \to \infty$, the average-case performance bound N/D can be made arbitrarily close to B_λ. ∎

To show the average-case performance bound B_λ in Theorem 5, we let $m = 1024$, and choose λ in such a way that the mean task size

$$\bar{\pi} = \frac{1}{\lambda} - \frac{e^{-\lambda}}{1 - e^{-\lambda}}$$

takes the values $1/(2r)$ for $r = 1, 2, ..., 10$, so that a comparison can be made between performance bounds of H_m under the uniform and the exponential distributions.

$\lambda = 0.0001813...,\qquad B_\lambda = 1.2898305...$
$\lambda = 3.5935119...,\qquad B_\lambda = 1.2731064...$
$\lambda = 5.9030000...,\qquad B_\lambda = 1.2145755...$
$\lambda = 7.9781077...,\qquad B_\lambda = 1.1640016...$
$\lambda = 9.9954411...,\qquad B_\lambda = 1.1273400...$
$\lambda = 11.9991145...,\qquad B_\lambda = 1.1021181...$
$\lambda = 13.9998370...,\qquad B_\lambda = 1.0846745...$
$\lambda = 15.9999711...,\qquad B_\lambda = 1.0722076...$
$\lambda = 17.9999950...,\qquad B_\lambda = 1.0629307...$
$\lambda = 19.9999991...,\qquad B_\lambda = 1.0557653...$

As shown in the above list, B_λ is slightly smaller than $\pi^2/3 - 2$, when $\bar{\pi} = 0.5$, i.e, $r = 1$, due to distribution imbalance in $(0,1]$. However, B_λ is larger than B_r for all $r > 1$, because $E(n_1)$ is never null.

3. Part II: Precedence Constrained Parallel Tasks

3.1. Algorithm LLH$_m$

The structure of a parallel computation $C = \langle P, T, \prec, \pi, \tau \rangle$ can be represented by a directed acyclic graph $G = (T, \prec)$, where nodes stand for tasks in T, and arcs stand for precedence constraints in $\prec$. Strictly speaking, since the size n of C is a variable, G represents a family of graphs. A directed acyclic task graph can be decomposed into levels, which are denoted by $V_1, V_2, ..., V_L$. Tasks with no predecessors (called initial tasks) constitute level

1. Generally, a task T_i is in level V_l if the number of nodes on the longest path from some initial task to T_i is l. Note that all tasks in the same level are independent of each other, and hence, they can be scheduled using algorithm H_m. Let L be the number of levels in G, and $n_l = |V_l|$ be the number of tasks in V_l, where $1 \leq l \leq L$. Define

$$\beta_n = \frac{L}{n},$$

and

$$\eta_n = \frac{1}{n}\left(\sqrt{\frac{n_1}{2}} + \sqrt{\frac{n_2}{2}} + \cdots + \sqrt{\frac{n_L}{2}}\right).$$

A task graph (actually, a family of graphs) G is said to be *wide* if

$$\beta_\infty = \lim_{n \to \infty} \frac{L}{n} = 0.$$

The above condition also implies that

$$\eta_\infty = \lim_{n \to \infty} \frac{1}{n}\left(\sqrt{\frac{n_1}{2}} + \sqrt{\frac{n_2}{2}} + \cdots + \sqrt{\frac{n_L}{2}}\right)$$
$$\leq \lim_{n \to \infty} \frac{L}{n}\sqrt{\frac{n}{2L}} = \sqrt{\frac{\beta_\infty}{2}} = 0.$$

A task graph is *narrow* if the above condition is not satisfied. Informally, wide task graphs exhibit large degree of parallelism.

Algorithm LLH_m schedules tasks in T level by level. A task graph is processed in the order $V_1, V_2, ..., V_L$. Tasks in V_{l+1} cannot start their execution until all tasks in V_l are finished. For level V_l, we use algorithm H_m to generate its schedule.

3.2. Worst-Case Performance Analysis

The performance of LLH_m is limited by the level-by-level scheduling strategy, which makes the worst-case performance ratio of LLH_m unbounded. In fact, this statement is true for all level-by-level scheduling algorithms.

Theorem 6 *All level-by-level scheduling algorithms have unbounded worst-case performance ratio.*

Proof. Let us consider a computation $C = \langle P, T, \prec, \pi, \tau \rangle$ consisting of $2n$ tasks, i.e., $T = \{T_1, T_2, ..., T_n, T'_1, T'_2, ..., T'_n\}$, where $n = P$. Tasks $T_1, T_2, ..., T_n$ are "short" tasks with $\pi(T_i) = P$ and $\tau(T_i) = 1$, for all $1 \leq i \leq n$. Tasks $T'_1, T'_2, ..., T'_n$ are "long" tasks with $\pi(T'_i) = 1$ and $\tau(T'_i) = K$, for all $1 \leq i \leq n$. The precedence constraints are $T_i \prec T_{i+1}$, $T_i \prec T'_{i+1}$, for all $1 \leq i \leq n-1$. (See Figure 1 for an illustration.) Clearly, $A(C) = P(K+1)$ for every level-by-level scheduling algorithm A, and $OPT(C) = P+K$. As $K \to \infty$, the ratio

$$\frac{A(C)}{\text{OPT}(C)} = \frac{PK + P}{P + K}$$

approaches P, which is an unbounded parameter in our problem specification. ∎

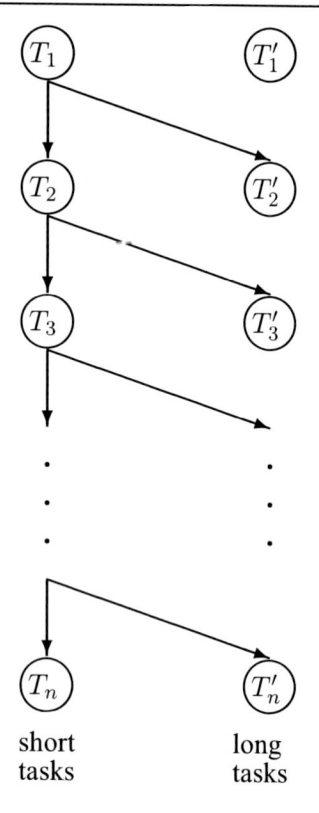

Figure 1. An example task graph.

3.3. Average-Case Performance Analysis

Let $\bar{\pi}$ be the mean task size, i.e.,

$$\bar{\pi} = \int_0^1 xf(x)dx,$$

and b be the probability that the size of a task exceeds $1/2$, i.e.,

$$b = \int_{\frac{1}{2}}^1 f(x)dx.$$

Define

$$D = \max(\bar{\pi}, b) = \max\left(\int_0^1 xf(x)dx, \int_{\frac{1}{2}}^1 f(x)dx\right).$$

Now we present the main result of the section.

Theorem 7 *Under the assumptions (A1)-(A3) on task sizes and execution times, we have the following average-case performance bound for algorithm* LLH_m:

$$\bar{R}_{\text{LLH}_m}^n = \frac{E(\text{LLH}_m(C))}{E(\text{OPT}(C))} \leq \frac{1}{D}\left(\sum_{k=1}^{m-1}\frac{1}{k}\int_{\frac{1}{k+1}}^{\frac{1}{k}} f(x)dx + \frac{m}{m-1}\int_0^{\frac{1}{m}} xf(x)dx\right.$$

$$\left. + \beta_n(m-1) + \beta_n\frac{\sqrt{2}}{3}m^{1.5}c + \eta_n c\right).$$

(*Remark.* The above bound depends on three factors, namely, $f(x)$: probability distribution of task sizes; μ and σ: parameters of task execution times; β_n and η_n: characterizations of a task graph.)

Proof. Let the area of a task T_i be defined as $\pi(T_i)\tau(T_i)$, i.e., the product of its size and execution time. It is clear that $\text{OPT}(C)$ is bounded from below by the total area of the tasks in T, that is, $E(\text{OPT}(C)) \geq n\bar{\pi}\mu$. Since the tasks with sizes exceeding $1/2$ have to be executed sequentially, we have $E(\text{OPT}(C)) \geq bn\mu$. Thus, Equation (8) can be easily extended to

$$E(\text{OPT}(C)) \geq \max(n\bar{\pi}\mu, bn\mu) = Dn\mu. \tag{13}$$

It is clear that the level-by-level scheduling method yields

$$E(\text{LLH}_m(C))) = E(\text{H}_m(V_1)) + E(\text{H}_m(V_2)) + \cdots + E(\text{H}_m(V_L)),$$

where, by Equation (12),

$$E(\text{H}_m(V_l)) \leq \left(\sum_{k=1}^{m-1} \frac{1}{k} \int_{\frac{1}{k+1}}^{\frac{1}{k}} f(x)dx + \frac{m}{m-1} \int_0^{\frac{1}{m}} xf(x)dx \right) n_l \mu$$

$$+ (m-1)\mu + \left(\frac{\sqrt{2}}{3} m^{1.5} + \sqrt{\frac{n_l}{2}} \right) \sigma.$$

Hence, we obtain the following bound for $E(\text{LLH}_m(C))$:

$$E(\text{LLH}_m(C)) \leq \left(\sum_{k=1}^{m-1} \frac{1}{k} \int_{\frac{1}{k+1}}^{\frac{1}{k}} f(x)dx + \frac{m}{m-1} \int_0^{\frac{1}{m}} xf(x)dx \right) n\mu$$

$$+ L(m-1)\mu + L\frac{\sqrt{2}}{3} m^{1.5}\sigma + \left(\sum_{l=1}^{L} \sqrt{\frac{n_l}{2}} \right) \sigma. \tag{14}$$

Combining Equations (13) and (14), we get

$$\frac{E(\text{LLH}_m(C))}{E(\text{OPT}(C))} \leq \frac{1}{D} \left(\sum_{k=1}^{m-1} \frac{1}{k} \int_{\frac{1}{k+1}}^{\frac{1}{k}} f(x)dx + \frac{m}{m-1} \int_0^{\frac{1}{m}} xf(x)dx \right.$$

$$\left. + \frac{L}{n}(m-1) + \left(\frac{L}{n}\right) \frac{\sqrt{2}}{3} m^{1.5} \left(\frac{\sigma}{\mu}\right) + \frac{1}{n} \left(\sum_{l=1}^{L} \sqrt{\frac{n_l}{2}} \right) \frac{\sigma}{\mu} \right).$$

This proves the theorem. ∎

It is clear that as $n \to \infty$, we get the following asymptotic average-case performance bound by the definition of wide task graphs.

Theorem 8 *For wide task graphs, we have the following asymptotic average-case performance bound for algorithm* LLH_m:

$$\bar{R}_{\text{LLH}_m}^{\infty} = \lim_{n \to \infty} \left(\frac{E(\text{LLH}_m(C))}{E(\text{OPT}(C))} \right) \leq \frac{\sum_{k=1}^{m-1} \frac{1}{k} \int_{\frac{1}{k+1}}^{\frac{1}{k}} f(x)dx + \frac{m}{m-1} \int_0^{\frac{1}{m}} xf(x)dx}{\max \left(\int_0^1 xf(x)dx, \int_{\frac{1}{2}}^1 f(x)dx \right)}.$$

(Remark. Note that the bound only depends on $f(x)$.)

The bound in Theorem 8 is exactly the same as that in Theorem 3. This means that as a wide task graph gets larger, there is more and more parallelism and the performance of algorithm LLH_m in scheduling precedence constrained parallel tasks approaches that of algorithm H_m in scheduling independent parallel tasks.

The following results are consequences of Theorem 8.

Theorem 9 *For wide task graphs, if the $\pi(T_i)$'s are i.i.d. random variables uniformly distributed in the range $(0, 1/r]$, we have $\bar{R}^\infty_{\text{LLH}_m} \leq B_r$, that is,*

$$E(\text{LLH}_m(C)) \leq B_r E(\text{OPT}(C)),$$

as $n \to \infty$, where

$$B_r = 2r^2 \left(\frac{\pi^2}{6} - \frac{1}{r} - \left(1 + \frac{1}{2^2} + \cdots + \frac{1}{(r-1)^2} \right) \right),$$

as $m \to \infty$.

Theorem 10 *For wide task graphs, if the $\pi(T_i)$'s are i.i.d. random variables exponentially distributed in the range $(0, 1]$, we have $\bar{R}^\infty_{\text{LLH}_m} \leq B_\lambda$, that is,*

$$E(\text{LLH}_m(C)) \leq B_\lambda E(\text{OPT}(C)),$$

as $n \to \infty$, where

$$B_\lambda = \frac{\sum_{k=1}^\infty \frac{1}{k} \cdot \frac{e^{-\lambda/(k+1)} - e^{-\lambda/k}}{1 - e^{-\lambda}}}{\frac{1}{\lambda} - \frac{e^{-\lambda}}{1 - e^{-\lambda}}},$$

as $m \to \infty$.

The proofs of Theorems 9 and 10 are similar to those of Theorems 4 and 5.

3.4. Example Task Graphs

In this section, we provide several example wide task graphs to demonstrate our bound in Theorem 7 for the average-case performance ratio of algorithm LLH_m. These task graphs include iterative computations, partitioning algorithms, and linear algebra task graphs. They have been extensively used to study the scheduling of precedence constrained parallel tasks [21, 25, 26, 31].

Iterative Computations. An iterative computation is organized as a series of alternating sequential and parallel phases (see Figure 2). There is a master task that is active in

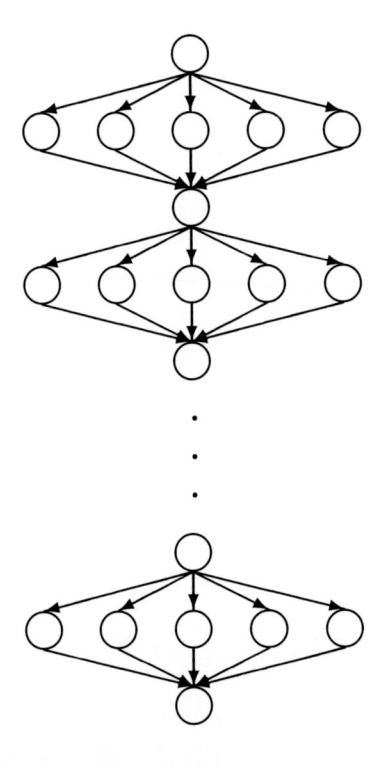

Figure 2. An iterative computation with $s = 5$.

sequential phases, which represent synchronization, communication, collection and distribution of partial results. There are s slave tasks that are active during parallel phases, which represent actual computations. There are numerous applications that fall into this category, such as relaxation methods for solving partial differential equations, iterative algorithms for solving linear and nonlinear systems of equations, searches for extreme values of functions, and smoothing in image processing, etc. In an iterative computation with s slave tasks and t repetitions, we have $L = 2t + 1$, $n_l = 1$ for $l = 1, 3, 5, ...$, $n_l = s \geq 2$ for $l = 2, 4, 6, ...$, $n = (s + 1)t + 1$, and

$$\beta_n = \frac{2t+1}{(s+1)t+1},$$

$$\eta_n = \frac{1}{(s+1)t+1}\left(\frac{t+1}{\sqrt{2}} + t \cdot \sqrt{\frac{s}{2}}\right).$$

If we fix s and use t, the number of repetitions, as an indication of the size of a computation, then

$$\beta_\infty = \lim_{t \to \infty} \frac{2t+1}{(s+1)t+1} = \frac{2}{s+1} > 0,$$

and

$$\eta_\infty = \lim_{t \to \infty} \frac{(\sqrt{s}+1)t+1}{\sqrt{2}((s+1)t+1)} = \frac{\sqrt{s}+1}{\sqrt{2}(s+1)} > 0,$$

Table 1. Bound for $\bar{R}^n_{\text{LLH}_m}$ in Scheduling Iterative Computations.

r	$z=0$	$z=1$	$z=2$	$z=3$	$z=4$	$z=5$	$z=6$	$z=7$	$z=8$	$z=9$
1	1.3288	1.2965	1.2942	1.2933	1.2928	1.2924	1.2922	1.2920	1.2918	1.2917
2	1.2376	1.1729	1.1684	1.1665	1.1655	1.1648	1.1643	1.1639	1.1636	1.1633
3	1.2262	1.1292	1.1224	1.1196	1.1181	1.1170	1.1163	1.1157	1.1153	1.1149
4	1.2392	1.1098	1.1008	1.0971	1.0950	1.0936	1.0926	1.0919	1.0913	1.0908
5	1.2627	1.1010	1.0897	1.0851	1.0825	1.0807	1.0795	1.0785	1.0778	1.0772
6	1.2917	1.0976	1.0841	1.0785	1.0754	1.0733	1.0718	1.0707	1.0698	1.0690
7	1.3239	1.0974	1.0817	1.0752	1.0715	1.0691	1.0673	1.0660	1.0650	1.0641
8	1.3582	1.0994	1.0814	1.0740	1.0698	1.0670	1.0650	1.0635	1.0623	1.0613
9	1.3941	1.1028	1.0826	1.0743	1.0695	1.0664	1.0642	1.0625	1.0611	1.0600
10	1.4309	1.1074	1.0849	1.0756	1.0704	1.0669	1.0644	1.0625	1.0610	1.0598

that is, an iterative computation gives a narrow task graph. However, it is easy to see that if we fix t, and use s to indicate the size of a computation, then we have $\beta_\infty = \eta_\infty = 0$, that is, an iterative computation has a wide task graph.

In Table 1, we show the bound for $\bar{R}^n_{\text{LLH}_m}$ ($m = 20$) calculated using Theorem 7 in iterative computations with a uniform task size distribution in the range $(0, 1/r]$, where $r = 1, 2, ..., 10$. We assume that the coefficient of variation of task execution times is $c = \sigma/\mu = 1$. The number of iterations is $t = 100$, and the number of slave tasks is $s = 10000 + 100000z$ for $z = 0, 1, 2, ..., 9$. The following observations are made.

(O1) The performance bound is a decreasing function of the size of the computation. This means that the average-case performance of algorithm LLH_m improves when there is more parallelism.

(O2) Since m is fixed at a relatively small value, the performance bound is not a decreasing function of r in some columns of the table.

(O3) When the size of the computation is sufficiently large, the performance bound approaches a value very close to B_r given in Theorem 9, and B_r is a decreasing function of r.

(O4) As the amount of parallelism and m increase and the task sizes become smaller, the average-case performance ratio of algorithm LLH_m approaches one.

Partitioning Algorithms. A partitioning algorithm performs a divide-and-conquer computation. In a partitioning algorithm with branching factor $b \geq 2$ and height $h \geq 0$ (see Figure 3 where $b = 2$ and $h = 3$), we have $L = 2h + 1$, $n_l = b^{l-1}$ for $l = 1, 2, 3, ..., h+1$, and $n_l = b^{2h+1-l}$ for $l = h+2, h+3, ..., 2h+1$. The height h indicates the size of a computation. Levels $V_1, V_2, ..., V_h$ contain tasks which partition large problems into small subproblems. Level V_{h+1} includes tasks which solve base case problems. Levels $V_{h+2}, V_{h+3}, ..., V_{2h+1}$ have tasks which combine subsolutions into a grand solution. The parameters for the structure of the task graph are

$$n = b^0 + b^1 + b^2 + \cdots + b^{h-1} + b^h + b^{h-1} + \cdots + b^0$$

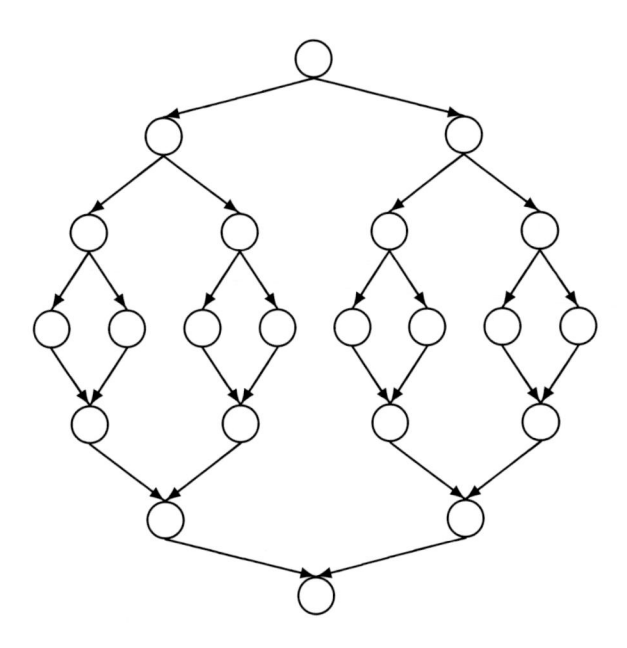

Figure 3. A partitioning algorithm with $b = 2$ and $h = 3$.

$$\begin{aligned}
&= \frac{b^{h+1} + b^h - 2}{b - 1}, \\
\beta_n &= \frac{(2h+1)(b-1)}{b^{h+1} + b^h - 2}, \\
\eta_n &= \frac{1}{n}\Big(2\Big(\sqrt{\frac{1}{2}} + \sqrt{\frac{b}{2}} + \sqrt{\frac{b^2}{2}} + \cdots + \sqrt{\frac{b^{h-1}}{2}}\Big) + \sqrt{\frac{b^h}{2}}\Big) \\
&= \Big(\frac{b-1}{b^{h+1} + b^h - 2}\Big)\Big(\sqrt{2}\Big(\frac{\sqrt{b^h} - 1}{\sqrt{b} - 1}\Big) + \sqrt{\frac{b^h}{2}}\Big) \\
&= \Big(\frac{\sqrt{b} + 1}{b^{h+1} + b^h - 2}\Big)\Big(\frac{\sqrt{b^{h+1}} + \sqrt{b^h} - 2}{\sqrt{2}}\Big).
\end{aligned}$$

Since $\beta_\infty = \eta_\infty = 0$, a partitioning algorithm has a wide task graph.

In Table 2, we show the bound for $\bar{R}^n_{\mathrm{LLH}_m}$ ($m = 20$) calculated using Theorem 7 in partitioning algorithms with a uniform task size distribution in the range $(0, 1/r]$, where $r = 1, 2, ..., 10$. We assume that the coefficient of variation of task execution times is $c = \sigma/\mu = 1$. The branching factor is $b = 2$, and the height is $h = 16, 17, ..., 25$. It is clear that observations (O1)–(O4) of algorithm LLH_m in scheduling iterative computations also hold for partitioning algorithms.

Linear Algebra Task Graphs. A linear algebra task graph with L levels (see Figure 4 where $L = 5$) has $n_l = L - l + 1$ for $l = 1, 2, ..., L$, $n = L(L+1)/2$, and

$$\beta_n = \frac{2}{L+1},$$

Table 2. Bound for $\bar{R}^n_{\text{LLH}_m}$ in Scheduling Partitioning Algorithms.

r	h = 16	h = 17	h = 18	h = 19	h = 20	h = 21	h = 22	h = 23	h = 24	h = 25
1	1.3212	1.3084	1.3011	1.2968	1.2942	1.2927	1.2917	1.2911	1.2907	1.2905
2	1.2223	1.1968	1.1821	1.1735	1.1684	1.1653	1.1634	1.1622	1.1614	1.1609
3	1.2033	1.1650	1.1430	1.1301	1.1224	1.1178	1.1150	1.1132	1.1120	1.1112
4	1.2087	1.1576	1.1282	1.1111	1.1009	1.0947	1.0909	1.0885	1.0869	1.0859
5	1.2245	1.1607	1.1240	1.1025	1.0898	1.0821	1.0773	1.0743	1.0723	1.0711
6	1.2459	1.1693	1.1252	1.0994	1.0841	1.0749	1.0692	1.0656	1.0632	1.0617
7	1.2704	1.1811	1.1296	1.0996	1.0818	1.0710	1.0643	1.0601	1.0574	1.0556
8	1.2971	1.1950	1.1362	1.1019	1.0815	1.0692	1.0615	1.0567	1.0536	1.0516
9	1.3253	1.2104	1.1442	1.1056	1.0827	1.0688	1.0602	1.0548	1.0513	1.0491
10	1.3546	1.2269	1.1534	1.1105	1.0850	1.0696	1.0600	1.0540	1.0502	1.0476

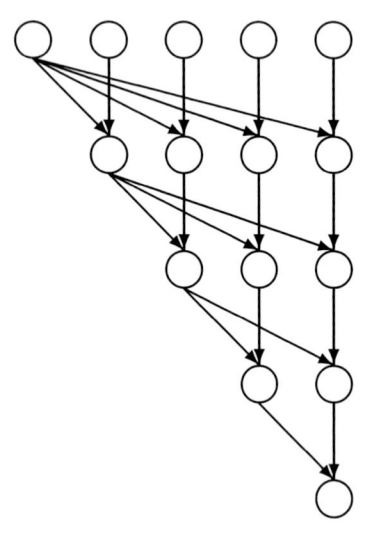

Figure 4. A linear algebra task graph with $L = 5$.

$$\eta_n = \frac{1}{n}\left(\sqrt{\frac{1}{2}} + \sqrt{\frac{2}{2}} + \sqrt{\frac{3}{2}} + \cdots + \sqrt{\frac{L}{2}}\right).$$

It is clear that a linear algebra task graph is wide. In Table 3, we show the bound for $\bar{R}^n_{\text{LLH}_m}$ ($m = 20$) calculated using Theorem 7 in linear algebra task graphs with a uniform task size distribution in the range $(0, 1/r]$, where $r = 1, 2, ..., 10$. We assume that the coefficient of variation of task execution times is $c = \sigma/\mu = 1$. The number of levels is $L = 50000z$ for $z = 1, 2, ..., 10$.

Table 3. Bound for $\bar{R}^n_{\text{LLH}_m}$ in Scheduling Linear Algebra Task Graphs.

r	$z=1$	$z=2$	$z=3$	$z=4$	$z=5$	$z=6$	$z=7$	$z=8$	$z=9$	$z=10$
1	1.3033	1.2984	1.2965	1.2954	1.2947	1.2942	1.2938	1.2936	1.2933	1.2931
2	1.1865	1.1767	1.1728	1.1707	1.1693	1.1683	1.1676	1.1670	1.1665	1.1661
3	1.1496	1.1349	1.1291	1.1259	1.1239	1.1224	1.1213	1.1204	1.1197	1.1191
4	1.1371	1.1174	1.1098	1.1055	1.1028	1.1008	1.0993	1.0981	1.0972	1.0964
5	1.1350	1.1104	1.1009	1.0956	1.0921	1.0897	1.0878	1.0864	1.0852	1.0842
6	1.1384	1.1089	1.0975	1.0911	1.0870	1.0840	1.0818	1.0800	1.0786	1.0774
7	1.1451	1.1107	1.0973	1.0899	1.0851	1.0816	1.0790	1.0770	1.0753	1.0739
8	1.1539	1.1146	1.0993	1.0908	1.0853	1.0814	1.0784	1.0760	1.0741	1.0725
9	1.1642	1.1199	1.1027	1.0932	1.0870	1.0826	1.0792	1.0766	1.0744	1.0726
10	1.1755	1.1264	1.1073	1.0967	1.0898	1.0848	1.0811	1.0782	1.0758	1.0738

4. Concluding Remarks

4.1. Summary

We have studied the problem of scheduling parallel tasks in parallel systems with identical processors and noncontiguous processor allocation. We proposed a simple approximation algorithm called H_m and performed combinatorial analysis for its worst-case performance and probabilistic analysis for its average-case performance. In particular, we proved the following results. (1) The asymptotic worst-case performance ratio $R^\infty_{H_m}$ is in the range $[1\frac{2}{3}..1\frac{13}{18}]$. (2) If the numbers of processors requested by the tasks are uniformly distributed i.i.d. random variables and task execution times are i.i.d. random variables with finite mean and variance, then the asymptotic average-case performance ratio is $\bar{R}^\infty_{H_m} \leq 1.2898680....$ In other words, less than 22.5% of the allocated computing power is wasted. (3) Both the worst- and average-case performance ratios improve significantly when tasks request for smaller numbers of processors. (4) Results similar to (2)–(3) also hold for the truncated exponential distribution of task sizes.

We have investigated the problem of scheduling precedence constrained parallel tasks. We observed that if a task graph is scheduled level by level, then the scheduling performance is determined by an algorithm for scheduling independent parallel tasks. The performance of algorithm H_m that uses the harmonic system partitioning scheme for noncontiguous processor allocation is superior to that of the largest-task-first algorithm that uses the binary system partitioning scheme for contiguous processor allocation. In particular, $R^\infty_{H_m}$ approaches one when task sizes are smaller and smaller. Therefore, we are able to develop an efficient algorithm LLH_m for scheduling precedence constrained parallel tasks in parallel systems with noncontiguous processor allocation. It is shown that for wide task graphs and some common task size distributions, as m increases and the task sizes become smaller, the asymptotic average-case performance ratio of algorithm LLH_m approaches one.

4.2. Further Research

It is still an open problem on whether there exists an approximation algorithm A which has finite asymptotic worst-case performance ratio R^∞_A or finite asymptotic average-case performance ratio $\bar{R}_A^\infty$ for scheduling precedence constrained parallel tasks. As a further research direction, it is of great importance to find such algorithms or to prove inapproximability of scheduling precedence constrained parallel tasks. It is also of great interest to see how our algorithms perform in scheduling real parallel computations on real parallel systems.

References

[1] B. S. Baker, D. J. Brown, and H. P. Katseff, "A 5/4 algorithm for two-dimensional packing," *Journal of Algorithms*, vol. 2, pp. 348-368, 1981.

[2] B. S. Baker and J. S. Schwarz, "Shelf algorithms for two-dimensional packing problems," *SIAM Journal on Computing*, vol. 12, pp. 508-525, 1983.

[3] S. Bischof and E. W. Mayr, "On-line scheduling of parallel jobs with runtime restrictions," *Proceedings of the 9th International Symposium on Algorithms and Computation, Lecture Notes in Computer Science*, vol. 1533, pp. 119-128, 1998.

[4] J. Blazewicz, J. K. Lenstra, and A. H. G. Rinnooy Kan, "Scheduling subject to resource constraints: classification and complexity," *Discrete Applied Mathematics*, vol. 5, pp. 11-24, 1983.

[5] E. G. Coffman, Jr., D. S. Johnson, P. W. Shor, and G. S. Lueker, "Probabilistic analysis of packing and related partitioning problems," in *Probability and Algorithms*, pp. 87-107, National Research Council, 1992.

[6] H. A. David, *Order Statistics*, John Wiley & Sons, New York, 1970.

[7] M. Drozdowski, "Scheduling multiprocessor tasks - an overview," *European Journal of Operational Research*, vol. 94, pp. 215-230, 1996.

[8] A. Feldmann, M.-Y. Kao, J. Sgall, and S.-H. Teng, "Optimal online scheduling of parallel jobs with dependencies," *Proceedings of the 25th ACM Symposium on Theory of Computing*, pp. 642-651, 1993.

[9] M. R. Garey and R. L. Graham, "Bound for multiprocessor scheduling with resource constraints," *SIAM Journal on Computing*, vol. 4, pp. 187-200, 1975.

[10] M. R. Garey, R. L. Graham, D. S. Johnson, and A. C.-C. Yao, "Resource constrained scheduling as generalized bin packing," *Journal of Combinatorial Theory (A)*, vol. 21, pp. 257-298, 1976.

[11] M. R. Garey and D. S. Johnson, *Computers and Intractability – A Guide to the Theory of NP-Completeness*, W. H. Freeman, New York, 1979.

[12] I. Golan, "Performance bounds for orthogonal oriented two-dimensional packing algorithms," *SIAM Journal on Computing*, vol. 10, pp. 571-582, 1981.

[13] R. L. Graham, "Bounds on multiprocessing timing anomalies," *SIAM J. Appl. Math.*, vol. 2, pp. 416-429, 1969.

[14] R. L. Graham, E. L. Lawler, J. K. Lenstra, and A. H. G. Rinnooy Kan, "Optimization and approximation in deterministic sequencing and scheduling: a survey," *Annals of Discrete Mathematics*, vol. 5, pp. 287-326, 1979.

[15] D. S. Hochbaum, ed., *Approximation Algorithms for NP-Hard Problems*, PWS Publishing, Boston, Mass., 1997.

[16] D. S. Hochbaum and D. B. Shmoys, "Using dual approximation algorithms for scheduling problems: practical and theoretical results," *Journal of the ACM*, vol. 34, pp. 144-162, 1987.

[17] K. K. Jain and V. Rajaraman, "Lower and upper bounds on time for multiprocessor optimal schedules," *IEEE Transactions on Parallel and Distributed Systems*, vol. 5, no. 8, pp. 879-886, 1994.

[18] D. S. Johnson, et al., "Worst-case performance bounds for simple one-dimensional packing algorithms," *SIAM Journal on Computing*, vol. 3, pp. 299-325, 1974.

[19] N. Karmarkar and R. M. Karp, "An efficient approximation scheme for the one-dimensional bin packing problem," *Proceedings of the 23rd Symposium on Foundations of Computer Science*, pp. 312-320, 1982.

[20] J. K. Lenstra and A. H. G. Rinnooy Kan, "Complexity of scheduling under precedence constraints," *Operations Research*, vol. 26, pp. 22-25, 1978.

[21] K. Li, "Stochastic bounds for parallel program execution times with processor constraints," *IEEE Transactions on Computers*, vol. 46, no. 5, pp. 630-636, 1997.

[22] K. Li, "Analysis of the list scheduling algorithm for precedence constrained parallel tasks," *Journal of Combinatorial Optimization*, vol. 3, pp. 73-88, 1999.

[23] K. Li, "Analysis of an approximation algorithm for scheduling independent parallel tasks", *Discrete Mathematics and Theoretical Computer Science*, vol. 3, no. 4, pp. 155-166, 1999.

[24] K. Li, "Scheduling precedence constrained parallel tasks on multiprocessors using the harmonic system partitioning scheme," *Journal of Information Science and Engineering*, vol. 21, no. 2, pp. 309-326, 2005.

[25] K. Li and Y. Pan, "Probabilistic analysis of scheduling precedence constrained parallel tasks on multicomputers with contiguous processor allocation," *IEEE Transactions on Computers*, vol. 49, no. 10, pp. 1021-1030, 2000.

[26] S. Madala and J. B. Sinclair, "Performance of synchronous parallel algorithms with regular structures," *IEEE Transactions on Parallel and Distributed Systems*, vol. 2, pp. 105-116, 1991.

[27] D. K. D. B. Sleator, "A 2.5 times optimal algorithm for bin packing in two dimensions," *Information Processing Letters*, vol. 10, pp. 37-40, 1980.

[28] J. Turek, *et al.*, "Scheduling parallelizable tasks to minimize average response time," *Proceedings of 6th ACM Symposium on Parallel Algorithms and Architectures*, pp. 200-209, 1994.

[29] J. D. Ullman, "NP-complete scheduling problems," *Journal of Computer and System Science*, vol. 10, pp. 384-393, 1975.

[30] Q. Wang and K. H. Cheng, "A heuristic of scheduling parallel tasks and its analysis," *SIAM Journal on Computing*, vol. 21, pp. 281-294, 1992.

[31] N. Yazıcı-Pekergin and J.-M. Vincent, "Stochastic bounds on execution times of parallel programs," *IEEE Transactions on Software Engineering*, vol. 17, no. 10, pp. 1005-1012, 1991.

Chapter 4

MULTI-CHANNEL PARALLEL ADAPTATION THEORY FOR RULE DISCOVERY

Li Min Fu[*]
Department of CISE, University of Florida

Abstract

In this paper, we introduce a new machine learning theory based on multi-channel parallel adaptation for rule discovery. This theory is distinguished from the familiar parallel-distributed adaptation theory of neural networks in terms of channel-based convergence to the target rules. We show how to realize this theory in a learning system named CFRule. CFRule is a parallel weight-based model, but it departs from traditional neural computing in that its internal knowledge is comprehensible. Furthermore, when the model converges upon training, each channel converges to a target rule. The model adaptation rule is derived by multi-level parallel weight optimization based on gradient descent. Since, however, gradient descent only guarantees local optimization, a multi-channel regression-based optimization strategy is developed to effectively deal with this problem. Formally, we prove that the CFRule model can explicitly and precisely encode any given rule set. Also, we prove a property related to asynchronous parallel convergence, which is a critical element of the multi-channel parallel adaptation theory for rule learning. Thanks to the quantizability nature of the CFRule model, rules can be extracted completely and soundly via a threshold-based mechanism. Finally, the practical application of the theory is demonstrated in DNA promoter recognition and hepatitis prognosis prediction.

Keywords: rule discovery, adaptation, optimization, regression, certainty factor, neural network, machine learning, uncertainty management, artificial intelligence.

1. Introduction

Rules express general knowledge about actions or conclusions in given circumstances and also principles in given domains. In the if-then format, rules are an easy way to represent cognitive processes in psychology and a useful means to encode expert knowledge. In

---
[*]E-mail address: lifu@patcar.org, Corresponding Author: Li Min Fu, 210 Rockview, Irvine, CA 92612, Phone: (626)922-8499.

another perspective, rules are important because they can help scientists understand problems and engineers solve problems. These observations would account for the fact that rule learning or discovery has become a major topic in both machine learning and data mining research. The former discipline concerns the construction of computer programs which learn knowledge or skill while the latter is about the discovery of patterns or rules hidden in the data.

The fundamental concepts of rule learning are discussed in [16]. Methods for learning sets of rules include symbolic heuristic search [3, 5], decision trees [17-18], inductive logic programming [13], neural networks [2, 7, 20], and genetic algorithms [10]. A methodology comparison can be found in our previous work [9]. Despite the differences in their computational frameworks, these methods perform a certain kind of search in the rule space (i.e., the space of possible rules) in conjunction with some optimization criterion. Complete search is difficult unless the domain is small, and a computer scientist is not interested in exhaustive search due to its exponential computational complexity. It is clear that significant issues have limited the effectiveness of all the approaches described. In particular, we should point out that all the algorithms except exhaustive search guarantee only local but not global optimization. For example, a sequential covering algorithm such as CN2 [5] performs a greedy search for a single rule at each sequential stage without backtracking and could make a suboptimal choice at any stage; a simultaneous covering algorithm such as ID3 [18] learns the entire set of rules simultaneously but it searches incompletely through the hypothesis space because of attribute ordering; a neural network algorithm which adopts gradient-descent search is prone to local minima.

In this paper, we introduce a new machine learning theory based on multi-channel parallel adaptation that shows great promise in learning the target rules from data by parallel global convergence. This theory is distinct from the familiar parallel-distributed adaptation theory of neural networks in terms of channel-based convergence to the target rules. We describe a system named CFRule which implements this theory. CFRule bases its computational characteristics on the certain factor (CF) model [4, 22] it adopts. The CF model is a calculus of uncertainty mangement and has been used to approximate standard probability theory [1] in artificial intelligence. It has been found that certainty factors associated with rules can be revised by a neural network [6, 12, 15]. Our research has further indicated that the CF model used as the neuron activation function (for combining inputs) can improve the neural-network performance [8].

The rest of the paper is organized as follows. Section 2. describes the multi-channel rule learning model. Section 3. examines the formal properties of rule encoding. Section 4. derives the model parameter adaptation rule, presents a novel optimization strategy to deal with the local minimum problem due to gradient descent, and proves a property related to asynchronous parallel convergence, which is a critical element of the main theory. Section 5. formulates a rule extraction algorithm. Section 6. demonstrates practical applications. Then we draw conclusions in the final section.

2. The Multi-channel Rule Learning Model

CFRule is a rule-learning system based on multi-level parameter optimization. The kernel of CFRule is a multi-channel rule learning model. CFRule can be embodied as an artificial neural network, but the neural network structure is not essential. We start with formal definitions about the model.

Definition 2.1 *The multi-channel rule learning model M is defined by k (k ≥ 1) channels (Ch's), an input vector (M_{in}), and an output (M_{out}) as follows:*

$$M \equiv (Ch_1, Ch_2, ..., Ch_k, M_{in}, M_{out}) \quad (1)$$

where $-1 \leq M_{out} \leq 1$ *and*

$$M_{in} \equiv (x_1, x_2, ..., x_d) \quad (2)$$

such that d is the input dimensionality and $-1 \leq x_i \leq 1$ *for all i.*

The model has only a single output because here we assume the problem is a single-class, multi-rule learning problem. The framework can be easily extended to the multi-class case.

Definition 2.2 *Each channel (Ch_j) is defined by an output weight (u_j), a set of input weights (w_{ji}'s), activation (ϕ_j), and influence (ψ_j) as follows:*

$$Ch_j \equiv (u_j, w_{j0}, w_{j1}, w_{j2}, ..., w_{jd}, \phi_j, \psi_j) \quad (3)$$

where w_{j0} is the bias, $0 \leq u_j \leq 1$, *and* $-1 \leq w_{ji} \leq 1$ *for all i. The input weight vector* $(w_{j1}, ..., w_{jd})$ *defines the channel's pattern.*

Definition 2.3 *Each channel's activation is defined by*

$$\phi_j = f_{cf}(w_{j0}, w_{j1}x_1, w_{j2}x_2, ..., w_{jd}x_d) \quad (4)$$

where f_{cf} is the CF-combining function [4, 22], as defined below.

Definition 2.4 *The CF-combining function is given by*

$$f_{cf}(x_1, x_2, ..., y_1, y_2, ...) = f_{cf}^+(x_1, x_2, ...) + f_{cf}^-(y_1, y_2, ...) \quad (5)$$

where

$$f_{cf}^+(x_1, x_2, ...) = 1 - \prod_i (1 - x_i) \quad (6)$$

$$f_{cf}^-(y_1, y_2, ...) = -1 + \prod_j (1 + y_j) \quad (7)$$

x_i's are nonnegative numbers and y_j's are negative numbers.

As we will see, the CF-combining function contributes to several important computational properties instrumental to rule discovery.

Definition 2.5 *Each channel's influence on the output is defined by*

$$\psi_j = u_j \phi_j \quad (8)$$

Definition 2.6 *The model output M_{out} is defined by*

$$M_{out} = f_{cf}(\psi_1, \psi_2, ..., \psi_k) \tag{9}$$

We call the class whose rules to be learned the *target class*, and define rules inferring (or explaining) that class to be the *target rules*. For instance, if the disease diabetes is the target class, then the diagnostic rules for diabetes would be the target rules. Each target rule defines a condition under which the given class can be inferred. Note that we do not consider rules which deny the target class, though such rules can be defined by reversing the class concept. The task of rule learning is to learn or discover a set of target rules from given instances called training instances (data). It is important that rules learned should be generally applicable to the entire domain, not just the training data. How well the target rules learned from the training data can be applied to unseen data determines the generalization performance.

Instances which belong to the target class are called positive instances, else, called negative instances. Ideally, a positive training instance should match at least one target rule learned and vice versa, whereas a negative training instance should match none. So, if there is only a single target rule learned, then it must be matched by all (or most) positive training instances. But if multiple target rules are learned, then each rule is matched by some (rather than all) positive training instances. Since the number of possible rule sets is far greater than the number of possible rules, the problem of learning multiple rules is naturally much more complex than that of learning single rules.

In the multi-channel rule learning theory, the model learns to sort out instances so that instances belonging to different rules flow through different channels, and at the same time, channels are adapted to accommodate their pertinent instances and learn corresponding rules. Notice that this is a mutual process and it cannot occur all at once. In the beginning, the rules are not learned and the channels are not properly shaped, both information flow and adaptation are more or less random, but through self-adaptation, the CFRule model will gradually converge to the correct rules, each encoded by a channel. The essence of this paper is to prove this property.

In the model design, a legitimate question is what the optimal number of channels is. This is just like the question raised for a neural network of how many hidden (internal computing) units should be used. It is true that too many hidden units cause data overfitting and make generalization worse [7]. Thus, a general principle is to use a minimal number of hidden units. The same principle can be equally well applied to the CFRule model. However, there is a difference. In ordinary neural networks, the number of hidden units is determined by the sample size, while in the CFRule model, the number of channels should match the number of rules embedded in the data. Since, however, we do not know how many rules are present in the data, our strategy is to use a minimal number of channels that admits convergence on the training data.

The model's behavior is characterized by three aspects:

- Information processing: Compute the model output for a given input vector.

- Learning or training: Adjust channels' parameters (output and input weights) so that the input vector is mapped into the output for every instance in the training data.

- Rule extraction: Extract rules from a trained model.

The first aspect has been described already.

3. Model Representation of Rules

The IF-THEN rule (i.e., If the premise, then the action) is a major knowledge representation paradigm in artificial intelligence. Here we make analysis of how such rules can be represented with proper semantics in the CFRule model.

Definition 3.1 *CFRule learns rules in the form of*

IF $A_1^+, ..., A_i^+,, ..., \neg A_1^-, . . ., \neg A_j^-, . . .$, THEN *the target class with a certainty factor.*

where A_i^+ is a positive antecedent (in the positive form), A_j^- a negated antecedent (in the negative form), and $\neg$ reads "not." Each antecedent can be a discrete or discretized attribute (feature), variable, or a logic proposition. The IF part must not be empty. The attached certainty factor in the THEN part, called the rule CF, is a positive real ≤ 1.

The rule's premise is restricted to a conjunction, and no disjunction is allowed. The collection of rules for a certain class can be formulated as a DNF (disjunctive normal form) logic expression, namely, the disjunction of conjunctions, which implies the class. However, rules defined here are not traditional logic rules because of the attached rule CFs meant to capture uncertainty. We interpret a rule by saying when its premise holds (that is, all positive antecedents mentioned are true and all negated antecedents mentioned are false), the target concept holds at the given confidence level. CFRule can also learn rules with weighted antecedents (a kind of fuzzy rules), but we will not consider this case here.

There is increasing evidence to indicate that good rule encoding capability actually facilitates rule discovery in the data. In the theorems that follow, we show how the CFRule model can explicitly and precisely encode any given rule set. We note that the ordinary sigmoid-function neural network can only implicitly and approximately does this. Also, we note although the threshold function of the perceptron model enables it to learn conjunctions or disjunctions, the non-differentiability of this function prohibits the use of an adaptive procedure in a multilayer construct.

Theorem 3.1 *For any rule represented by Definition 3.1, there exists a channel in the CFRule model to encode the rule so that if an instance matches the rule, the channel's activation is 1, else 0.*

(Proof): This can be proven by construction. Suppose we implement channel j by setting the bias weight to 1, the input weights associated with all positive attributes in the rule's premise to 1, the input weights associated with all negated attributes in the rule's premise to -1, the rest of the input weights to 0, and finally the output weight to the rule CF. Assume that each instance is encoded by a bipolar vector in which for each attribute, 1 means true and -1 false. When an instance matches the rule, the following conditions hold: $x_i = 1$ if x_i is part of the rule's premise, $x_i = -1$ if $\neg x_i$ is part of the rule's premise, and otherwise

x_i can be of any value. For such an instance, given the above construction, it is true that $w_{ji}x_i = 1$ or 0 for all i. Thus, the channel's activation (by Definition 2.3),

$$\phi_j = f_{\text{cf}}(w_{j0} = 1, w_{j1}x_1, w_{j2}x_2, ..., w_{jd}x_d) \tag{10}$$

must be 1 according to f_{cf}. On the other hand, if an instance does not match the rule, then there exists i such that $w_{ji}x_i = -1$. Since w_{j0} (the bias weight) = 1, the channel's activation is 0 due to f_{cf}. □

Theorem 3.2 *Assume that rule CF's > θ ($0 \le \theta \le 1$). For any set of rules represented by Definition 3.1, there exists a CFRule model to encode the rule set so that if an instance matches any of the given rules, the model output is > θ, else 0.*

(Proof): Suppose there are k rules in the set. As suggested in the proof of Theorem 3.1, we construct k channels, each encoding a different rule in the given rule set so that if an instance matches, say rule j, then the activation (ϕ_j) of channel j is 1. In this case, since the channel's influence ψ_j is given by $u_j\phi_j$ (where u_j is set to the rule CF) and the rule CF > θ, it follows that $\psi_j > \theta$. It is then clear that the model output must be > θ since it combines influences from all channels that ≥ 0 but at least one > θ. On the other hand, if an instance fails to match any of the rules, all the channels' activations are zero, so is the model output. □

4. Model Adaptation and Convergence

In neural computing, the backpropagation algorithm [19] can be viewed as a multilayer, parallel optimization strategy that enables the network to converge to a local optimum solution. The black-box nature of the neural network solution is reflected by the fact that the pattern (the input weight vector) learned by each neuron does not bear meaningful knowledge. The CFRule model departs from traditional neural computing in that its internal knowledge is comprehensible. Furthermore, when the model converges upon training, each channel converges to a target rule. How to achieve this objective and what is the mathematical theory are the main issues to be addressed.

4.1. Model Training Based on Gradient Descent

The CFRule model learns to map a set of input vectors (e.g., extracted features) into a set of outputs (e.g., class information) by training. An input vector along with its target output constitute a training instance. The input vector is encoded as a $1/-1$ bipolar vector. The target output is 1 for a positive instance and 0 for a negative instance.

Starting with a random or estimated weight setting, the model is trained to adapt itself to the characteristics of the training instances by changing weights (both output and input weights) for every channel in the model. Typically, instances are presented to the model one at a time. When all instances are examined (called an epoch), the network will start over with the first instance and repeat. Iterations continue until the system performance has reached a satisfactory level.

The learning rule of the CFRule model is derived in the same way as the backpropagation algorithm [19]. The training objective is to minimize the sum of squared errors in the data. In each learning cycle, a training instance is given and the weights of channel j (for all j) are updated by

$$u_j(t+1) = u_j(t) + \Delta u_j \tag{11}$$

$$w_{ji}(t+1) = w_{ji}(t) + \Delta w_{ji} \tag{12}$$

where u_j: the output weight, w_{ji}: an input weight, the argument t denotes iteration t, and Δ the adjustment. The weight adjustment on the current instance is based on gradient descent. Consider channel j. For the output weight (u_j),

$$\Delta u_j = -\eta(\partial E/\partial u_j) \tag{13}$$

(η: the learning rate) where

$$E = \frac{1}{2}(T_{out} - M_{out})^2$$

(T_{out}: the target output, M_{out}: the model output). Let

$$D = T_{out} - M_{out}$$

The partial derivative in Eq. (13) can be rewritten with the calculus chain rule to yield

$$\partial E/\partial u_j = (\partial E/\partial M_{out})(\partial M_{out}/\partial u_j) = -D(\partial M_{out}/\partial u_j)$$

Then we apply this result to Eq. (13) and obtain the following definition.

Definition 4.1 *The learning rule for output weight u_j of channel j is given by*

$$\Delta u_j = \eta D(\partial M_{out}/\partial u_j) \tag{14}$$

For the input weights (w_{ji}'s), again based on gradient descent,

$$\Delta w_{ji} = -\eta(\partial E/\partial w_{ji}) \tag{15}$$

The partial derivative in Eq. (15) is equivalent to

$$\partial E/\partial w_{ji} = (\partial E/\partial \phi_j)(\partial \phi_j/\partial w_{ji})$$

Since ϕ_j is not directly related to E, the first partial derivative on the right hand side of the above equation is expanded by the chain rule again to obtain

$$\partial E/\partial \phi_j = (\partial E/\partial M_{out})(\partial M_{out}/\partial \phi_j) = -D(\partial M_{out}/\partial \phi_j)$$

Substituting these results into Eq. (15) leads to the following definition.

Definition 4.2 *The learning rule for input weight w_{ji} of channel j is given by*

$$\Delta w_{ji} = \eta d_j(\partial \phi_j/\partial w_{ji}) \tag{16}$$

where

$$d_j = D(\partial M_{out}/\partial \phi_j)$$

Assume that

$$\phi_j = f_{cf}^+(w_{j1}x_1, w_{j2}x_2, ..., w_{jd'}x_{d'}) + f_{cf}^-(w_{jd'+1}x_{d'+1}, ..., w_{jd}x_d) \qquad (17)$$

Suppose $d' > 1$ and $d - d' > 1$. The partial derivative $\frac{\partial \phi_j}{\partial w_{ji}}$ can be computed as follows.

Case (a) If $w_{ji}x_i \geq 0$,

$$\frac{\partial \phi_j}{\partial w_{ji}} = (\prod_{l \neq i, l \leq d'} (1 - w_{jl}x_l))x_i \qquad (18)$$

Case (b) If $w_{ji}x_i < 0$,

$$\frac{\partial \phi_j}{\partial w_{ji}} = (\prod_{l \neq i, l > d'} (1 + w_{jl}x_l))x_i \qquad (19)$$

It is easy to show that if $d' = 1$ in case (a) or $d - d' = 1$ in case (b), $\frac{\partial \phi_j}{\partial w_{ji}} = x_i$.

4.2. Multi-channel Regression-Based Optimization

It is known that gradient descent can only find a local-minimum. When the error surface is flat or very convoluted, such an algorithm often ends up with a bad local minimum. Moreover, the learning performance is measured by the error on unseen data independent of the training set. Such error is referred to as generalization error. We note that minimization of the training error by the backpropagation algorithm does not guarantee simultaneous minimization of generalization error. What is worse, generalization error may instead rise after some point along the training curve due to an undesired phenomenon known as overfitting [7]. Thus, global optimization techniques for network training (e.g., [21]) do not necessarily offer help as far as generalization is concerned. To address this issue, CFRule uses a novel optimization strategy called multi-channel regression-based optimization (MCRO).

In Definition 2.4, f_{cf}^+ and f_{cf}^- can also be expressed as

$$f_{cf}^+(x_1, x_2, ...) = \sum_i x_i - \sum_i \sum_j x_i x_j + \sum_i \sum_j \sum_k x_i x_j x_k - ... \qquad (20)$$

$$f_{cf}^-(y_1, y_2, ...) = \sum_i y_i + \sum_i \sum_j y_i y_j + \sum_i \sum_j \sum_k y_i y_j y_k + ... \qquad (21)$$

When the arguments (x_i's and y_i's) are small, the CF function behaves somewhat like a linear function. It can be seen that if the magnitude of every argument is < 0.1, the first order approximation of the CF function is within an error of 10% or so. Since when learning starts, all the weights take on small values, this analysis has motivated the MCRO strategy for improving the gradient descent solution. The basic idea behind MCRO is to choose a starting point based on the linear regression analysis, in contrast to gradient descent which uses a random starting point.

If we can use regression analysis to estimate the initial influence of each input variable on the model output, how can we know how to distribute this estimate over multiple channels? In fact, this is the most intricate part of the whole idea since each channel's structure and parameters are yet to be learned. The answer will soon be clear.

In CFRule, each channel's activation is defined by

$$\phi_j = f_{\text{cf}}(w_{j0}, w_{j1}x_1, w_{j2}x_2, ...) \qquad (22)$$

Suppose we separate the linear component from the nonlinear component (R) in ϕ_j to obtain

$$\phi_j = \left(\sum_{i=0}^{d} w_{ji}x_i\right) + R_j \qquad (23)$$

We apply the same treatment to the model output (Definition 2.6)

$$M_{out} = f_{\text{cf}}(u_1\phi_1, u_2\phi_2, ...) \qquad (24)$$

so that

$$M_{out} = \left(\sum_{j=1}^{k} u_j\phi_j\right) + R_{out} \qquad (25)$$

Then we substitute Eq.(23) into Eq.(25) to obtain

$$M_{out} = \left(\sum_{j=1}^{k}\sum_{i=0}^{d} u_j w_{ji} x_i\right) + R_{acc} \qquad (26)$$

in which the right hand side is equivalent to

$$\left[\sum_{i=0}^{d}\left(\sum_{j=1}^{k} u_j w_{ji}\right)x_i\right] + R_{acc}$$

Note that

$$R_{acc} = \left(\sum_{j=1}^{k} u_j R_j\right) + R_{out}$$

Suppose linear regression analysis produces the following estimation equation for the model output:

$$M'_{out} = b_0 + b_1 x_1 + ...$$

(all the input variables and the output transformed to the range from 0 to 1).

Definition 4.3 *The MCRO strategy is defined by*

$$\sum_{j=1}^{k} u_j(t=0) w_{ji}(t=0) = b_i \qquad (27)$$

for each $i, 0 \leq i \leq d$

Table 1. The target rules in the simulation experiment.

rule 1:	IF x_1 and $\neg x_2$ and x_7	THEN the target concept
rule 2:	IF x_1 and $\neg x_4$ and x_5	THEN the target concept
rule 3:	IF x_6 and x_{11}	THEN the target concept

Table 2. Comparison of the MCRO strategy with random start for the convergence to the target rules. The results were validated by the statistical t test with the level of significance < 0.01 and < 0.025 (degrees of freedom = 48) for the training and test error rates upon convergence, respectively.

	MCRO	*Random Start*	*t-Value*	Level of Significance
Train error rate mean	0.010	0.026	2.47	0.01
Test error rate mean	0.012	0.033	2.34	0.025

That is, at iteration $t = 0$ when learning starts, the initial weights are randomized but subject to these $d + 1$ constraints.

To demonstrate this strategy, we designed an experiment. Assume there were 20 input variables and three targets rules as shown in Table 1. The training and test data sets were generated independently, each consisting of 100 random instances. An instance was classified as positive if it matched any of the target rules and as negative otherwise. The CFRule model for this experiment comprised three channels. The model was trained under MCRO and random start separately. For each strategy, 25 trials were run, each with a different initial weight setting. The same learning rate and stopping condition were used in every trial regardless of the strategy taken. The training and test error rates were measured. If the model converged to the target rules, then both training and test errors should be close to zero. We used the t test (one-sided hypothesis testing based on the statistical t distribution) to evaluate the difference in the means of error rates produced under the two strategies. Given the statistical validation result (as summarized in Table 2), we can conclude that MCRO is a valid technique.

4.3. Asynchronous Parallel Convergence

In the multi-channel rule learning theory, there are two possible modes of parallel convergence. In the synchronous mode, all channels converge to their respective target patterns at the same time, whereas in the asynchronous mode, each channel converges at a different time. In a self-adaptation or self-organization model without a global clock, the synchronous mode is not a plausible scenario of convergence. On the other hand, the asynchronous mode may not arrive at global convergence (i.e., every channel converging to its target pattern) unless there is a mechanism to protect a target pattern once it is converged upon. Here we examine a formal property of CFRule on this new learning issue.

Multi-channel Parallel Adaptation Theory for Rule Discovery

Theorem 4.1 *Suppose at time t, channel j of the CFRule model has learned an exact pattern $(w_{j1}, w_{j2}, ..., w_{jd})$ ($d \geq 1$) such that w_{j0} (the bias) $= 1$ and $w_{ji} = 1$ or -1 or 0 for $1 \leq i \leq d$. At time $t + 1$ when the model is trained on a given instance with the input vector $(x_0, x_1, x_2, ..., x_d)$ ($x_0 = 1$ and $x_i = 1$ or -1 for all $1 \leq i \leq d$), the pattern is unchanged unless there is a single mismatched weight (weight w_{ji} is mismatched if and only if $w_{ji}x_i = -1$). Let $\Delta w_{ji}(t+1)$ be the weight adjustment for w_{ji}. Then*
(a) If there is no mismatch, then $\Delta w_{ji}(t+1) = 0$ for all i.
(b) If there are more than one mismatched weight then $\Delta w_{ji}(t+1) = 0$ for all i.

(Proof): In case (a), there is no mismatch, so $w_{ji}x_i = 1$ or 0 for all i. There exists l such that $w_{jl}x_l = 1$ and $l \neq i$, for example, $w_{j0}x_0 = 1$ as given. From Eq. (18),

$$\frac{\partial \phi_j}{\partial w_{ji}} = (\prod_{l \geq 0, l \neq i}^{d} (1 - w_{jl}x_l))x_i = 0$$

Then from Eq. (16),

$$\Delta w_{ji}(t+1) = \eta d_j(\frac{\partial \phi_j}{\partial w_{ji}}) = 0$$

In case (b), the proof for matched weights is the same as that in case (a). Consider only mismatched weights w_{ji}'s such that $w_{ji}x_i = -1$. Since there are at least two mismatched weights, there exists l such that $w_{jl}x_l = -1$ and $l \neq i$. From Eq. (19),

$$\frac{\partial \phi_j}{\partial w_{ji}} = (\prod_{w_{jl}x_l = -1, l \neq i} (1 + w_{jl}x_l))x_i = 0$$

Therefore,

$$\Delta w_{ji}(t+1) = \eta d_j(\frac{\partial \phi_j}{\partial w_{ji}}) = 0$$

In the case of a single mismatched weight,

$$\frac{\partial \phi_j}{\partial w_{ji}} = x_i$$

which is not zero, so the weight adjustment $\Delta w_{ji}(t+1)$ may or may not be zero, depending on the error d_j. □

Since model training starts with small weight values, the initial pattern associated with each channel cannot be exact. When training ends, the channel's pattern may still be inexact because of possible noise, inconsistency, and uncertainty in the data. However, from the proof of the above theorem, we see that when the nonzero weights in the channel's pattern grow larger, the error derivative ($d_j \frac{\phi_j}{w_{ji}}$) generally gets smaller, so does the weight adjustment, and as a result, the pattern becomes more stable and gradually converges to a target pattern. A converged pattern does not move unless there is a near-miss instance (with a single feature mismatch against the pattern) that causes some error in the model output, in which case, the pattern is refined to be a little more general or specific. This analysis explains how the CFRule model ensures the stability of a channel once it is settled in a

Table 3. Asynchronous parallel convergence to the target rules in the CFRule model. Channels 1, 2, 3 converge to target rules 1, 2, 3, respectively. $w_{j,i}$ denotes the input weight associated with the input x_i in channel j. An epoch consists of a presentation of all training instances.

epoch	$w_{1,1}$	$w_{1,2}$	$w_{1,7}$	$w_{2,1}$	$w_{2,4}$	$w_{2,5}$	$w_{3,6}$	$w_{3,11}$
1	.016	-.073	.005	.144	-.166	.087	.387	.479
5	.202	-.249	.133	.506	-.348	.385	1.00	.948
10	.313	-.420	.256	.868	-.719	.725	1.00	1.00
15	.462	-.529	.440	1.00	-.920	.893	1.00	1.00
20	.851	-.802	.789	1.00	-.983	1.00	1.00	1.00
25	1.00	-.998	.996	1.00	-1.00	1.00	1.00	1.00
30	1.00	-1.00	1.00	1.00	-1.00	1.00	1.00	1.00

target pattern. Note that the output weight of a channel with a stable pattern can still be modified toward global error minimization and uncertainty management. In asynchronous parallel convergence, each channel is settled in its own target pattern with a different time frame. Without the above pattern stabilizing property, global convergence is difficult to achieve in the asynchronous mode. This line of arguments imply that CFRule admits asynchronous parallel convergence. Theorem 4.1 is unique for CFRule. That property has not been provable for other types of neural networks or learning methods (e.g., [16]).

Asynchronous parallel convergence for rule learning can be illustrated by the example in Section 4.2.. Table 3 shows how each channel converges to a target rule in the training course when the model was trained on just 100 random instances (out of 2^{20} possible instances). For instance, given $\neg x_2$ in the premise of rule 1 (Table 1), we observe the corresponding weight $w_{1,2}$ of channel 1 converged to -1 (Table 3); also, for x_6 mentioned in rule 3, we see the weight $w_{3,6}$ of channel 3 converged to 1. Only the significant weights that converge to a magnitude of 1 are shown. Unimportant weights ending up with about zero values are omitted. The convergence behavior can be better visualized in Figure 1. It clearly shows that convergence occurs asynchronously for each channel. It does not matter which channel converges to which rule. This correspondence is determined by the initial weight setting and the data characteristics. Note that given k channels in the model, there are $k!$ equivalent permutations in terms of their relative positions in the model. It matters, though, whether the model as a whole converges to all the needed target rules.

5. Rule Extraction

As illustrated by the example in Section 4.3., when a channel converges to a target rule, the weights associated with the input attributes contained in the rule's premise grow into large values, whereas the rest of input weights decay to small values. The asymptotic absolute weight values upon convergence approach either 1 or 0 ideally, but this case does not necessarily happen in practical circumstances involving data noise, inconsistency, uncertainty,

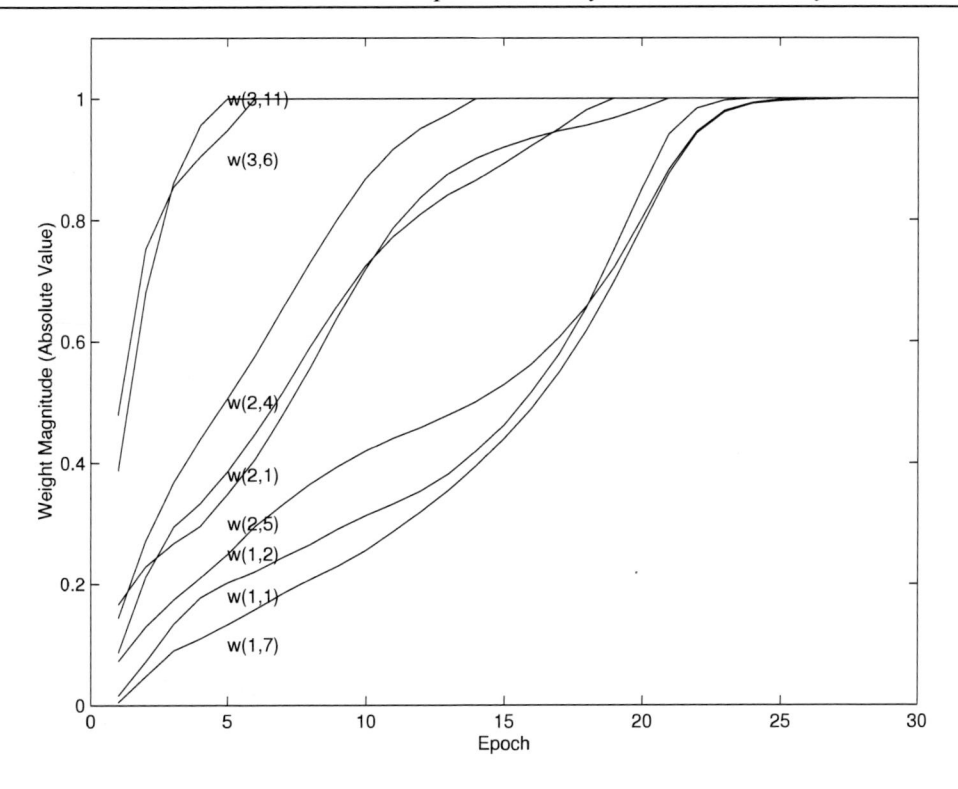

Figure 1. The temporal curves of asynchronous parallel convergence for rule learning.

and inadequate sample sizes. However, in whatever circumstances, it turns out that a simple thresholding mechanism suffices to distinguish important from unimportant weights in the CFRule model. Since the weight absolute values range from 0 to 1, it is reasonable to use 0.5 as the threshold, but this value does not always guarantee optimal performance. How to search for a good threshold in a continuous range is difficult. Fortunately, thanks to the quantizability nature of the system adopting the CF model [9], only a handful of values need to be considered. Our research has narrowed it down to four candidate values: 0.35, 0.5, 0.65, and 0.8. A larger threshold makes extracted rules more general, whereas a smaller threshold more specific. In order to lessen data overfitting, our heuristic is to choose a higher value as long as the training error is acceptable. Using an independent cross-validation data set is a good idea if enough data is available. The rule extraction algorithm is formulated below.

The CFRule Rule Extraction Algorithm

- Select a rule extraction threshold r ($0 < r < 1$).
- For each channel j,

    [1] $P := nil$ (an empty set)
    [2] $C :=$ the target class

[3] Normalize the input weights w_{ji}'s so that the maximum weight absolute value is 1.

[4] For each input weight w_{ji} ($1 \leq i \leq d$, d: the input dimensionality),

    a. If $w_{ji} \geq r$, then add x_i to P.

    b. If $w_{ji} \leq -r$, then add $\neg x_i$ to P.

    c. Else, do nothing.

[5] Form a rule: "IF P, THEN C with CF = u_j" (u_j: the output weight based on the rule).

- Remove subsumed rules and rules with low CFs.

The threshold-based algorithm described here is fundamentally different from the search-based algorithm in neural network rule extraction [7, 9, 20]. The main advantage with the threshold-based approach is its linear computational complexity with the total number of weights, in contrast to polynomial or even exponential complexity incurred by the search-based approach. Furthermore, the former approach obviates the need of a special training, pruning, or approximation procedure commonly used in the latter approach for complexity reduction. As a result, the threshold-based, direct approach should produce better and more reliable rules. Notice that this approach is not applicable to the ordinary sigmoid-function neural network where knowledge is entangled. The admissibility of the threshold-based algorithm for rule extraction in CFRule can be ascribed to the CF-combining function.

6. Applications

Two benchmark data sets were selected to demonstrate the value of CFRule on practical domains. The promoter data set is characterized by high dimensionality relative to the sample size, while the hepatitis data has a lot of missing values. Thus, both pose a challenging problem.

The decision-tree-based rule generator system C4.5 [18] was taken as a control since it (and with its later version) is the currently most representative (or most often used) rule learning system, and also the performance of C4.5 is optimized in a statistical sense.

6.1. Promoter Recognition in DNA

In the promoter data set [23], there are 106 instances with each consisting of a DNA nucleotide string of four base types: A (adenine), G (guanine), C (cytosine), and T (thymine). Each instance string is comprised of 57 sequential nucleotides, including fifty nucleotides before (minus) and six following (plus) the transcription site. An instance is a positive instance if the promoter region is present in the sequence, else it is a negative instance. There are 53 positive instances and 53 negative instances, respectively. Each position of an

Table 4. The promoter (of prokaryotes) consensus sequences.

Region	DNA Sequence Pattern
Minus-35	@-36=T @-35=T @-34=G @-33=A @-32=C @-31=A
Minus-10	@-13=T @-12=A @-11=T @-10=A @-9=A @-8=T

instance sequence is encoded by four bits with each bit designating a base type. So an instance is encoded by a vector of 228 bits along with a label indicating a positive or negative instance.

In the literature of molecular biology, promoter (of prokaryotes) sequences have average constitutions of -TTGACA- and -TATAAT-, respectively, located at so-called minus-35 and minus-10 regions [14], as shown in Table 4.

The CFRule model in this study had 3 channels, which were the minimal number of channels to bring the training error under 0.02 upon convergence. Still, the model is relatively underdetermined because of the low ratio of the number of instances available for training to the input dimension. However, unlike our previous approach [9], we did not use any pruning strategy. The model had to learn to cope with high dimensionality by itself. The learning rate was set to 0.2, and the rule extraction threshold 0.5 (all these are default values). The model was trained on the training data under the MCRO strategy and then tested on the test data. The stopping criterion for training was the drop of MSE (mean squared error) less than a small value per epoch. Rules were extracted from the trained model.

Cross-validation is an important means to evaluate the ability of learning. Domain validity is indicated if rules learned based on some data can be well applied to other data in the same domain. In the two-fold cross-validation experiment, the 106 instances were randomly divided equally into two subsets. CFRule and C4.5 used the same data partition. The rules learned on one subset were tested by the other and vice versa. The average prediction error rate on the test set was defined as the cross-validation *rule* error rate. The cross-validation experiment with CFRule was run 5 times, each with a different initial weight setting. The average cross-validation error was reported. CFRule had a significantly smaller cross-validation rule error rate than C4.5 (12.8% versus 23.9%, respectively), as shown in Table 5. Note that the prediction accuracy and the error rate were measured based on exact symbolic match. That is, an instance is predicted to be in the concept only if it matches exactly any rule of the concept, else it is not in the concept. If, however, prior domain knowledge is used and exact symbolic match is not required, the error rate based on leave-one-out can be as low as 2% [7].

Both CFRule and C4.5 learned three rules from the 106 instances. The rules are summarized in Table 6. In the aspect of rule quality, CFRule learned rules of larger size than C4.5 under inadequate samples. This is because CFRule tends to keep attributes sufficiently correlated with the target concept, whereas C4.5 retains only attributes with verified statistical significance and tends to favor more general rules. In terms of domain validity, the

Table 5. The average two-fold cross-validation error rates of the rules learned by C4.5 and CFRule, respectively.

Domain	C4.5	CFRule
Promoters (without prior knowledge)	23.9%	12.8%
Hepatitis	7.1%	5.3%

Table 6. The promoter prediction rules learned from 106 instances by CFRule and C4.5, respectively. ¬: not. @: at.

	Rule	DNA Sequence Pattern
CFRule	#1	@-34=G @-33=¬G @-12=¬G
	#2	@-36=T @-35=T @-31=¬C @-12=¬G
	#3	@-45=A @-36=T @-35=T
C4.5	#1	@-35=T @-34=G
	#2	@-36=T @-12=A
	#3	@-36=T @-35=T @-34=T

rule's accuracy based on cross-validation is more reliable than other quality measures. Another interesting discovery made by CFRule (but not by C4.5) is @-45=A (in rule #3) which plays a major role in the so-called conformation theory for promoter prediction [11].

The data for this research are available from a machine learning database located in the University of California at Irvine with an ftp address at ftp.ics.uci.edu/pub/machine-learning-databases.

6.2. Hepatitis Prognosis Prediction

In the data set concerning hepatitis prognosis [1], there are 155 instances, each described by 19 attributes. Continuous attributes were discretized, then the data set was randomly partitioned into two halves (78 and 77 cases), and then cross-validation was carried out. CFRule and C4.5 used exactly the same data to ensure fair comparison. The CFRule model for this problem consisted of 2 channels. Again, CFRule was superior to C4.5 based on the cross-validation performance (see Table 5). However, both systems learned the same single rule from the whole 155 instances, as displayed in Table 7. To learn the same rule by two fundamentally different systems is quite a coincidence, but it suggests the rule is true in a global sense.

---

[1] This data set is an old version previously used in our research work [7].

Table 7. The hepatitis rules for predicting (bad) prognosis learned from 155 instances by CFRule and C4.5, respectively. ¬: not. @: at.

	Rule	Premise
CFRule	# 1	MALE and NO STEROID and ALBUMIN < 3.7
C4.5	# 1	MALE and NO STEROID and ALBUMIN < 3.7

7. Conclusions

If global optimization is a main issue for automated rule discovery from data, then current machine learning theories do not seem adequate. For instance, the decision-tree and neural-network based algorithms, which dodge the complexity of exhaustive search, guarantee only local but not global optimization. In this paper, we introduce a new machine learning theory based on multi-channel parallel adaptation that shows great promise in learning the target rules from data by parallel global convergence. The basic idea is that when a model consisting of multiple parallel channels is optimized according to a certain global error criterion, each of its channels converges to a target rule. While the theory sounds attractive, the main question is how to implement it. In this paper, we show how to realize this theory in a learning system named CFRule.

CFRule is a parallel weight-based model, which can be optimized by weight adaptation. The parameter adaptation rule follows the gradient-descent idea which is generalized in a multi-level parallel context. However, the central idea of the multi-channel rule-learning theory is not about how the parameters are adapted but rather, how each channel can converge to a target rule. We have noticed that CFRule exhibits the necessary conditions to ensure such convergence behavior. We have further found that the CFRule's behavior can be attributed to the use of the CF (certainty factor) model for combining the inputs and the channels.

Since the gradient descent technique seeks only a local minimum, the learning model may well be settled in a solution where each rule is optimal in a local sense. A strategy called multi-channel regression-based optimization (MCRO) has been developed to address this issue. This strategy has proven effective by statistical validation.

We have formally proven two important properties that account for the parallel rule-learning behavior of CFRule. First, we show that any given rule set can be explicitly and precisely encoded by the CFRule model. Secondly, we show that once a channel is settled in a target rule, it barely moves. These two conditions encourage the model to move toward the target rules. An empirical weight convergence graph clearly showed how each channel converged to a target rule in an asynchronous manner. Notice, however, we have not been able to prove or demonstrate this rule-oriented convergence behavior in other neural networks.

We have then examined the application of this methodology to DNA promoter recognition and hepatitis prognosis prediction. In both domains, CFRule is superior to C4.5 (a rule-learning method based on the decision tree) based on cross-validation. Rules learned are also consistent with knowledge in the literature.

In: Concurrent and Parallel Computing...
Editor: Alexander S. Becker, pp. 113-131

ISBN 978-1-60456-274-3
© 2008 Nova Science Publishers, Inc.

Chapter 5

AN OVERVIEW OF PARALLEL AND DISTRIBUTED JAVA FOR HETEROGENEOUS SYSTEMS: APPROACHES AND OPEN ISSUES

Jameela Al-Jaroodi[1],[*] *Nader Mohamed*[1],[†] *Hong Jiang*[2],[‡] *and David Swanson*[2],[§]
[1]The Electrical and Computer Engineering Department
Stevens Institute of Technology, Hoboken, NJ 07030
[2]Department of Computer Science and engineering,
University of Nebraska-Lincoln, 115 Ferguson Hall, Lincoln, NE 68588-0115

Abstract

Java is gaining considerable recognition as the most suitable language for developing distributed applications in heterogeneous systems due to its portability and machine independence. However, standard Java does not provide easy-to-use features for parallel application development. Therefore, considerable research has been conducted and is underway to provide users with tools and programming models to write parallel applications in Java. This paper reviews a number of representative research projects and outlines the primary approaches used in these projects that enable Java to provide high performance parallel and distributed computing in heterogeneous systems. The study shows that most projects fit within one of the following parallel programming models: (1) message (or object-) passing, (2) distributed shared address (or object), (3) multi-threaded, and (4) transparent (or towards seamless) parallelization. Within these categories, the different implementation approaches are discussed. The paper also identifies and discusses a number of related problems and open issues such as benchmarks, porting legacy applications, distributed environment overhead and security.

Keywords: parallel Java, programming languages, heterogeneous systems

AMS Subject Classifications: 68N19, 68N15

---

[*]E-mail address: jaljaroo@stevens.edu
[†]E-mail address: nmohamed@stevens.edu
[‡]E-mail address: jiang@cse.unl.edu
[§]E-mail address: dswanson@cse.unl.edu

1. Introduction

Clusters, computational grids and heterogeneous networked systems can provide processing power comparable to special-purpose multi-processor systems for a fraction of the cost. Moreover, it is essential to have application software that can support such systems and provide the user with transparent and efficient utilization of the multiple resources available. Java emerges as a natural development environment for such architectures because it is portable, extendible and currently provides basic features that support distributed application development. However, standard Java is still not suitable for efficient parallel programming.

This paper studies and classifies a number of representative research projects that empower Java with parallel and distributed capabilities for clusters and heterogeneous networked systems. The classification is based on the programming model used. Within each model, projects are compared in terms of the implementation approaches, the level of user involvement, and the compatibility with the Java virtual machine (JVM). In addition, the paper discusses some of the problems, open issues and challenges facing such projects.

The paper provides some background information in section 2. Section 3 reviews the projects and classifies them in categories based on the programming models they embody. A discussion of the primary approaches used in these projects is presented in Section 4, which also identifies the problems and open issues in the area, while Section 5 concludes the study.

2. Background

Java in its current state provides features and classes that facilitate distributed application development. However, the development process of large scale distributed applications is usually very complex and time consuming. Some of the features Java provides are:

1. The reflection API, which represents, or reflects, the classes, interfaces, and objects in the current Java Virtual Machine [15].

2. Object serialization [45], which is used to store and retrieve objects in a serialized form by representing the state of objects using byte streams in sufficient details that allows for reconstructing the object(s) [15].

3. The Java class loader is responsible for loading the Java classes (bytecode) onto a JVM. Java allows programmers to override the default class loader by writing their own method for class loading. This is an important feature in Java for facilitating remote and dynamic class loading in a distributed environment.

4. Sockets, in Java, provide programmers with the flexibility to write efficient distributed applications, but they tend to make the development process lengthy and complex due to the low level details that need to be attended to.

5. Java Native Interface (JNI) [27] is a standard programming interface for writing Java native methods and embedding the JVM into native applications, thus making the application more efficient on the target machine. This provides binary compatibility of

native method libraries across all JVM implementations on a given platform. However, using JNI compromises the portability of the Java application since parts of the code will be machine dependant.

6. Remote Method Invocation (RMI) [43] was introduced as a more user-friendly alternative to socket programming. It creates a layer that hides the details of communications to the level of procedure call (method invocation) from the developer. However, this layer increases the costs of communications.

These same features can be used to develop parallel applications in Java. However, the process becomes even more complex and requires considerable effort to handle not just the communication aspects, but also the synchronization and process distribution, to mention just a few. In addition, some of these features are inefficient or introduce high overhead that offsets the efficiency of the parallel application. Therefore, some research groups have tried to enhance or modify them for their projects.

On the other hand, message-passing provides other programming languages such as C with a simpler tool to develop parallel applications in a distributed environment. The most well known standard for message-passing is the Message Passing Interface (MPI) [33]. MPI provides a number of library functions to exchange messages among processes, such as point-to-point and group communication primitives, synchronization and other functions. MPI-2 is an extension of MPI-1, adding more functionality such as process creation and management, extended collective operations, I/O, and additional language bindings such as C++ bindings.

Object-Oriented MPI was introduced recently to provide C++ programmers with abstract message-passing methods. A number of extensions were developed to provide object orientation for C++ and FORTRAN 90, such as OOMPI [46, 37], Charm++ [31] and ABC++ [8]. More recently, with the success of Java as a programming language for regular and distributed applications, some effort has been made to provide extensions of MPI that can be used in Java. The Java Grande Forum [26] has developed a draft standard for message-passing in Java (MPJ) [17] based on MPI.

3. Programming Models

In this section, we discuss the different programming models for parallel and distributed application development. Figure 1 shows a logical view of these models in increasing level of user involvement and awareness of the parallelization process, and the efficiency of the system adopting to the model. The message-/object-passing model is the most efficient in terms of computation performance, but requires full user awareness of the parallelization details (e.g. explicit data distribution). On the other hand; while transparent parallelization tries to completely hide the parallelization details from the user, it is arguably the least efficient in terms of resource utilization and speedup. The models' logical view also shows the implementation dependencies among the models. In a distributed environment, message-/object-passing is essential to support the other models. In addition, it is possible to implement each model by utilizing the features and functionality of the model(s) below. This may explain the great interest in developing and optimizing message-/object-passing models for Java in order to benefit future implementations of the higher-level models. The sub-sections that follow will discuss the different research projects in light of these models. As mentioned earlier, the projects discussed here are a representative subset of the available projects and is by no means a comprehensive list.

```
User
Awareness     | Transparent (Automatic)
& Efficiency  | Parallelization
              |--------------------------
              | Multi-Threaded
              | Programming Model
              |--------------------------
              | Distributed Shared
              | Memory (Object) Model
              |--------------------------
              | Message-Passing and
              | Object-Passing Model
    ▼
```

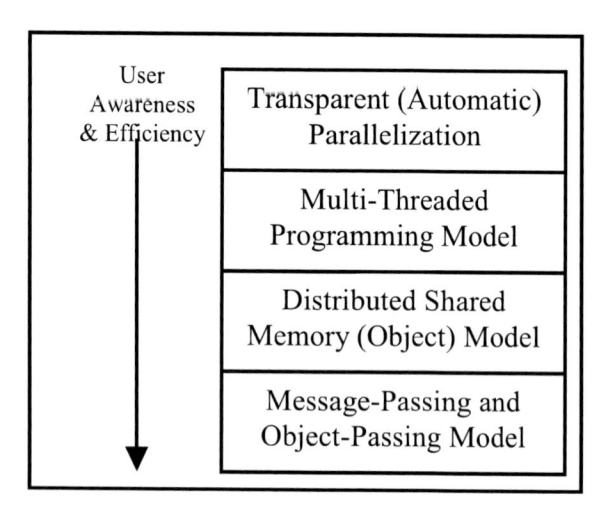

Figure 1. An overview of the organization of the programming models used for parallel Java (the arrow indicates increased user awareness (involvement) and increased efficiency).

3.1. Information Passing

In this category, systems provide certain mechanisms for some form of information exchange between processes, as in message- (object-) passing. This approach requires the utilization of a run-time support system to handle the application deployment and process allocation, in addition to the message or object exchanges between the participating machines. This environment can be implemented in many different ways such as using a pure Java implementation based on socket programming, native marshaling, RMI, utilizing the Java native interface (JNI), Java-to-C interface (JCI), parallel virtual machine (PVM) and others. In terms of the API provided, a number of systems were found to have tried to comply with MPI and MPJ [17], while others were based on a new set of class libraries for message (object) passing interfaces.

3.1.1. Java Object-Passing Interface [1, 32]

Developed at The University of Nebraska-Lincoln, the Java Object Passing Interface (JOPI) [32] provides the user with a class library of APIs very similar to the MPI and MPJ interface. Moreover, JOPI also exploits the object-oriented nature of Java by exchanging objects instead of data elements, which simplifies the process of writing parallel programs and facilitates the exchange of complex structures and logic. JOPI is a pure Java implementation and the applications written with JOPI can execute on any JVM. Furthermore, the interprocess communication is implemented using socket programming to ensure efficiency and flexibility for the parallel application.

A run-time environment to support the parallel programming capabilities in JOPI is provided [1]. Using this environment, parallel Java applications written with JOPI can execute on homogeneous multi-processor systems or on heterogeneous systems. The system is portable, which makes it possible to utilize different machines of varying architectures to execute the user applications. Software agents [1] were used to coordinate and manage the parallel processes and to schedule multiple user jobs among the available processors. The agents help deploy and run the user processes on the remote machines as threads from the memory. This approach reduces the I/O overhead, consumes fewer resources, and enhances the system security.

3.1.2. University of Waterloo and York University Research Projects

A series of projects were developed here that facilitate parallel Java application development:

ParaWeb [13] allows users to utilize the Internet computing resources seamlessly. It enables users to upload and execute programs on multiple machines on a heterogeneous system. Using ParaWeb, clients can download and execute a single Java application in parallel, on a network of workstations, or they can automatically upload and execute programs on remote compute servers. ParaWeb has two implementations:

1. Java Parallel Class Library (JPCL): It facilitates remote creation and execution of threads and provides communication using message-passing.

2. Java Parallel Runtime System (JPRS): the Java interpreter is modified to provide the illusion of a global shared address space for the multi-threaded application.

Ajents [24] is a collection of Java classes and servers, written in standard Java, that provide seamless implementation of distributed and parallel Java applications. It requires no modifications to Java language or the JVM and uses Java security features to protect the servers. Ajents provides many features such as remote object creation, remote class loading, asynchronous RMI, object migration, and checkpointing, rollback and restart of objects.

Babylon [23], a Java based system to support object distribution, inherits Ajents' features, in addition to a few new features. It allows object creation and migration at any time, seamlessly handles arrival and departure of compute servers, and provides I/O through the originating machine.

3.1.3. MPIJ - MPI for Java [34]

MPIJ was built as part of the DOGMA project [19], but it can be used as stand alone system. This is a pure Java implementation of message-passing interface for Java and it is compliant with MPJ. The MPIJ communication is built using native marshaling, which provides efficient communication primitives. The pure Java implementation makes MPIJ portable. Another useful feature of MPIJ is that it is independent of the application frameworks; therefore, it can be utilized to support different distributed applications such as DOGMA.

3.1.4. CCJ - Collective Communication in Java [36]

CCJ adds classes to Java to support MPI-like message-passing and collective communication operations. CCJ utilizes the object-oriented framework in Java to provide these operations. CCJ is a pure Java implementation on top of Manta RMI, which is a modified implementation of RMI on Myrinet. The use of Manta RMI reduces the overhead and utilizes the faster Myrinet infrastructure.

3.1.5. JPVM - Java Parallel Virtual Machine [21]

Java Parallel Virtual Machine is a PVM-like library of object classes implemented purely in Java to achieve portability. The main goal is to enable a system to utilize the available computing resources in a heterogeneous system. It allows explicit message-passing parallel programming in Java. However, programs written for JPVM cannot be ported to JVM. Experiments were conducted to measure the overhead of creating tasks and communications. The task creation and communication overhead is high, which implies that JPVM is most suitable for coarse grain parallelization.

3.1.6. HPJava Language [39, 22]

HPJava is being developed at the Syracuse University under the Parallel Compiler Runtime Consortium (PCRC) [39]. HPJava [22]is a dialect of Java for message-passing parallel programming, specifically designed for SPMD programming with distributed arrays added as language primitives. By design, applications written in HPJava can be preprocessed straightforwardly to standard Java with calls to kernel runtime functions. Java bindings of various runtime functions have been implemented and one of the useable components of the HPJava environment is the mpiJava [9, 35] binding of MPI. mpijava uses JNI to link the parallel Java constructs and methods to the MPI library.

3.2. Shared Address Space

Here we discuss the systems that provide parallel Java capabilities through the shared address space model or the shared object model. In both cases, the parallel application is given the illusion of having a single address or object space where all data or objects are available to all the participating processes. Using a distributed shared address or object space, the user has less concern with the particular details of communicating information. However, it is still necessary to provide some parallelization information and directives in the application. The underlying infrastructure can be implemented in different ways, for example, using an existing distributed shared memory (DSM) system, or utilizing a message- or object-passing infrastructure. The systems discussed here used different approaches to handle the various issues of shared space such as information (data or objects) integrity and consistency, synchronization and coherence.

3.2.1. Titanium [47]

Developed at the University of California-Berkeley, Titanium is a Java dialect used for large scale scientific computing, where applications run in a shared address space. It provides parallelization primitives in a Java-like language, including immutable classes, flexible and efficient multi-dimensional arrays, and distributed data structures. One advantage is that programs written for shared memory can be executed in a distributed system without modification. The Titanium compiler compiles Titanium programs into C, thus it is not compatible with JVM; however, it inherits some of the safety features of Java.

3.2.2. UIUC Project [29]

A research group at the University of Illinois at Urbana-Champaign has been working on a prototype extension of Java to provide dynamic creation of remote objects with load balancing, and object groups [29]. The language constructs, based on those of Charm++ [31], provide a shared address space. The parallel Java extension is implemented using the Converse interoperability framework [28], which makes it possible to integrate parallel libraries written in Java with modules in other parallel languages in a single application. Existing libraries written in C and MPI, Charm++, PVM, etc. can be utilized in a new application, with new modules written in Java using the provided parallelization runtime library.

The system is designed for multi-lingual parallel programming. To achieve parallelism, proxy objects and serialization are utilized in addition to asynchronous remote method invocation and JNI to interface with converse messaging layer. The main implementation goals of this system are to minimize native code and copying.

3.2.3. PARASLAX [38]

Paraslax is a collection of Java packages that provide distributed shared object environment. The interface allows users to define and share objects on remote nodes and provides efficient consistency protocols. The code for a shared object is similar to an ordinary object with some modifications using Paraslax classes and methods.

3.3. Multi-threading

Many research projects aim to provide seamless utilization of a distributed environment by executing multi-threaded programs on multiple connected machines. The main goal here is to be able to run concurrent multi-threaded applications in parallel without having to modify or rewrite them. This requires the system to transparently distribute the threads among the different processors without any user involvement. This is made possible by the inherent concurrency of multiple threads that can be translated into parallel processes on the distributed environment. In this case, the implementation issues are similar to the shared space model in the sense that all data and objects used by the threads need to be sharable. The underlying run-time support requires data sharing or exchange mechanisms to provide thread distribution and information sharing.

3.3.1. cJVM - Clustered JVM [4, 5, 6, 7, 18]

cJVM is a clustered Java virtual machine that allows multi-threaded applications to run on multiple nodes of a cluster. The main objective is to allow existing multi-threaded server applications to be executed in a distributed fashion without the need for rewriting them.

cJVM creates a single system image (SSI) of the traditional JVM to transparently exploit the power of a cluster. It is an object-oriented model that can make use of the possibility of having remote and consistent replicated objects on different nodes.

The shared object model was implemented by having a master object (the original object defined by the programmer) and proxies. Proxy objects, located on other nodes, are created by the cJVM run time environment to provide mechanism for other threads located on different nodes to remotely access the master object in a transparent way. Different optimization techniques to reduce the amount of communication among the nodes were employed. All these techniques enhance data locality by using cashing based on locality of execution and object migration. In addition, to enhance data locality, the master copy of an object is placed where it will be used not where it was created. cJVM is a new JVM that replaces the standard JVM.

3.3.2. JavaParty [25, 40]

JavaParty provides facilities for transparent remote objects in Java and allows easy porting of multi-threaded Java programs to distributed systems such as clusters. The JavaParty environment can be viewed as a Java virtual machine that is distributed over several computers. Object migration is one way of adapting the distribution layout to changing locality requirements of the application. In JavaParty, objects that are not declared as residents can migrate from one node to another. JavaParty extends the Java language with one modifier, called remote, to declare a JavaParty remote class or thread. The fields and methods of a remote object instantiated from a remote class can be accessed transparently, while the JavaParty environment deals with locality and communication optimizations.

The JavaParty environment uses a pre-processor and a runtime system. The pre-processor translates the JavaParty source program to Java code and RMI hooks. The runtime system is a set of components distributed on all the nodes with a central component, called RuntimeManager, which maintains the locations of contributing node objects. To reduce the access latency to a remote object while maintaining compatibility with the JVM, different optimization efforts were attempted, including more efficient object serialization and optimized RMI (KaRMI).

3.3.3. Hyperion [3]

Developed at The University of New Hampshire, Hyperion is an automatic distribution framework. It is aimed towards high performance execution of multithreaded Java applications on distributed systems. Hyperion consists of two parts: a Java bytecode-to-c compiler that compiles the Java classes into native C code, and a portable run-time system that is used to facilitate the communication and distribution of the generated code. Using Hyperion, a multithreaded Java application can be compiled and linked with the run-time system and then executed over a distributed shared memory system, thus alleviating the burden of explicitly parallelizing the application for the distributed environment. In addition, Hyperion provides a round-robin type of load distribution (of active threads) to achieve a basic level of load balancing. However, using the native code limits the portability of Hyperion to a set of predetermined UNIX systems and defies the original purpose for using Java.

3.4. Transparent (Seamless) Parallelization

In this category, some systems provide transparent parallelization of Java programs written in standard Java by modifying the JVM, while others utilize preprocessors to achieve this goal. Still others provide seamless utilization of resources or communication mechanisms to simplify the parallelization process. In general, the systems introduced in this category aim to hide the parallelization process details as much as possible, in an effort to get closer to the fully transparent parallelization of sequential applications. Thus, they try to relieve the developer of all details of parallelizing the application and of running existing applications in parallel without (or with minor) modifications. Again, a run-time support is needed to execute the generated parallel programs. The run-time support may be built from scratch or utilizing some facilities provided in the infrastructures described in the above three categories. For example, a distributed shared memory (DSM) system can be used to support the execution of a preprocessed parallel code.

3.4.1. ProActive [10, 16, 41]

ProActive includes a library for parallel, distributed, and concurrent (PDC) programming in Java. It provides a metacomputing framework to convert an object to a thread running in a pre-defined remote address space. Objects are classified into passive objects (non-thread objects) and active object (thread objects). A passive object can be activated as thread object running on another node. All method invocations to any of the methods in the active object will be transparently transferred to the node where the object is running and the results will be transparently returned to the caller address space.

A sequential Java program can be transformed to a distributed program by converting some of the passive objects to active objects using the ProActive APIs. The rest of the sequential code requires no changes. Asynchronous RMI is used to allow the main thread to continue its execution without waiting for the result. The invocation of active object method immediately returns a future object, which is a reference to where the result of the method invocation will be placed. The caller thread will be suspended when it needs to use the result of the previously invoked remote method. This is called wait-by-necessity, which is a data-driven synchronization mechanism among the distributed threads. In addition, ProActive provides active object migration and group communication. Moreover, the latest releases of ProActive provide a framework using XML and monitors for supporting dynamic code loading on dynamically changing environments such as the Grid systems.

3.4.2. JAVAR [12] and JAVAB [11]

Developed at the Syracuse University, JAVAR [12] is a prototype restructuring preprocessor that parallelizes existing Java code by converting loops and recursive calls into multi-threaded structures to run in parallel. In the same spirit, JAVAB [11] is a prototype preprocessor that parallelizes loops in the Java bytecode. Similar to JAVAR, JAVAB generates a multi-threaded version that can then be executed in parallel.

3.5. Others Approaches

Some of the systems we encountered could not be classified directly under any of the four main categories identified above. This is mainly due to the hybrid approaches they have taken. One example is the Do! System [30], which transforms multithreaded applications into distributed applications while requiring user involvement in the process. In Do!, the user needs to use the classes provided to identify the parrallelizable threads and remote object mappings. This approach, however, hides the details of the distribution and communication from the user. Another example is the JavaSymphony [20], which provides flexible controls over hardware/software resources and load balancing. Although JavaSymphony provides explicit parallel programming APIs, as in the message passing model, it does not follow that model. Instead, it provides an independent set of APIs for parallel and distributed programming. Java Symphony provides a Java class library written entirely in Java, thus maintaining compatibility with the JVM. This library provides many features, such as access to system parameters, user controlled mapping of objects, asynchronous RMI and selective remote class loading.

4. Classifications and Open Issues

Although Java is very suitable for distributed and multi-threaded applications, the features available in Java for distribution are not fine-tuned for tightly coupled processes as in the conventional parallel programming. Lately, many research groups have started working on providing parallel environments for Java. Most of them, as described above, have targeted clusters and heterogeneous networks of workstations because of Java's portability and machine independence. The projects, compiled in the table in Figure 2, are some typical examples of the different approaches and programming models identified in this area of research.

4.1. Comparison and Classification

Based on the programming models used, the available parallel Java systems are classified into the following four different groups:

1. Systems supporting message-passing or object-passing among parallel and distributed processes. In this group, each system provides its own interface for users to utilize message-passing or object-passing. Many choose to provide MPI binding for Java such that the interface becomes compatible with MPI and MPJ. However, this limits the utilization of the object-oriented nature of Java. One system, an agent-based parallel Java provides an interface for object-passing (JOPI). Others choose to use existing infrastructure and features, such as using JNI (mpijava), or linking to C MPI or other libraries (UIUC project). Still another provides a pure Java implementation to maintain portability. This approach requires using different techniques such as RMI (in CCJ), native marshaling (MPIJ), or sockets (JOPI) for communication. A pure Java implementation gives the system the advantage of portability since it will be possible to simultaneously execute the parallel program on a heterogeneous collection of systems.

An Overview of Parallel and Distributed Java for Heterogeneous Systems

Project Name	Main Features	Approach used	User involvement	JVM Compatibility
Message-Passing and Object-Passing				
JOPI, U. Nebraska-Lincoln	Uses Software agents. JOPI	Class library	Need to learn JOPI (similar to MPI)	Compatible
ParaWeb, Waterloo & York	Runs parallel Java programs on heterogeneous systems	Class library / run-time machine modifications	Need to learn class methods	Java interpreter is modified
Ajents, Waterloo & York	Provide object migration. Uses RMI	Class library	Need to learn class methods	Compatible
Babylon, Waterloo & York	Adds scheduling and load balancing features	Class library	Need to learn class methods	Compatible
MPIJ, Brigham Young U.	Pure Java, MPJ compliant, uses native marshaling	Class library	API similar to MPI	Compatible
CCJ, Indiana U.	Pure Java, uses Manta RMI, MPJ compliant, optimized group communication	Class library	API similar to MPI	Compatible
JMPI (commercial)	object-oriented bindings to MPI	JNI bindings to MPI	API similar to MPI	Not Compatible
HPJava, PCRC Group	MPJ compliant	JNI bindings to MPI	API similar to MPI	Not Compatible
JPVM, Univ. of Virginia	Provides native parallel environment	Create new Java virtual machine	Need to know PVM	Not compatible
Shared Address (Object) Space				
Titanium, Univ. California-Berkley	Java dialect. Scientific computing.	Language (compiles to C)	Must learn new language	Not compatible
UIUC Project	Multi-language parallel programs support. Remote objects and load balancing	Combine different languages. Uses Converse and JNI	Need to know how to use the system libraries	Not compatible
Paraslax (commercial)	Pure Java, provides consistency protocols.	Uses TCP sockets, fixed No. of nodes.	Need to learn some API primitives	Compatible
Multi-Threaded Programming Model				
Clustered JVM, IBM	Creates single system image to distribute multi-threaded applications. Modified JVM	Transparent parallelization of multi-threaded apps.	Need to write multi-threaded programs	Not compatible
JavaParty, U. Karlsruhe	Distributed applications Uses RMI	Transparent parallelization of multi-threaded applications	Need to write multi-threaded programs	Compatible Pre-compiler needed
Hyperion U. New Hampshire	Distributes multithreaded applications on a DSM system	Transparent parallelization of multi-threaded applications	Need to write multi-threaded programs	Not compatible, compiles to C, runs on UNIX systems
Transparent (Automatic) Parallelization				
ProActive, Université de Nice - Sophia Antipolis	Active objects. Migration. Based on RMI	Class library. Creates remote thread for objects.	Need to define active objects	Compatible, no preprocessing needed
JAVAR, U. Syracuse	Parallelize loops and recursive calls in Java code	Preprocessor	Preprocess code before compilation	Depends on run-time system
JAVAB, U. Syracuse	Parallelize loops in bytecode	Preprocessor	Preprocess bytecode before execution	Depends on run-time system

Figure 2. Summary of the systems studied.

2. Systems providing a shared address space or shared object space. These systems provide the user with mechanisms to write parallel Java programs that logically share some data or objects. Most of these systems required changes in the JVM, resulting in such systems becoming dependent on the modified JVM. A very small number of implementations, such as Paraslax, attempted to keep the system compatible with the standard JVM by adding classes to handle the required mechanisms for making data or objects available on all remote machines.

3. Systems executing regular multi-threaded Java applications on multiple processors. In this case, the system transparently executes a multi-threaded program in parallel by

distributing the threads among the participating processors. Some systems, such as cJVM, provide a different JVM that creates a single system image (SSI), thus hiding the details of the underlying infrastructure from the application. The main advantage of this model is that existing multi-threaded applications can run seamlessly in parallel without any (or with minor) modifications. However, a disadvantage in this approach is that optimizations for communication and locality are difficult. In addition, cJVM has the disadvantage of having a modified JVM, rendering its support for portability and heterogeneity difficult. While JavaParty does not change the JVM, it requires more user involvement (such as defining the remote objects).

4. Systems capable of transparent and relatively seamless parallelization of existing Java applications. Although this may be the most attractive model (from the application development viewpoint), it is the one that is the least explored. A system in this category should provide some mechanisms to transparently parallelize an application. However, some of the systems in this category require some help from the programmer to make it possible (as in ProActive). Prototypes of preprocessors are also available that try to parallelize loops and recursive calls in a Java code or bytecode. The transparent parallelization model is very attractive, but until now, there is no simple way to achieve it. The complexity and diversity of the application is one main barrier and maintaining efficiency is another challenge.

On the other hand, the systems discussed above may be examined in a different four-category classification, from an implementation point of view, as follows [2]:

1. Developing a run-time environment based on existing technologies and infrastructures. This approach utilizes current techniques such as JNI bindings to MPI, JCI, distributed shared memory (DSM) systems, among others, to support the parallel Java environment. An advantage of this approach is that most of the underlying technologies have been optimized for efficiency and widely used and tested. However, these implementations limit the use of parallel Java to the systems and platforms that support these techniques and make the parallel Java programs non-portable. Examples in this category include ParaWeb (the JPRS implementation), the project at UIUC, mpijava, and Hyperion.

2. Replacing the JVM by a modified version to support parallel and distributed Java. The advantage of this approach is the total control the developers have over the environment (The new JVM), thus enabling an efficient implementation. However, one major disadvantage is that the modified JVM will not be compatible with other JVMs, leading to loss of portability. In addition, enhancements or changes in the standard JVM cannot be easily incorporated into the new system. Moreover, adding more machines to the system becomes non-trivial. Some examples of this category are the JPVM that creates a new JVM for parallel processing and the Clustered JVM (cJVM).

3. Providing new parallel languages that are dialects of Java. The main advantage here is the ability to provide different functionalities in the new language without having to fully comply with the Java language specifications while keeping the desirable

features in Java. The main disadvantage, again, is the machine dependence of the new language, hence making it difficult to port the applications to other platforms. Examples in this category are Titanium and HPJava

4. Providing a pure Java implementation by extending Java with class libraries to provide explicit parallelization functions. Such implementations require some form of run-time support to exist on the participating machines. This approach preserves the portability and machine independence of Java, which enables the parallel application to run on different architectures, thus providing support for heterogeneity. Another advantage is that the addition of more machines to the system is effortless. One disadvantage is that users must be aware of the parallelization process and need to learn the added classes. Some implementations make this process simpler by providing an interface that is similar to MPI such as JOPI, MPIJ, and CCJ. Another drawback is the loss in efficiency due to the overhead introduced to support remote objects and message-passing. This overhead is higher for systems using RMI, such as Ajents and Babylon. In addition, using class libraries limits the features that can be provided and the flexibility in development. Some examples in this category include ParaWeb (the JPCL implementation), Ajents, Babylon, JOPI, CCJ and Paraslax.

In addition, some of the projects provide mechanisms for dynamic class loading as part of the system or the support environment such as in JOPI, JavaParty, ProActive and Java Symphony, while others do not discuss the process/class deployment mechanisms. Regardless of the approaches taken and the implementation techniques used in these projects, the nature of a distributed environment imposes some limits on the performance of the parallel or distributed application. The major issue is the cost of communication since the processors are not tightly coupled as in a MPP or SMP. Here the overhead makes such environments mostly suitable for coarse grain parallel applications where communication is relatively small and infrequent and the computation-to-communication ratio is high. This limitation should gradually be overcome by advancements in the processing and communications technologies.

4.2. The Open Issues

This study shows a steadily growing interest in creating environments for high performance parallel and distributed computing in Java. While many design and implementation approaches have been used by various research projects and prototypes, numerous problems and open issues remain to be addressed. The following is a discussion of some of the issues related to these systems.

1. Since all systems are based on a distributed infrastructure, they all experience some inevitable overhead introduced by the distributed nature of the system. Generally, some methods have to be used to migrate objects and exchange information. At the present, RMI and socket programming have been the most widely used methods for information exchange. A few projects such as cJVM, CCJ and JavaParty have tried to refine their techniques to reduce the overhead. Nevertheless, reducing communication overhead remains a difficult challenge.

2. The lack of a general agreement on what is a suitable implementation approach has led to many different implementations and various types of APIs. To further complicate the situation, the rapid advancement in the supporting (underlying) technology has meant that some implementations thought to be inefficient before could become efficient now or in the near future and the trade-off between simplicity and performance in implementations could be shifting immensely. For example, using RMI was considered inefficient by some, yet an improved RMI for specific implementations (such as KaRMI and Manta RMI) has made it much more efficient while keeping the flexibility of development associated with RMI. Another example is the use of JNI to bind with MPI, which had to be done manually before research suggested an automated model to generate the JNI bindings.

3. Benchmarking research projects, especially with macro benchmarks and live applications, is difficult since each one has a different design, implementation approach and API. Until now, the available benchmarks are limited to micro benchmarks of specific operations or to specific implementations such as mpijava and JMPI, which are written based on MPJ [14]. Many others have written their own benchmark applications, which make the comparison of the results of different projects difficult and inaccurate. Therefore, it is necessary to have some general benchmarks that can be easily ported to measure and compare the performance of the different parallel Java systems.

4. Conforming (or not conforming) with MPI or MPJ is another debated issue. Not conforming to a standard allows the developers to freely exploit the object-oriented nature of Java to simplify the parallelization process. However, this creates a new set of APIs that the user needs to learn, making it difficult to benchmark. On the other hand, conforming to some standard like MPI will limit the capabilities of parallel Java, while providing a familiar interface to the user and making benchmarking easier. Some projects have tried to combine the opposing approaches by providing an MPI-like interface and object-passing methods.

5. Legacy applications written in other languages such as C and FORTRAN need to be considered. Do we want to port such applications to Java? Alternatively, do we need to link Java with these applications? Porting legacy codes would require a considerable amount of effort, which can be further increased by the many different approaches and APIs taken to design and implement the parallel Java environment. On the other hand, the alternative would limit the portability of the parallel Java programs due to links to machine dependant codes. An example of the second approach is the UIUC project. The issues of efficiency, portability and scalability become more important in such implementations.

6. The security of the participating machines and user applications must also be considered. To run parallel Java programs on multiple machines, users are allowed to upload their programs and execute them on the remote machines, where caution must be given to the possibility of malicious programs. The JOPI system, for example, provides a starting point to providing security for the participating machines. More

measures need to be considered to enhance security and to protect the machines and users.

7. Scheduling, dynamic load balancing and fault tolerance issues need to be addressed. Many parallel Java implementations do not consider these issues or only slightly touch on them. Since parallel Java is targeted for heterogeneous systems, where reliability is relatively low and performance of participating machines vary significantly, these issues must be considered in more details by designing efficient algorithms and protocols to attack such problems.

These are some issues to be addressed for a successful design and implementation of a parallel Java environment. While it may be difficult, if not impossible, to address all these issues at the same time, a particular implementation might judiciously choose to emphasize more on some specific issues than others, depending on the available underlying technology and infrastructure.

5. Conclusion

This paper conducted a survey that provides a concise study and classification of research projects involved in providing parallel and distributed environments for Java. Most of the studied systems target heterogeneous systems and clusters because of Java's portability and machine independence. The projects selected are representative of the different approaches and programming models known in this area. While each of them has its own unique features, advantages and disadvantages, they all aim towards the goal of having a parallel and distributed Java. We observed that almost all projects follow one of the following programming models: (1) Message- or object-passing, (2) shared address (or object) space, (3) multi-threading, and (4) transparent/seamless parallelization. From an implementation point of view, we were able to classify these projects based on the following four implementation approaches: (1) Utilizing the available infrastructure, (2) building a different JVM, (3) providing pure Java implementation by extending Java with class libraries, and (4) building new Java dialects for parallel programming. The study further identified a number of problems and open issues in this area that remain to be addressed in order to provide a robust, reliable and scalable high performance parallel and distributed Java environment for clusters and heterogeneous networked systems.

Acknowledgments

This work was partially supported by a National Science Foundation grant (EPS-0091900) and a Nebraska University Foundation grant. We would like to thank members of the secure distributed information (SDI) group [44] and the research computing facility (RCF) [42] at UNL their continuous support.

References

[1] J. Al-Jaroodi, N. Mohamed, H. Jiang, and D. Swanson, An agent-based infrastructure for parallel Java on heterogeneous clusters, *Proceedings of International Conference on Cluster Computing (CLUSTER'02)*, Chicago, IL, September 2002, IEEE, 19-27.

[2] A comparative study of parallel and distributed Java projects for heterogeneous systems, *Proceedings of IPDPS 2002, workshop on Java for Parallel and Distributed Computing*, Fort Lauderdale, FL, April 2002, IEEE.

[3] G. Antoniu, L. Boug, P. Hatcher, M. MacBeth, K. McGuigan, and R. Namyst, The Hyperion system: Compiling multithreaded java bytecode for distributed execution, *Parallel Computing*, 27, (2001), 1279-1297.

[4] Y. Aridor, M. Factor, and A. Teperman, Implementing Java on clusters, *technical report*, IBM Research Lab, MATAM, Advanced Technology Center, Haifa, ISRAEL, 1998.

[5] cJVM: a single system image of a JVM on a cluster, *Proceedings of International Conference on Parallel Processing*, IEEE, 1999.

[6] Y. Aridor, M. Factor, A. Teperman, T. Eilam, and A. Schuster, A high performance cluster JVM presenting a pure single system image, *Proceedings of The Java Grande conference*, ACM, June 2000.

[7] Transparently obtaining scalability for Java applications on a cluster, *Journal of Parallel and Distributed Computing*, 60, (2000), 1159-1193 (*special issue - Java on Clusters*).

[8] E. Arjomandi, W. O'Farrell, I. Kalas, G. Koblents, F. C. Eigler, and G. R. Gao, ABC++ - concurrency by inheritance in C++, *IBM Systems Journal*, 34 (1995), 120-137 (IBM Corp. Riverton, NJ, USA).

[9] M. Baker, B. Carpenter, G. Fox, S. H. Ko, and S. Lim, mpiJava: an object-oriented Java interface to MPI, *tech. report, School of Computer Science*, University of Portsmouth and Syracuse University, January 1999 (*Presented at International Workshop on Java for Parallel and Distributed Computing IPPS/SPDP*).

[10] F. Baude, D. Caromel, L. Mestre, F. Huet, and J. Vayssire, Interactive and descriptor-based deployment of object-oriented grid applications, *Proceedings of The 11th International Symposium on High Performance Distributed Computing*, IEEE, July 2002.

[11] A. Bik and D. Gannon, JAVAB: a prototype bytecode parallelization tool, *tech. report*, Syracuse University, 2002. http://www.extreme.indiana.edu/ ajcbik/JAVAB/ index.html.

[12] JAVAR: a prototype Java restructuring tool, *tech. report*, Syracuse University, 2002. http://www.extreme.indiana.edu/~ajcbik/JAVAR/index.html.

[13] T. Brecht, H. Sandhu, M. Shan, and J. Talbot, ParaWeb: towards world-wide supercomputing, *Proceedings of The 7th ACM SIGOPS European Workshop*, Connemara, Irland, September 1996, ACM. http://bbcr.uwaterloo.ca/~brecht/papers/html/paraweb/.

[14] J. Bull, A. Smith, M. Westhead, D. Henly, and R. Dary, A benchmark suite for high performance Java, *Concurrency - Practice and Experience*, **12**, (2000), 375-388.

[15] M. Campione, K. Walrath, A. Huml, and the Tutorial Team, The Java Tutorial Continued: The Rest of the JDK, *The Java Series*, Addison-Wesley Publication Co., 1998. http://java.sun.com/docs/books/tutorial/index.html.

[16] D. Caromel, W. Klauser, and J. Vayssiere, Towards seamless computing and meta-computing in Java,*Concurrency - Practice and Experience*, **10**, (1998), 1043-1061.

[17] B. Carpenter, V. Getov, G. Judd, T. Skjellum, and G. Fox, MPI for Java: position document and draft API specification, *Technical report JGF-TR-03*, Java Grande Forum, November 1998. http://www.npac.syr.edu/projects/pcrc/reports/MPIposition/position/position.html.

[18] cJVM, Clustered JVM - IBM, 2003. http://www.haifa.il.ibm.com/projects/systems/cjvm/index.html.

[19] DOGMA, The DOGMA Project, 2003. http://dogma.byu.edu.

[20] T. Fahringer, JavaSymphony: a system for development of locality-oriented distributed and parallel Java application, *Proceedings of International Conference on Cluster Computing (CLUSTER2000)*, Chemnitz, Germany, December 2000, IEEE.

[21] A. Ferrari, JPVM: network parallel computing in Java, *Technical Report CS-97-29*, Department of Computer Science, University of Virginia, December 1997. http://www.cs.virginia.edu/~ajf2j/jpvm.html.

[22] HPJava, The HPJava home Project. http://www.npac.syr.edu/projects/pcrc/mpiJava/index.html.

[23] M. Izatt, Babylon: A Java-based distributed object environment, *m.sc. thesis*, Department of Computer Science, York University, Canada, July 2000.

[24] M. Izatt, T. Brecht, and P. Chan, Ajents: Towards an environment for parallel distributed and mobile Java applications, *Proceedings of The ACM Java Grande Conference*, ACM, June 1999.

[25] JavaParty, September 2003. http://wwwipd.ira.uka.de/JavaParty/.

[26] JGF, *The Java Grande Forum*, 2003. http://www.javagrande.org/.

[27] JNI, *Java native interface*, 2003. http://java.sun.com/products/jdk/1.2/docs/guide/jni/.

[28] L. Kale, M. Bhandarkar, and T. Wilmarth, Converse: An interoperable framework for parallel programming, *Proceedings of the 10th International Parallel Processing Symposium*, Honolulu, Hawaii, April 1996, 212-217.

[29] Design and implementation of parallel Java with global object space, *Proceedings of Conference on Parallel and Distributed Processing Technology and Applications*, Las Vegas, Nevada, 1997. http://charm.cs.uiuc.edu/papers/ParJavaPDPTA97.html.

[30] P. Launay and J. Pazat, Easing parallel programming for clusters with Java, *Future Generation Computer Systems*, **18**, (2001), 253-263.

[31] V. Laxmikant and S. Krishman, Charm++: a portable concurrent object oriented systems based on C++, *Proceedings SIGPLAN Notices for Conference on Object Oriented Programming, Systems, Languages and Applications (OOPSLA '93)*, vol. 28, Washington, D.C., October 1993, ACM.

[32] N. Mohamed, J. Al-Jaroodi, H. Jiang, and D. Swanson, JOPI: a Java object-passing interface, *Proceedings of the Joint ACM Java Grande-ISCOPE (International Symposium on Computing in Object-Oriented Parallel Environments) Conference (JGI2002)*, Seattle, Washington, November 2002, ACM, 37-45.

[33] MPI, *The message passing interface forum*, 2003. http://www.mpi-forum.org/.

[34] MPIJ, *MPI for Java online documentation*, 2002. http://dogma.byu.edu/.

[35] mpiJava, 2003. http://www.npac.syr.edu/projects/pcrc/mpiJava/mpiJava.html.

[36] A. Nelisse, J. Maassen, T. Kielmann, and H. Bal., CCJ: object-based message passing and collective communication in Java, *Proceedings of the Joint ACM Java Grande - ISCOPE (JGI'01)*, Stanford University, CA, June 2001, ACM.

[37] OOMPI, *Object-oriented MPI*, 2003. http://www.mpi.nd.edu/research/oompi.

[38] Paraslax, 2002. http://www.paraslax.com.

[39] PCRC, *Parallel compiler runtime consortium*, 2003. http://www.npac.syr.edu/projects/pcrc/.

[40] M. Philippsen and M. Zenger, JavaParty: transparent remote objects in Java, (*Concurrency - Practice and Experience*, **9**, (1997), 1225-1242.

[41] ProActive, 2003. http://www-sop.inria.fr/oasis/ProActive/.

[42] RCF, *Research computing facility at UNL*, 2003. http://rcf.unl.edu.

[43] RMI, *Java remote method invocation documentation*, 2003. http://java.sun.com/products/jdk/rmi/.

[44] SDI, *Secure distributed information at UNL*, 2003. `http://rcf.unl.edu/~sdi/front.php3`.

[45] Serialization, *Obejct serialization information*, 2003. `http://java.sun.com/j2se/1.4/docs/guide/serialization/`.

[46] J. Squyres, J. Willock, B. McCandless, and P. Rijks, Object oriented MPI (OOMPI): A C++ class library for MPI, *Proceedings of the POOMA Conference*, Santa Fe, New Mexico, February 1996.

[47] Titanium, 2003. `http://www.cs.berkeley.edu/Research/Projects/titanium/`.

Chapter 6

THE PERFORMANCE OF ROUTING ALGORITHMS UNDER BURSTY TRAFFIC LOADS

Timothy Mark Pinkston[*] *and Jeonghee Shin*[†]
SMART Interconnects Group
Department of Electrical Engineering - Systems
University of Southern California
Los Angeles, CA 90089-2562, USA

Abstract

Routing algorithms are traditionally evaluated under Poisson-like traffic distributions. This type of traffic is smooth over large time intervals and has been shown not necessarily to be representative to that of real network loads in parallel processing and communication environments. Bursty traffic, on the other hand, has been shown to be more representative of the type of load generated by multiprocessor and local area network (LAN) applications, but it has been seldom used in the evaluation of network routing algorithms. This chapter investigates how bursty traffic—specifically, self-similar traffic—affects the performance of well-known interconnection network routing algorithms. Various packet sizes, network resources (i.e., virtual channels) and spatial traffic patterns are used in the analysis. This allows the ability to evaluate performance under load non-uniformities in both time and space which differs from previous research that applies non-uniformity in only the space domain, such as with bit-reversal, matrix transpose, and hot-spot traffic patterns.

1. Introduction

The performance of multiprocessor systems depends not only on how effectively communication and computation loads are balanced over each processor, but also on how efficiently processor nodes communicate with one another. The routing algorithm is one of the most important design factors of an interconnection network—the backbone for communication in a parallel processor environment. It significantly impacts the performance characteristics

---

[*]E-mail address: tpink@charity.usc.edu. Tel: (213) 740-4482, Fax: (213) 740-4418
[†]E-mail address: jeonghee@charity.usc.edu

(latency and throughput) of a network under various workloads as well as resource cost. For this reason, many routing algorithms have been proposed over the last decade that incorporate several cost/performance enhancing techniques, including cut-through switching [1], virtual channel flow [2] and increased adaptivity [3]. These techniques can improve both latency and throughput in various ways. For example, adaptive routing allows the path taken by packets in the network to be decided dynamically —based on the local state of network resources—in order to more evenly distribute the traffic load over those resources, thus averting congested and/or faulty areas. As the routes taken are non-deterministic, it is important for the routing algorithm to effectively handle any anomalous behavior that may arise (such as deadlock, livelock, or starvation) by either avoiding [4] or recovering [5] from it.

Traditionally, most routing algorithms have been evaluated under traffic following a Poisson-like distribution [3][5][6]. This type of traffic is smooth over large time intervals and has been shown not necessarily to be representative to that of real network loads in a parallel processing or communication environment [7][8]. Nevertheless, according to extensive evaluations based on this traffic assumption, adaptive routing algorithms are shown to have superior performance over deterministic ones as they supposedly do a better job of balancing the traffic load over network resources and avoiding congested regions. Recovery-based true-fully-adaptive routing algorithms are shown to have higher saturation throughput capability than fully-adaptive and deterministic avoidance-based schemes given their unrestricted ability to use network virtual channel resources [5]. The question arises, however, as to how results may be affected under a more realistic traffic model. Bursty traffic, for example, has been shown to be more representative of the type of load generated by multiprocessor and local area network (LAN) applications such as Splash-2 benchmarks and Ethernet traffic [7][9][10], but it has been seldom used in the evaluation of network routing algorithms. With the emergence of new bursty traffic models such as self-similar traffic, the performance of routing algorithms can be re-evaluated through simulation. It is now possible to find out whether the load balancing and head-of-line blocking benefits of adaptive routing and virtual channel flow remain, become more pronounced, or diminish in the presence of bursty traffic. It is also interesting to determine how packet size and switching technique can further affect network behavior under bursty traffic. Comparisons can also be made across varying degrees of traffic burstiness and "hot spots" occurring both in time and space to challenge our current understanding of the benefits of previously proposed techniques.

This chapter investigates how bursty traffic may affect the performance of well-known interconnection network routing algorithms proposed for multiprocessor and network-based computing systems. Various packet sizes, network resources (i.e., virtual channels) and spatial traffic patterns are used in the analysis. We evaluate performance under various degrees of non-uniformities in load in both the time and space domains. This differs from previous research that applies non-uniformity only in the space domain, such as with bit-reversal, matrix transpose, and hot-spot traffic patterns. Such analysis allows us to reason about the relative benefits of well-known techniques and to understand how they can be modified to perform better under more realistic communication scenarios.

The next section describes how to synthetically generate self-similar traffic. It goes on to prove that traffic generated this way indeed has self-similarity (bursty) behavior. Sec-

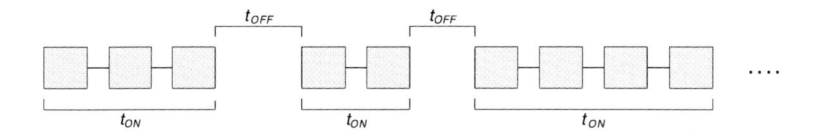

Figure 1. The packet train model.

tion 3. presents the evaluation methodology, results, and analysis. Possible ways in which the performance degradation can be reduced is also presented. Related research is described in Section 4.. Finally, Section 5. presents the main conclusions.

2. Self-Similar Traffic Generation

In this section, a way of generating self-similar traffic is described. This traffic is used in the performance evaluation presented in the next section. In addition, to ensure that the generated traffic has self-similarity characteristics prevalent in real traffic, a verification process is performed.

Self-similar traffic has the property of appearing and behaving similarly across different time scales [11]. In other words, the time sequence exhibits a similar pattern regardless of the degree of resolution. This means that self-similar traffic is bursty in both small and large time scales (i.e., has long-range dependence). This is opposed to Poisson-like traffic which is bursty only in small time scales but is smooth in large time scales (i.e., has short-range dependence).

One of the most popular approaches for synthetically generating self-similar traffic is by superimposing many Pareto-like ON/OFF sources [12]. In the ON/OFF source model or packet train model suggested in [13], packets arrive at regular intervals during ON-periods, i.e., the train length, while OFF-periods are periods without packet arrivals, i.e., the inter-train distances. Each source alternates between an ON (t_{ON}) and an OFF period (t_{ON}) as shown in Figure 1. These ON- and OFF-periods on each source have high variability, which follows a Pareto distribution with parameter α (i.e., the probability distribution function $F(x) = 1 - x^{-\alpha}$ where $1 < \alpha < 2$ and x is a non-negative value). The superposition of many ON/OFF sources produces aggregate network traffic, which is self-similar with Hurst parameter H. The Hurst parameter represents the degree of self-similarity of the aggregate traffic stream, where $H = (3 - \alpha)/2$; thus, $1 < \alpha < 2$ implies $0.5 < H < 1$.

The benefit of this approach is that a traditional Poisson-like traffic generator can be used for generating self-similar traffic simply by adding an ON/OFF controller to it. During ON-periods, bursty traffic consisting of Poisson generated packets during both the current ON-period and in the previous OFF-period is injected into the network. During OFF-periods, no newly generated packets are injected into the network. As is stated, the length of ON- and OFF-periods is Pareto distributed: $F(x) = 1 - x^{-\alpha}$, where $1 < \alpha < 2$. Let R be a random number with a uniform distribution between 0 and 1. Then, $x = (1 - R)^{-1/\alpha}$.

According to a sampling of 1994 Ethernet traffic [12], α is around 2.0 for ON-periods (t_{ON}) and between 1.0 and 1.5 for OFF-periods (t_{OFF}). Therefore, $t_{ON} = (1-R)^{-1/\alpha_{ON}}$,

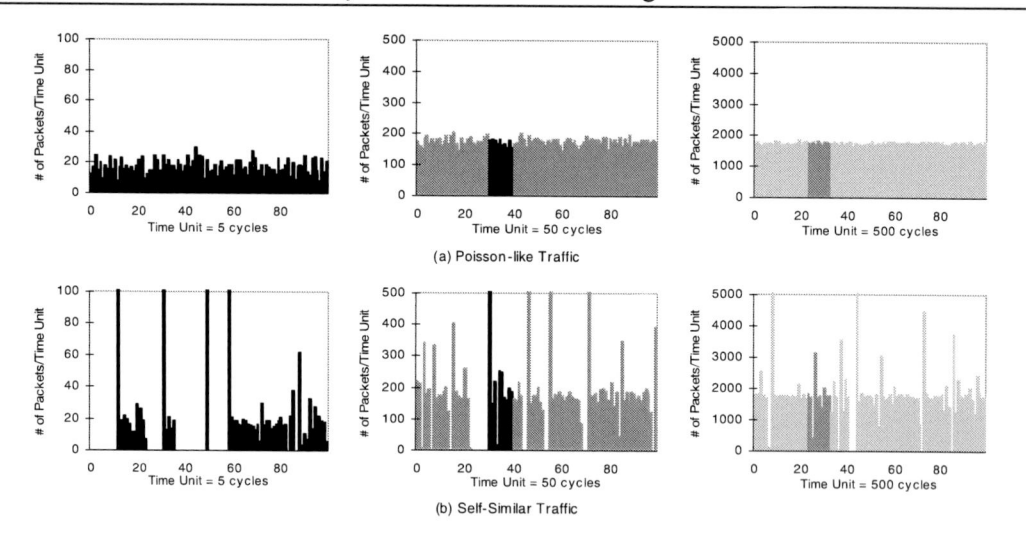

Figure 2. Degree of burstiness of the two traffic generation models: (a) Poisson-like traffic and (b) self-similar traffic.

where $\alpha_{ON} \approx 2.0$, and $t_{OFF} = (1 - R)^{-1/\alpha_{OFF}}$, where $1.0 < \alpha_{OFF} < 1.5$. Such generated traffic with parameter $\alpha_{ON} = 1.9$ and $\alpha_{OFF} = 1.25$, which is used for the experiments with 16-flit packets on 16×16 two-dimensional torus discussed in the next section, is shown in Figure 2. The number of packets generated during 500, 50 and 5 cycle time intervals are shown versus the number of time intervals over which statistics were gathered. The same segments of traffic with different time intervals are indicated by the same gray levels. As seen in Figure 2, self-similar traffic maintains burstiness characteristics, while Poisson-like traffic smooths out and loses its burstiness characteristics as the time scale increases.

Another way to prove whether or not traffic generated synthetically exhibits self-similarity is through the use of variance-time plots [11]. The variance of the m-aggregated time series $X^{(m)}$ of self-similar processes for large m is described by the following:

$$Var(X^{(m)}) \equiv Var(X)/m^{\beta}, \text{ where } H = 1 - (\beta/2).$$

This can be rewritten as follows:

$$log[Var(X^{(m)})] \equiv log[Var(X)] - \beta log(m).$$

Here, a slope of $-\beta$ in $Var(X^{(m)})$ versus m on a variance-time plot implies the degree of self-similarity. As β approaches 0 (alternatively, 1), traffic has a higher (alternatively, lower) degree of self-similarity. A variance-time plot of the generated traffic is shown in Figure 3, where self-similar traffic with 16-, 32- and 128-flit packets is compared against Poisson-like traffic with 16-flit packets. As given by the larger slope, self-similar traffic indeed has more self-similarity than Poisson-like traffic. Moreover, the Hurst parameter H of self-similar traffic with 16-flit packets is 0.92, which is close to the Hurst parameter of multiprocessor systems [10] ($H = 0.93$ on average) as well as Ethernet traffic [12] ($H = 0.9$). Thus, the synthetic traffic used for performance evaluation in this work highly

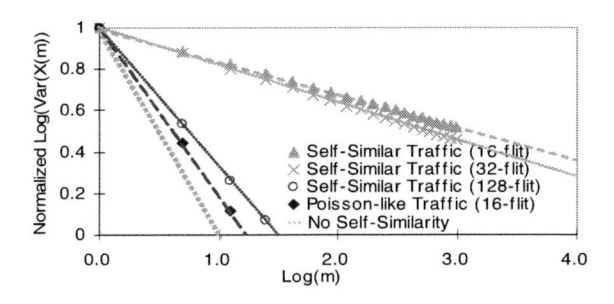

Figure 3. Degree of self-similarity of generated traffic.

reflects real traffic occurring in parallel processing and communication environments. The relationship between the Hurst parameter of self-similar traffic and the packet size will be discussed further in Section 3.2..

3. Evaluation Methodology and Results

In prior studies, interconnection network routing algorithms have been evaluated under spatially non-uniform but temporally uniform traffic known as the Poisson traffic model, which is less realistic than the self-similar traffic model. To observe the effect of self-similar traffic or temporally non-uniform traffic, the performance of well-known routing algorithms is re-evaluated in this section. The performance evaluation will provide answers to how much performance degradation results from non-uniform traffic in time, if any, and whether the benefits of adaptive routing and virtual channels remain even under temporally non-uniform traffic.

The performance evaluation is carried out with various routing algorithms, network design parameters and spatial traffic patterns. A deterministic routing algorithm and two adaptive routing algorithms are evaluated with different packet sizes (16, 32, and 128 flits), and four or eight virtual channels. Deterministic routing algorithms, such as E-cube, always supply the same routing paths between source and destination nodes while adaptive routing algorithms allow the routing paths to be decided dynamically, based on network state. In adaptive routing, deadlock due to non-deterministic path decisions can be resolved by restricting the use of virtual channels (i.e., escape channels) or recovering from the deadlock if it occurs owing to not restricting the use of virtual channel resources. The former is called avoidance-based fully-adaptive routing algorithms, such as Duato's Protocol [4], and the latter is referred to as recovery-based true-fully-adaptive routing algorithms, such as Disha [5]. In terms of the spatial traffic pattern, uniform and non-uniform traffic (bit-reversal and hot spot) are used. Under uniform traffic each node sends packets to all other nodes with equal probability. On the other hand, a node sends messages to the node with its reversal coordinates under bit-reversal traffic. In case of hot spot traffic, up to 5% of the network traffic is sent to a single hot spot in the network; the other 95% is uniform traffic. All simulations are run on a 16×16 two-dimensional wormhole torus with full-duplex links.

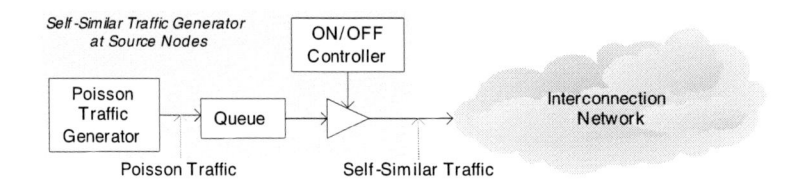

Figure 4. Self-similar traffic generator.

As is described in Section 2., Poisson-like traffic created by a traditional traffic generator is modulated by an ON/OFF controller to produce self-similar traffic generation at each source node. Figure 4 depicts the self-similar traffic generator. During OFF-periods, generated Poisson traffic is queued in the self-similar generator, while during ON-periods, the queued traffic and newly generated Poisson traffic are presented to the network. In generating the self-similar traffic, the controller has a length of ON- and OFF-periods which is Pareto distributed with the parameter $\alpha = 1.9$ and 1.25, respectively. In generating the Poisson traffic, the controller maintains a 100% duty factor (i.e., always ON state with no OFF state).

In each simulation, the first 10,000 cycles are excluded from the performance measurements (throughput and latency) so that the network reaches steady state before collecting data. Latency and throughput are plotted versus applied load rate. In all cases, applied load rate is defined as a fraction of the full bisection bandwidth of a network assuming uniform traffic distributed evenly over both space and time. Throughput is measured as the number of arrived flits at each node per cycle and latency is measured as the average number of cycles needed to deliver each packet—from the time they are generated to the time they are delivered.

3.1. Comparison of the Benefits of Increased Routing Adaptivity

A performance comparison of the routing algorithms under different spatial traffic patterns with 16-flit packets and 4 virtual channels is provided in Figure 5(a) - (c), where solid and dotted lines indicate self-similar (SS) and Poisson (PO) traffic, respectively. Figure 5(a) shows that under spatially uniform and self-similar traffic, the deterministic routing algorithm (E-cube) has slightly better performance than the adaptive ones (Disha and Duato). This not only indicates that the performance degradation of the adaptive routing algorithms is worse than that of the deterministic routing algorithm (as is seen in Figure 5(a), adaptive routing has over 40% performance degradation while deterministic routing has only 5%) but it also indicates that bursty traffic makes the adaptive routing networks saturate at a slightly lower load rate, compared with the deterministic routing networks. In the adaptive routing algorithms, the number of channels available for injecting new packets into the network may be larger than that in the deterministic routing algorithms since routing adaptivity provides more choices of channels for injecting the packets into the network. These channels occupied by the injected packets may then be released earlier by providing multiple routing paths. The packets can be routed though different paths instead of waiting for a particular path to be released, thus they can be more quickly distributed over the network. Therefore, a larger portion of bursty traffic could be accepted into the adaptive routing networks, thus causing the network to be saturated at lower load rate. On the contrary, bursty traffic is throttled in the deterministic routing network due to a lack of available channels to inject the packets.

The performance of self-similar traffic with different spatial traffic patterns is shown in Figure 5(d), where U, BR and HS denote uniform, bit-reversal and hot-spot traffic, respectively. An interesting result is that throughput in the adaptive routing algorithms is about the same under uniform or bit-reversal traffic with self-similarity. The reason for this is that the adaptive routing network under non-uniform traffic in *time* reaches an early saturation point, thus no more performance degradation is caused by adding non-uniformity in *space*. On the other hand, for the deterministic routing algorithm, a 30% decrease in throughput between uniform and bit-reversal traffic with self-similarity is observed because the self-throttling effect is overshadowed by the inflexible routings. Consequently, adaptive routing algorithms have better performance than deterministic ones under both spatial and temporal non-uniform traffic.

From these results, it can be concluded that routing adaptivity is an important factor in relieving spatial bursts, but it is not sufficient for relieving temporal bursts. This is clearly revealed by Figure 5(e). In adaptive routing algorithms (Duato and Disha), self-similar traffic with uniform traffic pattern (U,SS) which has only temporal non-uniformity produces more performance degradation than bit-reversal traffic with a Poisson distribution (BR,PO) which has only spatial non-uniformity. On the other hand, in deterministic routing algorithms (E-cube), spatial non-uniformity causes more performance degradation than temporal non-uniformity.

3.2. Comparison of the Benefits of Increased Packet Size

A performance comparison of different packet sizes with 4 virtual channels and uniform traffic is presented in Figure 6. Compared to 16-flit packets in Figure 5(a), larger packets mitigate performance degradation caused by bursty traffic since larger packets are injected less often than smaller ones with the same load-rate, thus making traffic less bursty. For example, assume that 4096 flits are injected into the network at a given load rate. In case of 16-flit packets, at most 256 nodes inject a packet at the same time (i.e., 256 flits/cycle for 16 cycles), while at most 32 128-flit packets are simultaneously injected by at most 32 nodes (i.e., 32 flits/cycle for 128 cycles). That is, larger packets have an effect of distributing packet injection over time. Hence, 16-flit packets generate more bursts than 128-flit packets. This fact is also well represented by a variance-time plot which indicates the degree of self-similarity, i.e., burstiness in Figure 3. The Hurst parameter for 32-flit packets, $H = 0.91$, is slightly less than that of 16-flit packets, $H = 0.92$, while in case of 128-flit packets the Hurst parameter value of $H = 0.67$ is close to 0.5, which means no burstiness or Poisson-like distribution.

A couple of other factors which affect performance can be considered as well. Larger packets with the same load-rate occupy fewer virtual channels, thus providing more freedom in the use of virtual channels. In addition, as packet size increases, transmission time per flit decreases due to less set-up time [6]. Therefore, messages consisting of larger packets could be delivered faster than the same size of messages consisting of smaller packets.

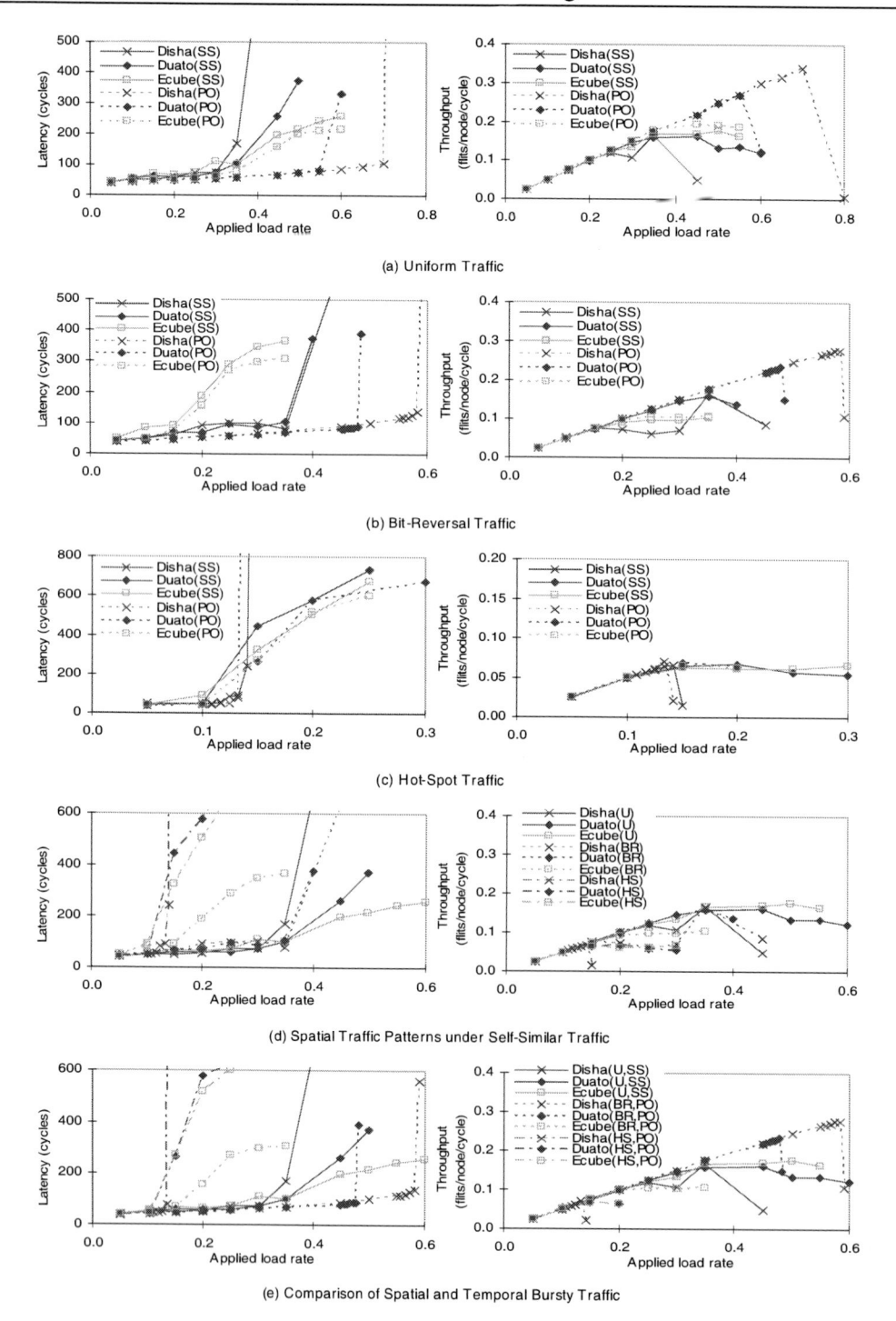

Figure 5. Performance comparison of deterministic and adaptive routing algorithms for various spatial traffic patterns generated by self-similar and Poisson processes. The x-axis represents the applied load rate which is a fraction of the full bisection bandwidth of the network.

(a) 32-flit Packets

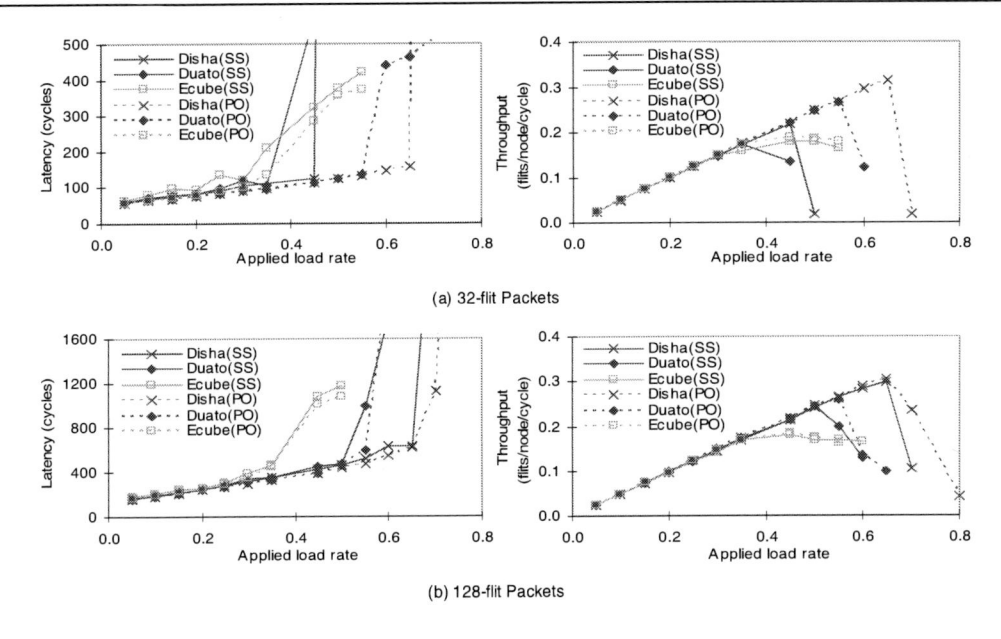

(b) 128-flit Packets

Figure 6. Performance comparison of deterministic and adaptive routing algorithms for different packet sizes under uniform traffic generated by self-similar and Poisson processes (4 virtual channels). The x-axis represents the applied load rate which is a fraction of the full bisection bandwidth of the network.

This fact might cause less traffic to be present in the network, thus saturating the network more slowly. A performance comparison under non-uniform traffic in space is provided in Figure 8 and 9. Similar observations to spatially uniform traffic are obtained with bit-reversal or hot-spot traffic patterns—with the same channel resources (4 or 8 virtual channels) performance degradation decreases as the packet size increases.

3.3. Comparison of the Benefits of Increased Virtual Channels

To observe the effect of the number of virtual channels, twice more virtual channels than in Figure 5 and Figure 6 are provided in Figure 7. Compared with 4 virtual channels, Figure 7 shows that the increase in the number of virtual channels improves throughput of all routing algorithms regardless of traffic uniformities in time. In particular, it alleviates performance degradation of routing algorithms under bursty traffic since more virtual channels are helpful to distribute traffic over the network and relieve burstiness. In case of 128-flit packets, performance degradation is almost resolved by using twice more virtual channels. The same benefits of increased virtual channels are also observed under spatially non-uniform traffic in Figure 8 and 9.

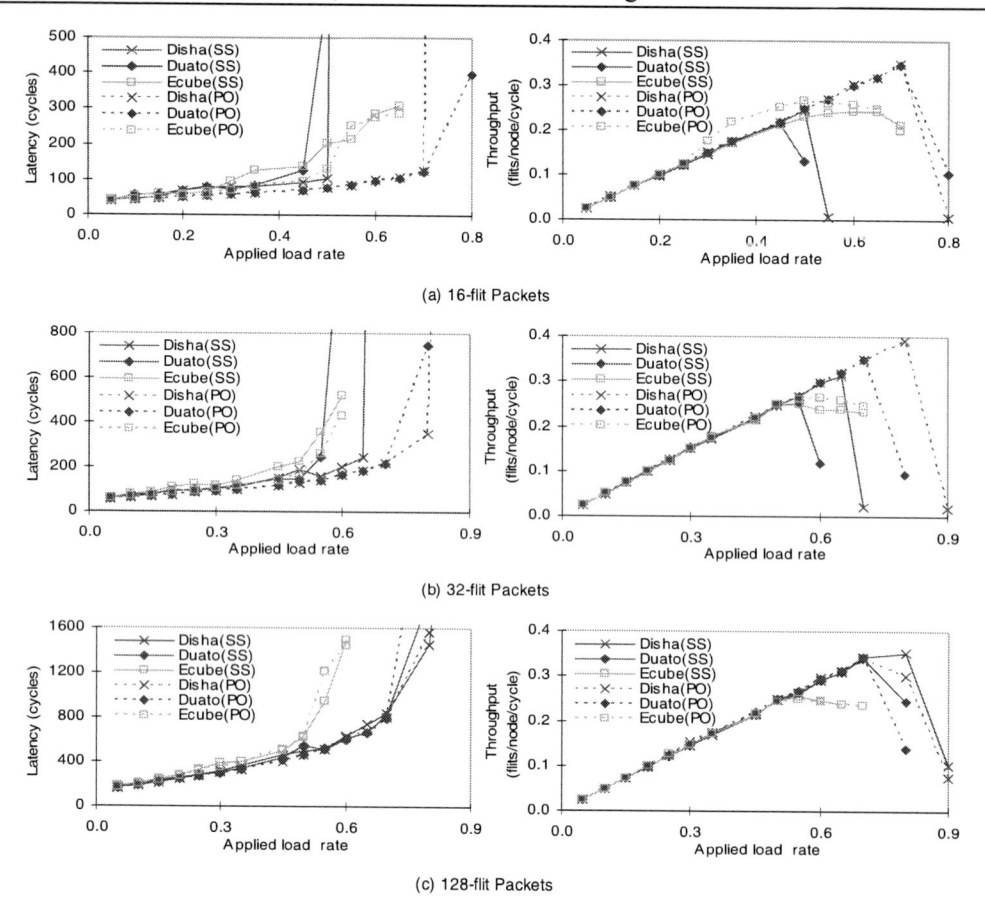

Figure 7. Performance comparison of deterministic and adaptive routing algorithms for different packet sizes under uniform traffic generated by self-similar and Poisson processes (8 virtual channels). The x-axis represents the applied load rate which is a fraction of the full bisection bandwidth of the network.

3.4. Discussion

As is shown in the performance results above, burstiness in traffic causes severe performance degradation. The aggressive way to improve the performance under this traffic is to make injected traffic smooth even though bursty traffic is generated. To do so, a congestion control mechanism can be employed in the packet-injection module at the end nodes. The mechanism controls the amount of injected traffic with the information of local or global network condition and ensures that the amount does not exceed a certain maximum level, thus helping the network to avoid being saturated. In prior work, several congestion control mechanisms [14][15][16] have been proposed, and the self-tuning mechanism proposed in [12] works well under loads created by alternating low loads and high loads, which is not exactly self-similar. As is discussed in Sections 3.2. and 3.3., an appropriate network configuration such as more virtual channels or larger packets could also help to smooth out bursty traffic to improve performance.

The Performance of Routing Algorithms under Bursty Traffic Loads 143

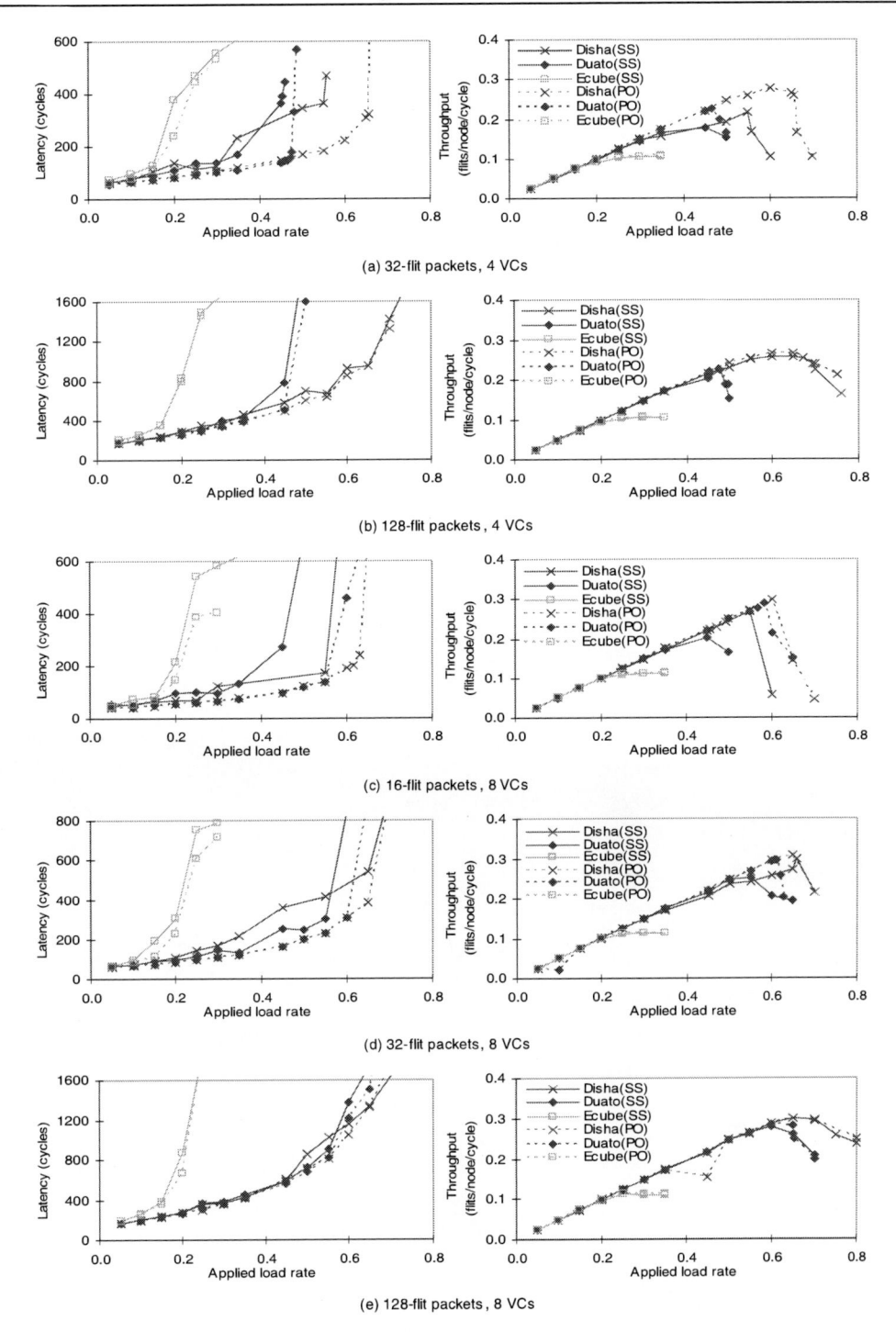

(a) 32-flit packets, 4 VCs

(b) 128-flit packets, 4 VCs

(c) 16-flit packets, 8 VCs

(d) 32-flit packets, 8 VCs

(e) 128-flit packets, 8 VCs

Figure 8. Performance comparison of deterministic and adaptive routing algorithms under bit-reversal traffic generated by self-similar and Poisson processes. The x-axis represents the applied load rate which is a fraction of the full bisection bandwidth of the network.

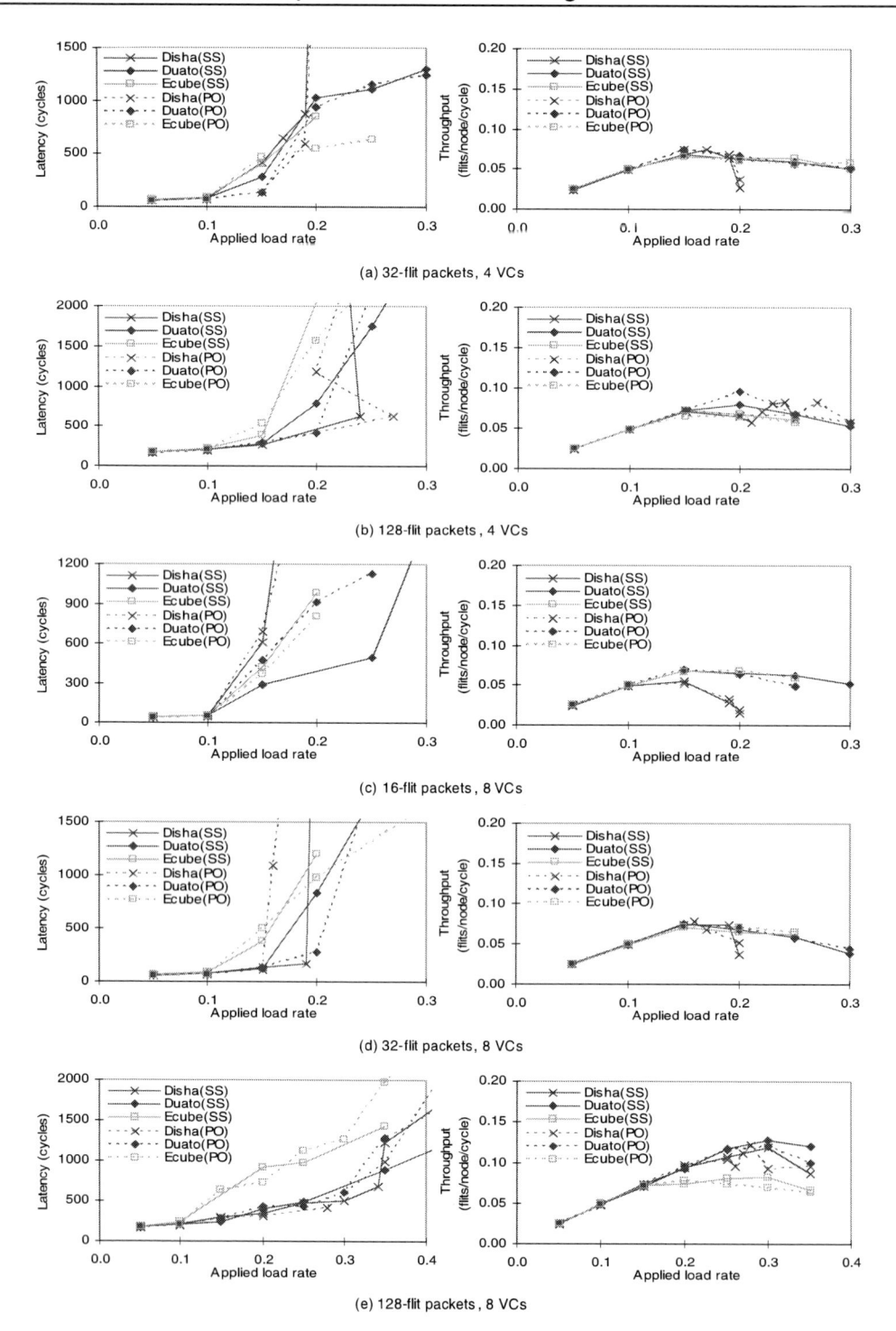

Figure 9. Performance comparison of deterministic and adaptive routing algorithms under 5% hot-spot traffic generated by self-similar and Poisson processes. The x-axis represents the applied load rate which is a fraction of the full bisection bandwidth of the network.

4. Related Work

Previously, many network applications and models for LAN or WAN were re-evaluated under self-similar traffic [9]. Recently, this traffic has been explored in multiprocessor systems as well [8][10][17]. In particular, the observation of self-similarity in interconnection network traffic generated among multiprocessors [10] motivated the performance re-evaluation of interconnection network properties proposed for multiprocessor systems.

The performance of SeverNet SAN—the wormhole-routed and point-to-point network for server systems—was re-evaluated under self-similar traffic in order to improve the routers and end devices, and to modify the optimization method which was developed on the basis of Poisson-like traffic [8]. That work is limited to the design consideration and evaluation results in the specific system. However, this chapter discusses results which can be applicable for generic systems.

In addition, an analytical performance model for self-similar traffic [17] has been proposed recently. It supports pipelined circuit switching (PCS) routing algorithms with uniform traffic patterns in k-ary n-cubes. Various environments such as the wormhole-routed tori, adaptive wormhole routing, and circuit-switched networks are currently being researched in [17]. That performance model does not consider burstiness of traffic in both space and time, and it measures performance only in terms of latency. However, throughput is one of the most important quantities to measure performance and should not be ignored. In this chapter, the effect of burstiness in both time and space is analyzed, and performance is measured by both latency and throughput.

5. Conclusion

This chapter investigates the effect of self-similar traffic on the performance of well-known routing algorithms with various spatial traffic patterns, packet sizes and number of virtual channels. Consequently, adaptive routing algorithms under non-uniform traffic in both time and space have better performance than deterministic ones. However, compared with deterministic routing algorithms, adaptive routing algorithms have more performance degradation caused by temporally bursty traffic. This implies that routing adaptivity is not enough to relieve temporal non-uniformity. Additional congestion control mechanisms to relieve temporal burstiness prove to be useful. Furthermore, larger packet sizes and more virtual channels also help to smooth out bursty traffic to improve performance.

Acknowledgement

This work was supported in part by NSF grants CCR-0209234 and CCR-0311742, and by WiSE funding at USC.

References

[1] Parviz Kermani, and Leonard Kleinrock, "Virtual cut-through: a new computer communication switching technique," *Computer Networks*, Vol. 3, No. 4, pp. 267-286, September 1979.

[2] William J. Dally, "Virtual-Channel Flow Control," *IEEE Transactions on Parallel Distributed Systems*, Vol. 3, No. 2, pp. 194-205, March 1992.

[3] Patrick T. Gaughan and Sudhakar Yalamanchili, "Adaptive Routing Protocols for Hypercube Interconnection Networks," *IEEE Computer*, Vol. 26, No. 5, pp. 12-23, May 1993.

[4] Jose Duato, "A New Theory of Deadlock-Free Adaptive Routing in Wormhole Networks," *IEEE Transactions on Parallel and Distributed Systems*, Vol. 4, No. 12, pp. 1320-1331, December 1993.

[5] Anjan K. V. and Timothy M. Pinkston, "An Efficient Fully Adaptive Deadlock Recovery Scheme: DISHA," *Proceedings of the 22nd International Symposium on Computer Architecture*, pp. 201-210, June 1995.

[6] Jose Duato, Sudhakar Yalamanchili, and Lionel Ni, "*Interconnection Networks: An Engineering Approach*," Morgan Kaufmann Publisher, 2003.

[7] Will E. Leland, Murad S. Taqqu, Walter Willinger, and Daniel V. Wilson, "On the self-similar nature of Ethernet traffic", *Proceedings of ACM SIGCOMM*, pp. 183-193, September 1993.

[8] Dimiter R. Avresky, Vladimir Shurbanov, Robert W. Horst, and Pankaj Mehra, "Performance Evaluation of the ServerNetR SAN under Self-Similar Traffic", *Proceedings of the 13th International Parallel Processing Symposium and 10th Symposium on Parallel and Distributed Processing*, April 1999.

[9] Walter Willinger, Murad S. Taqqu, and Ashok Erramilli, "A Bibliographical Guide to Self-Similar Traffic and Performance Modeling for Modern High-Speed Networks", *Stochastic Networks: Theory and Applications*, pp. 339-366, Oxford University Press, 1996.

[10] J. Sahuquillo, T. Nachiondo, J.C. Cano, J.A. Gil, and A. Pont, "Self-Similarity in SPLASH-2 Workloads on Shared Memory Multiprocessors Systems," *Proceedings of the 8th Euromicro Workshop on Parallel and Distributed Processing*, pp. 293-300, January 2000.

[11] William Stallings, "High-Speed Networks: TCP/IP and ATM Design Principles," Prentice Hall, 1998.

[12] Walter Willinger, Murad S. Taqqu, Robert Sherman, and Daniel V. Wilson, "Self-similarity through high-variability: statistical analysis of Ethernet LAN traffic at the source level", *IEEE/ACM Transactions on Networking*, Vol. 5, No. 1, pp. 71-86, February 1997.

[13] Raj Jain and Shawn A. Routhier, "Packet trains: Measurements and a new model for computer network traffic", *IEEE Journal on Selected Areas in Communications*, Vol. 4, No. 6, pp. 986-995, September 1986.

[14] Mithuna Thottethodi, Alvin R. Lebeck, and Shubhendu S. Mukherjee, "Self-Tuned Congestion Control for Multiprocessor Networks," *Proceedings of the 7th International Symposium on High-Performance Computer Architecture*, January 2001.

[15] E. Baydal, P. Lopez, and J. Duato, "A Simple and Efficient Mechanism to Prevent Saturation in Wormhole Networks," *Proceedings of th 14th International Parallel and Distributed Processing Symposium*, pp. 617-622, Cancun, Mexico, May 2000.

[16] Abdel-Halim Smai and Lars-Erik Thorelle, "Global Reactive Congestion Control in Multicomputer Networks," *Proceedings of the 5th International Conference on High Performance Computing*, pp. 179-186, December 1998.

[17] Geyong Min and Mohamed Ould-Khaoua, "A Performance Model for k-Ary n-Cube Networks with Self-Similar Traffic", *Proceedings of the 16th International Parallel and Distributed Processing Symposium*, April 2002.

In: Concurrent and Parallel Computing...
Editor: Alexander S. Becker, pp. 149-164
ISBN 978-1-60456-274-3
© 2008 Nova Science Publishers, Inc.

Chapter 7

AN EXTENSION OF AMBIENT CALCULUS FOR UN-NESTED STRUCTURES

Masaki Murakami
Department of Computer Science
Graduate School of Natural Science and Technology,
Okayama University
3-1-1 Tsushima-Naka, Okayama, 700-0082, Japan

Abstract

One of the important issues on management of data materials such as documents, databases and/or softwares is access control. This paper presents a formal model of access control of data materials in an organization that consists of a number of user groups. The model presented here is an extension of ambient calculus. As ambient calculus is introduced to model behavior of mobile systems such as agents accessing firewalls, it assumed that target systems have nested structures. We extend the calculus to represent unnested structures of user groups of materials. An example of user authentication protocol is presented.

1. Introduction

Access control of data materials such as documents, databases and/or softwares is important for safe and secure management in companies, universities or institutes. Access from unauthorized user must be rejected. Management of data materials are sometimes implemented on a heterogeneous system in one organization. Different sections may use different hardwares, operating systems and/or programming languages for implementation of management system. Then platform independent specifications of access control task are required for consistent implementation of access control. A formal model of access control to support such platform independent specifications is an important issue.

Access control of data materials is basically management of user groups whose members have privilege for access to the materials. When materials belong to sections in an organization and each of the materials is under the control of the section, the organization of privileged groups in an organization reflects the architecture of the organization. For example, when a material with confidential data belongs to a section, the members of the section have access privilege to the material and who is not a member of the section does not have. Many enterprises have hierarchical architecture in their organization as Fig. 1. Then the access groups can be organized as hierarchically. Namely membership of sections have nested structures as Fig 2.

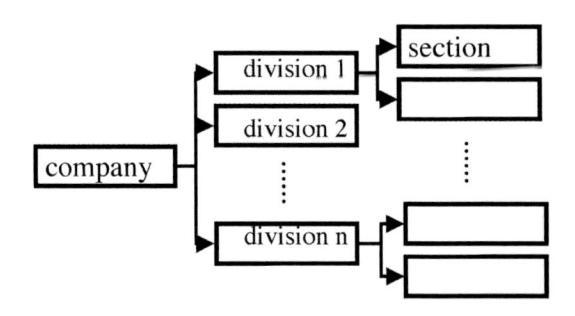

Figure 1. Hierarchical structure in an organization.

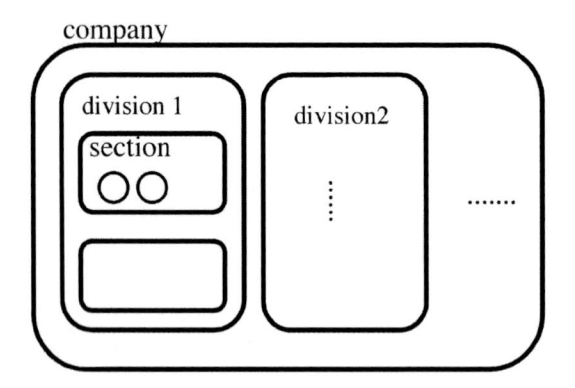

Figure 2. Nested Structure of organization.

Such nested structure is modeled by ambient calculus [1]. Ambient calculus is introduced to model mobile agents that move across the boundary of LAN, domain or site. For example, the model of agent authentication and access control for firewall are presented using the calculus. Ambient calculus represents hosts, users (user processes), websites (files and directories), LANs, domains and firewalls as *ambients*. Ambients are nested collection of spaces with boundaries. The ambients can access each other only if they have the common innermost boundary. The access for a firewall F by host A is represented as entry of A into F.

We adopt this idea for modeling of access control for data materials in organizations, as access control of data materials and authentication of mobile agents have something common with each other.

However the original ambient calculus is not enough for modeling of access control for data materials. The original ambient calculus allows nested (or disjoint) groups but can not represent a unnested intersecting groups. Network domains are well organized as hierarchical structures at least in some layer. Then a network consists of hosts, LANs, local domains, sites and global domains has a nested structure. On the other hand, groups of authenticated users are not well organized as hierarchy of network domains. Some member m in a section S_1 may also be a member of the other section S_2 and may be able to access a material that only members in S_2 can access.

Then it is difficult by the original ambient calculus to represent the situation such that m is a member both of S_1 and S_2 which are not nested. When m is a member of group S_1 and wants to join the other group S_2, he must quit S_1 at first and join S_2 or whole of S_1 must join S_2 in the original ambient calculus model. In order to represent the situation that S_1 is extruded to let m join S_2, intersecting S_1 and S_2 must be represented (Fig 3).

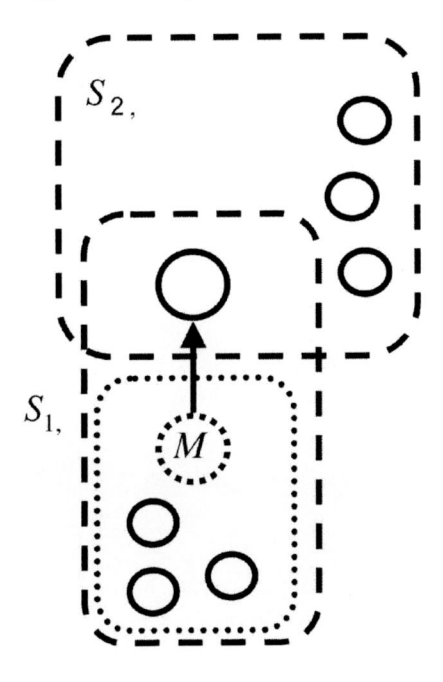

Figure 3. Unnested case.

This paper presents that can represent unnested structures. The original ambient calculus is based on the framework like process algebra such as π-calculus [4, 10]. We extend ambient calculus based on graph rewriting models [2,3,5,9,11] rather than process algebra. We represent an organization structure that consists of sections, unnested groups of members and materials using a partially ordered set. A (finite) partially ordered set is represented as a directed acyclic graph. A tree structure derived from an term of the original ambient calculus that represents a nested organization is a special case of directed acyclic graph. In this sense, the model presented here is a proper extension of the original ambient calculus. An operational semantics is defined as a set of rules for graph rewriting.

2. Ambient Calculus: An Informal Introduction

This section presents the outline of the ambient calculus. The basic notions of the calculus are used in this paper also. *An ambient* is a *bounded* place where computation such as access to data happens. For example, a host (a computer), a local domain connected with

LAN, a site or a global domain are ambients. In addition to them, data materials such as files, directories, folders and databases are also ambients. We also regard processes and messages as ambients.

An ambient is something that can be nested within other ambients. A folder contains a number of subdirectory folders and a subdirectory has subdirectories and so on. A file also can be a nested structure of ambients as it is a collection of something contains data values, for example, columns in a spreadsheet, tuples in a relational database and lines in a text file.

Each ambient has a name. The name of an ambient is used to control access. A folder has its name, a file has its name. Each tuple in a relational database has a primary key to access a certain data value.

Furthermore an ambient is something that can be moved as a whole. A file can be moved into a folder and a new data item is added to a file. If a folder A is moved into another folder B, the files in A also move together with A into B.

The behavior of an ambient is represented of three capabilities: *entry capability*, *exit capability* and *open capability*. If M_1 has an entry capability:

$$in\ M_2,$$

the capability instructs M_1 to enter an adjacent ambient (the ambient that has the common innermost surrounding ambient with M_1) named M_2 (Fig. 4).

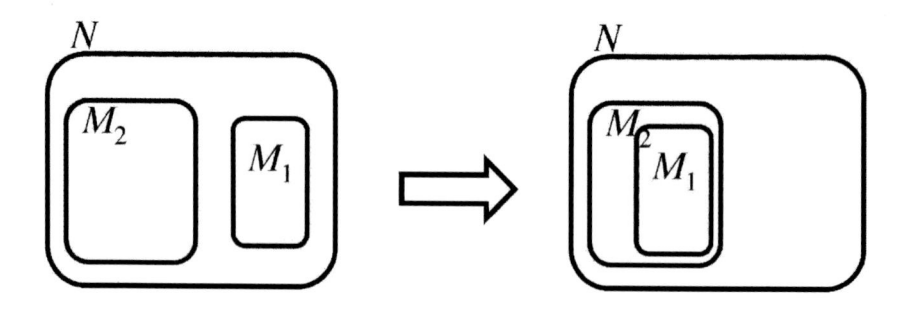

Figure 4. Entry capability.

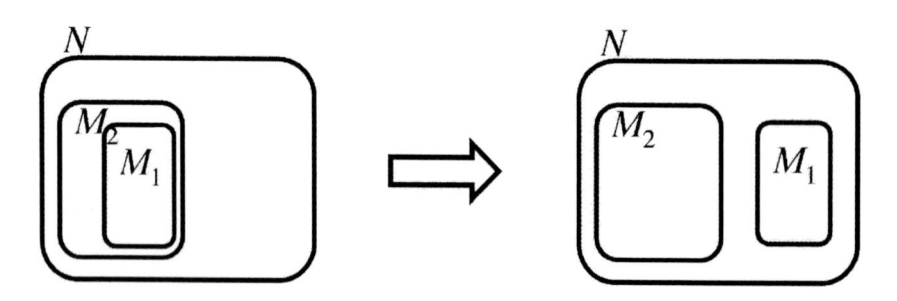

Figure 5. Exit capability.

If M_1 has an exit capability:

$$out\ M_2,$$

it instructs to M_1 to exit out of the parent ambient M_2(Fig. 5).

If M_1 has an open capability:

$$open\ M_2,$$

it provides a way to dissolving the boundary of an adjacent ambient named M_2 (Fig. 6).

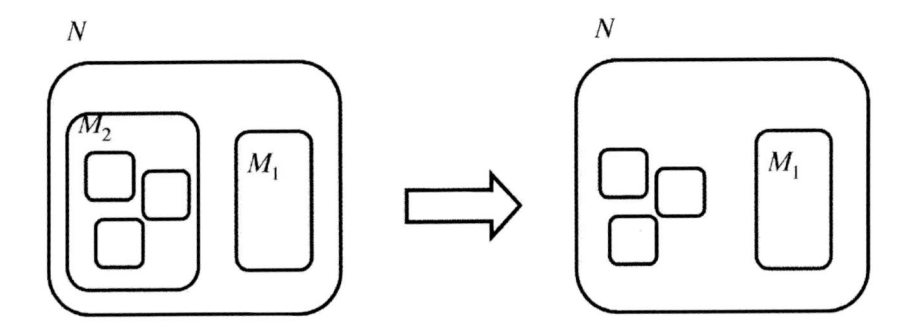

Figure 6. Open capability.

The calculus has primitives to pass a data value to a variable. If there is a data value $\langle a \rangle$ and a receiver $(x).P$ in an adjacent place, $\langle a \rangle$ is consumed by the receiver and a is substituted to variable x in P. The consumed data disappears from the system.

A message to send a value a from ambient M to N is:

$$out\ M.in\ N.\langle a \rangle$$

(if M and N has the common innermost surrounding ambient.)

To get a value stored in ambient M and send it to N, it is possible with the following command.

$$in\ M.(x).(out\ M.in\ N.\langle x \rangle)$$

In [1], examples such as mobile agent authentication and firewall access protocol are presented using these primitives. However, examples with unnested structure are not mentioned. It is difficult to deal with the unnested structure for the original ambient calculus that is based on process algebra. Then we introduce an extension of ambient calculus based on graph rewriting.

3. An Extension of Ambient Calculus: Formal Definitions

3.1. Primitives

We represent systems using directed acyclic graph instead of process algebraic formulas. An ambient (groups, members and messages) in a system is a node in the graph. When the innermost ambient that involves M is N, there is an arc from N to M.

Definition 3.1 (capability) Let n be *a name. A capability* : C is *in n*, *out n* or *open n*.

Definition 3.2 (sequential processes, ambients, processes) Let $n_1, n_2, \ldots$ be names and C be a capability. *Sequential processes*, *processes*, *ambients* and *ambient systems* are defines as follows.

- **0** is a sequential process.

- For a capability C and a process P, $C.P$ is a sequential process.

- For a variable x and a process P, $(x).P$ is a sequential process.

- For a process P, $!P$ is a sequential process.

- For a name n, $\langle n \rangle$ is a sequential process.

- $id : [n, \Gamma, \Pi]$ is an ambient where id is an ambient identifier, n is a name, Γ is a multiset of processes and Π is a set of ambient identifiers such that $id \notin \Pi$.

- A finite set of ambients $\mathcal{S}$:

$$\{id_1 : [n_1, \Gamma_1, \Pi_1], \ldots, id_k : [n_k, \Gamma_k, \Pi_k]\}$$

is an ambient system if it is a partially ordered set. Namely,

  - For every $1 \leq i, j \leq k$, id_i and id_i are distinct,
  - Π_i is a subset of $\{id_1, \ldots, id_k\}$ for every $1 \leq i \leq k$ and
  - the following graph P:
    1. The set of nodes are $id_i (1 \leq i \leq k)$ and
    2. there is an arc from id_i to id_j if and only if $id_j \in \Pi_i$.
       satisfies the following conditions:
       (a) P is acyclic and
       (b) for any two nodes id_i and id_j in P, if there is an arc from id_i to id_j then it is the only path from id_i to id_j.

- A process is a sequential process or an ambient system.

0 is an inactive process that does nothing and used to denote a process whose execution is terminated.

We introduce an *anonymous ambient* :

$$id : [\_, \Gamma, \Pi]$$

as a special case of ambients for technical convenience. An anonymous ambient with empty Γ and empty Π, $id : [\_, \emptyset, \emptyset]$ acts like **0**.

3.2. Operational Semantics

Definition 3.3 (maximal elements) For an ambient system $\mathcal{S}$, $L \in \mathcal{S}$ is a *maximal element* in $\mathcal{S}$ if id_L does not occur in Π_i for any $A_i \in \mathcal{S}$ where

$$A_i = id_i : [m, \Gamma_i, \Pi_i] \text{ and } L = id_L : [n, \Gamma, \Pi].$$

Definition 3.4 (normalization) For two ambient systems : $\mathcal{S}$ and $\mathcal{S}'$,

1. $\mathcal{S} \stackrel{\text{nrm}}{\to} \mathcal{S}'$ if and only if

   - $A \in \mathcal{S}$, $A = id_A : [n, \Gamma, \Pi]$ and $\mathcal{S}_0 \in \Gamma$ for an ambient system $\mathcal{S}_0$:

   $$\mathcal{S}_0 = \{A_0, \ldots A_i\} \cup \{L_1, \ldots, L_k\}$$

   where $L_1, \ldots, L_k$ are all maximal elements in $\mathcal{S}_0$ and $A_0, \ldots A_i$ other elements and

   - $\mathcal{S}' = \mathcal{S} \cup \mathcal{S}_0 \setminus \{A\} \cup \{A'\}$ where

   $$A' = id_A : [n, \Gamma \setminus \{\mathcal{S}_0\}, \Pi \cup \{L_1, \ldots, L_k\}].$$

2. $\mathcal{S}'$ is a *normal form* of $\mathcal{S}$ if and only if

   - There is no $\mathcal{S}''$ such that $\mathcal{S}' \stackrel{\text{nrm}}{\to} \mathcal{S}''$ and
   - $\mathcal{S} = \mathcal{S}'$ or $\mathcal{S} \stackrel{\text{nrm}}{\to} \mathcal{S}_1$ and $\mathcal{S}'$ is a normal form of $\mathcal{S}_1$.

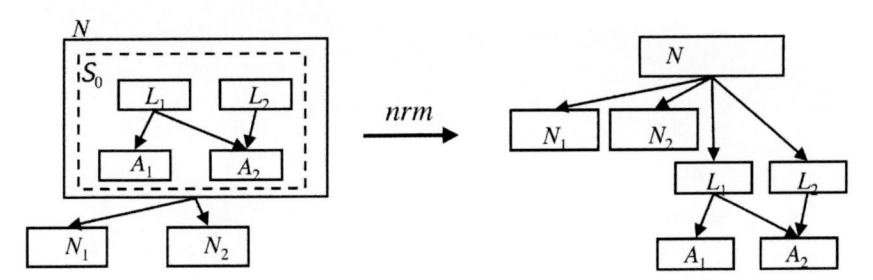

Figure 7. Normalization.

Normalization *unfolds* a recursive node to a subgraph of the system. If a node N have an ambient system $\mathcal{S}_0$ in Γ, the all nodes in $\mathcal{S}_0$ are placed under N preserving the partial order in $\mathcal{S}_0$ as Fig. 7. As we must maintain the uniqueness of ambient identifier, we redefine the identifier id of each ambients in $\mathcal{S}_0$ as $id_A; id$ prefixed with id_A after normalization if necessary.

Definition 3.5 (bound variables) If a name x occurs in a subprocess of the form $(x).P$ in a process $\mathcal{S}$, x is *a bound variable* in $\mathcal{S}$.

We can assume that y is not x nor a without loosing generality in the following definition, because bound variables can be renamed if necessary.

Definition 3.6 (substitution) For a process P and names a and a variable x, $P\{a/x\}$ is a process defined as follows.

- $0\{a/x\} = 0$

- $((y).P)\{a/x\} = (y).(P\{a/x\})$

- $!P\{a/x\} = !(P\{a/x\})$

- $\langle s \rangle \{a/x\} = \begin{cases} \langle a \rangle & \text{if } s = x \\ \langle s \rangle & \text{otherwise} \end{cases}$

-
  - $(in\ m.P)\{a/x\} = in\ m'.(P\{a/x\})$
  - $(out\ m.P)\{a/x\} = out\ m'.(P\{a/x\})$
  - $(open\ m.P)\{a/x\} = open\ m'.(P\{a/x\})$

  where
  $$m' = \begin{cases} a & \text{if } m = x \\ m & \text{otherwise} \end{cases}$$

- $id\colon [n, \Gamma, \Pi]\{a/x\} = id\colon [n', \Gamma\{a/x\}, \Pi]$ where
  $$n' = \begin{cases} a & \text{if } n = x \\ n & \text{otherwise} \end{cases}$$
  and $\Gamma\{a/x\} = \{A\{a/x\} \mid A \in \Gamma\}$.

- $\mathcal{S}\{a/x\} = \{id\colon [n, \Gamma, \Pi]\{a/x\} \mid id\colon [n, \Gamma, \Pi] \in \mathcal{S}\}$

Definition 3.7 (reduction relation) For two ambient systems: $\mathcal{S}$ and $\mathcal{S}'$, $\mathcal{S} \rightharpoonup \mathcal{S}'$ holds if and only if one of the followings holds.

in : $N_0, M_1, M_2 \in \mathcal{S}$ where
$$\begin{aligned} M_1 &= id_1\colon [m_1, \Gamma_1, \Pi_1], \\ &in\ m_2.P \in \Gamma_1, \\ M_2 &= id_2\colon [m_2, \Gamma_2, \Pi_2], \\ N_0 &= id_0\colon [n, \Gamma_0, \Pi_0], \\ &id_1, id_2 \in \Pi_0, \end{aligned}$$

and
$$\mathcal{S}' = \mathcal{S} \setminus \{N_{01}, \ldots, N_{0l}, M_1, M_2\} \cup \{N'_{01}, \ldots, N'_{0l}, M'_1, M'_2\}$$

where $N_{0k}(1 \leq k \leq l)$ is the collection of all ambients such that

$$N_{0k} = id_{0k} : [n_k, \Gamma_{0k}, \Pi_{0k}],$$
$$id_1, id_2 \in \Pi_{0k},$$
$$N'_{0k} = id_{0k} : [n_k, \Gamma_{0k}, \Pi'_{0k}] \text{ for each } k,$$
$$M'_1 = id_1 : [m_1, \Gamma'_1, \Pi_1],$$
$$M'_2 = id_2 : [m_2, \Gamma_2, \Pi'_2],$$
$$\Pi'_{0k} = \Pi_{0k} \setminus \{id_1\} \text{ for each } k,$$
$$\Gamma'_1 = \Gamma_1 \setminus \{in\ m_2.P\} \cup \{P\},$$
$$\Pi'_2 = \Pi_2 \cup \{id_1\}$$

out : $M_1, M_2 \in \mathcal{S}$, where

$$M_1 = id_1 : [m_1, \Gamma_1, \Pi_1],$$
$$M_2 = id_2 : [m_2, \Gamma_2, \Pi_2],$$
$$id_1 \in \Pi_2,$$
$$out\ m_2.P \in \Gamma_1,$$

and

$$\mathcal{S}' = \mathcal{S} \setminus \{N_{01}, \ldots, N_{0l}, M_1, M_2\} \cup \{N'_{01}, \ldots, N'_{0l}, M'_1, M'_2\}$$

where $N_{0k}(1 \leq k \leq l)$ is the collection of all ambients such that

$$N_{0k} = id_{0k} : [n_k, \Gamma_{0k}, \Pi_{0k}],$$
$$id_2 \in \Pi_{0k} \text{ for all } k,$$
$$N'_{0k} = id_{0k} : [n_k, \Gamma_{0k}, \Pi'_{0k}],$$
$$M'_1 = id_1 : [m_1, \Gamma'_1, \Pi_1],$$
$$M'_2 = id_2 : [m_2, \Gamma_2, \Pi'_2],$$
$$\Pi'_{0k} = \Pi_{0k} \cup \{id_1\} \text{ for each } k,$$
$$\Pi'_2 = \Pi_2 \setminus \{id_1\},$$
$$\Gamma'_1 = \Gamma_1 \setminus \{out\ m_2.P\} \cup \{P\}$$

open : $N_0, M_1, M_2 \in \mathcal{S}$, where

$$N_0 = id_0 : [n, \Gamma_0, \Pi_0],$$
$$M_1 = id_1 : [m_1, \Gamma_1, \Pi_1],$$
$$M_2 = id_2 : [m_2, \Gamma_2, \Pi_2],$$
$$id_1, id_2 \in \Pi_0,$$
$$open\ m_2.P \in \Gamma_1,$$

and

$$S' = S \setminus \{N_{01}, \ldots, N_{0l}, N_1, N_2\} \cup \{N'_{01}, \ldots, N'_{0l}, M'_1, M'_2\}$$

where $N_{0k} (1 \leq k \leq l)$ is the collection of all ambients such that

$$N_{0k} = id_{0k} : [n_k, \Gamma_{0k}, \Pi_{0k}],$$
$$id_2 \in \Pi_{0k},$$
$$N'_{0k} = id_{0k} : [n_k, \Gamma'_{0k}, \Pi'_{0k}],$$
$$M'_1 = id_1 : [m_1, \Gamma'_1, \Pi_1],$$
$$\Gamma'_{0h} = \Gamma_{0h} \cup \Gamma_2$$

for some h $(1 \leq h \leq l)$ such that $id_1 \in \Pi_{0k}$,

$$\Gamma'_{0k} = \Gamma_{0k} \text{ for other } k \ (k \neq h, 1 \leq k \leq l),$$
$$\Pi'_{0k} = \Pi_{0k} \cup \Pi_2,$$
$$\Gamma'_1 = \Gamma_1 \setminus \{open\ m_2.P\} \cup \{P\}.$$

replication : $M \in S$ where

$$M = id : [m, \Gamma, \Pi]$$
$$!P \in \Gamma$$

and

$$S' = S \setminus \{M\} \cup \{M'\}$$

where

$$M' = id : [m, \Gamma', \Pi] \ \Gamma' = \Gamma \cup \{P\}$$

comm : $N_1 \in S$, where

$$N_1 = id_0 : [n, \Gamma_0, \Pi_0],$$
$$\langle n \rangle, (x).P \in \Gamma_0,$$

and

$$S' = S \setminus \{N_1\} \cup \{N'_1\}$$

where

$$N'_1 = id_0 : [n, \Gamma'_0, \Pi_0], \Gamma'_0 = \Gamma_0 \setminus \{\langle n \rangle, (x).P\} \cup \{P\{n/x\}\}$$

remove 0 : $N_1 \in \mathcal{S}$ where

$$N_1 = id_0 : [n, \Gamma_0 \cup \{\mathbf{0}\}, \Pi_0],$$

and $\mathcal{S}' = \mathcal{S} \setminus \{N_1\} \cup \{N_1'\}$ where

$$N_1' = id_0 : [n, \Gamma_0, \Pi_0].$$

remove anonymous : $N_1 \in \mathcal{S}$ where

$$N_1 = id_0 : [n, \Gamma_0, \Pi_0 \cup \{A\}],$$
$$A = id_A : [\_, \emptyset, \emptyset]$$

and $\mathcal{S}' = \mathcal{S} \setminus \{N_1\} \cup \{N_1'\}$ where

$$N_1' = id_0 : [n, \Gamma_0, \Pi_0].$$

For each ambient $A = id : [n, \Gamma, \Pi]$, if there is a sequential process $C.P \in \Gamma$, then A has C as a *top capability*. In rules **in**, **out** and **open**, M_1 is the *subject ambient* and M_2 is the *object ambient* of the rule.

Note that the rules for *in, open* capabilities require that the subject ambient and the object ambient must have at least one common parent ambient. And the rule for *out* require that the object must be one of the (direct) parent of the subject ambient.

in rule says that if the subject ambient M_1 that has *in* m_2 as a top capability to enter M_2 and the object ambient M_2 have the common parent node, arcs to M_1 is deleted for every common parent N_{0i} of M_1 and M_2 and a new arc from M_2 to M_1 is created (Fig. 8).

out rule says that if there is an arc from the object ambient M_2 to the subject ambient M_1 that has *out* m_2 as a top capability to exit M_2, then the arc from M_2 to M_1 is deleted and arcs from the parent nodes of M_2 to M_1 are created (Fig. 9).

open rule says that if the subject ambient M_1 with *open* m_2 as a top capability to open M_2 and the object ambient M_2 have the common parent node, then the object node M_2 is deleted and all elements in Γ_2 is moved to one of the common parents and arcs from the all parent nodes to all elements in Π_2 are created(Fig 10).

replication rule creates a new instance of P from $!P$ in Γ. If P is an ambient system, an application of the normalization rule to P follows to this rule in typical case.

comm rule is value passing to substitute the value n to the receiver. **remove anonymous** and **remove 0** are rules for deleting inactive ambients.

Definition 3.8 $\mathcal{S} \to \mathcal{S}'$ if and only if there exist $\mathcal{S}_1$ and $\mathcal{S}_1'$ such that $\mathcal{S}_1 \rightharpoonup \mathcal{S}_1'$, $\mathcal{S}_1$ is a normal form of $\mathcal{S}$ and $\mathcal{S}'$ is a normal form of $\mathcal{S}_1'$.

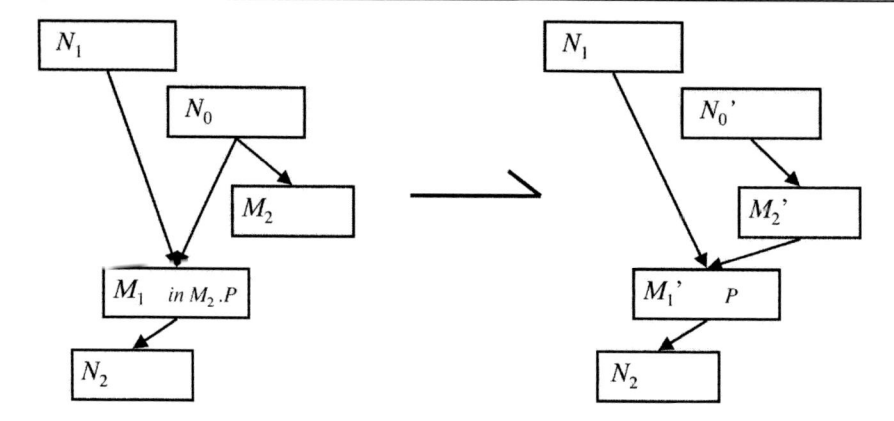

Figure 8. **in** rule.

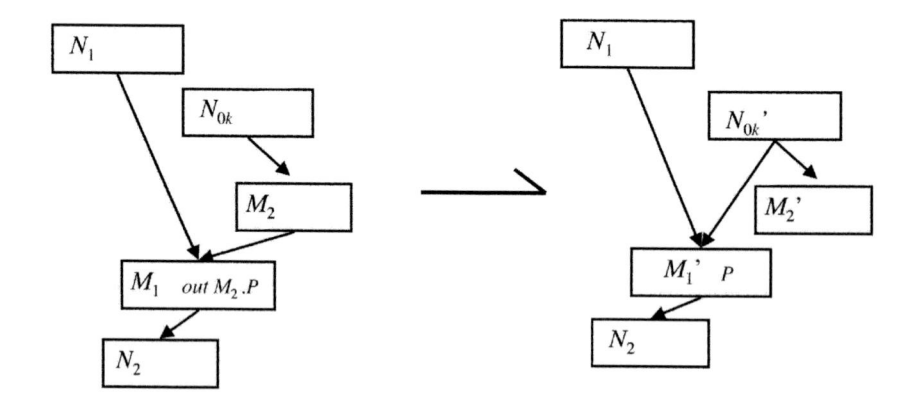

Figure 9. **out** rule.

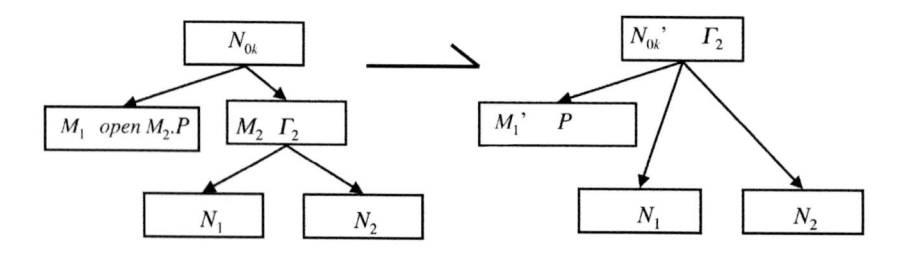

Figure 10. **open** rule.

4. Example

We present an example of authentication of a new member of a group. The system that consists of the group of authenticated members, the administrator and a newcomer (and other ambients not mentioned here). The membership of the group is controlled by the administrator. The newcomer process is going to join the group. At first he/she sends his/her name to the administrator to get a permission to join the group. The administrator issues a password (that is the name of the group here) to the newcomer (if the application is verified). Then the reply from the administrator is received by the newcomer and he/she can join the group.

The behavior of the newcomer is defined as the following ambient. We assume that the name of the group g is a secret name that is known only by the members authenticated by the administrator. Namely, *Newcomer* who is going to join the group does not know g until he/she was informed the name.

$$Newcomer : [m, \Gamma_m, \Pi_m],$$

$$\Gamma_m = \{(X).in\ X.M\},$$

$$\Pi_m = \{Message, Opener_r\},$$

$$Message : [e, \{out\ m.in\ a.in\ r.\langle m \rangle\}, \emptyset],$$

$$Opener_r : [\_, \{open\ r.\mathbf{0}\}, \emptyset]$$

The behavior of the administrator is defined as the following ambient.

$$Administrator : [a, \Gamma_a, \Pi_a],$$

$$\Pi_a = \{Reply : [r, \Gamma_r, \Pi_r]\},$$

$$\Gamma_r = \{(M).(out\ a.in\ M.\langle g \rangle)\},$$

$$\Pi_r = \{Opener_e\},$$

$$Opener_e : [\_, \{open\ e.\mathbf{0}\}, \emptyset].$$

Group ambient is :

$$Group : [g, \Gamma_g, \Pi_g].$$

First, *Newcomer* ambient sends its name to *Administrator*. The name of *Newcomer* ambient m is carried by *Message* ambient. *Message* ambient moves out of *Newcomer* by the application of **out** rule to the *Message* and *Newcomer*. Then *Administrator* ambient receives the name of *Newcomer* ambient, and send the secret name g to access the group to *Newcomer* (after some verification procedure that is 1not mentioned here). These steps are as follows. *Message* moves into *Administrator* by the application of **in** rule for *Message* and *Administrator* and then moves into *Reply* with **in** rule again. After normalization of *Administrator* and applications of **open** rule, the name $\langle m \rangle$ meets with $(M).(out\ a.in\ M.\langle g \rangle)$ in *Reply*. The **comm** rule is applied. Thus *Reply* moves out of *Administrator* by **out** rule and go into *Newcomer*. Then $\langle g \rangle$ is delivered to the *Newcomer*. Applying **comm** rule to *Newcomer*, it can move into the *Group* by **in** rule.

The implementation presented here works even if *Newcomer* ambient is already involved in the other groups. It is not necessary to move out of the other groups to join *Group*. Then a unnested structure is represented.

5. Name Restriction

We did not mentioned name restriction that the original ambient calculus has in previous sections. The name restriction operator is convenient to represent situations such that there are names which are secret to some ambient as name g of the example in the previous section. However, as we allowed unnested structure in our calculus, the scopes of restricted names are also not nested. We cannot use the restriction operation of the original ambient calculus because that assumes the scopes of names are nested. So we need other method to represent scope restriction of names. We have an idea that can represent unnested scopes of names [8]. It is possible to adopt the idea in our extended ambient calculus.

The basic idea is as follows. The scope of each name is represented with a binary relation on processes and names. Namely a system is a tuple:

$$[\![S, \mathcal{R}]\!]$$

where S is an ambient system defined in section **2** and $\mathcal{R}$ is a binary relation that is a subset of $\mathcal{P}_S \times \mathcal{N}_S$ where $\mathcal{N}_S$ is the set of all names other than bound variables that occur in S and $\mathcal{P}_S$ is the set of all occurrences of processes in S. The formal definition of $\mathcal{P}_S$ is as follows.
Definition 5.1

- $\mathcal{P}_\mathbf{0} = \{\mathbf{0}\}$,

- $\mathcal{P}_{\langle n \rangle} = \{\langle n \rangle\}$,

- $\mathcal{P}_{C.P} = \mathcal{P}_P \cup \{C.P\} \setminus \{P\}$

- $\mathcal{P}_{(x).P} = \mathcal{P}_P \cup \{(x).P\} \setminus \{P\}$

- $\mathcal{P}_{!P} = \mathcal{P}_P \cup \{!P\} \setminus \{P\}$

- for a multiset of of processes Γ, $\mathcal{P}_\Gamma = \bigcup_{Q \in \Gamma} \mathcal{P}_Q$

- for a ambient system $S = \{id_1 : [n_1, \Gamma_1, \Pi_1], \ldots, id_k : [n_k, \Gamma_k, \Pi_k]\}$,

$$\mathcal{P}_S = \bigcup_{1 \leq i \leq k} \mathcal{P}_{\Gamma_i}$$

Note that we assume that $\mathcal{P}_S$ is the set of occurrences of processes. It means that $\mathcal{P}_S$ is a multiset of processes.
Definition 5.2 (Ambient system with name restriction) : *Ambient system with name restriction* is a tuple $[\![S, \mathcal{R}]\!]$ where S is an ambient system and $\mathcal{R} \subset \mathcal{P}_S \times \mathcal{N}_S$ where for each $P \in \mathcal{P}_S$ and for each occurrence of name n in P, $(P, n) \in \mathcal{R}$.

The reduction rules for ambient systems with name restrictions are defined as follows based on the reduction relation defined in section **3**. In the following definition, for each application of the rule, *the principal process of the rule* is *in* $m_2.P$ of **in** rule, *out* $m_2.P$ of **out** rule, *open* $m_2.P$ of **open** rule or $!P$ of **replication** rule respectively. For **comm** rule, both of $\langle n \rangle$ and $(x).P$ are the principal processes. And *the updated process of the rule* is P of **in** rule, **out** rule, **open** rule or **replication** rule or $P\{n/x\}$ of **comm** rule respectively.

Definition 5.3 (reduction relation with name restriction) For two systems with name restrictions: $[\![\mathcal{S}, \mathcal{R}]\!]$ and $[\![\mathcal{S}', \mathcal{R}']\!]$,

$$[\![\mathcal{S}, \mathcal{R}]\!] \rightharpoonup [\![\mathcal{S}', \mathcal{R}']\!]$$

holds if and only if $\mathcal{S} \rightharpoonup \mathcal{S}'$ and

- if it is derived with **in** rule, **out** rule, **open** rule, **replication** rule or **comm** rule and Q is the principal process then $\mathcal{R}'$ is the relation that is obtained from $\mathcal{R}$ by replacing each (Q, m) with (Q', m) where Q' is the updated process of the rule.

- if is derived from **remove 0** rule or **remove anonymous**, then $\mathcal{R}'$ is the relation that is obtained from $\mathcal{R}$ by replacing each (N_1, m) with (N_1', m) where N_1 and N_1' are defined in the rule respectively.

Definition 5.4 (normalization with restriction) For two systems with name restrictions: $[\![\mathcal{S}, \mathcal{R}]\!]$ and $[\![\mathcal{S}', \mathcal{R}]\!]$,

$$[\![\mathcal{S}, \mathcal{R}]\!] \stackrel{\text{nrm}}{\rightharpoonup} [\![\mathcal{S}', \mathcal{R}]\!]$$

holds if and only if $\mathcal{S} \stackrel{\text{nrm}}{\rightharpoonup} \mathcal{S}'$.

For the example in the previous section, the situation such that the name of the group g is a secret name that is known only by the members authenticated by the administrator is represented with the following relation when the whole system is represented with the set $\mathcal{S}$.

$$\mathcal{R} = \{(P_a, g) | P_a \in \mathcal{P}_{\Gamma_a} \cup \mathcal{P}_{\Gamma_m}, \ id \in \Pi_g, \ id : [m, \Gamma_m, \Pi_m] \in \mathcal{S}\}$$

And if *Newcomer* is not a member of the group, $(Q, g) \notin \mathcal{R}$ for any $Q \in \mathcal{P}_{\Gamma_m}$.

6. Conclusion

This paper presented an extension of ambient calculus for applications of access control of data materials. The early idea to extend ambient calculus to allow unnested structure is reported in [6]. That paper uses multidimensional representation for inclusion relationship between ambients. That is inspired by the idea introduced in [7]. However, the expressive power is not enough for many practical examples. Our extended model can represent structures that consists of groups that are not nested.

References

[1] Cardelli, L. and A. D. Gordon, Mobile Ambients, *Theoretical Computer Science* **240**, pp. 177-213 (2000)

[2] Fournet, C., and G. Gonthier, A Calculus of Mobile Agents, *Proc. of CONCUR '96* (1996)

[3] Lafont, Y., Interaction Nets. *Proc. of POPL'90, ACM*, pp. 95-108, (1990)

[4] Milner, R.: *Communication and Mobile Systems: The π-Calculus*, Cambridge University Press (1999)

[5] Milner, R., Bigraphical Reactive Systems, *Proc. of CONCUR'01, LNCS* **2154**, Springer, pp. 16-35 (2001)

[6] Morinaga A., An Extension of Ambient Calculus for Representations of Unnested Structures, (in Japanese) Okayama University (2002)

[7] Murakami M., Run Time Transformation of Concurrent Processes Using Multi Dimensional Representation of Linear Logic, *Proc. of ISPSE '00* (2000)

[8] Murakami M., A Formal Model of Concurrent Systems BAsed on Bipartite Directed Acyclic Graph, *Science of Computer Programming* **61**, 38-47 (2006)

[9] Odersky, M. Functional Nets, *Proc. of European Symposium on Programming 2000, Lecture Notes in Computer Science* **1782**, Springer Verlag, (2000)

[10] Sangiorgi, D. and D. Walker, *The π-calculus, A Theory of Mobile Processes*, Cambridge University Press, (2001)

[11] Ueda, K. and N. Kato, Programming with Logical Links: Design of the LMNtal language, *Proc. of PPL'03, JSSST*, pp. 20-31 (2003)

Phys. Lett. B **70**, 59 (1977).

In: Concurrent and Parallel Computing...
Editor: Alexander S. Becker, pp. 165-184

ISBN: 978-1-60456-274-3
© 2008 Nova Science Publishers, Inc.

Chapter 8

EFFICIENT EXPLOITATION OF GRIDS FOR LARGE-SCALE PARALLEL APPLICATIONS

Young Choon Lee[*], *Riky Subrata*[**] *and Albert Y. Zomaya*[***]

Advanced Networks Research Group, School of Information Technologies,
The University of Sydney, NSW 2006, Australia

Abstract

The grid computing platform has become a promising alternative to high-performance parallel computing systems including supercomputers, mainly due to its affordability, scalability, and capability. Over the past decade, many different types of grids have been constructed to mostly deal with large-scale problems in science and engineering—high-energy physics, bioinformatics, and data-mining. Numerous parallel applications have been developed, and deployed onto grids to solve these problems. Bag-of-tasks (BoT) is a typical application model identified in those parallel applications. An application in this model consists of a large number of independent tasks. Although the scheduling of BoT applications seems to be simple, the heterogeneity and dynamicity of resources on grids much complicate this scheduling. Due to the NP-hardness of the BoT scheduling problem, most previously proposed scheduling algorithms are heuristics. This chapter surveys various BoT scheduling approaches proposing a taxonomy of such algorithms. A set of projects closely related to BoT scheduling on grids are then presented followed by a discussion on the issues, in BoT scheduling, that need further investigation.

1. Introduction

The need for powerful processing capability and/or massive amount of storage capacity to solve many scientific and engineering problems, has led to the development of various high-performance computing systems, such as supercomputers, computer clusters, and more recently grids. Generally, the powerful performance of these computing systems is achieved

---

[*] E-mail address: yclee@it.usyd.edu.au
[**] E-mail address: efax@it.usyd.edu.au
[***] E-mail address: zomaya@it.usyd.edu.au

by their parallel processing capability; however, applications deployed onto them are actually the primary source to gain such performance. Therefore, many applications in science and engineering have been devised using parallel processing facilities—MPI [1], PVM [2], OpenMP [3], POSIX pThreads [4], High Performance Fortran (HPF) [5], split C [6], HyperC [7] and pC++ [8]. Although these tools have successfully demonstrated their capabilities in tightly coupled computing systems, their applicability to loosely coupled computing systems (e.g., grids) is limited, because unlike many traditional parallel computers built with homogeneous resources and individually administered, grids are composed of geographically dispersed heterogeneous resources owned by multiple administrative domains.

Grids have emerged as an attractive computing platform in terms of cost-effectiveness, scalability and capability. However, due to the dynamic and heterogeneous nature of grids, their efficient use is a crucial issue; here, scheduling particularly plays a key role. While scheduling decisions in traditional scheduling are made primarily on the basis of static information, those in grid scheduling are more heavily relied on dynamic information. In general, an information service such as the Globus monitoring and discovering service (MDS) [9] is provided in a grid. Both static and dynamic information about grid resources can be obtained from such information service; however, since grid dynamics is highly unpredictable, perfectly accurate dynamic information is not readily available.

An increasing number of applications have been developed and many existing applications have been ported for grid environments. Bag-of-tasks (BoT) applications are a typical application model, found particularly in science and engineering, and deployed in grids. Well-known examples are '@home' type of applications (e.g., SETI@home [10], Folding@home [11] and Einstein@Home [12]), BLAST [13], MCell [14] and INS2D [15]. Although these applications are composed of independent tasks, there are a number of issues that complicate scheduling them on grids. These issues include (i) tasks of a BoT application are generally considerably different in both computation and communication cost, (ii) resources on a grid are heterogeneous, and (iii) capacities and availabilities of these resources fluctuate.

In this chapter, we survey various BoT scheduling approaches proposing a taxonomy of such algorithms. Due to the NP-hardness of the BoT scheduling problem, heuristics are the single most popularly adopted technique in the literature. In addition to heuristics, other interesting approaches, such as game theory and linear programming are discussed. There have been many projects related to grid computing at various levels, ranging from architecture, middleware and simulation to application. Since our main interest in this chapter is BoT scheduling on grids, we present a set of closely related projects to our interest. Finally, we identify and discuss the issues, in BoT scheduling, that need further investigation. This chapter is not meant to be a comprehensive survey of techniques and research efforts in the area of BoT scheduling; instead, it covers a set of noteworthy approaches.

2. Scheduling Model

To efficiently utilize a grid and its rich set of services, much attention should be paid to scheduling in the grid. Due to the unique characteristics of the grid, scheduling on grids is far more complex than traditional multiprocessor scheduling. Grid scheduling differs from traditional multiprocessor scheduling in the following three respects.

- *Lack of control*—Resources in the grid are dispersed across multiple administrative domains that are often in different geographical locations. This implies resources belonging to a particular administrative domain are more dedicated to the local users of the domain than those in other administrative domains; that is, the alien users have less control over those resources than the local users, and resources in a grid may not be equally accessible to all the users.
- *Dynamicity of resource*—The availability and capacity of resources can change dynamically. This is one of the greatest hurdles to scheduling on grids. Resources join and disjoin the grid at any time.
- *Application diversity*—It is often the case that a particular conventional parallel computing system is used by a group of users for applications in specific fields, such as bioinformatics and astrophysics; that is, the applications run in the system are of a similar model, if not the same. However, applications deployed in grids are typically from numerous disciplines, and are thus of different application models.

2.1. BoT Application Model

BoT applications are the 'embarrassingly parallel' type of applications in many scientific and engineering disciplines. An application J of this model consists of a number of n heterogeneous tasks $\{T_1, T_2, ..., T_n\}$ without inter-task communications or dependencies. Parameter-sweep applications (PSA) are typical of this model. A PSA is composed of a set of multiple 'experiments', each of which is executed with a distinct set of parameters [16]. BoT applications are typically classified into computationally intensive, or data/communication-intensive; however, in some cases this distinction is not clearly identified. Here, the terms application and job are used interchangeably.

Computationally intensive bag-of-tasks (CBoT) model

A CBoT application usually consists of a large number of independent tasks, each involving a massive amount of computation. The workload (computation time) of each task in the CBoT model varies and can be estimated. The input data transfer for each task is negligible and the size of the task itself is small; thus, communication does not greatly influence the completion time of the task. Computation is a dominant factor when scheduling such applications.

SETI@home [10] and similar follow-up projects, such as Folding@home [11] and Einstein@Home [12], are well-known examples of the CBoT model. With SETI@home tasks, each task performs a total of 3.9 trillion floating-point operations, or about 10 hours on a 500 MHz Pentium II, yet requires only 350 KB of input data and produces 1 KB of output [10].

Data-intensive bag-of-tasks (DBoT) model

A task T_i in a DBoT application J is associated with a set I_i of input data objects $\{I_{i,1}, I_{i,2}, ..., I_{i,d}\}$. In the DBoT model, the input data transfer for each task is a more influential factor than its computation for task execution. Input data required by a task need to be transferred to the site on which the task is scheduled, if those data are on the scheduled site. A group of tasks in an application may share one or more input data objects. This data-sharing pattern varies between applications. Three typical data-sharing patterns occurring in DBoT applications are 'one-to-many', 'partitioned' and 'random' (Figure 1).

Generally, the amount of output data produced by the DBoT applications is assumed to be significantly smaller and negligible than input data.

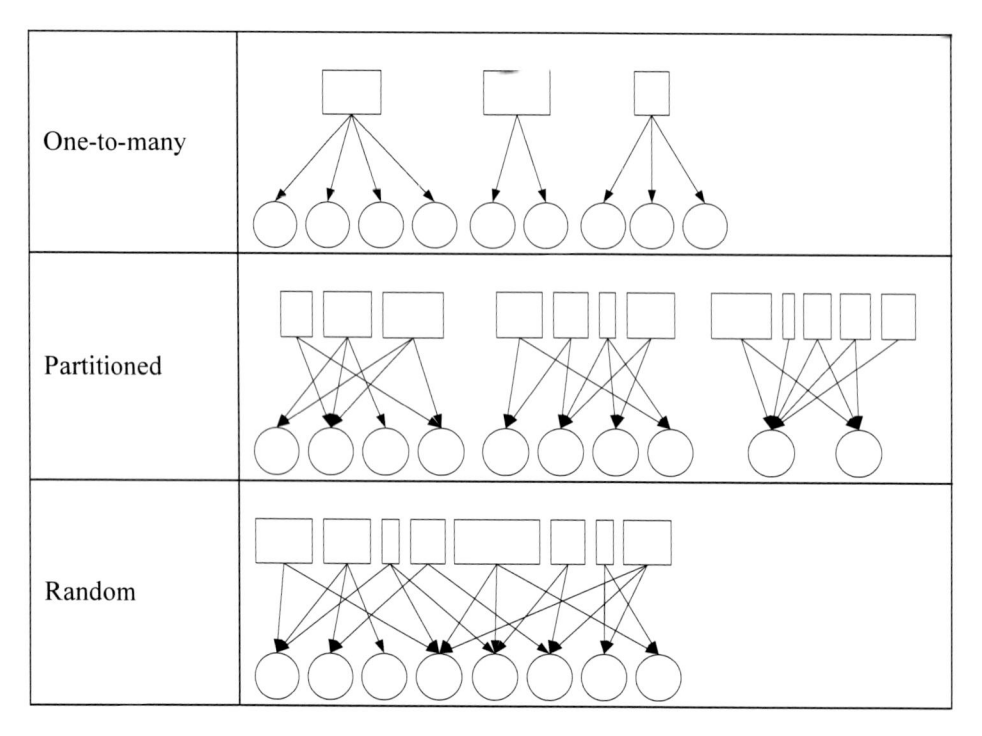

Figure 1. Data sharing patterns.

2.2. Grid System Model

The grid G consists of a number of sites in each of which a set of m computational hosts is participating in a grid (Figure 2). More formally,

$$G = \{S_1, S_2, ..., S_r\}, \text{ and } S_i, 1 \leq i \leq r, = \{H_{i,1}, H_{i,2}, ..., H_{i,m}\} \cup D_i$$

where S_i is the ith site participating in G, and H_i and D_i are a set of host machines and data repository/storage at S_i, respectively. Let $H = \{H_1, H_2, ..., H_r\}$ denote a superset of all host sets in G.

Each site is an autonomous administrative domain with own local users. These sites are connected through WAN. Hosts are composed of both space- and time-shared machines with different processing speeds. These resources are not entirely dedicated to the grid, but are used for both local and grid jobs. Each host has one or more processors, memory and disk. We assumed that data repositories of hosts in the same site are equally accessible, as if the hosts access their own; in other words, a set of data repositories in a site can be viewed as a single aggregated data repository because, in general, a site connects its hosts through a high-bandwidth LAN.

The availability and capacity of resources such as hosts and network links fluctuates. Therefore, the accurate completion time of a task on a particular host is difficult, if not impossible, to determine *a priori*. Moreover, a task may fail to complete due to the failure of the resource on which it is running.

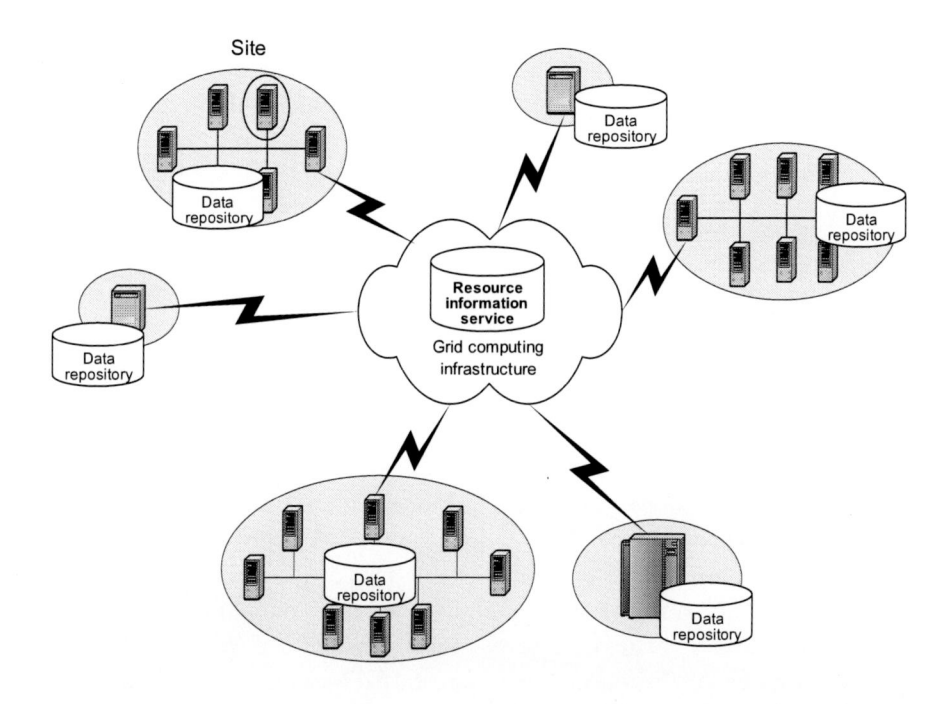

Figure 2. Grid system model.

2.3. BoT scheduling problem and Performance metrics

The grid scheduling problem addressed in this study is task scheduling of a set J of n independent tasks, comprising a BoT application, onto $|H|$ heterogeneous hosts dispersed across multiple sites in a grid. The BoT scheduling problem is of 'discrete scheduling' (i.e., scheduling of each particular application is independent). The primary goal of this scheduling is to make as many appropriate task-host matches as possible, so that the *makespan*, also called schedule length (SL), of a BoT application can be minimized. Resource utilization, average response time, and fairness are other commonly used performance metrics.

Schedule length
The precise definition of SL may vary between scheduling problems, due to application-specific characteristics. However, for a given application (i.e., a set of tasks), an ultimate definition of SL applicable to the scheduling problem instances in this chapter is the amount of time taken from the initiation of the earliest starting task to the completion of the latest finishing task. The following are two definitions of SL, each specific to a particular application type.

- *Scheduling of CBoT applications.* The time from the start of the first task to the end of the last task.
- *Scheduling of DBoT applications.* The time from the start of the first input data transfer to the end of the last task.

Resource utilization/wastage

The single most important objective in constructing grids is the exploitation of underutilized resources (i.e., better resource utilization); however, attention should be paid not to misuse (e.g., overload) grids by blindly dispatching jobs redundantly. In traditional parallel algorithm design, resource utilization can be defined as the percentage of resources kept busy during the execution of a parallel application. More formally, $U_p = \frac{O_p}{pT_p}$, where O_p is the actual total number of unit operations performed by a p-processor machine, while pT_p represents the number of operations that could have been performed with p processors in T_p time units. However, this measure is inappropriate to apply for heterogeneous and dynamic resources in grids; in other words, grids may be composed of space- and time-shared computing resources, and tasks can be suspended and/or killed for local jobs. For this reason, resource wastage is a more widely adopted measure when discussing resource utilization in grids. Many scheduling algorithms for BoT applications incorporate task duplication. Consequently, there might be some resources redundantly used for replica tasks. For a given application, resource utilization accounting for resource wastage can be defined as the amount of time that actually contributed to the execution of the application over the total amount of time used including wasted time. Alternatively, relative resource waste can be used that is defined to be the amount of wasted time over the total amount of time used including wasted time.

Fairness to users

Fairness to users is often measured in the sense that all users should receive the same level of utility from the system. If different users receive different level of utility, then the scheduling scheme can be considered unfair, as it gives some users an advantage, while it gives some other users a disadvantage. Fairness is another important performance measure for scheduling schemes beside time related completion of tasks, and relates directly to the Quality of Service (QoS) provided to users. A well-known fairness criterion is the max-min fairness, whereby the aim is to maximize the minimum utility of a user.

As scheduling scheme becomes distributed (as opposed to centralized) to address the issue of fault tolerance and scalability, the issue of fairness to users among the different decentralized schedulers becomes important. In the context of distributed schedulers, fairness to users can be measured in the sense that users should receive the same level of utility no matter which schedulers are responsible for them. In this sense, and using the average measure, fairness is achieved when the average utility to users for each of the scheduler is the same. Fairness is important in this regard, as a scheduling scheme that results in a few schedulers having extremely low utilities (e.g. long delays) may not be preferable, as these few schedulers would become "unwanted" schedulers for the users in the system—though arbitrary they may be. Fairness in such distributed scheduling system is discussed in [17].

A fairness index given by

$$FI = \frac{\left(\sum_{i=1}^{n} T_i\right)^2}{n \sum_{i=1}^{n} T_i^2}$$

where T_i is the average job completion time of *entity i* (or other utility measure), was discussed in [18] to quantify the fairness of scheduling schemes. If a scheduling scheme is 100% fair, then *FI* is 1.0. A fairness index close to 1.0 indicates a relatively fair scheduling scheme.

3. A Taxonomy of Bot Scheduling Algorithms

BoT scheduling algorithms can be classified into a number of different categories; however, a typical hierarchical taxonomy does not appropriately show relationships between these categories. Thus, we present a contrast-based taxonomy in the rest of this section. A BoT scheduling algorithm is classified as either category in each of the following classifications.

3.1. Static vs. Dynamic

At the highest level, BoT scheduling, as in traditional task scheduling, can be classified as static (batch) and dynamic (online). These are distinguished by the time at which the scheduling decisions are made. With static scheduling, the necessary information, such as the processing requirements of tasks and the processing capacities of resources, are identified and schedules are determined *a priori*. Conversely, scheduling information in a dynamic scheduling scheme is obtained on the fly. Dynamic scheduling attempts to reduce scheduling overheads and job completion time. Both of these scheduling models have been studied widely and intensively.

Although static scheduling can be used and has been used for BoT scheduling, it is an unrealistic approach in ever-changing grid environments. Rather, scheduling decisions should be made reflecting changes in a given grid, such as resource/task failures; however, the information of these changes is also dynamic in nature. A simple, yet frequently adopted, example of dynamic scheduling is first-come-first-serve (FCFS) that performs reasonably in many cases with a very low time complexity.

3.2. Performance Prediction Information Dependent vs. Independent

Generally, the quality of schedules is highly dependent on performance estimates on both resources and applications; in other words, the more comprehensive and accurate performance information a scheduling algorithm can get, the shorter SL it delivers. Performance estimates of jobs are relatively easy to obtain than those of grid resources. While some researchers have made many efforts to develop performance estimation tools (e.g., the network weather service (NWS) [19–21]) for accurate performance estimates, others have focused on designing performance information independent—more precisely, performance prediction information independent—scheduling algorithms.

In conventional tightly coupled heterogeneous computing systems, such as computer clusters, the acquisition of accurate performance information is not an issue; however, this is not true in the grid where users have very limited knowledge of the participating resources. Usually, grid information services (GIS) are implemented to resolve this matter. Both static and dynamic information are accumulated and maintained by the GIS. The Globus MDS [9] is one widely implemented and deployed GIS. Since the accuracy of performance prediction information particularly on resources is hardly guaranteed, other techniques, such as advance reservation (e.g., [22]) have been actively studied.

3.3. Fault-Tolerant vs. Non-fault-Tolerant

In a grid environment, failure is the rule, not the exception; hence, fault tolerance must be considered. Resources constituted in a grid are autonomous; thus, their availabilities and capacities are subject to change. In addition to resources, applications deployed in grids vary significantly. Example sources of these uncertainties are resource disconnection, resource anomaly/failure, process suspension and abortion, bugs in applications, and grid middleware faults. Therefore, it is not an option, but essential to design scheduling algorithms to be fault-tolerant/resilient.

A scheduling scheme typically deals with resource/application failures either implicitly or explicitly. Task duplication is the most common technique to implicitly tolerate these failures, whereas checkpoint and migration, and rescheduling are two dominant explicit fault-tolerance strategies.

Task duplication—particularly in BoT scheduling in grids—plays a significant role in three respects: (1) fault-tolerance, (2) the improvement of resource utilization, and (3) the reduction of SL. On the contrary, replica tasks may result in resource wastage; thus, the number of replicas and the selection of replication candidate tasks among many other issues should be carefully considered when designing a duplication scheme.

Rescheduling takes place not only for fault-tolerance, but for other purposes, such as balancing load and increasing throughput. For example, while the job is running, if other powerful resources previously allocated to other jobs become available and the grid scheduler estimates they will enable better performance for the job, a decision to reschedule may be made. Although rescheduling is an attractive alternative to improve performance, there are challenging issues to be addressed, such as checkpointing if migration is involved. There are occasions when migrating a job is too costly due to time-consuming checkpointing [23].

4. A Survey of Bot Scheduling Algorithms

This section presents a set of well-known scheduling algorithms (Table 1) and other interesting approaches that can be used for grids. They are selected from many other previously proposed scheduling algorithms for both their simplicity and practicality.

Table 1. BoT scheduling algorithms

Algorithm	Application model	Scheduling mode	Fault-tolerance	Performance info dependency
RR [24]	CBoT	dynamic	implicit	no
Max-min and *min-min* [27, 28]	CBoT & DBoT	static	no	yes
Sufferage [27, 28]	CBoT & DBoT	static	no	yes
XSufferage [16]	DBoT	static	no	yes
SA [29]	DBoT	dynamic	implicit	no
MQD [30]	CBoT	dynamic	implicit	no
SIL [30]	DBoT	dynamic	implicit	no

4.1. List Scheduling with Round-Robin Order Replication (RR) Algorithm

RR [24] is a grid-scheduling algorithm for independent coarse-grained tasks. As the name implies, its distinctiveness comes from the round-robin order replication scheme that makes replicas of running tasks in a round-robin fashion after conducting list scheduling for all of the unscheduled tasks. *RR* first randomly assigns a task to each host in the grid, and waits until one or more of those assigned hosts complete their tasks. On the completion of a task, the next unscheduled task is dispatched to the host on which the completed task has run. In this way, faster resources are likely to receive more tasks. Once all of the tasks are dispatched, *RR* starts replicating running tasks in the expectation that some or all of these replicas will finish earlier than their originals. *RR* performs scheduling without dynamic information on resources and tasks; despite this, the algorithm is comparable in performance to other scheduling heuristics that do require such performance information. Similar approaches can be found in [23, 24] with minor differences in their replication schemes and fault-tolerance mechanism.

4.2. *Max-min* and *min-min* Algorithms

Max-min [27, 28] selects the unscheduled task, for which the minimum earliest completion time over all the hosts is the longest among all of the unscheduled tasks. The selected task is allocated to the host on which the minimum earliest completion time is expected. The only difference in distinguishing *min-min* [27, 28] from *max-min* is the task selection scheme. Specifically, *min-min* gives priority to the task with the shortest, earliest completion time. At the time of each scheduling event, *max-min* is more likely to schedule the longest task, and *min-min* the shortest task.

4.3. *Sufferage* Algorithm

Sufferage [27, 28] makes scheduling decisions on the basis of the sufferage value of a task, defined as the difference between its earliest and second-earliest completion times. At each scheduling decision, *Sufferage* computes sufferage values of all of the unscheduled tasks, and schedules the task for which the sufferage value is the largest. This approach can be effective, since it avoids a significant increase in makespan, although it is no guarantee that the overall SL will be shortened.

4.4. *XSufferage* Algorithm

XSufferage [16] extends the *Sufferage* scheduling heuristic [27, 28] by accounting for data-sharing. It makes scheduling decisions on the basis of the sufferage value of a task, which in *XSufferage* is defined as the difference between its earliest and second-earliest site-level completion times. While sufferage values used in *Sufferage* are host-level, those used by *XSufferage* are site-level. The sufferage value of a task is used as a measure of possible increase on makespan; that is, a task with a large sufferage value indicates that the completion time of the task increases significantly, causing a probable increase in makespan, if the task is not assigned to the host on which the earliest site-level completion time is attainable. Therefore, the larger the sufferage value of a task, the higher its scheduling priority.

For each scheduling decision, *Xsufferage* computes sufferage values of all of the unscheduled tasks, and schedules the task for which the sufferage value is the largest. This approach can be effective, since it avoids a significant increase in makespan, although it is no guarantee that the overall makespan will be shortened. *XSufferage* assumes access to 100% accurate performance information on resources and tasks.

4.5. Storage Affinity (SA) Algorithm

SA [29] primarily aims to minimise data transfer by making scheduling decisions incorporating the location of transferred data. It considers task replication as soon as a host becomes available between the time the last unscheduled task is assigned and the time the last running task completes its execution.

SA determines task–host assignments on the basis of 'the storage affinity metric'. The storage affinity of a task to a host is the amount of the task's input data already stored in the site to which the host belongs. Although the scheduling decision *SA* makes is between task and host, storage affinity is calculated between task and site; this is because, in the grid model used for *SA*, each site in the grid uses a single data repository that can be equally accessible by the hosts in the site.

For each scheduling decision, SA calculates the storage affinity values of all unscheduled tasks and dispatches the task with the largest storage affinity value. If none of the tasks has a positive storage affinity value, one is scheduled at random. By the time this initial scheduling is completed, there will be as many as $|H|$ running tasks, leaving all $|H|$ hosts busy. On the completion of any of these running tasks, *SA* starts task replication. Each of the remaining running tasks is considered for replication, and the best one is selected. The selection decision is based on the storage affinity value and the number of replicas.

4.6 Multiple Queues with Duplication (MQD) Algorithm

MQD [30] makes scheduling decisions that account for the recent workload pattern of resources. The rationale behind *MQD* is that computational hosts receive tasks as proportional as possible to their recent performance. It also adopts a duplication scheme to significantly improve resource utilization, leading to better schedules.

MQD consists of three major phases—initial scheduling, main scheduling, and duplication. The $|H|$ smallest tasks in a given BoT application are initially assigned to computing resources to more realistically identify the current performance of these resources. In the meantime, the remaining tasks are grouped and placed into a number of queues. On completion of a task, the performance ranking of the host on which the task is completed is computed. The performance of a host used for computing its performance ranking is quantified by dividing the workload of the last task the host completed by the amount of time taken for that task. This performance ranking indicates queue from which the next task for the host is selected; for example, if the performance ranking of a host is the second best among all the hosts, the first unscheduled task in the second queue will be selected for scheduling. When the selected queue is empty, *MQD* considers task duplication with first the queues before it and after it. Task duplications may take place in spite of the existence of some unscheduled tasks, for the sake of efficient task-host mapping, i.e., better load balancing. Every scheduled and yet uncompleted task has equal opportunity to get duplicated; that is, the number of replicas for each running task is intended to be the same.

4.7. Shared-Input-Data-Based Listing (SIL) Algorithm

Like *XSufferage* and *SA*, *SIL* [30] is specifically designed for scheduling DBoT applications on grids. As an increasing number of applications—particularly in bioinformatics, data mining, and image processing—deal with massive amounts of data, a fundamental scheduling issue arises when exploiting grids with these types of applications: the minimization of data transfer.

SIL uses an intuitive approach to detect data-sharing patterns in DBoT applications. Specifically, for tasks of a given application, it identifies data-sharing-patterns in these tasks, and then groups the tasks into a number of lists, each of which is intended to be scheduled onto the same site in the grid to minimize data transfer. These task lists are further rearranged according to the actual transfer amount (ATA) of a task. The actual transfer amount is defined as:

$$ATA(T_j, S_i) = TA(T_j) - \sum_{d \in (I_j \cap DAT(D_i))} |d|$$

where $TA(T_j)$ is the original transfer amount of T_j, $DAT(D_i)$ is the data already transferred to D_i, and $|d|$ is the amount of data object d. Since the performance of grid resources fluctuates, the lists are reorganized dynamically during application runtime. To efficiently deal with the dynamicity of grid resources, *SIL* adopts task duplication, which helps to avoid serious schedule increases. For example, one or more tasks may run for unexpectedly long durations, significantly increasing the overall schedule due to the overload or abnormal behaviors of the resources on which they run or are transferred.

4.8. Other Approaches

FIFO protocol
As the name suggests, the first-in-first-out (FIFO) scheduling protocol ensures that the first task presented to the system is the first one completed; such a property may be desirable in terms of fairness to users. One such protocol is studied in [31]. In the study, the system consists of a set of workstations whose computational power is heterogeneous; the underlying communication network is assumed to be homogeneous. The bag of tasks to be scheduled is assumed to be independent, and have identical computation and communication sizes. The aim is then to minimize the workspan, which in the context of the study is to complete the required amount of work, using the assigned set of workstations, in as little amount of time as possible. An equivalent problem for the above set of conditions is to complete as much work as possible within a set amount of time.

The paper shows that under the aforementioned assumptions, the FIFO protocol provides an asymptotically optimal solution to the bag of task scheduling problem. In other word, given a large enough time periods, the FIFO protocol completes as much work as any other scheduling protocols. It should be noted that in a FIFO scheduling protocol, one has to present the execution order of tasks to the system; the FIFO protocol then ensures the completion order is the same as the initial order of the tasks. The study of [31] shows that the initial order completely determines the schedule of tasks to the system. That is, given an initial ordering of tasks, there is a unique solution that determines the work to be assigned to each workstation, as well as the associated communications. Further, the asymptotical optimality of the FIFO protocol holds for any initial ordering of tasks. That is, for any pair of tasks ordering Σ_1, Σ_2, the work output $W(\Sigma_1) = W(\Sigma_2)$.

Linear programming
While the scheduling problem in general is NP-hard, certain constraints and assumptions reduces the problem to a tractable one that can be solved in polynomial time using methods as well known as linear programming (LP). In [32], the problem for scheduling bag of task applications on networks structured as single-level trees as well as multi-level trees are discussed. The processors, as well as the underlying communication network are assumed to be heterogeneous. The problem considered is that of fair and efficient scheduling of applications on the target network. For simplicity it is assumed that the tasks for an application have the same computation and communication requirements, although they can differ between applications. In the context of fairness, a linear utility function is assumed for each application; the well-known max-min fairness criterion is used in the paper, whereby the aim is to maximize the minimum utility of an application. A linear programming formulation, providing max-min fair solution is then presented. The solution can be computed in polynomial time. The results in the paper give an interesting insight as to the criteria for max-min fairness in star networks (i.e., a one-level rooted tree): applications with higher communication to computation ratio are scheduled on processors with higher bandwidth.

While such a characteristic may be expected and has been used in scheduling heuristics, the paper has given proof that this is the case for star networks.

Non-cooperative scheduling

In recent years, there has been an interest in the use of game theoretic models for the design and analysis of distributed systems, including scheduling [33, 17]. In the context of scheduling, non-cooperative scheduling involves multiple schedulers (players) that act independently and selfishly. The aim of each scheduler is to maximize its own utility (regardless of the other schedulers); as a consequence, the system as a whole would tend towards the Nash equilibrium. The Nash equilibrium for the game is a *strategy profile* $\mathbf{r} = \{\mathbf{r}_1, \mathbf{r}_2, \cdots, \mathbf{r}_n\}$ in which no player (scheduler) can decrease its utility by unilaterally changing its strategy. In [33], a non-cooperative scheduling framework is presented for bag of task applications. The results show their framework yields a relatively inefficient Nash equilibrium.

Algorithms for cycle stealing

Within the field of distributed computing and volunteer computing, a relatively new term "cycle stealing" has emerged. A typical scenario involves a user and a provider, whereby a user uses the resources of the provider whenever it is idle—the owner is absent. Once the owner returns, the resources of the provider are no longer available to the user; depending on the context of the problem this may imply losing all computed results since the last "save-point".

Cycle stealing is studied in [35, 36], where a user is assumed to have large amount of identical tasks (i.e., bag of tasks with uniform computation and communication sizes) to be executed. The conflicting problem for the user is then the following: on the one hand there is assumed to be a *large* fixed overhead for communication setup between the user and the provider, meaning the user is inclined to send large amount of work at once and communicate infrequently; on the other hand, the possible lost of all work by the return of the owner means the user should send small amount of work each time and therefore communicate more frequently. There are at least two debatable points with the suggested problem: (1) whether a relatively large communication setup is reasonable in practice, and (2) the possibility of work being suspended but not lost when the owner returns. In [34], the author discusses schedules for the above cycle stealing problem, given that the probability distribution of the provider's availability is known. Optimal schedules are shown when the probability distributions are concave. Approximate schedules are discussed for heavy-tailed distribution. The work presented in [34] builds on earlier results and study in [35, 36].

5. Related Projects

As grids become a new generation of high-performance computing systems, an increasing number of organizations, including universities, research laboratories, and companies, have initiated various grid projects. In the late 1990's, most of these projects focused on developing architectural components and middleware. Representative examples are the Globus toolkit [37], Condor [38, 39], AppLes [40, 41], NetSolve/GridSolve [42, 43] and Nimrod/G [44]. However, in recent years, a much broader range of projects—to better use grids—have formed. In this section, we introduce a set of recent projects that are closely related to our interest (i.e., BoT scheduling on grids).

5.1. Bayanihan

The Bayanihan computing .NET framework [45, 46] enables its users to mainly run computationally intensive parallelizable applications on volunteered computers through web services. Specifically, users (computational clients) submit their tasks (e.g., BoT applications) via 'computational web services' and these tasks are further sent to a *PoolService* web service, which creates pools of these tasks, dispatches them to idle volunteered computers, and retrieves and returns results (Figure 3); thus, the technical details of the grid resources used for the tasks are transparent to users. Since web services play a key role in Bayanihan computing .NET, any devices, e.g., PDAs and mobile phones—capable of accessing web services—can be used to launch tasks. As its name, Bayanihan computing .NET, imples, it is based on Microsoft .NET [47]. Resources exploited by tasks using this framework are primarily individual computing resources (e.g., PCs) registered for 'volunteer computing [48].' This idea is similar to projects, such as SETI@home and Folding@home; however, the use of Bayanihan computing .NET is not confined to a specific type of applications; hence, it is a generic grid computing framework.

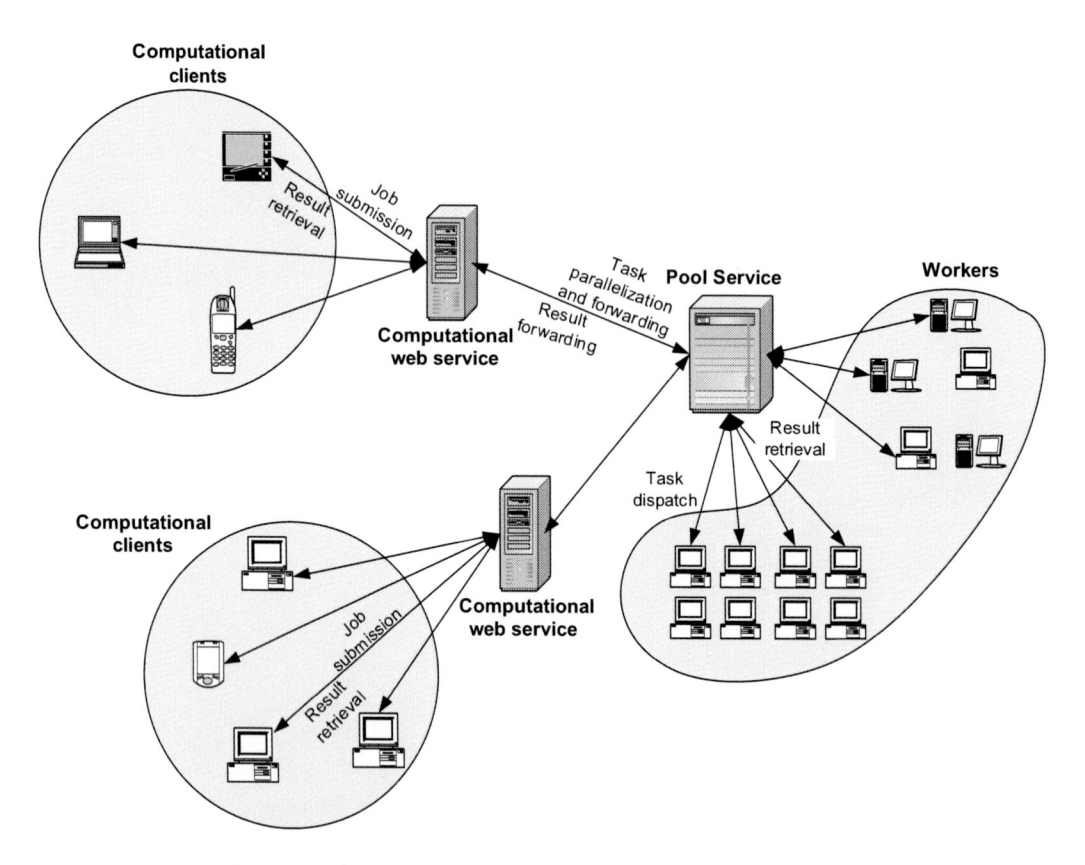

Figure 3. Volunteer computing using Bayanihan computing .NET.

5.2. Berkeley Open Infrastructure for Network Computing (BOINC)

BOINC [49, 50] is a software platform that allows primarily scientists to perform their 'computational experiments' on individually owned computers (e.g., PCs and Macintoshes) around world. It was initially developed for the SETI@home project; however, the use of this free/open source middleware system is now beyond its original purpose. Any volunteer computing projects can be set up with BOINC. Like Bayanihan computing .NET, the main idea is to exploit idle computing power for large-scale scientific projects. Diverse applications and operating systems including Windows, Unix/Linux and Mac OS X are supported. Two core components of BOINC are (1) a server complex—composed of scheduling and data servers—playing as a coordinating system, and (2) client software running actual project-specific applications on participating computers. They communicate with each other to distribute, process, and return work units. BOINC is the single most dominant platform for volunteer computing projects from famous SETI@home, Einstein@Home and Rosetta@home [51] to more recent PrimeGrid [52], HashCrash@home [53] and Cosmology@Home [54].

5.3. OurGrid

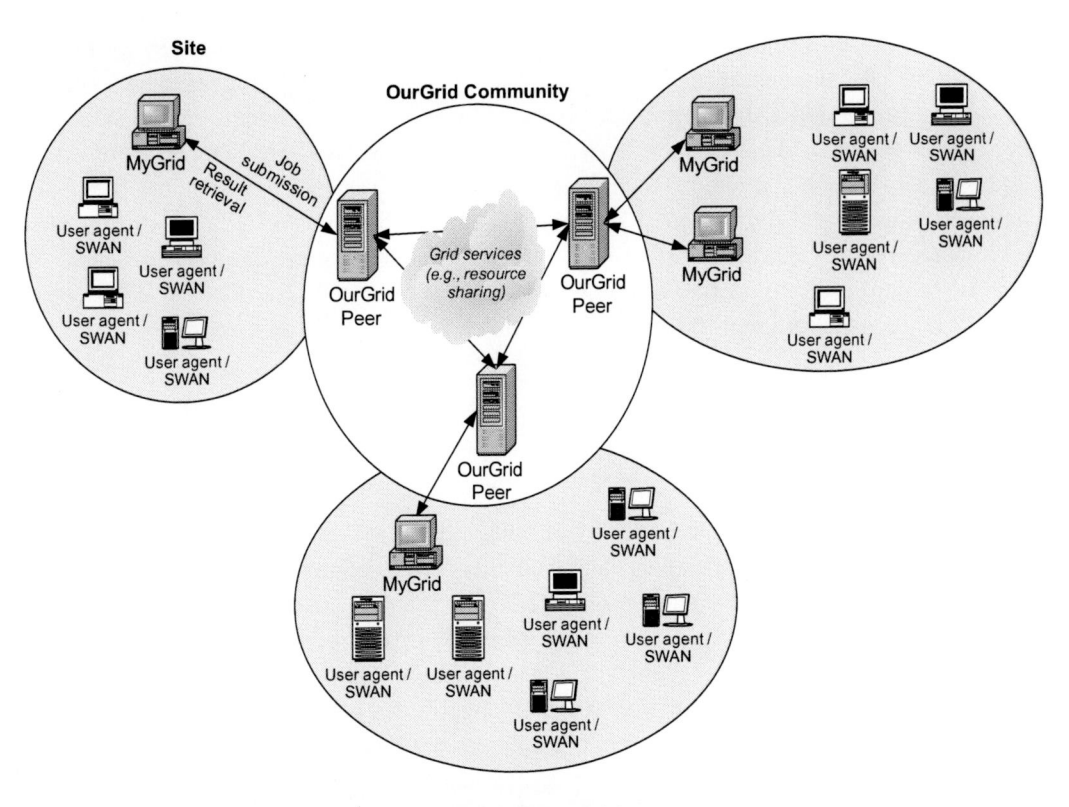

Figure 4. OurGrid.

The main idea behind OurGrid [55, 56] is to provide massive computing capacity primarily to BoT applications by aggregating idle computing power of workstations and PCs at participating entities (small and medium size research laboratories); in other words, OurGrid, as in most other CPU cycle stealing projects, aims at better resource utilization. The OurGrid software package largely relies on Java technology [57], and it is available for Linux and Windows (NT family). It consists of four major components (Figure 4)—Peer, MyGrid, User agent, and SWAN. Each site in OurGrid designates an OurGrid Peer that coordinates with other Peers (sites) to facilitate resource sharing between sites. A user launches jobs using the MyGrid broker and the execution of these jobs is managed by the User agent component. SWAN is the sandboxing component that protects grid resources from unexpected behaviors of grid jobs.

5.4. XtremWeb

XtremWeb [58, 59] is a middleware software platform for Global computing—also known as 'volunteer computing', 'public-resource computing' or 'peer-to-peer computing. In essence, it is similar to BOINC in that its primary design goal is to use underutilized computational resources (i.e., volunteered and previously registered PCs) to support large-scale and computationally intensive scientific projects. Another similarity is that XtremWeb is non-profit and free/open source software. The supported operating systems are Linux and Windows (NT family). XtremWeb consists of three software components: (1) worker for executing actual computation on participated machines, (2) client for submitting tasks and retrieving results, and (3) server as a central controller that maintains different project applications and their data, and that coordinates between workers and clients. Note that, a computer can be either a client or worker, or both. The worker on a volunteer computer continually monitors if the computer becomes available (i.e., idle) for XtremWeb originated tasks. Three typical scenarios used to determine the availability are the user presence, the presence of non-interactive tasks, and time. The scheduler in XtremWeb firsts selects a group of tasks and dispatches them to the actual scheduler for allocating appropriate resources for the tasks.

6. Conclusion

In this chapter, we have presented a survey of scheduling algorithms for BoT applications —a typical class of parallel applications deployed in grid environments. The application and system models were detailed with common performance metrics used in BoT scheduling. We have classified BoT applications into two categories: computationally intensive and data-intensive, although in some cases, this distinction is blurred. Our taxonomy on the approaches employed in BoT scheduling is structured as a contrast-based model that is different from the typical hierarchical counterpart. According to our taxonomy, a BoT application can be described using a combination of those contrasted classes. To more clearly understand how different BoT scheduling approaches can be classified using this taxonomy, a set of representative algorithms have been presented. In addition to these well-known algorithms, several other interesting approaches including linear programming and game theoretic were introduced to provide a more comprehensive survey to readers. Finally, grid projects that are closely related to BoT scheduling were described.

Over the past decade, an increasing number of grid scheduling algorithms for the BoT application model have been proposed. Despite these efforts, most of them have difficulty in guaranteeing good quality of schedules. Like these algorithms, we previously approached the problem of scheduling BoT applications with an assumption that a BoT application consists of either computationally or data-intensive tasks [30]. Most existing algorithms have been developed with this assumption; in other words, a scheduling algorithm is specific to either of these two types, because a particular algorithm for computationally intensive BoT applications makes scheduling decisions almost exclusively depending on the performance of computing resources, where as that for data-intensive BoT applications performs its scheduling based heavily on data transfers. Consequently, it is difficult to use a single algorithm for BoT applications regardless of application characteristics. This assumption should be reviewed and loosened when designing algorithms in BoT scheduling. Another future research needed is regarding the use and estimation of performance information on both applications and resources. As mentioned earlier, grids are very dynamic and heterogeneous in nature; thus, the assumption that the acquisition of perfect performance information is possible should not be made. However, such information may be accurately estimated in some scenarios with specific applications and platforms. In this case, the incorporation of performance information into scheduling algorithms would be a great advantage leading to good schedules, or even optimal schedules.

References

[1] Message Passing Interface Forum. (1994). MPI: a message passing interface standard. *International Journal of Supercomputer Applications*, **8**(3/4), 165–414.

[2] Geist, A., Beguelin, A., Dongarra, J., Jiang, W., Manchek, R., and Sunderam, V. S. (1994). PVM: Parallel Virtual Machine: A Users' Guide and Tutorial for Networked Parallel Computing, Cambridge, MA: The MIT Press.

[3] OpenMP Architecture Review Board. (1997). *The OpenMP: A Proposed Industry Standard API for Shared Memory Programming.* http://www.openmp.org.

[4] *IEEE, Threads Extension for Portable Operating Systems* (Draft 10), 1996.

[5] High Performance Fortran Forum. (1992). High Performance Fortran Language Specification, *Technical Report*. Rice University.

[6] Krishnamurthy, A., Culler, D. E., Dusseau, A., Goldstein, S. C., Lumetta, S., von Eicken, T., and Yelick, K. (1993). Parallel programming in Split-C. *Proceedings of the 1993 ACM/IEEE conference on Supercomputing*, Oregon, OR: IEEE Computer Society Press, 262–273.

[7] Clermont, P., and Paris, N. (1994). HyperC: portable parallel programming in C. *Proceedings of the eighth international parallel processing symposium*. H.J. Siegel, Eds., Cancu´n, NM: IEEE Computer Society Press, 682–687.

[8] Bodin, F., Beckman, P., Gannon, D., Yang, S., Kesavan, S., Malony, A., and Mohr, B. (1993). Implementing a parallel C++ runtime system for scalable parallel systems. *Proceedings of the 1993 ACM/IEEE conference on Supercomputing*, Oregon, OR: IEEE Computer Society Press, 588–597.

[9] Globus Monitoring and Discovering Service (MDS), http://www.globus.org/toolkit/mds/.
[10] Anderson, D. P., Cobb, J., Korpela, E., Lebofsky, M., and Werthimer, D. (2002). SETI@home: An experiment in public-resource computing. *Communications of the ACM*, **45**(11):56–61.
[11] Larson, S. M., Snow, C. D., Shirts, M., and Pande, V. S. (2003). Folding@Home and Genome@Home: Using distributed computing to tackle previously intractable problems in computational biology. *Computational Genomics*.
[12] Einstein@Home, http://einstein.phys.uwm.edu/.
[13] Altschul, S. F., Gish, W., Miller, W., Myers, E. W., and Lipman, D. J. (1990). Basic local alignment search tool. *Journal of Molecular Biology*, **1**(215):403–410.
[14] Stiles, J., Bartol, T., Salpeter, E., and Salpeter, M. (1998). Monte Carlo simulation of neuromuscular transmitter release using MCell, a general simulator of cellular physiological processes. *Computational Neuroscience*, 279–284.
[15] Rogers, S., and Ywak, D. (1991). Steady and Unsteady Solutions of the Incompressible Navier-Stokes Equations. *AIAA Journal*, **29**(4):603–610.
[16] Casanova, H., Legrand, A., Zagorodnov, D., and Berman, F. (2000). Heuristics for scheduling parameter sweep applications in grid environments. *Proceedings of the 9th Heterogeneous Computing Workshop (HCW)*, 349–363.
[17] Subrata, R., Zomaya, A. Y., and Landfeldt, B. Game Theoretic Approach for Load Balancing in Computational Grids. *IEEE Transactions on Parallel and Distributed Systems*, in press.
[18] Jain, R. (1991). *The Art of Computer Systems Performance Analysis: Techniques for Experimental Design, Measurement, Simulation and Modelling*. New York: Wiley-Interscience.
[19] Wolski, R. (1998). Dynamically forecasting network performance using the network weather service. *Journal of Cluster Computing*, **1**(1):119–132.
[20] Wolski, R., Spring, N. T., and Hayes, J. (1999). The network weather service: A distributed resource performance forecasting system, *Journal of Future Generation Computing Systems*, **15**(5):757–768.
[21] The network weather service home page, http://nws.cs.ucsb.edu.
[22] Smith, W., Foster, I., and Taylor, V. (2000). Scheduling with advanced reservations. *Proceedings of the 14th International Parallel and Distributed Processing Symposium*, IEEE Computer Society, Cancun, pp. 127–132.
[23] MacLaren, J., Sakellariou, R., Krishnakumar, K. T., Garibaldi, J., and Ouelhadj, D. (2004). Towards Service Level Agreement Based Scheduling on the Grid, *position paper in Workshop on Planning and Scheduling for Web and Grid Services*, www.isi.edu/ikcap/icaps04-workshop/final/maclaren.pdf.
[24] Fujimoto, N., and Hagihara, K. (2003). Near-optimal dynamic task scheduling of independent coarse-grained tasks onto a computational grid. *Proceedings of Int'l Conf. Parallel Processing*, 391–398.
[25] da Silva, D. P., Cirne, W., and Brasileiro, F. V. (2003). Trading Cycles for Information: Using Replication to Schedule Bag-of-Tasks Applications on Computational Grids. *Proceedings of the 9th international European conference on parallel processing*, Klagenfurt, Austria, 169–180.

[26] Anglano, C., and Canonico, M. (2005). Fault-Tolerant Scheduling for Bag-of-Tasks Grid Applications. *Proceedings of European Grid Conference*, Amsterdam, The Netherlands, 630–639.
[27] Ibarra, O. H., and Kim, C. E. (1977). Heuristic Algorithms for Scheduling Independent Tasks on Nonidentical Processors, *Journal of the ACM*, **24**(2):280–289.
[28] Maheswaran, M., Ali, S., Siegel, H. J., Hensgen, D., and Freund, R.(1999). Dynamic Matching and Scheduling of a Class of Independent Tasks onto Heterogeneous Computing Systems, *Proceedings of the eighth IEEE Heterogeneous Computing Workshop*, 30–44.
[29] Santos-Neto, E., Cirne, W., Brasileiro, F., and Lima, A. (2004). Exploiting Replication and Data Reuse to Efficiently Schedule Data-Intensive Applications on Grids, *Proceedings of the tenth Workshop on Job Scheduling Strategies for Parallel Processing*, 210–232.
[30] Lee, Y. C., and Zomaya, A. Y. (2007). Practical Scheduling Bag–of–Tasks Applications on Grids with Dynamic Resilience, *IEEE Transactions on Computers*, **56**(6):815–825.
[31] Adler, M., Gong, Y., and Rosenberg, A. L. (2003). Optimal Sharing of Bags of Tasks in Heterogeneous Clusters. *Proceedings of the fifteenth annual ACM symposium on parallel algorithms and architectures*, ACM Press, New York, USA, 1–10.
[32] Beaumont, O., Carter, L., Ferrante, J., and Legrand, A. Centralized versus Distributed Schedulers for Bag-of-Tasks Applications. *IEEE Transactions on Parallel and Distributed Systems*, in press.
[33] Legrand, A., and Touati, C. (2007). Non-Cooperative Scheduling of Multiple Bag-of-Task Applications. *Proceedings of the 26th IEEE International Conference on Computer Communications (INFOCOM)*, Anchorage, Alaska, USA, 427–435.
[34] Rosenberg, A. L. (2002). Optimal Schedules for Cycle-Stealing in a Network of Workstations with a Bag-of-Tasks Workload. *IEEE Transactions on Parallel and Distributed Systems*, **13**(2):179–191.
[35] Bhatt, S. N., Chung, F. R. K., Leighton, F. T., and Rosenberg, A. L. (1997). On Optimal Strategies for Cycle-Stealing in Networks of Workstations. *IEEE Transactions on Computers*, **46**(5):545–557.
[36] Rosenberg, A. L. (1998). Guidelines for Data-Parallel Cycle-Stealing in Networks of Workstations. *Proceedings of the 12th. International Parallel Processing Symposium on International Parallel Processing Symposium (IPPS/SPDP)*, 519–523.
[37] The Globus project, http://www.globus.org/.
[38] The Condor Project, University of Wisconsin Condor: High Throughput Computing, http://www.cs.wisc.edu/condor/
[39] Litzkow, M. J., Livny, M., Mutka, M. W. (1988). Condor—A hunter of idle workstations. *Proceedings of the 8th International Conference on Distributed Computer Systems*, IEEE Computer Society, San Jose, 104–111.
[40] Berman, F., and Wolski, R. (1997). The AppLeS Project: A Status Report, *8Pth NEC Research Symposium*, Berlin, Germany.
[41] Casanova, H., Obertelli, G., Berman, F., and Wolski, R. (2000). The AppLeS Parameter sweep template: User-level middleware for the Grid, *Scientific Programming*, **8**: 111–126.

[42] Casanova, H., Dongarra, J. (1997). Netsolve: A network-enabled server for solving computational science problems. *International Journal of Supercomputer Applications and High Performance Computing*, **11**:212–223.

[43] Project Description—GridSolve: A system for Grid-enabling general purpose scientific computing environments, http://icl.cs.utk.edu/netsolvedev/files/gridsolve/GridSolve-description.pdf.

[44] Buyya, R., Ahramson, D., and Giddy, J. (2000). Nimrod/G: An architecture for a resource management and scheduling system in a global computational grid. *Proceedings of HPC ASIA'2000*, China, IEEE Computer Society, 283–289.

[45] Sarmenta, L. F. G., Chua, S. J. V., Echevarria, P., Mendoza, J. M., Santos, R.-R., Tan, S., and Lozada, R. (2002). Bayanihan Computing .NET: Grid Computing with XML Web Services. *Proceedings of 2nd IEEE International Symposium on Cluster Computing and the Grid (CCGrid 2002)*, Berlin, Germany, IEEE Computer Society, 434–435.

[46] Bayanihan Computing Group, http://www.bayanihancomputing.net, accessed on September 21, 2007.

[47] Microsoft Corporation, Roadmap for XML in the .NET Framework, http://support.microsoft.com/kb/313651, accessed on September 20, 2007.

[48] Sarmenta, L. F. G. (2001). Volunteer computing. Ph.D. thesis, Massachusetts Institute of Technology, http://www.cag.lcs.mit.edu/bayanihan.

[49] Anderson, D. P. (2004). BOINC: A System for Public-Resource Computing and Storage. *Prooceedings of the 5th IEEE/ACM International Workshop on Grid Computing*.

[50] Berkeley Open Infrastructure for Network Computing (BOINC), http://boinc.berkeley.edu/, accessed on September 21, 2007.

[51] Rosetta@home, http://boinc.bakerlab.org/rosetta/, accessed on September 21, 2007.

[52] PrimeGrid, http://www.primegrid.com/, accessed on September 21, 2007.

[53] HashCrash, http://boinc.banaan.org/hashclash/, accessed on September 21, 2007.

[54] Cosmology@Home, http://cosmos.astro.uiuc.edu/cosmohome/, accessed on September 21, 2007.

[55] OurGrid, http://www.ourgrid.org/, accessed on September 22, 2007.

[56] Cirne, W., Brasileiro, F., Andrade, N., Costa, L., Andrade, A., Novaes, R., and Mowbray, M. (2006). Labs of the World, Unite!!!. *Journal of Grid Computing*, **4**(3):225–246.

[57] Java technology, http://java.sun.com, accessed on September 22, 2007.

[58] Fedak, G., Germain, C., N'eri, V., and Cappello, F. (2001). XtremWeb: A Generic Global Computing System. *Proceedings of IEEE Int. Symp. on Cluster Computing and the Grid*.

[59] XtremWeb, http://www.lri.fr/~fedak/XtremWeb/, accessed on September 21, 2007.

Chapter 9

SUPPORT AND EFFICIENCY OF NESTED PARALLELISM IN OPENMP IMPLEMENTATIONS

Panagiotis E. Hadjidoukas and Vassilios V. Dimakopoulos[†]*
Department of Computer Science
University of Ioannina
Ioannina, Greece, GR-45110

Abstract

Nested parallelism has been a major feature of OpenMP since its very beginnings. As a programming style, it provides an elegant solution for a wide class of parallel applications, with the potential to achieve substantial utilization of the available computational resources, in situations where outer-loop parallelism simply can not. Notwithstanding its significance, nested parallelism support was slow to find its way into OpenMP implementations, commercial and research ones alike. Even nowadays, the level of support is varying greatly among compilers and runtime systems.

In this work, we take a closer look at OpenMP implementations with respect to their level of support for nested parallelism. We classify them into three broad categories: those that provide full support, those that provide partial support and those that provide no support at all. The systems surveyed include commercial and research ones. Additionally, we proceed to quantify the efficiency of the implementation. With a representative set of compilers that provide adequate support, we perform a comparative performance evaluation. We evaluate both the incurred overheads and their overall behavior, using microbenchmarks and a full-fledged application. The results are interesting because they show that full support of nested parallelism does not necessarily guarantee scalable performance.

1. Introduction

OpenMP [27] has become a standard paradigm for programming symmetric shared memory multiprocessors (SMP), as it offers the advantage of simple and incremental parallel program development, in a high abstraction level. Its usage is continuously increasing as small

---
*E-mail address: phadjido@cs.uoi.gr
[†]E-mail address: dimako@cs.uoi.gr

SMP machines have become the mainstream architecture even in the personal computer market. Nested parallelism, a major feature of OpenMP, has the potential of benefiting a broad class of parallel applications to achieve optimal load balance and speedup, by allowing multiple levels of parallelism to be active simultaneously. This is particularly relevant these days in emerging SMP environments with multicore processors.

For applications that have enough (and balanced) outer-loop parallelism, a small number of coarse threads is usually enough to produce satisfactory speedups. In many other cases though, including situations with multiple nested loops, or recursive and irregular parallel applications, threads should be able to create new teams of threads because only a large number of threads has the potential to achieve good utilization of the computational resources.

Although many OpenMP compilation systems provide support for nested parallelism, there has been no comprehensive study up to now regarding the level and the efficiency of such a support. It can be seen that the existing OpenMP implementations exhibit significant runtime overheads which are mainly due to their adopted kernel-level threading model. In general, there are several design issues and performance limitations that need to be addressed effectively.

This work deals with the main issues that are related to the runtime support of nested parallelism in OpenMP. We survey existing implementations and discuss the type of support they offer. Based on previous knowledge and infrastructure, we also develop a set of appropriate microbenchmarks that measure the runtime overheads of OpenMP when nested parallelism is exploited. A comparative performance evaluation assesses the advantages and limitations of several OpenMP implementations, both commercial and research ones.

The rest of this chapter is organized as follows: in Section 2. we discuss nested parallelism in general. We also present the mechanisms OpenMP provides for controlling nested parallelism. In Section 3. we survey existing OpenMP implementations and discuss the level of nested parallelism support they provide; both commercial and research compilers are examined. Section 4. is devoted to the evaluation of the performance of a number of compilers when it comes to nested parallelism, while Section 5. summarizes the results of this study.

2. Nested Parallelism

Nested parallelism is becoming increasingly important as it enables the programmer to express a wide class of parallel algorithms in a natural way and to exploit efficiently both task and loop-level parallelism. Several studies with production codes and application kernels have shown the significant performance improvements of using nested parallelism. Despite some deficiencies in the current support of nested parallelization, many OpenMP applications have benefited from it and managed to increase their scalability mainly on large SMP machines [1,2,5,31].

2.1. What OpenMP Specifies

Nested parallelism in OpenMP is effected either by a nested `parallel` construct (i.e. a `parallel` region within the lexical extend of another `parallel` region) or by an *orphaned* construct, where a `parallel` region appears in a function which is called within the dynamic extend of another `parallel` region in the program.

In Fig. 1 the classic example of Fibonacci numbers is shown; the nth Fibonacci number is calculated recursively as the sum the $(n-1)$th and the $(n-2)$th, through an orphaned `parallel` construct. In each recursive call, two threads are spawned resulting in an exponential total population. Recursion-based nested parallelism is an elegant programming methodology but can easily lead to an overwhelming number of threads.

```
int fib(int n)
{
  int f1,f2;
  if (n < 2) return 1;
  #pragma omp parallel sections num_threads(2)
  {
    #pragma omp section
      f1 = fib(n-1);           /* Recursive call */
    #pragma omp section
      f2 = fib(n-2);           /* Recursive call */
  }
  return f1+f2;
}
```

Figure 1. Fibonacci numbers using nested parallelism.

The OpenMP specifications leave support for nested parallelism as optional. Implementations are considered compliant even if they don't support nested parallelism; they are allowed to execute the nested `parallel` region a thread encounters, by a team of just 1 thread, i.e. nested `parallel` regions may be serialized. Because of the difficulty in handling a possibly huge number of threads, many implementations provide support for nested parallelism but with certain limitations. For example, there may exist an upper limit on the depth of nesting or on the total number of simultaneously active threads.

Nested parallelism can be enabled or disabled either during program startup through the `OMP_NESTED` environment variable or dynamically (any time at runtime) through an `omp_set_nested()` call. The `omp_get_nested()` call queries the runtime system whether nested parallelism is enabled or not. In runtime systems that do not support nested parallelism, enabling or disabling it has no effect whatsoever.

To control the number of threads that will comprise a team, the current version of OpenMP (2.5) provides the following mechanism: the default number of threads per `parallel` region is specified through the `OMP_NUM_THREADS` environment variable. In the absence of such a variable, the default is implementation dependent. The `omp_set_num_threads()` call can be used at runtime to set the number of threads that will be utilized in subsequent `parallel` regions. Finally, a `num_threads(n)` clause that appears in a `parallel` directive requests this particular region to be executed by n threads.

However, the actual number of threads dispatched in a `parallel` region depends also on other things. OpenMP provides a mechanism for the *dynamic adjustment* of the number of threads which, if activated, allows the implementation to spawn fewer threads than what is specified by the user. In addition to dynamic adjustment, factors that may affect the actual number of threads include the nesting level of the region, the support/activation of nested parallelism and the peculiarities of the implementation. For example, some systems maintain a fixed pool of threads, usually equal in size to the number of available processors. Nested parallelism is supported as long as free threads exist in the pool, otherwise it is dynamically disabled. As a result, a nested `parallel` region may be executed by a varying number of threads, depending on the current state of the pool.

OpenMP has been architected mainly with the first (outer) level of parallelism in mind and certain features are not thoroughly thought out. For one, in the first version of the specifications [24, 25] there was no way to control the number of threads in inner levels, since `omp_set_num_threads()` can only be called from the sequential parts of the code; the `num_threads` clause was added in the second version of OpenMP [26] to overcome this limitation. There are also a few parts in the specifications which are unclear when applied to nested levels, e.g. the exact meaning of the persistence of threadprivate variable values between `parallel` regions. Finally, there are some features that are completely lacking; ancestor-descendant interaction and intra-team shared variables are only two of them.

The upcoming version of the OpenMP specifications is expected to clarify some ambiguities and provide a richer functional API for nested parallelism; [7] discloses the following self-explanatory calls:

```
omp_get_nested_level()
omp_set_max_nested_levels()
omp_get_max_nested_levels()
omp_set_thread_limit()
omp_get_thread_limit()
```

while it will be possible to call `omp_set_num_threads()` from within `parallel` regions, so as to control the number of threads for the next nesting level. There seem to also exist provisions for identifying one's parent (i.e. the master thread of a team), as well as any other ancestor.

3. Support in Compilers

According to the OpenMP specifications, an implementation which serializes nested `parallel` regions, even if nested parallelism is enabled through the OMP_NESTED environment variable or the `omp_set_nested()` call, is considered *compliant*. An implementation can claim *support* of nested parallelism if nested `parallel` regions (i.e. at levels greater than 1) may be executed by more than 1 thread. Nowadays, several commercial and research compilers support nested parallelism, either fully or partially. Partial support implies that there exists some kind of limit imposed by the implementation. For example, there exist systems that support a fixed number of nesting levels; some others allow an unlimited number of nested levels but have a fixed number of simultaneously active threads. In the latter case, a nested `parallel` region may be executed by a smaller number of threads than the one requested, if there are not enough free threads. The decision of the team size is made at the beginning of a `parallel` region. If later, however, some threads become idle, they will not be able to participate in the parallel execution of that region.

Notice that a nested `parallel` region which includes a `num_threads(n)` clause must be executed by exactly n threads, as requested, unless dynamic adjustment of the number of threads is turned on. Thus, those systems that limit the number of simultaneously active threads cannot be used with a disabled dynamic adjustment. Consequently, we consider an implementation as providing *full support* if it imposes no limit on the number of nesting levels or the number of simultaneously active threads and does not serialize nested regions when dynamic adjustment of threads is disabled.

The majority of OpenMP implementations instantiate their OpenMP threads with kernel-level threads, utilizing either the POSIX-threads API or the native threads provided by the operating system. The utilization of kernel threads limits the size of the thread pool and consequently the maximum number of OpenMP threads. In addition, it introduces significant overheads in the runtime library, especially if multiple levels of parallelism are exploited. When the number of threads that compete for hardware recourses significantly exceeds the number of available processors, the system is overloaded and the parallelization overheads outweigh any performance benefits. Finally, it becomes quite difficult for the runtime system to decide the distribution of inner-level threads to specific processors in order to favor computation and data locality.

3.1. Proprietary Compilers

Not all proprietary compilers support nested parallelism and some support it only in part. Below, we provide a summary of the level of support in various known systems.

- **Fujitsu**: The Fujitsu PRIMEPOWER compilers in the Parallelnavi software package [19] support nesting of `parallel` regions. Moreover, a high performance OpenMP runtime library is available for OpenMP applications with single-level parallelism.

- **HP**: The HP compilers for the HP-UX 11i operating system support dynamically nested parallelism [16]. When nested parallelism is enabled, the number of threads used to execute nested `parallel` regions is determined at runtime by the underlying OpenMP runtime library. The maximum number of threads is dependent upon the load on the system, the amount of memory allocated by the program and the amount of implementation dependent stack space allocated to each thread. The latest releases of HP-UX contain new thread functionality, providing the possibility for multiple POSIX threads of a process to map to a smaller number of kernel threads. Therefore, the OpenMP runtime library takes advantage of the hybrid (M:N) threading model.

- **Intel**: The basic mechanism for threading support in the Intel compilers [36] is the thread pool. The threads are not created until the first `parallel` region is executed, and only as many as needed by that `parallel` region are created. Additional threads are created as needed by subsequent `parallel` regions. Threads that are created by the OpenMP runtime library are not destroyed. Instead, they join the thread pool until they are called upon to join a team and are released by the master thread of the subsequent team. Since the Intel compiler maps OpenMP threads to kernel threads, its runtime library uses the KMP_MAX_THREADS environment variable to set the maximum number of threads that it will use. This gives the user the freedom to utilize any number of threads or to limit them to the number of physical processors, so that an application or a library used by an application does not over-subscribe the system with OpenMP threads. The library will attempt to use as many threads as requested at every level, until the KMP_MAX_THREADS limit is reached.

- **Microsoft**: Visual C++ 2005 provides a new compiler switch that enables the compiler to understand OpenMP directives [11]. Visual C++ allows nested parallel regions, where each thread of the original parallel region becomes the master of its own thread team. Nested parallelism can continue to further nest other parallel regions. This process of creating threads for each nested parallel region can continue until the program runs out of stack space.

- **Sun**: The OpenMP runtime library of the Sun Studio compilers [30] maintains a pool of threads that can be used as slave threads in parallel regions. When a thread encounters a parallel construct and needs to create a team of more than one thread, the thread will check the pool and grab idle threads from the pool, making them slave threads of the team. The master thread might get fewer slave threads than it needs if there is not a sufficient number of idle threads in the pool. When the team finishes executing the parallel region, the slave threads return to the pool. The user can control both the number of threads in the pool and the maximum depth of nested parallel regions that may utilize more than one thread. This is performed through the SUNW_MP_MAX_POOL_THREADS and SUNW_MP_MAX_NESTED_LEVELS environment variables respectively.

Full support for nested parallelism is also provided in the latest version of the well known open-source GNU Compiler Collection, **GCC 4.2**. libGOMP [23], the runtime library of the system, is designed as a wrapper around the POSIX threads library, with some target-specific optimizations for systems that provide lighter weight implementation of certain primitives. The GOMP runtime library allows the reuse of idle threads from a pre-built pool only for non-nested parallel regions, while threads are created dynamically for inner levels.

In contrast to the aforementioned cases, several other OpenMP compiler vendors do not currently support nested parallelism. The **MIPSpro** compiler and runtime environment on the SGI Origin does not support nested parallelism. Instead, it supports multi-loop parallelization for loops that are perfectly nested [35]. The current implementation of the **IBM XL** compiler does not provide true nested parallelism. Instead of creating a new team of threads for nested parallel regions, the OpenMP threads that are currently available are re-used [17, 18, 22]. The **PathScale** Compiler Suite is a family of compilers for the AMD64 processor family, compatible with the latest specification of the OpenMP programming model (2.5). Its Fortran version supports nested parallelism [28], as long as the number of threads does not exceed 256 and parallel regions are not lexically nested; nested regions should be orphaned (i.e. appear in different subroutines). Finally, the **Portland Group** (PGI) compilers do not support and thus ignore nested OpenMP parallel constructs. The omp_set_nested() function, which allows enabling and disabling of nested parallel regions, has currently no effect [33].

3.2. Research and Experimental Compilers

Most research OpenMP compilers are source-to-source compilation systems that transform OpenMP-annotated source code (C/Fortran) to equivalent multithreaded code in the same base language, ready to be compiled by the native compiler of the platform. The code also includes calls to a runtime library that supports and controls the execution of the program. Thread creation is based mostly on the *outlining* technique [8], where the code inside a `parallel` region is moved to a separate function or routine, which is executed by the spawned threads.

The next four experimental systems provide full support of nested parallelism through the use of the appropriate runtime libraries.

- **GOMP/Marcel**: MaGOMP [34] is a port of GOMP on top of the Marcel threading library [32] in which BubbleSched, an efficient scheduler for nested parallelism, is implemented. More specifically, a Marcel adaptation of libGOMP threads has been added to the existing abstraction layer. MaGOMP relies on Marcel 's fully POSIX compatible interface to guarantee that it will behave as well as GOMP on POSIX threads. Then, it becomes possible to run any existing OpenMP application on top of BubbleSched by simply relinking it.

- **OdinMP**: The Balder runtime library of OdinMP [20] is capable of fully handing OpenMP 2.0 including nested parallelism. Balder uses POSIX threads as its underlying thread library, provides efficient barrier and lock synchronization, and uses a pool of threads, which is expanded whenever it is necessary.

- **Omni**: The Omni compiler [29] supports full nested parallelism but requires a user-predefined fixed size for its kernel thread pool, where threads for the execution of `parallel` regions are extracted from. Specifically, an OpenMP program creates a fixed number of worker threads at the beginning of its execution and keeps a pool of idle threads. Whenever the program encounters a `parallel` construct, it is parallelized if there are idle threads at that moment. Omni/ST [31], an experimental version of Omni equipped with the StackThreads/MP library, provided an efficient though not portable implementation of nested irregular parallelism.

- **OMPi**: OMPi [10] is a source-to-source translator that takes as input C source code with OpenMP directives and outputs equivalent multithreaded C code, ready to be built and executed on a multiprocessor. It has been enhanced with lightweight runtime support based on user-level multithreading. A large number of threads can be spawned for every `parallel` region and multiple levels of parallelism are supported efficiently, without introducing additional overheads to the OpenMP library. A more detailed description of OMPi is provided in section 3.3..

There also exist other experimental compilation systems, some of them being quite advanced, which either provide a limited form of nested parallelism or do not support it at all.

- **CCRG**: CCRG OpenMP Compiler [9] aims to create a freely available, fully functional and portable set of implementations of the OpenMP Fortran specification for a variety of different platforms, such as SMPs as well as Software Distributed Shared Memory (sDSM) systems. CCRG uses the approach of the source-to-source translation and runtime support to implement OpenMP. The CCRG OpenMP Compiler fully implemented OpenMP 1.0 and in part features of OpenMP 2.0 Fortran API. Its runtime library for SMP is based on the standard POSIX threads interface.

- **NanosCompiler**: The NanosCompiler [3] for Fortran does not fully support nested parallelism. Instead, it supports multilevel parallelization based on the concept of thread groups, without allowing the total number of threads to exceed that of available processors. A group of threads is composed of a subset of the total number of threads available in the team to run a `parallel` construct. In a `parallel` construct, the programmer may define the number of groups and the composition of each one. When a `parallel` directive defining groups is encountered, a new team of threads is created. The new team is composed of as many threads as the number of groups. The rest of the threads are used to support the execution of nested `parallel` constructs. In other words, the definition of groups establishes an allocation strategy for the inner levels of parallelism. To define groups of threads, NanosCompiler supports the GROUPS clause extension to the `parallel` directive. The NanosCompiler has been recently replaced by its successor, the Nanos Mercurium compiler.

- **Nanos Mercurium**: The objective of the Nanos Mercurium compiler [4] is to offer a compilation platform that OpenMP researchers can use to test new language features. It is build on top of an existing compilation platform, the Open64 compiler, and uses templates of code for specifying the transformations of the OpenMP directives. The compiler implements most of OpenMP 2.0 along with extensions such as dynamic sections, a relaxation of the current definition of SECTIONS, to allow parallelization of programs that use iterative structures (such as while loops) or recursion. Since it is based on the runtime library of the NanosCompiler, Nanos Mercurium does not fully support nested parallelism.

- **OpenUH**: OpenUH [21] is a portable OpenMP compiler based on the Open64 compiler infrastructure with a unique hybrid design that combines a state-of-the-art optimizing infrastructure with a source-to-source approach. OpenUH is open source, supports C/C++/Fortran 90, includes numerous analysis and optimization components, and is a complete implementation of OpenMP 2.5. The thread creation transformations used in OpenUH are different from the standard outlining approach; the approach is similar to the MET (Multi-Entry Threading) technique employed in the Intel OpenMP compiler. The compiler generates a microtask to encapsulate the code lexically contained within a `parallel` region and the microtask is nested into the original function containing that `parallel` region. OpenUH does not support nested parallelism.

The above discussion is summarized in Table 1, where we list all the aforementioned compilers, their present status and the level of support for nested parallelism they provide.

Table 1. OpenMP implementations.

Entries marked with a star (⋆) represent compiler projects that seem to be dormant.

OpenMP compiler	Nested parallelism	Availability
CCRG 1.0 (Fortran)	no	freeware (⋆)
GCC 4.2.0	yes	freeware
Fujitsu	yes	commercial
HP (for HP-UX 11i)	yes	commercial
IBM XL (C v9.0, F v11.1)	no	commercial
Intel 10.0	yes	commercial, free
MaGOMP (GCC 4.2.0)	yes	freeware
Microsoft Visual C++ 2005	yes	commercial
Nanos Mercurium 1.2	limited	freeware
NanosCompiler (Fortran)	limited	freeware (⋆)
OdinMP 0.287.2 (C only)	yes	freeware (⋆)
Omni 1.6	yes	freeware (⋆)
OMPi 0.9.0 (C only)	yes	freeware
OpenUH alpha (Fortran)	no	freeware
PathScale 3.0	limited	commercial
PGI 7.0.6	no	commercial
SGI MIPSpro 7.4	no	commercial
Sun Studio 12	yes	commercial, free

3.3. OMPi

OMPi's runtime system has been architected with an internal threading interface that facilitates the integration of arbitrary thread libraries. It comes with two core libraries that are based on POSIX threads; one is optimized for single-level (non-nested) parallelism, while the other provides nested parallelism support through a fixed pool of threads (the size of which is determined at startup through the OMP_NUM_THREADS environment variable). In order to efficiently support unlimited nested parallelism, an additional library based on user-level threads has been developed [15], named psthreads.

The psthreads library implements a two-level thread model, where user-level threads are executed on top of kernel-level threads that act as *virtual processors*. Each virtual processor runs a dispatch loop, selecting the next-to-run user-level thread from a set of ready queues, where threads are submitted for execution. The queue architecture allows the runtime library to represent the layout of physical processors. For instance, a hierarchy can be defined in order to map the coupling of processing elements in current multicore architectures.

Although user-level multithreading has traditionally implied machine dependence, the psthreads library is completely portable because its implementation is based entirely on the POSIX standard. Its virtual processors are mapped to POSIX threads, permitting the interoperability of OMPi with third-party libraries and the coexistence of OpenMP and POSIX threads in the same program. The primary user-level thread operations are provided by Uth-Lib (Underlying Threads Library), a platform-independent thread package. An underlying thread is actually the stack that a `psthread` uses during its execution. Synchronization is based on the POSIX threads interface. Locks are internally mapped to POSIX mutexes or spinlocks, taking into account the non-preemptive threads of the library.

The application programming interface of `psthreads` is similar to that of POSIX threads. Its usage simplifies the OpenMP runtime library since spawning of threads is performed explicitly, while thread pooling is provided by the thread library. The thread creation routine of `psthreads` allows the user to specify the queue where the thread will be submitted for execution and whether it will be inserted in the front or in the back of the specified queue. Moreover, there exists a variant of the creation routine that accepts an already allocated thread descriptor. This is useful for cases where the user implements his own management of thread descriptors.

Efficient thread and stack management is essential for nested parallelism because a thread with a stack should always be created as the runtime library cannot know a priori whether the running application will spawn a new level of parallelism. An important feature of `psthreads` is the utilization of a lazy stack allocation policy. According to this policy, the stack of a user-level thread is allocated just before its execution. This results in minimal memory consumption and simplified thread migrations. Lazy stack allocation is further improved with stack handoff, whereby a finished thread re-initializes its own state by replacing its descriptor with the subsequent thread's descriptor and resumes its execution.

In the `psthreads` library, an idle virtual processor extracts threads from the *front* of its local ready queue but steals from the *back* of remote queues. This allows the OpenMP runtime library to employ an adaptive work distribution scheme for the management of nested parallelism. In particular, threads that are spawned at the first level of parallelism are distributed cyclically and inserted at the *back* of the ready queues. For inner levels, the threads are inserted in the front of the ready queue that belongs to the virtual processor they were created on. The adopted scheme favors the execution of inner threads on a single processor and improves data locality.

4. A Comparative Evaluation

In this section, we evaluate an implementation's efficiency with respect to nested parallelism. We measure both the incurred overheads and the overall behavior of a representative set of compilers, using microbenchmarks and an application that makes substantial use of nested parallelism. We performed all our experiments on a Compaq Proliant ML570 server with 4 Intel Xeon III CPUs running Debian Linux (2.6.6). We provide comparative performance results for two free commercial and three freeware OpenMP C compilers that fully support nested parallelism. The commercial compilers are the Intel C++ 10.0 compiler (ICC) and Sun Studio 12 (SUNCC) for Linux. The freeware ones are GNU GCC 4.2.0, Omni 1.6 and OMPi 0.9.0 with the `psthreads` library. We have used GCC as native back-end compiler for both OMPi and Omni.

4.1. Overheads

The EPCC microbenchmark suite [6] is the most commonly used tool for measuring runtime overheads of individual OpenMP constructs. This section describes the extensions we have introduced to the EPCC microbenchmark suite for the evaluation of OpenMP runtime support for nested parallelism.

Synchronization and loop scheduling operations can all be significant sources of overhead in shared memory parallel programs. The technique used by the EPCC microbenchmarks to measure the overhead of OpenMP directives, is to compare the time taken for a section of code executed sequentially with the time taken for the same code executed in parallel enclosed in a given directive. A full description of this method is given in [6]. To obtain statistically meaningful results, each overhead measurement is repeated several times and the mean and standard deviation are computed over all measurements. This way, the microbenchmark suite neither requires exclusive access to a given machine nor is seriously affected by background processes in the system.

To study how efficiently OpenMP implementations support nested parallelism, we have extended both the synchronization and the scheduling microbenchmarks. According to our approach, the core benchmark routine for a given construct is represented by a task. Each task has a unique identifier and utilizes its own memory space for storing the runtime measurements, i.e. its mean overhead time and standard deviation. When all tasks finish, we measure their total execution time and compute the global mean of all measured runtime overheads. Our approach, as applied to the synchronization benchmark, is outlined in Fig. 2. The loop that issues the tasks expresses the outer level of parallelism, while each benchmark routine includes the inner one.

If the outer loop is not parallelized, the tasks are executed in sequential order. This actually corresponds to the original version of the microbenchmarks, having each core benchmark repeated more than once. On the other hand, if nested parallelism is evaluated, the loop is parallelized and the tasks are executed in parallel. The number of simultaneously active tasks is bound by the number of OpenMP threads that constitute the team of the first level of parallelism. To ensure that the OpenMP runtime library does not assign fewer threads to inner levels than in the outer one, dynamic adjustment of threads is disabled.

By measuring the aggregated execution time of the tasks, we use the microbenchmark as an individual application. This time includes not only the parallel portion of the tasks, i.e. the time the tasks spend on measuring the runtime overhead, but also their sequential portion. This means that even if the mean overhead increases when tasks are executed in parallel, as expected due to the higher number of running threads, the overall execution time may decrease.

In OpenMP implementations that provide full nested parallelism support, inner levels spawn more threads than the number of physical processors, which are mostly kernel-level threads. Thus, measurements exhibit higher variations than in the case of single-level parallelism. To resolve this issue, we increase the number of internal repetitions for each microbenchmark, so as to achieve the same confidence levels.

```
void test_nested_bench(func_t f)
{
  int task_id;

  <get current time>
  #ifdef NESTED_PARALLELISM
  #pragma omp parallel for schedule(static,1)
  #endif
  for (task_id = 0; task_id < NTASKS; task_id++) {
    (*f)(task_id);
  }
  <get current time>

  <compute global mean time and standard deviation>
  <print construct name, elapsed time and mean values>
}

main ()
{
  <compute reference time>
  test_nested_bench(testpr);
  test_nested_bench(testfor);
  ...
}
```

Figure 2. Outline of the extended EPCC microbenchmarks for nested parallelism.

4.2. A Data clustering Application

Except overheads, we evaluate nested parallelism using a full application. For our purpose we have chosen PCURE (Parallel Clustering Using REpresentatives) [14], the OpenMP implementation of a well-known hierarchical data clustering algorithm (CURE). Data clustering is one of the fundamental techniques in scientific data analysis and data mining. The problem of clustering is to partition a data set into a number of segments (called clusters) that contain similar data. CURE [12] is a very efficient clustering algorithm with respect to the quality of clusters because it identifies arbitrary-shaped clusters and handles high-dimensional data. However, its worst-case time complexity is O($n^2 \log n$), where n is the number of data points to be clustered. The OpenMP parallelization of CURE copes with the quadratic time complexity of the algorithm and allows for efficient clustering of very large data sets.

Fig. 3 outlines the main clustering algorithm: since CURE is a hierarchical agglomerative algorithm, every data point is initially considered as a separate cluster with one representative, the point itself. The algorithm initially computes the closest cluster for each cluster. Next, it starts the agglomerative clustering, merging the closest pair of clusters until only k clusters remain. According to the merge procedure, the centroid of the new cluster is the weighted mean of the two merged clusters. Moreover, the new r representative points are chosen between the $2r$ points of the two merged clusters.

Fig. 4 presents in pseudocode the most computationally demanding routine in the clustering phase, which includes the update of the nearest neighbors (update_nnbs(), lines

```
1. Initialization: Compute distances and find nearest neighbors
   pairs for all clusters

2. Clustering: Perform hierarchical clustering until the
   predefined number of clusters k has been computed

   while (number of remaining clusters > k) {
       a.  Find the pair of clusters with the minimum distance
       b.  Merge them
             i. new_size = size1 + size2
            ii. new_centroid = a1*centroid1 + a2*centroid2,
                where a1 = size1/new_size and a2 = size2/new_size
           iii. find r new representative points
       c.  Update the nearest neighbors pairs of the clusters
       d.  Reduce the number of remaining clusters
       e.  If conditions are satisfied, apply pruning of clusters
   }

3. Output the representative points of each cluster
```

Figure 3. Outline of the CURE data clustering algorithm.

1–10). The parallelism in PCURE is expressed with the two parallel nested loops, found at lines 3 and 17 respectively. For a given cluster with index i, the algorithm finds its closest cluster among those with smaller index ($j < i$). Moreover, as the algorithm evolves, the number of valid clusters gradually decreases. Therefore, the computational cost of loop iterations cannot be estimated in advance.

The efficiency of PCURE strongly depends on the balanced distribution of computations to processors. Due to the highly irregular clustering algorithm, such distribution is not straightforward, though. As shown in [13], the algorithm scales efficiently only if nested parallelism is exploited.

4.3. Experimental Results

Synchronization overheads Our first experiment uses the extended synchronization benchmark to measure the overhead incurred by the `parallel` and `for` constructs. Both the OMP_NUM_THREADS environment variable and the number of tasks are equal to the number of physical processors in the system (4). Fig. 5 and 6 present the measured overhead for both constructs respectively. As the number of active threads increases when nested parallelism is enabled, the overheads are expected to increase accordingly. We observe, however, that the `parallel` construct does not scale well for the Intel, GCC and Omni compilers. For all three of them, the runtime overhead is an order of magnitude higher in the case of nested parallelism. On the other hand, both OMPi and SUNCC clearly scale better and their overheads increase linearly. SUNCC, however, exhibits higher overheads than OMPi for both single level and nested parallelism. The `for` construct (Fig. 6) behaves similarly bad except for the case of GCC, which shows significant but not excessive increase; this is attributed to the platform-specific atomic primitives that GCC uses. Although OMPi does not currently use atomic operations, it manages to deliver the best performance for

```
1.  void update_nnbs(int pair_low, int pair_high)
2.  {
3.    for (i=pair_low+1; i<npat; i++)
4.    {
5.      if (entry #i has been invalidated) continue;
6.      if (entry #i had neighbor pair_low or pair_high)
7.        find_nnb (i, &nnb[i].index, &nnb[i].dist);
8.      else if (pair_high < i)
9.        if ((dist = compute_distance(pair_high, i))) < nnb_dist[i])
10.         nnb[i].index = pair_high, nnb[i].dist = dist;
11.   }
12. }
13.
14. void find_nnb(int i, int *index, double *distance)
15. {
16.   min_dist = +inf, min_index = -1;
17.   for (j=0; j<i; j++)
18.   {
19.     if (entry #j has been invalidated) continue;
20.     if ((dist = compute_distance(i, j)) < min_dist)
21.       min_dist = dist, min_index = j;
22.   }
23.   *index = min_index; *distance = min_dist;
24. }
```

Figure 4. Pseudocode for the update of the nearest neighbors.

both microbenchmarks mainly due to its lower contention between OpenMP threads.

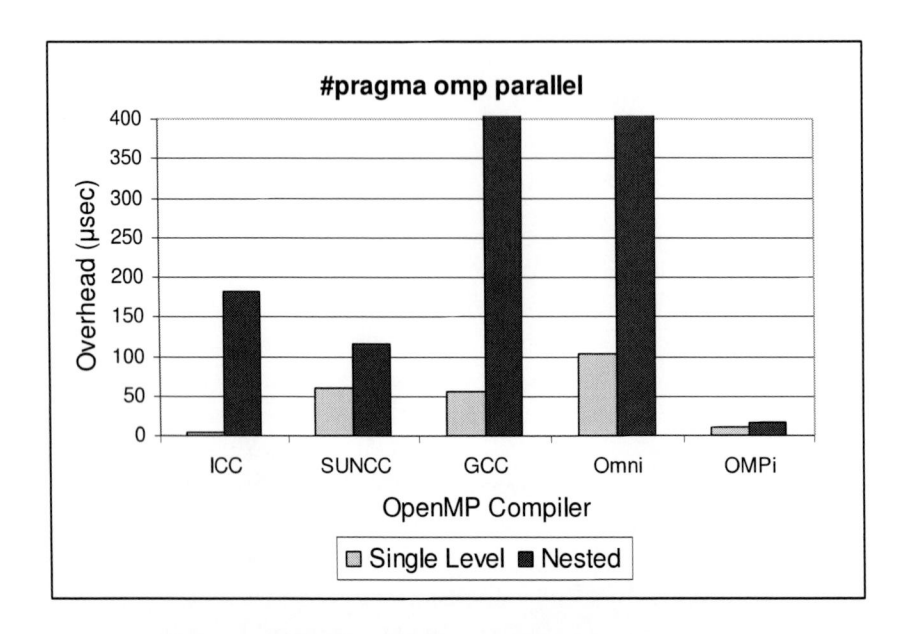

Figure 5. Runtime overhead of the OpenMP `parallel` construct (μsec).

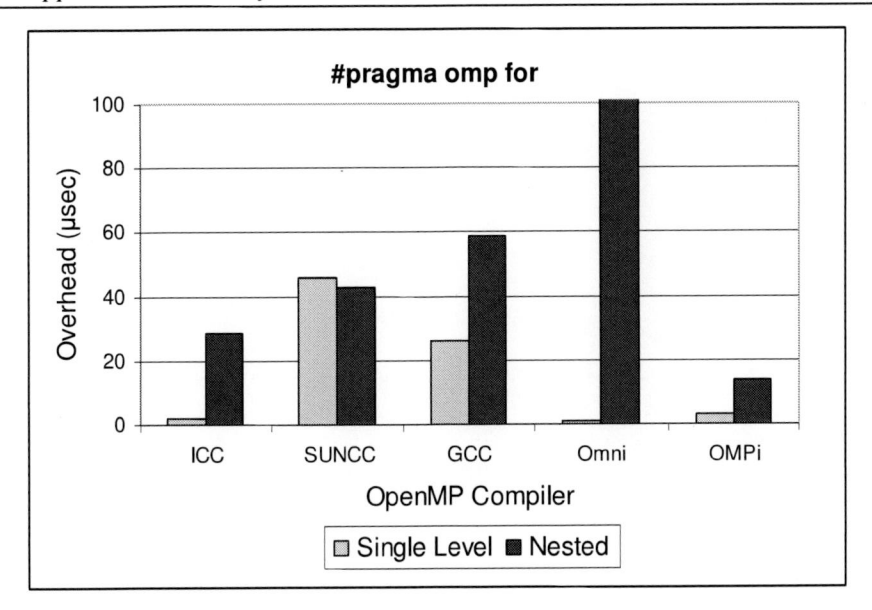

Figure 6. Runtime overhead of the OpenMP `for` construct (μsec).

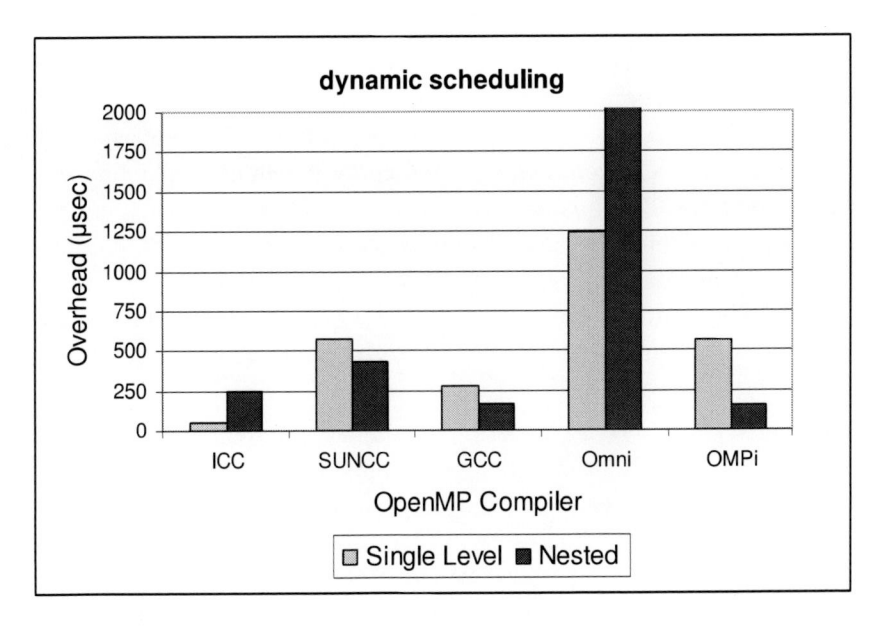

Figure 7. Runtime behavior of the dynamic scheduling policy (μsec).

Scheduling overheads In the second experiment, we use the loop scheduling benchmark to study the efficiency of OpenMP when several independent parallel loops are executed concurrently. We provide measurements for the dynamic and guided scheduling policies using their default chunk size, which is equal to one. This chunk size was chosen in order to measure the highest possible scheduling overhead. As shown in Fig. 7, the overhead of the dynamic scheduling policy increases substantially for the Intel and Omni compilers and decreases for SUNCC, GCC, and OMPi. The scheduling overhead depends strongly

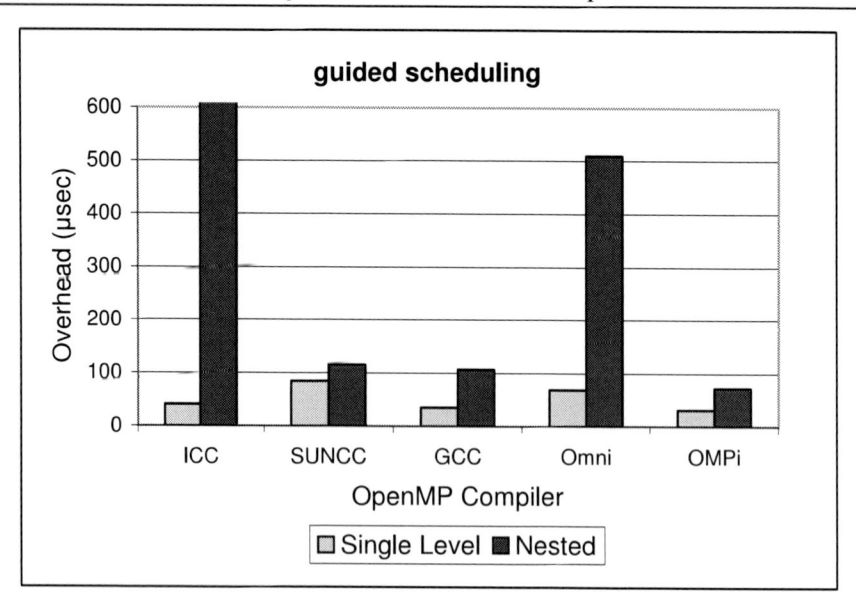

Figure 8. Runtime behavior of the guided scheduling policy (μsec).

on the mechanism that OpenMP threads use to get the next chunk of loop iterations. Appropriate use of atomic primitives and processor yielding can significantly reduce thread contention during the dynamic assignment of loop iterations. This appears to be the case for the Sun Studio and GCC compilers, for which the dynamic scheduling overhead decreases when nested parallelism is exploited. OMPi with user-level threading achieves the same goal because it is able to assign each independent loop to a team of non-preemptive user-level OpenMP threads that mainly run on the same virtual processor. The overhead of the guided scheduling policy, as depicted in Fig. 8, is lower than that of the dynamic policy and increases for all the OpenMP implementations when nested parallelism is exploited.

Parallel data clustering The last experiment evaluates the runtime support of nested parallelism running PCURE on a data set that contains 5000 points with 24 features. The guided scheduling policy is used for both loops of the update procedure. We provide performance results after 1000 and 4000 clustering steps, depicted in Fig. 9 and 10 respectively. With the exception of OMPi, all OpenMP compilers utilize kernel threads. If OMP_NUM_THREADS equals T, these compilers use T^2 total kernel threads. On the other hand, OMPi initializes its user-level threads library with T virtual processors and creates T^2 user-level threads. The Intel and Omni compilers perform best when $T=2$ because the actual number of kernel threads from both levels of parallelism is equal to the system's processor count (4). For $T=4$, where 16 threads are created in total, the speedup drops mostly due to the higher threading overhead and the increased memory traffic and contention. For both SUNCC and GCC, the speedup is improved slightly on 4 threads, although this improvement declines as the number of steps increases. On the other hand, PCURE scales well in both experiments for the OMPi compiler. Let us note here that PCURE is a data intensive application, so its scalability is limited by the low memory bandwidth of the bus-based SMP machine.

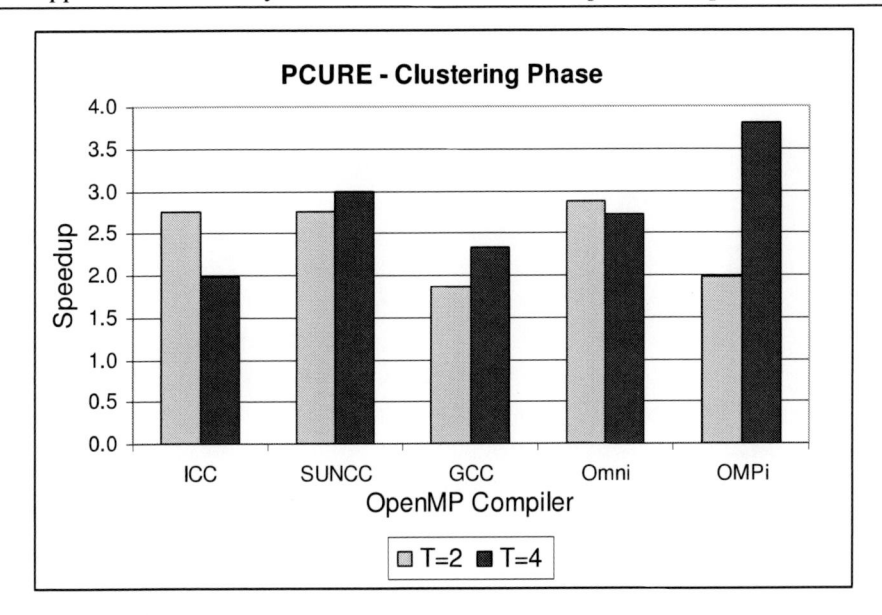

Figure 9. Speedups for 1000 steps of the parallel data clustering algorithm.

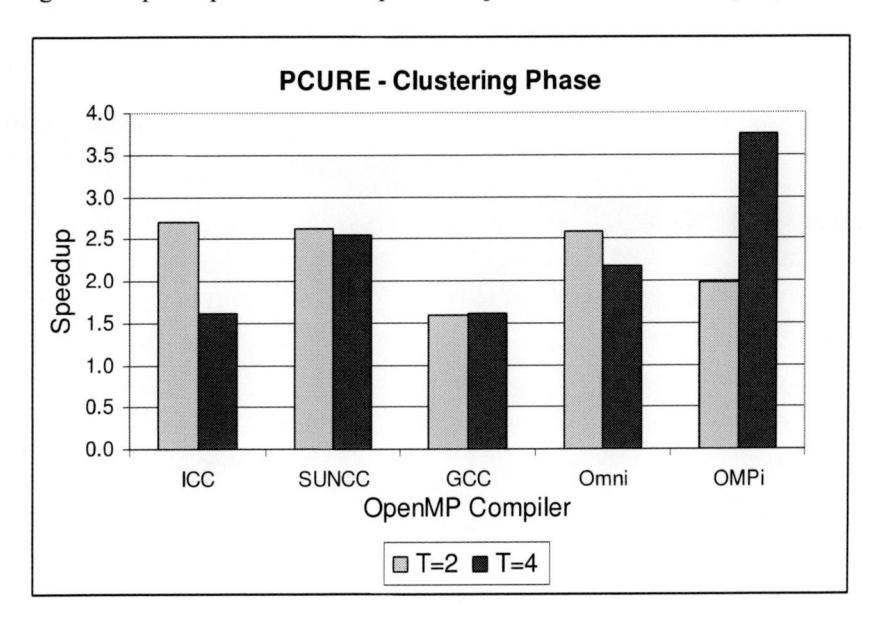

Figure 10. Speedups for 4000 steps of the parallel data clustering algorithm.

5. Conclusion

In this chapter we performed an in-depth analysis of nested parallelism in OpenMP. We examined both what the OpenMP specifications provide to the programmer for controlling nested parallelism and what the known implementations support. We surveyed commercial as well as research / experimental systems and categorized them according to the level of support they offer. After a decade since the first version of the OpenMP specifications came out, nested parallelism support is still at its infancy. There exist compilation systems that provide no support at all, but fortunately we found many systems that provide either partial or full support (i.e. the implementation does not limit dynamically the number of threads created).

However, we discovered that most implementations have scalability problems when nested parallelism is enabled and the number of threads increases beyond the number of available processors. Through specially designed microbenchmarks it was shown that the overheads increase dramatically even when moving merely to the second nesting level, in all but the OMPi compiler. In order to see the effect on the overall performance, a hierarchical data clustering application was also employed. The overheads manifested themselves as significantly lower-than-optimal attainable speedups, which got worse as the number of threads increased. It is clear that there are several design issues and performance limitations related to nested parallelism support that implementations have to address in an efficient way. The most important seems to be the kernel-level threading model which all but the OMPi compiler have adopted.

Last but not least, OpenMP still has a long way to go with respect to nested parallelism. A number of issues in the specifications have to be clarified and a richer functional API for the application programmers must be provided.

References

[1] D. an Mey, S. Sarholz, and C. Terboven. Nested Parallelization with OpenMP. *International Journal of Parallel Programming*, **35**(5):459–476, October 2007.

[2] E. Ayguade, M. Gonzalez, X. Martorell, and G. Jost. Employing Nested OpenMP for the Parallelization of Multi-zone Computational Fluid Dynamics Applications. In *Proc. of the 18th Int'l Parallel and Distributed Processing Symposium*, Santa Fe, New Mexico, USA, April 2004.

[3] E. Ayguade, M. Gonzalez, X. Martorell, J. Labarta, N. Navarro, and J. Oliver. NanosCompiler: Supporting Flexible Multilevel Parallelism in OpenMP. *Concurrency: Practice and Experience*, **12**(12):1205–1218, October 2000.

[4] J. Balart, A. Duran, M. Gonzalez, X. Martorell, E. Ayguade, and J. Labarta. Nanos Mercurium: A Research Compiler for OpenMP. In *Proc. of the 6th European Workshop on OpenMP (EWOMP '04)*, Stockholm, Sweden, October 2004.

[5] R. Blikberg and T. Sorevik. Nested Parallelism: Allocation of Processors to Tasks and OpenMP Implementation. In *Proc. of the 28th Int'l Conference on Parallel Processing (ICCP '99)*, Fukushima, Japan, September 1999.

[6] J. M. Bull. Measuring Synchronization and Scheduling Overheads in OpenMP. In *Proc. of the 1st European Workshop on OpenMP (EWOMP '99)*, Lund, Sweden, September 1999.

[7] J. M. Bull. Towards OpenMP V3.0. In *Proc. of the Int'l Conference on Parallel Computing: Architectures, Algorithms and Applications (PARCO '07)*, Aachen, Germany, September 2007.

[8] Jyh-Herng Chow, L. E. Lyon, and Vivek Sarkar. Automatic parallelization for symmetric shared-memory multiprocessors. In *Proc. of the 1996 conference of the Centre for Advanced Studies on Collaborative Research (CASCON '96)*, Toronto, Canada, November 1996.

[9] H. Chun and Y. Xuejun. CCRG OpenMP Compiler: Experiments and Improvements. In *Proc. of the 1st Int'l Workshop on OpenMP*, Eugene, Oregon, USA, June 2005.

[10] V. V. Dimakopoulos, E. Leontiadis, and G. Tzoumas. A Portable C Compiler for OpenMP V.2.0. In *Proc. of the 5th European Workshop on OpenMP (EWOMP '03)*, Aachen, Germany, October 2003.

[11] K. S. Gatlin and P. Isensee. OpenMP and C++: Reap the Benefits of Multithreading without All the Work. In *MSDN Magazine*, October 2005.

[12] S. Guha, R. Rastogi, and K. Shim. CURE: An Efficient Clustering Algorithm for Large DataBases. In *Proc. of the ACM SIGMOD Int'l Conference on Management of Data*, 1998.

[13] P. E. Hadjidoukas and L. Amsaleg. Portable Support and Exploitation of Nested Parallelism in OpenMP. In *Proc. the 6th European Workshop on OpenMP (EWOMP '04)*, Stockholm, Sweden, October 2004.

[14] P. E. Hadjidoukas and L. Amsaleg. Parallelization of a Hierarchical Data Clustering Algorithm Using OpenMP. In *Proc. the 2nd Int'l Workshop on OpenMP (IWOMP '06)*, Reims, France, June 2006.

[15] P.E. Hadjidoukas and V.V. Dimakopoulos. Nested Parallelism in the OMPi OpenMP C Compiler. In *Proc. of the European Conference on Parallel Computing (EUROPAR '07)*, Rennes, France, August 2007.

[16] Hewlett-Packard Development Company. *Parallel Programming Guide for HP-UX Systems, 8th Edition*. 2007.

[17] International Business Machines (IBM) Corporation. *IBM XL C/C++ Enterprise Edition for AIX, V9.0: Compiler Reference*. 2007.

[18] International Business Machines (IBM) Corporation. *IBM XL Fortran Enterprise Edition for AIX, V11.1: Compiler Reference*. 2007.

[19] H. Iwashita, M. Kaneko, M. Aoki, K. Hotta, and M. van Waveren. On the Implementation of OpenMP 2.0 Extensions in the Fujitsu PRIMEPOWER compiler. In *Proc. of the Int'l Workshop on OpenMP: Experiences and Implementations (WOMPEI '03)*, Tokyo, Japan, November 2003.

[20] S. Karlsson. A Portable and Efficient Thread Library for OpenMP. In *Proc. of the 6th European Workshop on OpenMP (EWOMP '04)*, Stockholm, Sweden, October 2004.

[21] C. Liao, O. Hernandez, B. Chapman, W. Chen, and W. Zheng. OpenUH: An Optimizing, Portable OpenMP Compiler. In *Proc. the 12th Workshop on Compilers for Parallel Computers*, A Coruna, Spain, January 2006.

[22] K. Matsubara, E. Kwok, I. Rodriguez, and M. Paramasivam. Developing and Porting C and C++ Applications on AIX. In *SG24-5674-01, IBM Redbooks*, July 2003.

[23] D. Novillo. OpenMP and automatic parallelization in GCC. In *Proc. of the 2006 GCC Summit*, Ottawa, Canada, June 2006.

[24] OpenMP Architecture Review Board. *OpenMP Fortran Application Program Interface, Version 1.0*. October 1997.

[25] OpenMP Architecture Review Board. *OpenMP C and C++ Application Program Interface, Version 1.0*. October 1998.

[26] OpenMP Architecture Review Board. *OpenMP C and C++ Application Program Interface, Version 2.0*. March 2002.

[27] OpenMP Architecture Review Board. *OpenMP C and C++ Application Program Interface, Version 2.5*. May 2005.

[28] QLogic. *PathScale Compiler Suite User Guide, V.3.0*. 2007.

[29] M. Sato, S. Satoh, K. Kusano, and Y. Tanaka. Design of OpenMP Compiler for an SMP Cluster. In *Proc. of the 1st European Workshop on OpenMP (EWOMP '99)*, Lund, Sweden, September 1999.

[30] Sun Microsystems. Sun Studio 12: OpenMP API User's Guide, 2007. P.N. 819-5270.

[31] Y. Tanaka, K. Taura, M. Sato, and A. Yonezawa. Performance Evaluation of OpenMP Applications with Nested Parallelism. In *Proc. of the Fifth Workshop on Languages, Compilers and Run-Time Systems for Scalable Computers (LCR '00)*, Rochester, NY, USA, May 2000.

[32] Team RUNTIME INRIA. Marcel: A POSIX-Compliant Thread Library for Hierarchical Multiprocessor Machines. Available at: http://runtime.futurs.inria.fr/marcel.

[33] The Portland Group, STMicroelectronics, Inc. *PGI User's Guide: Parallel Fortran, C and C++ for Scientists and Engineers, 13th printing*. 2007.

[34] S. Thibault, F. Broquedis, B. Goglin, R. Namyst, and P-A Wacrenier. An Efficient OpenMP Runtime System for Hierarchical Architectures. In *Proc. of the 3rd Int'l Workshop on OpenMP (IWOMP '07)*, Beijing, China, June 2007.

[35] X. Tian, M. Girkar, S. Shah, D. Armstrong, E. Su, and P. Petersen. Compiler and runtime support for running openmp programs on pentium- and itanium-architectures. In *Proc. of the 17th Int'l Parallel and Distributed Processing Symposium (IPDPS '03)*, Washington, DC, USA, 2003.

[36] X. Tian, J. P. Hoeflinger, G. Haab, Y-K Chen, M. Girkar, and S. Shah. A compiler for exploiting nested parallelism in OpenMP programs. *Parallel Computing*, **31**:960–983, 2005.

In: Concurrent and Parallel Computing…
Editor: Alexander S. Becker, pp. 205-212

ISBN: 978-1-60456-274-3
© 2008 Nova Science Publishers, Inc.

Chapter 10

A PARALLEL IMPLEMENTATION OF AN ITERATIVE RECONSTRUCTION ALGORITHM USING A SPACE-BASED PROGRAMMING MODEL

P. Knoll[*] and S. Mirzaei

Dept. of Nuclear Medicine, Wilhelminenspital, Montleartstr. 37, 1171 Vienna, Austria

Abstract

Iterative algorithms to reconstruct single photon emission computerized tomography (SPECT) data are based on the mathematical simulation of the acquisition process. The reconstruction times of these methods are much longer than that of routinely used reconstruction methods (such as filtered back projection). Java, a platform independent programming language changed the way of software design by using Jini and JavaSpaces, new technologies that have been introduced recently. By applying JavaSpaces, a *space* is used to store objects persistently which can be used also for effective parallel processing. In this paper, we report a novel approach for iterative reconstruction of SPECT data by means of JavaSpaces, which uses only a standard personal computer equipment and results in significant improvement of reconstruction time due to the fact that several layers of the object are computed in parallel.

Key words: space-based programming model, iterative reconstruction, distributed computing, JavaSpaces

I. Introduction

Nuclear medicine is a medical speciality that applies small amounts of radioactive materials or radiopharmaceuticals, which are attracted to specific organs, bones, or tissues to diagnose and treat disease. Nuclear medicine imaging is unique because it documents organ function and structure, in contrast to diagnostic radiology, which is based upon anatomy. Nuclear medicine imaging techniques often identify abnormalities very early in the progression of the

---

[*] E mail address: peter.knoll@wienkav.at

disease – long before some medical problems are apparent with other diagnostic tests [1]. This early detection allows a disease to be treated early in its course when there may be a more successful prognosis. A radioactive tracer is intravenously injected and transported into the organ of interest from which the emitted photons pass through the body of the patient. These photons can be detected externally by a gamma camera. The radionuclides used for gamma cameras emit only a single photon and therefore a special "lens" known as a collimator, which is placed between detector surface and the patient, has to be used to select a ray orientation. The resulting scintigram represents the two-dimensional projection of the three-dimensional activity distribution and therefore the tomographic information is lost if only a single planar acquisition is performed. Rotating Anger gamma cameras have been developed to utilize this information and the single photon emission computed tomography (SPECT) acquisition technique is widely used. During a standard SPECT acquisition the head of the gamma camera rotates around the patient. In order to determine the three-dimensional activity distribution mathematical reconstruction algorithms are applied. The filtered back projection (FBP) algorithm currently is the standard reconstruction method in nuclear medicine [2]. The FBP involves projecting the acquired data back across the reconstruction matrix. At each angle, the counts from each ray sum are evenly distributed between each element on the ray. Applying this method results in reconstructed transaxial slices (cross sections of the object) [3], which are usually blurred by the presence of noise. These image artefacts of the reconstructed slices can only be partly controlled by a filter function but not totally eliminated [4]. Instead of back projecting the acquired projection data, iterative algorithms update an estimate of the image until calculated ray sums and measured projection data match adequately. Iterative algorithms have the advantage that a-priori information can be incorporated at each step of the reconstruction process [5]. Although different iterative solutions already exists, the clinical application is altered by the following fact: the mean square error between reconstructed and true activity improves in early iterations, but then degrades due to increasing noise [6]. The Java platform developed by Sun Microsystems [1] represents a new means of computation specially designed for network computing and based on the idea that computer software should run on different available computer hardware and operating systems. Software written in Java and compiled with the commercially available Java Development Kit 1.2 [2] runs different kinds of computers due to the Java virtual machine which enables the Java platform to host applications on any computer without rewriting the programming code. Java applications are already used in medicine, but mainly to distribute clinical information [3, 4]. However, it does not seem reasonable to translate already existing programs written in C/C++ into Java. A new programming language rather should influence the way of software designing. The Jini concept which is 100 % pure Java, is a brand new technology that can be used to create homogeneous distributed systems. The JavaSpaces technology kit (JSTK 1.0) [5], which has to be installed together with the Jini application programming interface (API) provides a fundamentally different programming model. This model considers application as a collection of processes cooperating via the flow of objects into and out of one or more *spaces*. In this context, these spaces are used as a shared and network accessible repository for data objects [4]. Therefore, the space-based model of distributing computing can also be elegantly used to solve computing-intensive problems faster by means of parallel application patterns.

Single photon emission computed tomography (SPECT) data can be reconstructed either by filtered back projection (FBP) or iterative methods. Instead of filtering and backprojecting the projection data, iterative algorithms try to simulate the acquisition process itself and minimize the difference between measured and simulated data [4]. This process is repeated until a "final" image is found. Due to the time-consuming iterative calculations, the reconstruction time of these methods are much longer than that of the FBP even if very simple acquisition models (no scatter, no attenuation, etc.) are applied. Therefore, the FBP is still the standard reconstruction method in nuclear medicine. By separating the algorithm into independent tasks, it is possible to shorten the computation time but existing methods mostly require either specialized hardware [7,8] or network computing [9]. Instead of using dedicated hardware or peer-to-peer network communication we present a new approach of successful parallel implementation of an iterative algorithm for reconstructing of SPECT data using a truly distributed system and a space-based programming model.

II. Methods

To accelerate iterative reconstruction, it is possible to decompose this computing intensive problem into smaller independent tasks that then can be computed simultaneously. Recently, Sun Microsystems introduced Jini and JavaSpaces which are new technologies that changed the way of software design fundamentally [6, 10].

Jini, built on top of Java, provides a homogeneous view of the network and does not require any centralized administration of available services as opposed to already existing communication patterns. JavaSpaces uses the Jini programming model and provides a simple mechanism for sharing objects in network resources based on Java technology[4]. As for any other Jini service it is necessary to run

- A HTTP server
- The Remote Method Invocation daemon (RMID)
- A lookup service
- A transaction manager [10, 11]

when applying Java Spaces. The Jini API includes a simple *HTTP server* which is necessary for exporting the code. The *RMID* uses a log file to keep track of the on demand activation and persistent service registration. Once a service has already been registered, it does not have to re-register after each reboot. Instead, RMID will restart it upon start-up [12]. *Lookup services* keep track of all services that have joined a Jini community. Jini services broadcast its presence by dropping a multicast packet to a certain IP/Port (4160) as defined in the Jini specification. Furthermore the Jini service also establishes a TCP server socket, that awaits incoming connections (Fig.1). The multicast request relies upon the User Datagram Protocol (UDP) which allows multicast (one-to-many) networking to function properly. Lookup services monitor IP/Port 4160 for incoming requests that provide information about the Jini service such as the IP/Port number. The lookup service uses this information to contact the Jini service directly using UDP, and receives and registers a proxy object of the Jini service (Fig. 2). The Jini client contacts the Jini lookup service, downloads the proxy object reference and uses that proxy to communicate directly with the Jini service (Fig. 3). Transactions are effective ways to organize a series of related operations resulting in only two possible outcomes: either all operations succeed or fail. Transactions, coordinated by a centralized *transaction manager*, are executed as if they were a single ("atomic") operation.

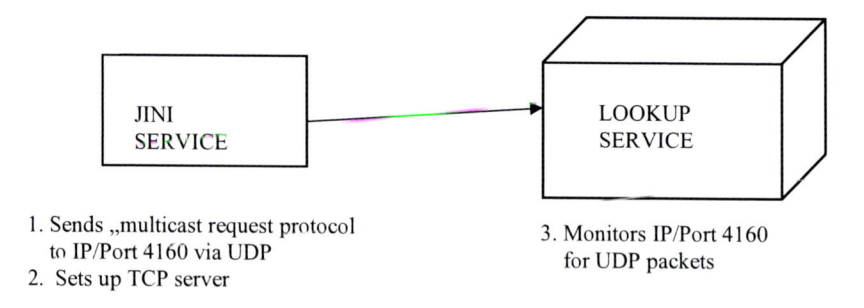

1. Sends „multicast request protocol to IP/Port 4160 via UDP
2. Sets up TCP server
3. Monitors IP/Port 4160 for UDP packets

Figure 1. Registering a Jini service I.

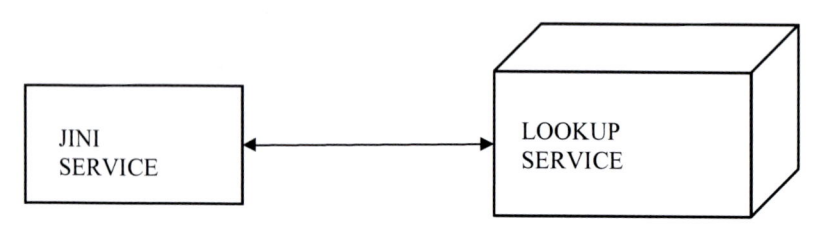

2. Gets information from the Lookup service
3. Sends proxy object reference to Lookup service
1. Contacts Jini service via TCP server
4. Receives proxy object reference

Figure 2. Registering a Jini service II.

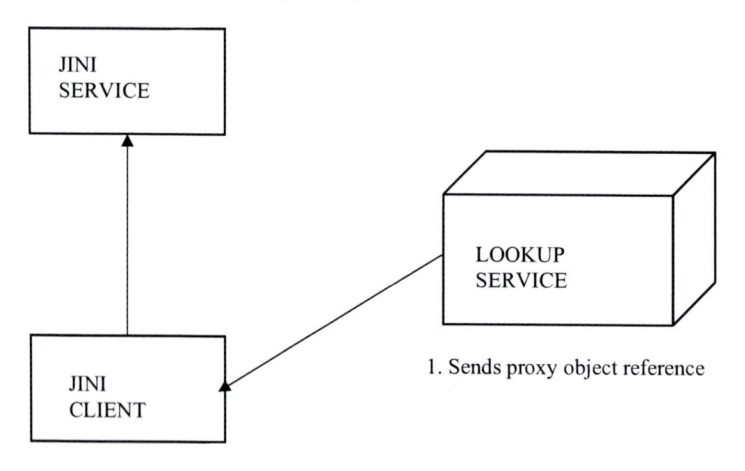

1. Sends proxy object reference
2. Communicates with the Jini service via proxy

Figure 3. Use of a Jini service.

The Jini API introduces a "leasing concept" that is able to clean up the whole system without human intervention if components have failed. Leasing is based on the idea that the resource is loaned to clients only for a fixed period of time. If this time interval expires, the resource is automatically removed.

If all these processes (HTTP server, RMID, lookup service and transaction manager) run on the host, a *space* can be created. In a distributed application, JavaSpaces act as virtual spaces between providers and users of Java objects. When applying this programming model, processes are loosely coupled because in this case processes interact indirectly through a *space* and not directly with other processes. One of the most common application pattern used for parallel computing is the replicated worker pattern. This pattern involves a master process along with a number of workers [6]. An iterative reconstruction algorithm based on the error back propagation method which is used in artificial neural networks [13, 14] was implemented and applies the space-based model with one master process and five reconstruction workers. The reconstruction software package was installed on 6 personal computers (PCs) routinely available in our department. The master process which runs on computer A simply writes the slice numbers and the projection data to be reconstructed into the *space using* a template matching mechanism. Each of the reconstruction workers which run on Computers B-F, takes one of the tasks, removes it from the space, and reconstructs only the slice that corresponds to this specific task. Since the task is removed from the *space*, exclusive access to this job is guaranteed. After reconstruction, the worker writes the reconstructed transaxial slice back into the space from where it will be collected by the master process. After the worker has finished his work, he looks into the *space again* for more available tasks. If successful, the worker starts to reconstruct the next slice. At the same time, the other workers reconstruct other slices and write them into the *space*. When all slices are reconstructed, the master process collects and views the reconstructed slices using a self developed Java slice viewer. The parallel implementation of this iterative reconstruction method shortens the reconstruction time significantly by a factor of approximately 20 as compared to a single processor.

III. Results

Reconstruction of In-111 Octreotide SPECT Images

SPECT raw data of a routine receptor study using In 111 octreotide in a patient with SCLC were used for reconstruction. After injection of 150 MBq In-111 octreotide a 360° SPECT was performed (acquisition. parameters: 64x64 matrix, 6°/step and 30 sec. per angular position) using a MEGP collimator. Acquired data were distributed among the workers by the master process and iteratively reconstructed. An iterative algorithm, based on the learning methods used by artificial neural networks [13, 14] needs approximately 15 seconds to reconstruct the whole object using the presented JavaSpaces implementation. When applying the same iterative reconstruction algorithm (and the same number of iterations), it takes approximately 3 minutes to reconstruct the data if a single processor implementation is used. The iteratively reconstructed slices were compared with those reconstructed with FBP. The iteratively reconstructed image (Fig. 4a) demonstrates a lesion (confirmed by CT) in the left suprarenal gland which is not shown by FBP (Fig. 4b).

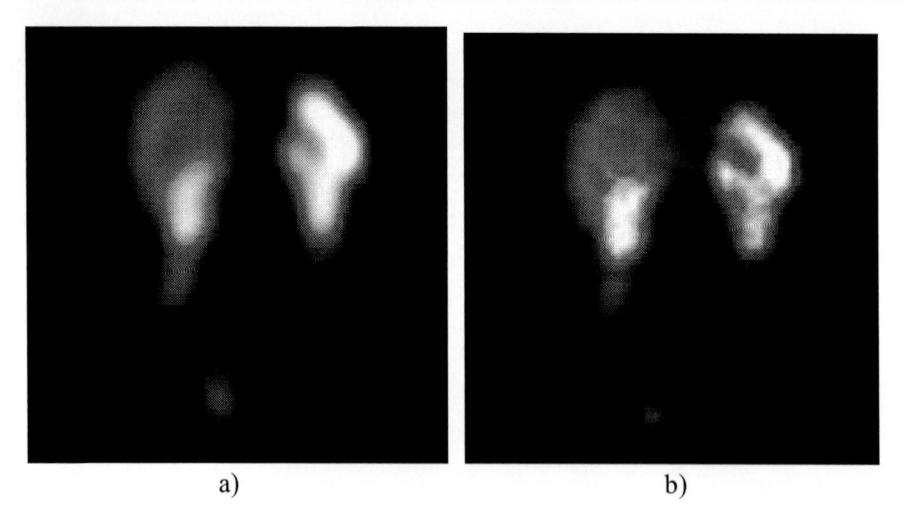

Figure 4. In 111 Octreotide image of the abdomen: a) Iterative reconstruction demonstrates a lesion in the left suprarenal gland. b) The lesion is not detected by FBP.

IV. Discussion

Distributed applications are - despite their advantages - difficult to design due to the complexity of the distributed environment which does not concern when writing standalone applications[15]. In the past, the variety of existing machine architectures and software platforms has prevented the development and proliferation of distributed applications [10]. JavaSpaces is a high-level coordination tool for combining processes into a distributed application by means of a network-accessible "space". This recently introduced technology [5, 6] can also be elegantly used to solve computational intensive tasks. In this paper, a new approach of the parallel implementation of an iterative reconstruction algorithm using Jini and JavaSpaces is presented, which reduces the computation time by several orders of magnitude. Although other attempts of parallel implementation for tomographic reconstruction methods using networking and/or dedicated hardware has been described before [7-9], a truly distributed system applying only standard PC equipment to reconstruct SPECT data has not been presented before. Applying JavaSpaces, the SPECT acquisition data are distributed by a master process between five reconstruction workers, which reside on different computers of our department's Intranet. Each reconstruction worker computes specific layers of the object. After successful computation of all the layers, the master process collects and views the reconstructed slices. The parallel implementation results in a significant acceleration of the reconstruction time, thus providing the possibility for additional implementation of physical properties (e.g. gamma camera resolution, scatter) into the algorithm, which further improves the quality of the reconstructed images. Use of an improved mathematical model will not necessarily lengthen the overall computation time, since the number of reconstruction workers can be incremented very easily. The significant acceleration of processing time is due to:

- Parallel implementation
- Loading of auxiliary data in advance

- Correct balance between computation and communication
- Processing and transfer time

The *parallel implementation* of the iterative algorithm enables reconstruction of several layers of the object at the same time. Reconstruction workers are able to *load auxiliary data*, needed for iterative reconstruction, in advance. A *correct balance between computation and communication* is difficult to achieve with other software design models [8]. Using a JavaSpaces implementation, the reconstruction workers stay busy and compute tasks in relation to their availability and ability to work. Consideration of both, the *processing and transfer time* is important for application in a clinical routine environment. The applied platform independent technology allows the use of hardware, which already exists in any department, thus avoiding communication bottlenecks since transfer time over the network connection is minimized. JavaSpaces technology does not only improve tomographic reconstruction but may also be used as a platform-independent, cost-effective means to shorten the computation time of other time-consuming computational tasks.

References

[1] http://www.sun.com
[2] http://java.sun.com/products/jdk1.2
[3] Malameteniou F., Vassilacopoulos G., Mantas J.: A search engine for virtual patient records. *Int. J. Med. Inf.* 1999 Aug;55(2):103-15
[4] Slomka P.,Elliot E., Driedger A.: Java-Based Remote Viewing and Processing of Nuclear Medicine Images: Toward "the Imaging Department without walls" *J. Nucl. Med.* 2000;41:111-118
[5] http://www.sun.com/jini/index.html
[6] Freeman E., Hupfer S., Arnold K.: JavaSpaces. *Principles, Patterns and Practice* Addison-Wesley, Massachusetts, USA 1999
[7] Passeri A., Formicioni A. R, de Cristofaro M., Pupi A. Meldolesi U.: High-performance computing and networking as tools for accurate emission computed tomography reconstruction. *Eur. J. Nucl. Med.* (1997) 24:390-397
[8] Comtat C., Defrise M., Morel C., Townsend D.: The FaVor Algorithm for 3D Pet Data and its Implementation using a Net of Transputers. *Phys. Med. Biol.*, Vol. 38; pp 929-944, 1993
[9] Kontaxakis G., Strauss L. G., vanKaick G.: Optimized Implementation and Perfromance Evaluation of Iterative Image Reconstruction Algorithms for PET on Distributed Pentium Systems and a Web-Based Interface. (Abs.) *J. Nucl. Med.* 1998; 39:8P
[10] Arnold K., Sullivan B., Scheifler R., Waldo J., Wollrath A.*: The Jini Specification Addison Wesley*, Massachusetts, USA, 1999
[11] Edwards K.: *Core Jini Prentice Hall*, NJ, USA, 1999
[12] Horstmann C, Cornell G.: Core Java 1.2: *Fundamentals Prentice Hall*, NJ, USA, 1999
[13] Knoll P., Mirzaei S., Müllner A., Koriska K., Köhn H., Neumann M.: An Artificial Neural Net and Error Backpropagation to Reconstruct Single Photon Emission Computerized Tomography Data. *Med. Phys.* 1999;26:244-248

[14] Knoll P, Mirzaei S., Krotla G., Koriska K., H, Köhn: Improvement in *Image Quality Using a Single Layered Artificial Neural Network to Reconstrcut SPECT data. Proceedings of the International Conference on Imaging Sciences*, Systems and Technology (CISST '98), LasVegas, USA 1998

[15] Farley J.: *Java Distributed Computing O'Reilly Associates Inc.*, CA, USA 1998

In: Concurrent and Parallel Computing...
Editor: Alexander S. Becker, pp. 213-233

ISBN: 978-1-60456-274-3
© 2008 Nova Science Publishers, Inc.

Chapter 11

SOLVING MAXIMUM CONCURRENT FLOW PROBLEMS IN A SIGNAL-CONTROLLED ROAD NETWORK

Suh-Wen Chiou[*]

Department of Information Management, National Dong Hwa University
1, Sec. 2, Da Hsueh Rd., Shou-Feng, Hualien, 97401. Taiwan

Abstract

An optimal design of concurrent flows in a signal-controlled road network is considered. The input to the problem is a traffic road network with signal-controlled junctions. A set of travel demands needs to be routed where route choices of users are taken into account. In this paper a mathematical optimization problem is formulated for which the objective is to find a delay-minimizing signal setting such that the largest value of a fraction of every demand can be simultaneously routed without exceeding the available capacities on edges. A fast algorithm globally solving signal settings and maximum concurrent flows is presented together with numerical calculations on example road networks. Improvement on a locally optimal search is achieved by combining the technique of parallel tangents with the gradient projection. As it shows, the proposed algorithm combines the locally optimal search and globally search heuristic achieved substantially promising performance with relatively less computational efforts when compared to traditional methods.

Keywords: concurrent flow; signal settings; road network; computational algorithms; equilibrium constraints; optimization.

1. Introduction

An optimal design of concurrent flows in a signal-controlled road network is considered. In this paper a mathematical optimization problem is formulated for signal settings while taking into account the route choice of users. In past decades, many researchers via the techniques of

---
[*] E-mail address: chiou@mail.ndhu.edu.tw

optimization have investigated the network design problem with concurrent flows [1, 3-4, 6, 9, 12]. In order to determine the signal settings, a good performance value can be achieved by optimizing a chosen objective function, in which the users' behavior of choice of routes is supposed to follow Wardrop's first principle. That is, a road user will choose his route between a specified origin-destination pair with the minimal travel time, which is in turn dependent on the choice of the network signal settings. Therefore, in the optimization process for concurrent network flows , not only the signal settings need to be considered but also the consequential effects on the equilibrium flows caused by the signal settings need to be taken into account. Abdulaal and LeBlanc [1] were the first ones who proposed the **Hooke-Jeeves (HJ)** method to solve the concurrent flow network design problem directly via continuous decision variables and obtained feasible solutions, which only confined to a small-scaled test network in practice due to the computation limit. Allsop and Charlesworth [2] proposed a **mutually consistent calculation (MC)** for the signal setting minimization problem and equilibrium network flows. The resulting mutually consistent signal settings and concurrent flows will, however, in general be a non-optimal solution.

The other alternative to solve the concurrent flows with signal settings is a bi-level programming approach [9, 12]. At the upper level, the system performance is optimized with respect to the signal setting variables, while at the lower level a user equilibrium traffic assignment problem is solved with concurrent flows. The dependence of equilibrium flows on the signal settings is regarded as a constraint for the upper level and is solved by the lower level problem. Therefore, the signal settings problem can be regarded as a constrained optimization problem. Using the bi-level programming to solve the signal settings problem, Heydecker and Khoo [7] firstly proposed a **linear constraint approximation (LCA)** to the equilibrium flows and solved the signal settings problem as a constrained optimization problem in a sequence of linear approximation. As it reported, the linear constraint approximation method has obtained good results as compared to other non bi-level programming approaches. Yang and Yagar [13] proposed a **sensitivity analysis based (SAB)** algorithm to solve the signal settings where a linearized sub-problem is formulated at current signal settings and solved by the simplex method. Because of the non-convexity of the signal settings problem, these two optimization based solution algorithms (**LCA** and **SAB**) can solve the network concurrent flow problem with signal settings only locally.

In this paper, the ways in optimally determining signal settings and network concurrent flows can be formulated as a bi-level problem. At the upper level an optimization problem of signal timings to find the maximal concurrent network flows is determined, among which the signal timing plan for coordinated fixed time control is defined by the common cycle time, the start and duration of greens. The performance index (PI) is defined as the sum of a weighted linear combination of rate of delay and number of stops per unit time for all traffic streams, which is evaluated by the traffic model from TRANSYT [10] in which vehicular platooning is considered on a simple traffic model. The corresponding approximate mathematical expressions for various components of the performance index and the average delay to a vehicle at the downstream junction in the TRANSYT model for both undersaturated and oversaturated links have been obtained. As a step toward finding solutions to the signal settings problem, the partial derivatives, with respect to signal setting variables and concurrent flows have been derived [5,11]. At the lower level a user equilibrium traffic assignment obeying Wardrop's first principle can be formulated as a minimization problem where the link travel time function is defined as the sum of the undelayed travel time on the link and the average delay incurred by vehicles at the downstream end of the link. Because the user equilibrium assignment constraint is non-linear, which leads the signal settings problem to be a non-convex problem, only locally optimal solutions can therefore be found.

In this paper a fast algorithm, **McNETS**, is proposed for the **Maximum concurrent NETwork flows and Signal settings**. The **McNETS** combines a locally optimal search and a global search heuristic, which can be specified in the following manner. For a locally optimal search, the gradient projection method is used to find an improving descent direction. For a global search heuristic, making equal and simultaneous changes in the starts of green for all signal settings at any one junction provides a wide search across the feasible region, thus a better local optimum can be identified. In order to enhance the efficiency of the locally optimal search, the technique combining parallel tangents (**PARTAN**) with gradient projection method is employed. By doing so, a good descent direction can be determined along which the value of objective function is consistently improved. Two example road networks have been used as illustrative examples for showing the efficiency and robustness of **McNETS** when solving the maximum concurrent network flows with signal settings.

The rest of the paper is organized as follows. In next section, formulations of the signal settings and concurrent network flows are given. In Section 3, a fast algorithm **McNETS** for the maximum concurrent network flows with signal settings is proposed where improvements in the performance index (PI) values can be further done by combining the technique of parallel tangents with the gradient projection method. In Section 4, a two-junction and Allsop and Charlesworth's example networks are illustrated for conducting numerical calculations. Conclusions and discussions for this paper are made in Section 5.

2. Problem Formulation

2.1. Notation

$G(N,L)$ denotes a directed road network, where N is the set of signal controlled junctions and L is the set of links.

W denotes the set of origin-destination (OD) pairs.

T denotes the travel demands for OD pairs.

R_w denotes the set of paths between OD pair w.

$\Psi = (\zeta, \theta, \phi)$ denotes the set of signal setting variables, respectively for the reciprocal of cycle time, start and duration of greens, where $\theta = [\theta_{jm}]$ and $\phi = [\phi_{jm}]$ represents the vector of starts θ_{jm} and durations of green ϕ_{jm} for signal group j at junction m as proportions of common cycle time.

u a common multiplier applied to the average flow.

Λ_a represents the duration of effective green for link a.

g_{jm} represents the minimum green for signal group j at junction m.

$\bar{c}_{jlm}$ represents the clearance time between the end of green for group j and the start of green for incompatible group l at junction m.

$\Omega_m(j,l)$ represents a collection of numbers 0 and 1 for each pair of incompatible signal groups at junction m; where $\Omega_m(j,l) = 0$ if the start of green for signal group j proceeds that of l, and $\Omega_m(j,l) = 1$, otherwise.

s_a represents saturation flow on link a.

D_a represents the rate of delay on link a.

S_a represents the number of stops per unit time on link a.

f denotes vector of path flows.

q denotes the link flows.

δ denotes the link-path incidence matrix.

Λ - denote the origin-destination-path incidence matrix.

c denotes the link travel times.

2.2. A Delay-Minimizing Concurrent Flow Signal Setting Problem

In order to determine the optimal signal settings Ψ and the maximal multiplier u attached to the demand matrix, a delay-minimizing concurrent flow signal setting problem can be formulated in the following manner.

$$\min_{\Psi, u} \quad Z = Z_0(\Psi, q^*(u, \Psi)) \tag{1}$$

$$= \sum_{a \in L} D_a W_{aD}^1 + S_a W_{aS}^1$$

subject to
$$\zeta_{min} \leq \zeta \leq \zeta_{max} \tag{2}$$

$$g_{jm}\zeta \leq \phi_{jm} \leq 1, \quad \forall j, m \tag{3}$$

$$uq_a \leq s_a \Lambda_a, \quad \forall a \in L \tag{4}$$

$$\theta_{jm} + \phi_{jm} + \overline{c}_{jlm}\zeta \leq \theta_{lm} + \Omega_m(j,l), \quad j \neq l, \forall j, l, m \tag{5}$$

where W_{aD}^1 and W_{aS}^1 are respectively link-specific weighting factors for the rate of delay and the number of stops per unit time used in TRANSYT. The first constraint is for the common cycle time and for each junction m the constraints (3-5) are for the green phase, link capacity and clearance time. Also the equilibrium flows can be found as follows. To find values $q^*(u, \Psi)$ such that

$$\mathbf{c}^t(\mathbf{q}(u,\Psi))(\mathbf{z}-\mathbf{q}(u,\Psi)) \geq 0 \tag{6}$$

for all $\mathbf{z} \in \mathbf{K} = \{\mathbf{q}(u,\Psi) : \mathbf{q}(u,\Psi) = \delta \mathbf{f}(u,\Psi), u\mathbf{T} = \Delta \mathbf{f}(u,\Psi), \mathbf{f}(u,\Psi) \geq 0\}$ where the superscript t denotes the matrix transpose operator.

2.3. Sensitivity Analysis

Suppose $(\mathbf{f}', u', \Psi')$ solves problem (6), the KKT system with Lagrange multipliers π' and μ' can be expressed as

$$\mathbf{C}(\mathbf{f}',\Psi') - \pi' - \Delta^t \mu' = 0 \tag{7}$$

$$\mathbf{diag}(\pi')\mathbf{f}'(u',\Psi') = 0$$

$$\Delta \mathbf{f}'(u',\Psi') - u\mathbf{T} = 0$$

$$\pi \geq 0$$

where $\mathbf{diag}(\cdot)$ denotes the diagonal matrix. Supposing with positive path flows, i.e. $\mathbf{f} > 0$ and $\pi = 0$ the KKT system of (7) can be re-expressed as

$$\mathbf{C}(\mathbf{f}',\Psi') - \Delta^t \mu' = 0 \tag{8}$$

$$\Delta \mathbf{f}'(u',\Psi') - u\mathbf{T} = 0$$

where $\pi = 0$ due to the complementarity condition. The first order partial derivatives of equilibrium flow and the associated Lagrange multiplier with respect to signal settings and the multiplier are of the following forms.

$$\begin{pmatrix} \nabla_\Psi \mathbf{f} \\ \nabla_\Psi \mu \end{pmatrix} = -\begin{pmatrix} \nabla \mathbf{C} & -\Delta^t \\ \Delta & 0 \end{pmatrix}^{-1} \begin{pmatrix} \nabla_\Psi \mathbf{C} \\ 0 \end{pmatrix} \tag{9}$$

$$\begin{pmatrix} \nabla_u \mathbf{f} \\ \nabla_u \mu \end{pmatrix} = -\begin{pmatrix} \nabla \mathbf{C} & -\Delta^t \\ \Delta & 0 \end{pmatrix}^{-1} \begin{pmatrix} 0 \\ -\mathbf{T} \end{pmatrix} \tag{10}$$

3. A Fast Algorithm for Concurrent Flows with Signal Settings

In this section, a fast algorithm McNETS is proposed to simultaneously solve problems (1-5), for which a search direction of descent is generated and a new iterate is created. The search process will be terminated at a KKT point or a new search direction can be generated. Consider the first order partial derivatives for the objective function in problems (1-5) evaluated at (u_0, Ψ_0, q_0), which can be expressed as

$$\begin{pmatrix} \nabla Z_\Psi(u_0,\Psi_0) \\ \nabla Z_u(u_0,\Psi_0) \end{pmatrix} = \begin{pmatrix} \nabla_\Psi Z_0(u_0,\Psi_0,q_0) \\ \nabla_u Z_0(u_0,\Psi_0,q_0) \end{pmatrix} + \nabla_q Z_0(u_0,\Psi_0,q_0)\nabla q(u_0,\Psi_0) \quad (11)$$

where the first order derivatives with respect to signal settings and the multiplier can be derived from [13], the second item are from the sensitivity analysis for network flows by eqs (9) and (10). Let **A** denote the coefficient matrix and **B** the constant vector in constrains (2-5) the problems (1-5) can be rewritten as

$$\underset{u,\Psi}{\text{Min}} \quad Z = Z_1(u,\Psi) \quad (12)$$

subject to $\quad A(u,\Psi) \leq B$

In the followings, we apply a gradient projection method to a linear constraint set as given in (12) by introducing a matrix in projecting the gradient of the objective function onto a null space of active constraints as in (2-5) with equality in order to efficiently search for feasible points.

Theorem 1. (Projected gradient method) Consider the problem in (12), a sequence of feasible iterates $\{u_k, \Psi_k\}$ can be generated according to

$$\begin{pmatrix} u_{k+1} \\ \Psi_{k+1} \end{pmatrix} = \begin{pmatrix} u_k \\ \Psi_k \end{pmatrix} + \alpha_{k+1} H_{k+1} d_{k+1} \quad (13)$$

where d_{k+1} is the gradient direction determined by the negative of (11) and α_{k+1} is the step length minimizing Z_1 along d_{k+1} for which (u_{k+1}, Ψ_{k+1}) is within the feasible region defined by (2-5). Suppose that M_{k+1} has full rank at (u_k, Ψ_k), which is the gradient of active constraints with equalities in (2-5) and the projection matrix H_{k+1} is of the following form.

$$H_{k+1} = I - M_{k+1}^t (M_{k+1} M_{k+1}^t)^{-1} M_{k+1} \quad (14)$$

The search direction s_{k+1} can be determined in the following form.

$$s_{k+1} = H_{k+1}d_{k+1} \qquad (15)$$

Then the sequence of feasible points $\{(u_k, \Psi_k)\}$ generated by the projected conjugate gradient method monotonically decreases the performance value,

$$Z_1(u_k, \Psi_k) > Z_1(u_{k+1}, \Psi_{k+1}), \qquad k = 1,2,3,\ldots \qquad (16)$$

whenever $H_{k+1}\nabla Z_1(u_k, \Psi_k) \neq 0$ and $\nabla Z_1(u_k, \Psi_k)$ is from (11). □

Theorem 2. (Projected gradient method as $H_{k+1}\nabla Z_1(u_k, \Psi_k) = 0$) In Theorem 1 when $H_{k+1}\nabla Z_1(u_k, \Psi_k) = 0$, if all the Lagrange multipliers corresponding to the active constraint gradients with equalities in (2-5) are positive or zeros, it implies the current (u_k, Ψ_k) is a KKT point. Otherwise choose one negative Lagrange multiplier, say μ_j, and construct a new $\hat{M}_{k+1}$ of the active constraint gradients by deleting the jth row of M_{k+1}, which corresponds to the negative component μ_j, and make the projection matrix of the following form

$$H_{k+1} = I - \hat{M}_{k+1}^t(\hat{M}_{k+1}\hat{M}_{k+1}^t)^{-1}\hat{M}_{k+1} \qquad (17)$$

The search direction then is determined by (15) and the results of Theorem 1 hold. □

Corollary 3 (Stopping condition) If (u_k, Ψ_k) is a KKT point for problem in (12) then the search process may stop; otherwise a new descent direction at (u_k, Ψ_k) can be generated according to Theorems 1-2. □

Consider the signal settings problem in (12), a fast algorithm, McNETS, for concurrent flows with signal settings can be specified in the following way. McNETS combines a local and global search as given below.

3.1. Local Search Step

Local search step is a locally optimal search for a full optimization with respect to the common cycle time, the start and duration of green at each junction for problem (12), which is conducted as follows.

Step 1. Start with (u_k, Ψ_k), set index $k = 0$.

Step 2. Solve a traffic assignment problem with signal settings and multiplier (u_k, Ψ_k), find the first order derivatives by (11).

Step 3. Use the projected gradient method to determine a search direction by (15). Go to Step 4.

Step 4. If $H_{k+1}\nabla Z_1(u_k,\Psi_k) \neq 0$, find a new (u_k,Ψ_k) in (13) and letting $k \leftarrow k+1$. Go to Step 2. If $H_{k+1}\nabla Z_1(u_k,\Psi_k) = 0$ and all the Lagrange multipliers corresponding to the active constraint gradients are non-negative, (u_k,Ψ_k) is the KKT point and stop. Otherwise, find the most negative Lagrange multiplier and cancel the corresponding constraint and find a new projection matrix and go to Step 3.

3.2. Global Search Step

Given the cycle time and duration of green at each junction, a global search is implemented in offsets to obtain a better point in another part of the feasible region as a reset point for local search. After a reset point with significant improvement in PI is found, conduct the local search in Section 3.1 again and locate new signal settings until the difference of the values of the performance index between successive iterations is negligible.

3.3. Integration with PARTAN

In order to effectively find local optimal points, in this section, an extension of McNETS in the locally optimal search integrated with PARTAN is presented in the following steps.

I-Step 1. Given initial values of (u_k,Ψ_k), start with step $k = 0$. Let I_0 be the set of indices of binding constraints.

I-Step 2. At step k, find the equilibrium flow q_k with fixed (u_k,Ψ_k).

I-Step 3. Calculate $\nabla q(u_k,\Psi_k)$ and obtain the gradient $\nabla Z_1(u_k,\Psi_k)$ from (11).

I-Step 4. Calculate the projection matrix and decide the search direction s_k. If $s_k = 0$, go to I-Step 5. If $k = 0$ go to I-Step 4-1; otherwise go to I-Step 4-2.

I-Step 4-1. Find the optimal step length α_{opt} in the search direction s_k along which the objective function value is minimized. Let

$$\begin{pmatrix} u_{k+1} \\ \Psi_{k+1} \end{pmatrix} = \begin{pmatrix} u_k \\ \Psi_k \end{pmatrix} + \alpha_{opt} s_k$$

and set $k \leftarrow k+1$ return to I-Step 2.

I-Step 4-2. Find the optimal step length α_{opt} in the search direction s_k along which the objective function value is minimized. Set

$$\begin{pmatrix} \overline{\mathbf{u}}_{k+1} \\ \overline{\mathbf{\Psi}}_{k+1} \end{pmatrix} = \begin{pmatrix} \mathbf{u}_k \\ \mathbf{\Psi}_k \end{pmatrix} + \alpha_{opt} \mathbf{s}_k$$

Go to I-Step 4-3.

I-Step 4-3. Conduct PARTAN line search and find λ^* such that

$$Z_1\left(\begin{pmatrix} \mathbf{u}_{k+1} \\ \mathbf{\Psi}_{k+1} \end{pmatrix} = \begin{pmatrix} \mathbf{u}_{k-1} \\ \mathbf{\Psi}_{k-1} \end{pmatrix} + \lambda^*\left(\begin{pmatrix} \overline{\mathbf{u}}_{k+1} \\ \overline{\mathbf{\Psi}}_{k+1} \end{pmatrix} - \begin{pmatrix} \mathbf{u}_{k-1} \\ \mathbf{\Psi}_{k-1} \end{pmatrix}\right)\right) = \underset{0 \leq \lambda \leq \lambda_{max}}{\text{Min}} \left\{ Z_1\left(\begin{pmatrix} \mathbf{u}_{k-1} \\ \mathbf{\Psi}_{k-1} \end{pmatrix} + \lambda\left(\begin{pmatrix} \overline{\mathbf{u}}_{k+1} \\ \overline{\mathbf{\Psi}}_{k+1} \end{pmatrix} - \begin{pmatrix} \mathbf{u}_{k-1} \\ \mathbf{\Psi}_{k-1} \end{pmatrix}\right)\right) \right\}$$

Where $\lambda_{max} = \min\{\underline{\lambda}, \overline{\lambda}\}$,

$$\underline{\lambda} = \min\left\{ \frac{\begin{pmatrix} u_{jk} \\ \Psi_{jk} \end{pmatrix}}{|s_{jk}|}, if \ s_{jk} < 0, \forall j \in L \right\}$$

and

$$\overline{\lambda} = \min\left\{ \frac{\mu_j - \begin{pmatrix} u_{jk} \\ \Psi_{jk} \end{pmatrix}}{s_{jk}}, if \ s_{jk} > 0, \forall j \in L \right\}$$

where s_{jk} and $\begin{pmatrix} u_{jk} \\ \Psi_{jk} \end{pmatrix}$ respectively denote the jth component of $\mathbf{s}_k$ and $\begin{pmatrix} \mathbf{u}_k \\ \mathbf{\Psi}_k \end{pmatrix}$. Go to I-Step 5.

I-Step 5. Check Lagrange multiplier $\boldsymbol{\mu}$ vector. If $\boldsymbol{\mu} \geq \mathbf{0}$ then $(\mathbf{u}_k, \mathbf{\Psi}_k)$ is KKT point and stop. Otherwise find μ_j the most negative component of vector $\boldsymbol{\mu}$ and set $I_0 \leftarrow I_0 - \{j\}$. Set $k \leftarrow k + 1$ and return to I-Step 2.

4. Numerical Examples and Computational Comparisons

In this section, numerical experiments are conducted twofold. Firstly, numerical computations were carried out for showing the effectiveness and robustness of the solution methods (LCA, SAB and McNETS) as compared to earlier conventional method Hooke-Jeeves (HJ) and the non-optimal mutually consistent (MC) solution method at a two-junction signal-controlled road network. Secondly, as illustrated on a medium-sized road network, numerical comparisons are made furthermore by conducting LCA, SAB and McNETS on Allsop & Charlesworth' s road network and the results are shown on a link-by-link basis.

4.1. Test Road Networks

The first test network contains two signal-controlled junctions, which has been modified from Braess's road network. The two-junction network consists of one OD pair and eight TRANSYT links. Link travel times are decided by the sum of the undelayed travel time along this link and the average delay incurred by traffic at the downstream junction. For each signal controlled junction, the travel times on entering links will be affected by the changes of the corresponding signal settings and for non-signal controlled links the travel times are constant throughout this computation process. Another test road network was given by [2]. This numerical test includes 22 pairs of trip-ends, 23 links at 6 signal-controlled junctions. Basic layouts of the example road networks and allocations for signal groups for each junction are given in Figs. 1-3. Fixed data for the example road networks are given in Tables 1-3. Using typical values found in practice, the minimum green time for each group is 7 seconds, and the clearance times are 5 seconds between incompatible signal groups. The maximum cycle time is set 130 seconds.

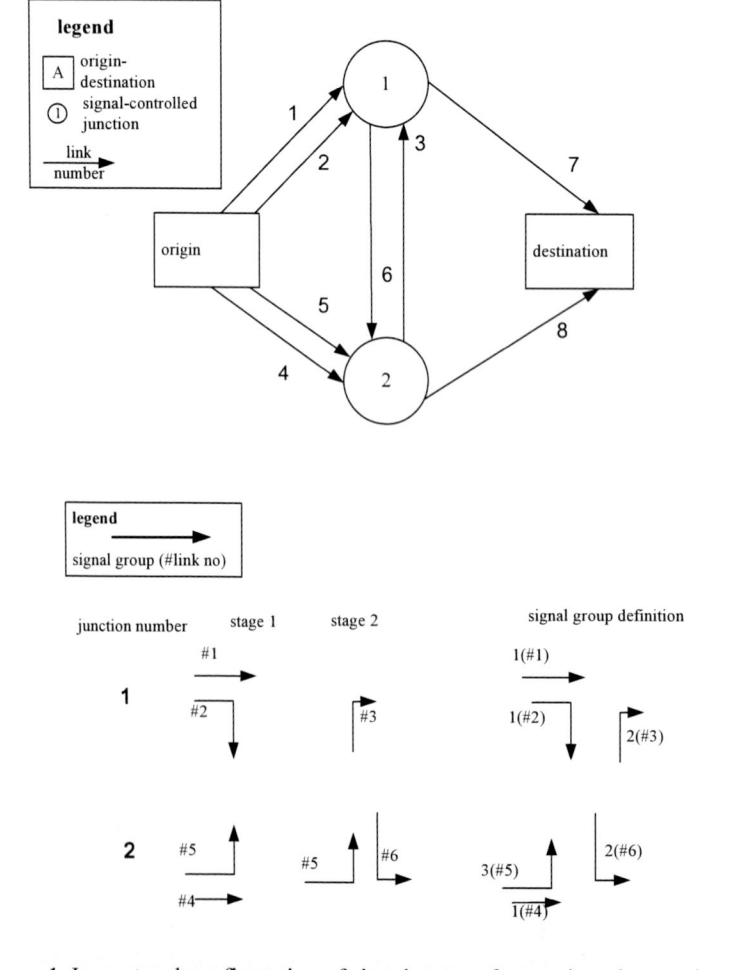

Figure 1. Layout and configuration of signal groups for two junction road network.

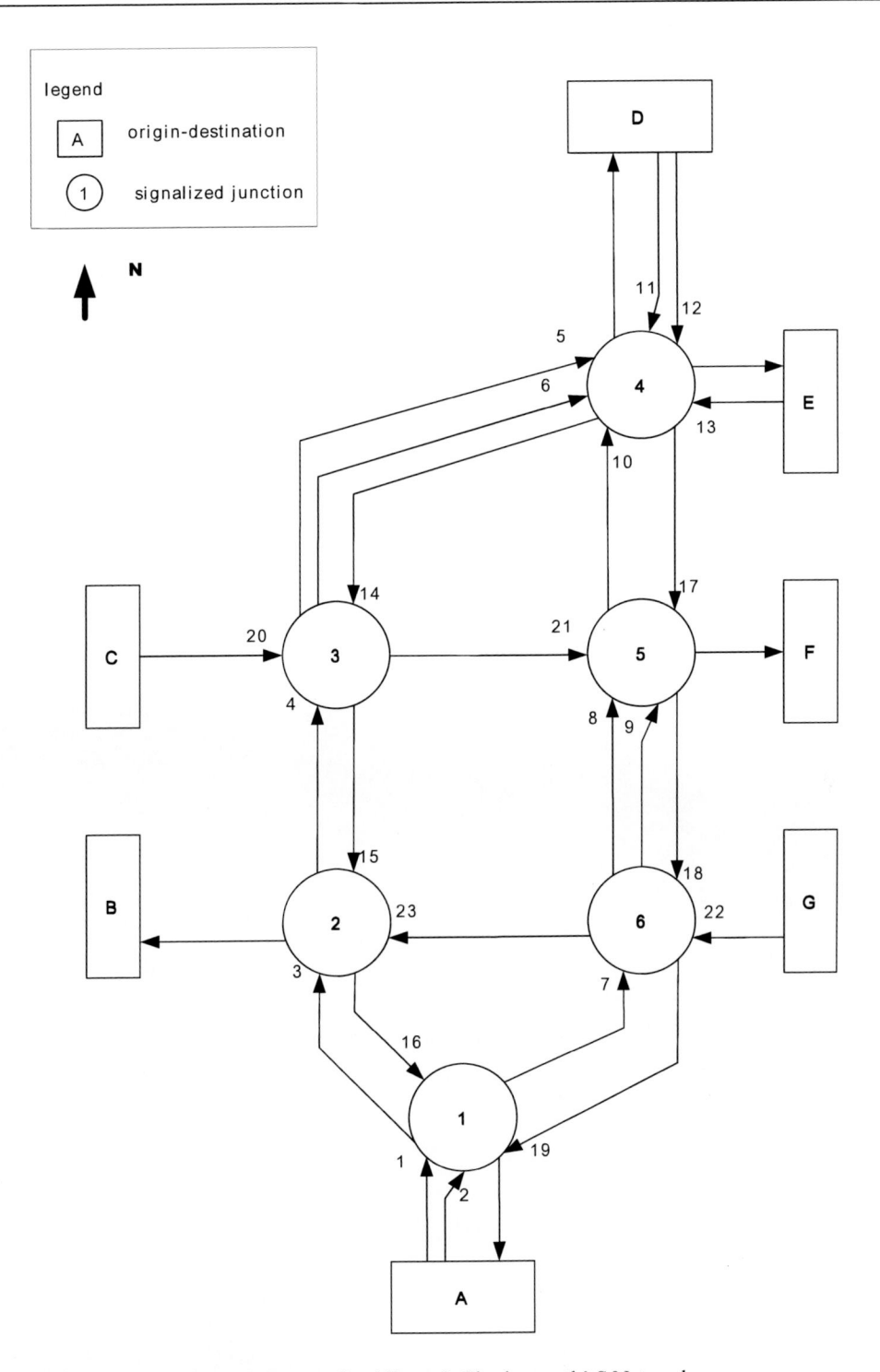

Figure 2. Layout for Allsop & Charlesworth' S Network.

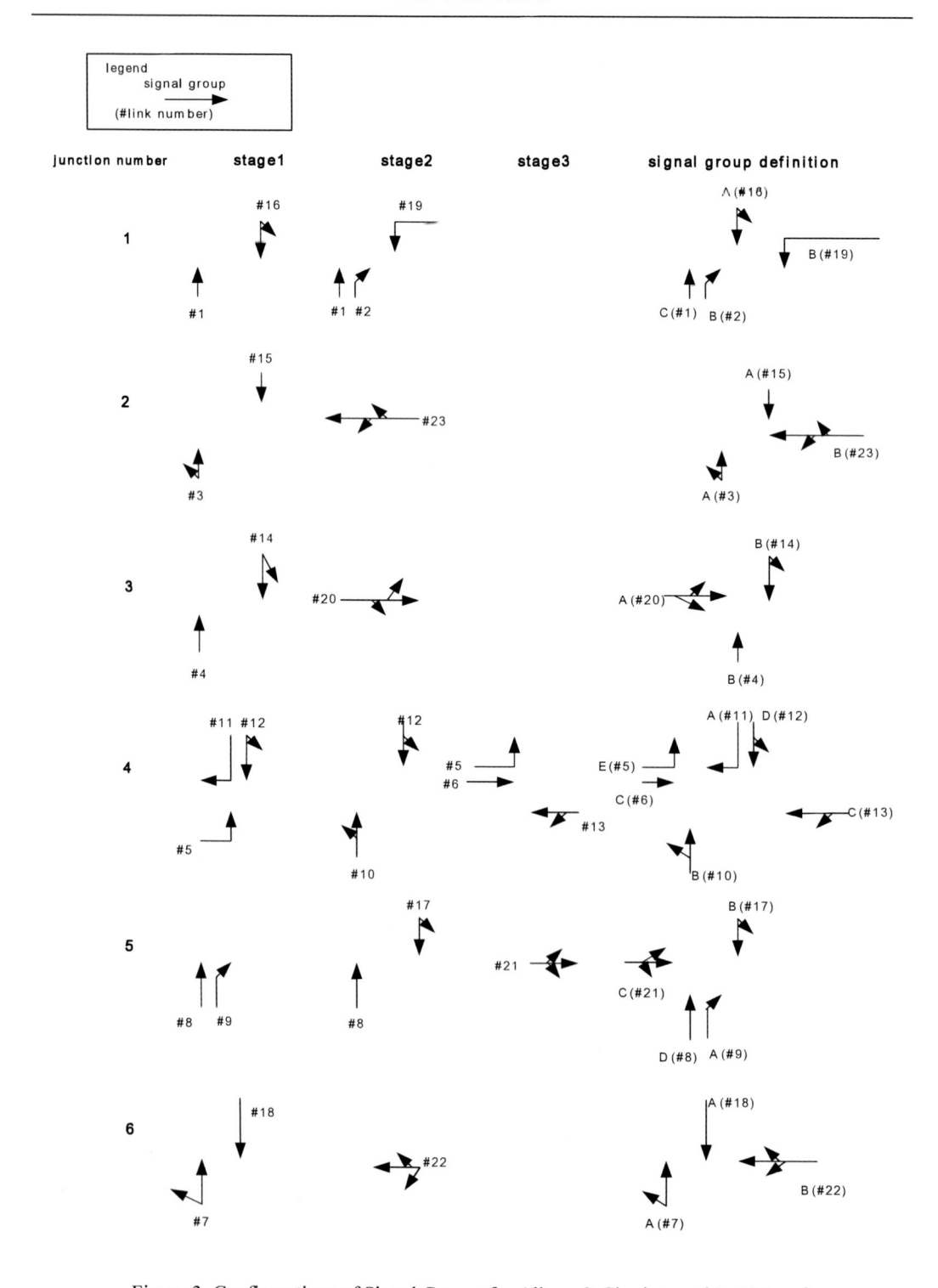

Figure 3. Configurations of Signal Groups for Allsop & Charlesworth's Network.

Table 1. Input Data for Two-Junction Road Network

\multicolumn{8}{c	}{Two-Junction Road Network}
Junction No.	Link No.	Cruise Travel Time (s)	Saturation Flow (in Veh/h)	Junction No.	Link No.	Cruise Travel Time (s)	Saturation Flow (in Veh/h)
1	1	20	1800	2	4	20	1800
1	2	20	1800	2	5	20	1800
1	3	20	1800	2	6	20	1800

where the non-signal controlled links 7 and 8 are given travel time of 10 seconds, the OD demand is set 1500 veh/h

Table 2. Input Data for Allsop and Charlesworth' S Road Network

\multicolumn{8}{c	}{Allsop & Charlesworth' s Road Network}
Junction No.	Link No.	Cruise Travel Time (s)	Saturation Flow (in Veh/h)	Junction No.	Link No.	Cruise Travel Time (s)	Saturation Flow (in Veh/h)
1	1	0	2000	4	5	20	1800
1	2	0	1600	4	6	20	1850
1	16	10	2900	4	10	10	2200
1	19	10	1500	4	11	0	2000
2	3	10	3200	4	12	0	1800
2	15	15	2600	4	13	0	2200
2	23	15	3200	5	8	15	1850
3	4	15	3200	5	9	15	1700
3	14	20	3200	5	17	10	1700
3	20	0	2800	5	21	15	3200
				6	7	10	1800
				6	18	15	1700
				6	22	0	3600

Table 3. Origin-Destination Trip Rates for Allsop and Charlesworth's Road Network

\multicolumn{7}{c	}{Allsop & Charlesworth' s Road Network}
Origin/Destination	A	B	D	E	F	Origin Totals
A	-	250	700	30	200	1180
C	40	20	200	130	900	1290
D	400	250	-	50	100	800
E	300	130	30	-	20	480
G	550	450	170	60	20	1250
Destination Totals	1290	1100	1100	270	1240	5000

4.2. Computational Results for Two-Junction Road Network

Computational results for conducting HJ, MC, LCA, SAB and McNETS at two-junction road network are shown in Table 4, where the optimal values of the performance index (PI) are achieved approximately as that did by the HJ solution method, but with quite different optimized solutions, which clearly shows the non-convexity of this problem with signal settings. As it reported in this case, the solution algorithms implemented in the two-junction road network improved the values of system performance to effectively the same extent as compared to those did by the solution method HJ, which provides a background to the subsequent numerical analysis using the MC, LCA, SAB and McNETS when a medium-sized road network is taken into account.

Table 4. Computational results for two-Junction road network

Variable/Algorithm	HJ	MC	LCA	SAB	McNETS
ϕ_{11}/ζ	43	58	43	43	43
ϕ_{21}/ζ	7	7	7	7	7
ϕ_{12}/ζ	43	58	43	43	43
ϕ_{22}/ζ	7	7	7	7	7
ϕ_{32}/ζ	60	75	60	60	60
q_1	750	750	750	750.3	750
q_2	0	0	0	0.1	0
q_3	0	0	0	0.1	0
q_4	750	750	750	749.6	750
q_5	0	0	0	0.1	0
q_6	0	0	0	0.1	0
$1/\zeta$	60	75	60	60	60
PI	3.08	3.09	3.09	3.11	3.09
u	0.95	0.95	0.95	0.95	0.95
#	37	11	9	10	9

where ϕ_{jm}/ζ denotes the duration of greens for signal group j at junction m measured in seconds and $1/\zeta$ denotes the common cycle time measured in seconds. q_a is measured in veh/h, PI denotes the performance index value measured in veh-h/h and # denotes the number of equilibrium assignment problems solved. Algorithm HJ, MC, LCA, SAB and McNETS are respectively short for Hooke-Jeeves, mutually consistent calculation, linearly constraint approximation, sensitivity analysis based and newly proposed method in this paper.

4.3. Computational Results on Allsop & Charlesworth's Road Network

Due to the computation limit of HJ when applies to a medium-sized test road network, in the following numerical calculations the methods MC, LCA, SAB and McNETS are chosen for comparisons. Computational results for conducting MC, LCA, SAB and McNETS on the medium-sized road network illustrated by [2] are summarized in Table 7 for two arbitrary sets of initial signal settings. Starting with two distinct sets of initial signal settings as given in

Tables 5-6, the solution algorithms LCA, SAB and McNETS achieve at their respective local optima with very close values whilst the corresponding signal settings are appreciably different from each other. On the other hand, the solutions given by MC, as it is observed in Table 7, showed greater sensitivity to the initial signal timings with relative difference about 48% in the resulting values of system performance than did those by other algorithms. For each kind of the solution methods, the performance index values PI reduced from the two initial signal timings are very similar. However, as far as the effectiveness of McNETS achieved in terms of the resulting PI values, McNETS did better than did SAB and LCA. For example, the solutions given by McNETS are about 15.3% and 13.8% lower than those did by SAB and LCA given by the first signal settings. Similarly, at the second set of initial signal settings those achieved by the McNETS are about 15.8% and 14.8% lower than those did by SAB and LCA respectively.

Table 5. Initial signal settings for Allsop and Charlesworth's road network

Variables	1st Set of Signal Settings	2nd Set of Signal Settings
ϕ_{11}/ζ	25	27
ϕ_{21}/ζ	25	38
ϕ_{31}/ζ	60	75
ϕ_{12}/ζ	25	27
ϕ_{22}/ζ	25	38
ϕ_{13}/ζ	25	37
ϕ_{23}/ζ	25	28
ϕ_{14}/ζ	15	15
ϕ_{24}/ζ	15	30
ϕ_{34}/ζ	15	15
ϕ_{44}/ζ	35	50
ϕ_{54}/ζ	35	35
ϕ_{15}/ζ	15	20
ϕ_{25}/ζ	15	20
ϕ_{35}/ζ	15	20
ϕ_{45}/ζ	35	45
ϕ_{16}/ζ	25	37
ϕ_{26}/ζ	25	28
$1/\zeta$	60	75
u	0.95	0.95
PI	115.36	124.96

Table 6. Initials for Allsop and Charlesworth's road network on link by link basis

	1st Set of Signal Settings		2nd Set of Signal Settings	
Link No.	Link Flows (in Veh/h)	PI (in Veh-h/h)	Link Flows (in Veh/h)	PI (in Veh-h/h)
1	950	3.28	810	2.41
2	230	2.97	370	2.33
3	950	3.97	810	4.48
4	840	3.6	770	2.49
5	880	4.98	700	6.10
6	150	1.33	140	1.65
7	230	2.57	470	2.82
8	250	2.22	350	1.61
9	90	1.62	210	2.24
10	260	2.02	500	2.85
11	500	9.87	430	11.31
12	300	1.38	370	1.55
13	480	6.33	480	8.86
14	740	3.01	640	1.89
15	790	5.04	700	5.22
16	610	2.56	620	3.39
17	460	6.11	610	11.16
18	350	2.46	590	4.6
19	680	9.24	670	5.58
20	1290	13.83	1290	10.86
21	1050	15.52	1160	10.61
22	1250	7.89	1250	16.59
23	810	3.56	1080	4.36
Total		115.36		124.96

Table 7. Computational results for Allsop & Charlesworth's road network

	1st Set of Signal Settings				2nd Set of Signal Settings			
Variable/Algorithm	MC	LCA	SAB	McNETS	MC	LCA	SAB	McNETS
ϕ_{11}/ζ	45	41	57	55	55	39	48	58
ϕ_{21}/ζ	52	55	35	50	60	60	56	42
ϕ_{31}/ζ	107	106	102	115	125	109	114	110
ϕ_{12}/ζ	60	68	57	56	65	51	55	55
ϕ_{22}/ζ	37	28	35	49	50	38	49	45
ϕ_{13}/ζ	53	42	36	45	47	43	44	44
ϕ_{23}/ζ	44	54	56	60	68	56	60	56
ϕ_{14}/ζ	42	37	35	40	35	35	35	43

Table 7. Continued

Variable/Algorithm	1st Set of Signal Settings				2nd Set of Signal Settings			
	MC	LCA	SAB	McNETS	MC	LCA	SAB	McNETS
ϕ_{24}/ζ	10	11	9	14	25	16	12	14
ϕ_{34}/ζ	40	43	43	46	50	43	52	38
ϕ_{44}/ζ	57	53	49	59	65	56	52	62
ϕ_{54}/ζ	87	85	83	91	90	83	92	86
ϕ_{15}/ζ	13	18	24	29	23	19	30	25
ϕ_{25}/ζ	23	17	14	18	20	19	15	17
ϕ_{35}/ζ	56	56	49	53	67	56	54	53
ϕ_{45}/ζ	41	40	43	52	48	43	50	47
ϕ_{16}/ζ	30	28	29	39	55	51	43	30
ϕ_{26}/ζ	67	68	63	66	60	48	61	70
$1/\zeta$	107	106	102	115	125	109	114	110
u	0.97	0.97	0.98	1.03	0.98	0.98	0.99	1.02
PI	55.57	45.22	46.04	39.00	108.22	45.91	46.48	39.12
#	108	32	16	21	128	35	14	24

Results for equilibrium concurrent network flows are shown in Tables 8-9 on a link-by-link basis, where the initial link flows are given in Tables 5-6. By the first set of signal settings, for example, the traffic streams with the largest PI values are the links 11, 19, 20, and 21. Three optimization based algorithms have successively decreased the PI values of those links either by increasing the durations of the greens for the corresponding signal groups or by transferring traffic flows via the alternative routes with less values of average delays. For instance, as it seen in Tables 8-9, that the southbound traffic via route in terms of links 11-14-15-16 is increasing while the other alternative in links of 12-17-18-19 is decreasing, and the average travel times keep decreasing after reallocating the durations of green among the junctions. Also the three optimization based algorithms induced relatively distinct traffic flows as seen in Tables 8-9. For example, at the first set of signal settings, the LCA method induced greater northbound traffic via junctions 2 and 3 while the SAB method induced more northbound traffic via junctions 6 and 5.

Comparisons for the final values of the local optimum as shown in Table 7: McNETS obtained one which is better than those found by the SAB and LCA, and in this numerical tests: the local optima found by the SAB and LCA are very close to each other although the corresponding signal settings and the maximum concurrent flows were appreciably different. Comparison of the computational efforts in terms of the number of the user equilibrium problems solved taken by the three optimization based algorithms shows that: SAB took fewer iterations to achieve its local optimum than did the McNETS and LCA, and LCA took more iterations than McNETS to find its local optimum, while MC took the most number iterations to converge to its local solutions in the both cases.

Table 8. Numerical results by the 1ST set of signal settings on link-by-link basis

	McNETS		SAB		LCA	
Link No	Link Flows (in Veh/h)	PI (in Veh-h/h)	Link Flows (in Veh/h)	PI (in Veh-h/h)	Link Flows (in Veh/h)	PI (in Veh-h/h)
1	1061	1.57	979	1.49	1044	1.81
2	119	0.31	201	0.80	136	0.35
3	1061	1.81	979	1.51	1044	1.44
4	874	2.28	835	2.63	958	3.10
5	891	1.87	909	2.00	953	2.49
6	155	0.39	138	0.34	178	0.52
7	114	0.38	196	0.85	136	0.65
8	215	0.59	222	0.68	165	0.59
9	89	0.41	118	0.61	52	0.37
10	247	2.16	242	3.78	159	1.80
11	558	3.02	577	3.93	594	4.29
12	242	0.41	223	0.45	206	0.41
13	480	1.25	480	1.21	480	1.40
14	992	3.55	1010	5.78	1069	4.73
15	1002	2.69	1044	2.47	1005	1.77
16	893	1.80	920	1.61	748	2.13
17	210	2.62	190	2.73	131	1.24
18	142	0.50	91	0.37	135	0.69
19	397	1.60	370	2.29	545	2.45
20	1290	4.42	1290	4.16	1290	6.53
21	1114	2.29	1044	2.10	1177	2.46
22	1250	1.53	1250	1.57	1250	1.58
23	805	1.55	827	2.68	602	2.42
Total		39.00		46.04		45.22

To extend the application of McNETS algorithm for finding better locally optimal solutions, improvements can be made on the local optimum found by the SAB and LCA by conducting the global search heuristic via searching the feasible region widely and locating better local optimal points in other neighborhoods. Results for this test have been reported in Table 10, where the initial values of the PI for the local optima obtained by the SAB and LCA have been decreased by carrying out the global search heuristic followed by performing the locally optimal searches to find better local optimal points until the changes in the values of PI for successive iterations are less than the predetermined threshold. As it is seen in Table 10, by the first set of signal settings, the new locally optimum found by the McNETS following the result of the SAB is slightly better than the one found by the McNETS originally, and similar results can be shown by the second signal settings for LCA. The other two are slightly less good but all four were within a range of less than 3 per cent.

Table 9. Numerical Results by the 2ND set of signal settings on link-by-link basis

Link No	McNETS Link Flows (in Veh/h)	McNETS PI (in Veh-h/h)	SAB Link Flows (in Veh/h)	SAB PI (in Veh-h/h)	LCA Link Flows (in Veh/h)	LCA PI (in Veh-h/h)
1	1033	1.44	953	1.42	880	1.20
2	147	0.39	227	0.61	300	0.69
3	1033	1.61	953	1.78	880	1.66
4	963	2.60	887	2.38	864	2.14
5	994	2.10	919	2.07	841	1.92
6	148	0.36	171	0.41	249	0.71
7	149	0.50	233	0.77	400	1.09
8	123	0.31	124	0.33	142	0.36
9	125	0.65	178	0.88	84	0.54
10	177	1.80	204	2.36	251	3.13
11	615	3.00	644	4.67	587	1.43
12	185	0.25	156	0.28	213	1.10
13	480	1.13	480	1.11	480	1.30
14	1084	4.26	1013	3.67	1012	3.19
15	1051	3.25	970	3.28	1016	3.64
16	985	1.46	864	2.37	860	2.82
17	145	2.17	191	3.48	238	2.93
18	120	0.44	180	0.60	258	0.67
19	306	1.31	426	1.67	430	1.19
20	1290	5.08	1290	5.58	1290	5.92
21	1145	1.58	1131	2.83	936	2.60
22	1250	1.22	1250	1.90	1250	3.07
23	966	2.21	935	2.03	976	2.61
Total		39.12		46.48		45.91

Table 10. Improvements in pi values (in veh-h/h) on SAB and LCA

Iteration Number	1st Set of Signal Settings SAB	1st Set of Signal Settings LCA	2nd Set of Signal Settings SAB	2nd Set of Signal Settings LCA
1	46.04	45.22	46.48	45.91
2	44.44	44.40	44.44	42.63
3	40.24	41.28	40.24	42.45
4	38.80	39.79	40.01	39.33
5				39.10

The implementations for carrying out the computational efforts on MC, LCA, SAB and McNETS have been conducted on SUN SPARC Ultra II workstation under operating system Unix SunOS 5.5.1 using C++ compiler gnu g++ 2.8.1 and C++ software library LEDA-R [8]. The stopping criterion for these solutions is set when the relative difference in the performance index value between the consecutive iterations less than 0.15%. Computational efforts for complete run of McNETS did not exceed 1 minute of CPU time.

5. Conclusion

In this paper, we presented a combined optimal design approach integrated with parallel tangents technique (McNETS) for delay-minimizing signal setting concurrent network flow problem. Numerical calculations for McNETS have been conducted in comparison with previous optimization algorithms for this problem. Two example road networks have been illustrated for showing the effectiveness of McNETS in improving on local optima found by other algorithms. Represented at a link-by-link level, changes in the values of the performance index can be easily observed to help to understand how these algorithms proceed. Improvements on the local optima found by SAB and by LCA can be made efficiently by using McNETS starting with the offset changes step and then using the local optimization steps to locate the better local optimal points within the corresponding neighborhoods.

It is envisaged to test McNETS on a wide range of general road networks. Further investigations will be made for the signal settings problem when integrated with a traffic model where vehicular behavior and queue set back are taken into account.

Acknowledgements

Thanks go to Taiwan National Science Council via grant NSC 96-2416-H-259-010-MY2.

References

[1] Abdulaal, M. & LeBlanc, L.J. (1979). Continuous equilibrium network design models. *Transportation Research,* **13B**, 19-32.

[2] Allsop, R. E. & Charlesworth, J. A. (1977). Traffic in a signal-controlled road network: an example of different signal timings inducing different routeings. *Traffic Engineering Control*, **18**, 262-264.

[3] Ban, J. X., Liu, H.X., Ferris, M. C. & Ran, B. (2006). A general MPCC model and its solution algorithm for continuous network design problem, *Mathematical and Computer Modelling*, **43**, 493-505.

[4]. Ceylan, H. & Bell, M.G.H. (2004). Traffic signal timing optimization based on genetic algorithm approach, including drivers routing, *Transportation Research Part B*, **38**, 329-342.

[5] Chiou, S-W. (2003). TRANSYT derivatives for area traffic control optimization with network equilibrium flows. *Transportation Research Part B*, **37**, 263-290.

[6] Friesz, T. L., Tobin, R. L., Cho, H-L & Mehta, N.J. (1990). Sensitivity analysis based algorithms for mathematical programs with variational inequality constraints. *Mathematical Programming*, **48**, 265-284.

[7] Heydecker, B. G. & Khoo, T. K. (1990). The equilibrium network design problem. *Proceedings of AIRO'90 Conference on Models and Methods for Decision Support,* Sorrento, pp. 587-602.

[8] Mehlhorn, K., Naher, S. & Uhrig, C. (1999). *The LEDA User Manual. Version 3.8.* Saarbrucken, Max-Planck-Institut fur Informatik.

[9] Suh, S. & Kim, T. J. (1992). Solving nonlinear bilevel programming models of the equilibrium network design problem: a comparative review. *Annals of Operations Research*, **34**, 203-218.

[10] Vincent, R. A., Mitchell, A. I. & Robertson, D. I. (1980). *User guide to TRANSYT*, version 8. TRRL Report, LR888, Crowthorne, Transport and Road Research Laboratory.

[11] Wong, S.C. (1995). Derivatives of the performance index for the traffic model from TRANSYT. *Transportation Research Part B*, **29**, 303-327.

[12] Yang, H. & Bell, M. G. H. (1998). Models and algorithms for road network design: a review and some new developments. *Transport Reviews*, **18**, 257-278.

[13] Yang, H. & Yagar, S. (1995). Traffic assignment and signal control in saturated road networks. *Transportation Research Part A*, **29**, 125-139.

INDEX

A

abdomen, 210
abortion, 172
access, vii, ix, 4, 11, 23, 40, 41, 42, 43, 46, 49, 50, 51, 53, 56, 57, 59, 60, 120, 122, 149, 150, 151, 152, 153, 161, 163, 168, 174, 195, 209
accounting, 170, 174
accuracy, 107, 108, 172
activation, 12, 94, 95, 97, 98, 101, 188, 207
adaptation, viii, 93, 94, 96, 102, 109, 191
adenine, 106
adjustment, 99, 103, 187, 188, 189, 195
administration, 207
agent, 1, 4, 122, 128, 150, 153, 179, 180
Alaska, 183
algorithm, vii, viii, x, 2, 16, 23, 57, 59, 67, 68, 69, 70, 71, 72, 74, 75, 79, 81, 82, 83, 84, 86, 87, 89, 90, 91, 92, 94, 98, 99, 100, 105, 106, 110, 133, 134, 137, 138, 139, 171, 173, 181, 196, 197, 201, 206, 207, 209, 210, 211, 213, 214, 215, 218, 219, 230, 232
alternative, ix, 115, 126, 165, 172, 214, 229
AMD, 26
AMS, 39, 113
Amsterdam, 183
AN, 113, 149, 205
anatomy, 205
argument, 9, 22, 99, 100
artificial intelligence, 93, 94, 97
assignment, 200, 214, 215, 219, 226, 233
assumptions, 16, 69, 75, 82, 176
asymptotic, viii, 67, 68, 69, 70, 71, 74, 75, 78, 79, 83, 89, 104
attachment, 9
attention, vii, 2, 39, 166, 170
Australia, 165
Austria, 182, 205
authentication, ix, 149, 150, 153, 161
availability, 14, 23, 167, 169, 177, 180, 211
avoidance, 134, 137
awareness, 115, 116

B

background information, 114
bandwidth, 138, 140, 141, 142, 143, 144, 168, 176, 200
barriers, 55, 57, 62
behavior, ix, x, 4, 8, 42, 58, 69, 96, 104, 109, 134, 149, 152, 161, 185, 194, 199, 200, 214, 232
Beijing, 204
benchmarking, 126
benchmarks, ix, 113, 126, 134
benefits, 134, 137, 141, 189
bias, 95, 98, 103
binding(s), 115, 118, 122, 123, 124, 126, 220
bioinformatics, ix, 165, 167, 175
blocks, 59
BoT, ix, 165, 166, 167, 169, 170, 171, 172, 173, 175, 178, 180, 181
bounds, 2, 73, 79, 80, 90, 91, 92
branching, 86, 87
Brazil, 39
buffer, 2, 5, 8, 9, 10, 15, 16, 18, 19, 20, 22, 23, 26, 29, 30, 59

C

C++, 10, 115, 128, 130, 131, 181, 190, 192, 193, 194, 203, 204, 206, 231
calculus, ix, 94, 99, 149, 150, 151, 153, 162, 163, 164
California, 108, 118, 123, 133
Canada, 39, 129, 203, 204

Index

Caravela, vii, 1, 2, 3, 5, 7, 9, 10, 11, 12, 13, 14, 15, 16, 17, 18, 19, 20, 21, 22, 23, 24, 25, 26, 27, 28, 29, 30, 31, 33, 34, 35, 37
case study, 30
category a, 125
CCR, 145
cell, 36
certainty, 93, 94, 97, 109, 110, 111
CFRule, viii, 93, 94, 96, 97, 98, 99, 100, 101, 102, 103, 104, 105, 106, 107, 108, 109
changing environment, 121
channels, 95, 96, 98, 101, 102, 104, 107, 108, 109, 137, 138, 139, 141, 145
charm, 130
Chicago, 128
children, 13
China, 184, 204
Chinese, 63
classes, 15, 45, 114, 117, 118, 119, 120, 122, 123, 125, 180
classification, 90, 110, 114, 124, 127
clients, 117, 178, 180, 209
closure, 47
clustering, 196, 197, 200, 201, 202
clusters, 114, 120, 122, 127, 128, 130, 165, 172, 196, 197
codes, 126, 186
coding, 25
coefficient of variation, 86, 87, 88
cognitive process, 93
coherence, vii, 39, 40, 41, 51, 52, 53, 54, 55, 56, 59, 60, 61, 62, 63, 64, 118
commodity, vii, 1, 2, 5, 34
communication, ix, 4, 18, 29, 39, 53, 54, 68, 85, 115, 116, 117, 118, 120, 121, 122, 123, 124, 125, 130, 133, 134, 137, 145, 166, 167, 176, 177, 207, 211
communication overhead, 118, 125
community, 207
compatibility, 7, 23, 114, 120, 122
compilation, 8, 123, 186, 191, 192, 201
compiler, 8, 11, 59, 119, 120, 123, 130, 189, 190, 191, 192, 193, 194, 200, 202, 203, 204, 231
complementarity, 217
complexity, 10, 64, 90, 94, 106, 109, 124, 171, 196, 210
components, 2, 43, 118, 120, 177, 179, 180, 192, 209, 214
composition, 192
computation, 2, 3, 5, 7, 10, 11, 12, 15, 26, 27, 28, 31, 34, 35, 37, 54, 68, 69, 71, 80, 81, 84, 85, 86, 115, 125, 133, 151, 166, 167, 176, 177, 180, 189, 206, 207, 210, 211, 214, 222, 226
Computational Fluid Dynamics, 202

computational grid, 114, 182, 184
computed tomography, 206, 211
computer software, 206
computers, 2, 35, 40, 120, 166, 178, 179, 206, 209, 210
computing, vii, viii, ix, 1, 2, 3, 4, 5, 10, 13, 14, 16, 18, 29, 35, 37, 52, 62, 68, 89, 93, 96, 98, 110, 117, 118, 123, 127, 129, 130, 134, 165, 166, 167, 169, 170, 172, 175, 177, 178, 179, 180, 181, 182, 184, 205, 206, 207, 209, 211
concentrates, 53
concurrency, 119, 128
confidence, 195
configuration, 142, 222
Congestion, 147
consensus, 107
constraints, viii, 67, 68, 69, 70, 71, 80, 81, 90, 91, 102, 176, 213, 216, 218, 220, 232
construction, 94, 98
consumption, 194
control, ix, 2, 5, 7, 9, 10, 42, 53, 106, 124, 142, 145, 149, 150, 152, 163, 167, 187, 188, 190, 214, 232, 233
convergence, viii, 93, 94, 96, 102, 104, 105, 107, 109
costs, 68, 115
coupling, 193
covering, 94
CPU, 2, 5, 7, 10, 21, 26, 30, 31, 32, 35, 180, 231
cross-validation, 105, 107, 108, 109
cycles, 136, 138, 139, 140, 141, 142, 143, 144
cytosine, 106

D

data analysis, 196
data distribution, 115
data mining, 94, 110, 196
data set, 106, 108, 196, 200
data structure, 12, 19, 20, 23, 24, 119
data transfer, 4, 167, 174, 175, 181
database, 108
data-mining, ix
decay, 104
decision trees, 94
decisions, 52, 137, 166, 171, 173, 174, 175, 181
decomposition, 31, 32, 33, 34
definition, 22, 42, 45, 49, 69, 83, 99, 155, 162, 163, 169, 192, 222, 224
degradation, 135, 137, 138, 139, 141, 145
degrees of freedom, 102
demand, x, 5, 207, 213, 216, 225
denoising, 31
derivatives, 214, 217, 218, 219, 232

designers, 5
detection, 31, 206
diabetes, 96
dimensionality, 95, 106, 107
directives, 118, 190, 191, 192, 195
discipline, 94
distributed applications, viii, 113, 114, 115, 117, 122, 210
distributed computing, vii, ix, 1, 2, 3, 10, 34, 35, 37, 68, 113, 125, 177, 182
distributed memory, 41
Distributed Shared Memory (DSM), vii, 39, 40, 41, 42, 43, 44, 45, 46, 47, 49, 50, 51, 52, 53, 54, 55, 56, 57, 59, 60, 61, 62, 63, 64, 65, 118, 121, 123, 124
distribution, viii, 67, 70, 78, 79, 80, 85, 86, 87, 88, 89, 102, 115, 117, 119, 120, 122, 134, 135, 139, 177, 189, 194, 197, 206
diversity, 124, 167
DNA, viii, 93, 106, 107, 108, 109
draft, 115, 129
duplication, 170, 172, 175
duration, 214, 215, 219, 220, 226

E

earth, 35
Einstein, 166, 167, 182
emission, 206, 211
encoding, 94, 98
encryption, 4
energy, 165
environment, vii, ix, 2, 3, 4, 7, 10, 13, 14, 16, 18, 22, 34, 37, 39, 44, 54, 113, 114, 115, 116, 117, 118, 119, 120, 123, 124, 125, 126, 127, 129, 133, 134, 187, 188, 189, 190, 193, 197, 210, 211
equality, 218
equilibrium, 177, 213, 214, 215, 216, 217, 220, 226, 229, 232, 233
equipment, x, 205, 210
execution, vii, viii, 1, 2, 3, 4, 5, 7, 9, 11, 12, 13, 14, 15, 16, 17, 18, 20, 21, 22, 23, 25, 26, 27, 28, 29, 34, 35, 37, 44, 45, 46, 47, 48, 49, 50, 51, 52, 53, 54, 55, 58, 64, 67, 68, 69, 70, 72, 73, 74, 75, 76, 77, 81, 82, 83, 86, 87, 88, 89, 91, 92, 117, 120, 121, 123, 128, 154, 167, 170, 174, 176, 180, 188, 191, 192, 193, 194, 195
exploitation, 170
extraction, 31, 94, 97, 105, 106, 107, 110

F

failure, 41, 54, 55, 169, 172
fairness, 169, 170, 171, 176
family, 48, 49, 80, 81, 180, 190
fault tolerance, vii, 39, 41, 54, 60, 61, 127, 170, 172
feedback, 3, 10, 15, 16, 17, 27, 29, 30, 34
FFT, 37
filters, 26
firewalls, ix, 149, 150
flexibility, 5, 17, 114, 116, 125, 126
float, 27, 33
floating, 5, 27, 167
focusing, 2, 5, 61
forecasting, 182
fragmentation, 71, 75
France, 64, 203
freedom, 139, 190
funding, 145

G

game theory, 166
garbage, 53, 54, 57
general knowledge, 93
generalization, 96, 100
generation, 17, 35, 57, 65, 136, 138, 177
genetic algorithms, 94
Georgia, 63, 64
Germany, 129, 183, 184, 202, 203
GIS, 172
gland, 209, 210
globus, 36, 182, 183
GLUT, 8, 35
goals, 3, 119
grants, 145
graph, viii, 67, 68, 71, 80, 81, 82, 83, 84, 86, 87, 88, 89, 109, 151, 153, 154
graphics processing units (GPUs), vii, 1, 2, 3, 5, 7, 8, 10, 15, 16, 18, 20, 21, 29, 30, 34, 35, 37
Greece, 61, 185
grid computing, ix, 165, 166, 178
grid environment, 166, 171, 172, 180, 182
grids, ix, 165, 166, 167, 170, 172, 175, 177, 178, 181
groups, ix, 70, 72, 73, 115, 119, 122, 149, 150, 151, 153, 162, 163, 175, 192, 216, 222, 223, 229
growth, 2
guanine, 106

H

Haifa, 37, 128

handoff, 194
hardness, ix, 165, 166
harmonic system partitioning scheme, viii, 67, 70, 71, 72, 74, 89, 91
Hawaii, 130
height, 70, 86, 87
hepatitis, viii, 93, 106, 108, 109
hepatitis d, 106
heterogeneity, ix, 124, 125, 165
heterogeneous systems, viii, ix, 113, 117, 123, 127, 128
Hm, vii, viii, 67, 70, 71, 72, 73, 74, 75, 76, 77, 78, 79, 80, 81, 83, 84, 89
host, 4, 9, 10, 15, 16, 21, 22, 23, 29, 30, 150, 151, 168, 169, 173, 174, 175, 206, 209
hot spots, 134
HPC, 184
Hurst parameter, 135, 136, 137, 139
hybrid, 40, 45, 49, 64, 122, 189, 192
hypercube, 56, 64
hypothesis, 52, 94, 102
hypothesis test, 102

I

identification, 24
illusion, 41, 117, 118
images, 210
imaging, 205
imaging techniques, 205
implementation, vii, ix, x, 3, 4, 11, 15, 20, 23, 30, 31, 34, 36, 37, 39, 40, 43, 44, 56, 62, 71, 113, 114, 115, 116, 117, 118, 119, 122, 123, 124, 125, 126, 127, 130, 149, 162, 185, 186, 187, 188, 189, 190, 191, 192, 193, 195, 196, 200, 201, 202, 209, 210, 211, 231
in situ, 185
incidence, 216
inclusion, 163
independence, viii, 113, 122, 125, 127
independent variable, 53
indication, 85
indices, 24, 220
induction, 110, 111
inequality, 232
infancy, 201
information exchange, 116, 125
information sharing, 119
infrastructure, 118, 122, 124, 125, 127, 128, 169, 186, 192
inheritance, 128
initiation, 169
insight, 176

institutions, 60
instruction, 8, 42, 45, 55
integration, 193
integrity, 118
interaction(s), vii, 54, 164, 188
interface, 2, 7, 8, 10, 11, 14, 15, 16, 19, 22, 23, 28, 29, 34, 35, 36, 37, 41, 59, 114, 116, 117, 119, 122, 125, 126, 129, 130, 181, 191, 192, 193, 194, 206
internet, 117
interoperability, 119
interval, 46, 56, 72, 73, 77, 209
intervention, 209
intravenously, 206
Israel, 37
iteration, 17, 18, 19, 23, 24, 25, 27, 30, 99, 102

J

Japan, 149, 202, 203
Java, viii, ix, x, 4, 36, 113, 114, 115, 116, 117, 118, 119, 120, 121, 122, 123, 124, 125, 126, 127, 128, 129, 130, 131, 180, 184, 205, 206, 207, 209, 211, 212
Java interface, 128
JavaSpaces, x, 205, 206, 207, 209, 210, 211
Jini, x, 205, 206, 207, 208, 209, 210, 211
jobs, 90, 117, 168, 170, 171, 172, 180

K

K^+, 81
kernel, 11, 27, 33, 55, 94, 118, 186, 189, 191, 193, 195, 200, 202

L

Lagrange multipliers, 217, 219, 220
LAN, 133, 145, 146, 150, 152, 168
language, viii, x, 7, 8, 10, 20, 35, 43, 59, 113, 115, 117, 118, 119, 120, 123, 124, 125, 191, 192, 205, 206
latency, 120, 134, 138, 145
LCA, 214, 221, 222, 225, 226, 227, 228, 229, 230, 231, 232
lead, 40, 49, 187
learning, viii, 93, 94, 95, 96, 99, 100, 102, 104, 105, 106, 107, 109, 110, 111, 209
learning behavior, 109
lens, 206
limitation, 13, 71, 125, 188
linear function, 100

linear programming, 166, 176, 180
links, 126, 137, 169, 214, 215, 222, 225, 229
literature, 41, 42, 45, 51, 54, 60, 68, 69, 107, 109, 166
LLHm, viii, 67, 68, 71, 80, 81, 82, 83, 84, 86, 87, 88, 89
load balance, 186
local area network (LAN), ix, 134
location, 9, 12, 14, 43, 44, 45, 174
logging, 54, 55
Los Angeles, 133

MPI, 4, 35, 37, 115, 116, 117, 118, 119, 122, 123, 124, 125, 126, 128, 129, 130, 131, 166, 181
multi-channel regression-based optimization, viii, 93, 100, 109
multicomputers, 63, 68, 71, 91
multidimensional, 163
multiple nodes, 119
multiple regression, 111
multiplication, 20
multiplier, 215, 216, 217, 218, 219, 220, 221
multi-threading, 127

M

machine learning, viii, 93, 94, 108, 109, 110
management, ix, 9, 11, 14, 15, 23, 42, 52, 93, 104, 115, 149, 194
mapping, 22, 27, 28, 42, 43, 55, 56, 122, 175
market, 2, 7, 186
Massachusetts, 184, 211
matrix, ix, 10, 28, 30, 31, 32, 133, 134, 206, 209, 216, 217, 218, 219, 220
measurement, 195
measures, 108, 127, 145
medicine, 111, 205, 206, 207
membership, 150, 161
memory, vii, 2, 7, 9, 10, 11, 12, 13, 15, 21, 23, 26, 29, 30, 39, 40, 41, 42, 44, 45, 46, 47, 48, 49, 50, 51, 52, 54, 55, 57, 59, 60, 61, 62, 63, 64, 65, 68, 117, 118, 119, 120, 121, 124, 168, 185, 189, 194, 195, 200, 203
memory capacity, 30
message passing, 1, 4, 36, 37, 39, 56, 122, 130, 181
messages, 53, 54, 59, 115, 137, 139, 152, 153
metapipeline, vii
Mexico, 131, 147, 202
microbenchmarks, x, 185, 186, 194, 195, 196, 198, 202
Microsoft, 8, 178, 184, 190, 193
migration, 12, 55, 58, 117, 120, 121, 123, 172
mining, 165, 175
MIT, 110, 111, 181
mobile phone, 178
modeling, 35, 150
models, viii, ix, 2, 3, 12, 13, 14, 15, 16, 17, 18, 19, 20, 22, 24, 25, 27, 34, 40, 44, 45, 47, 49, 51, 52, 60, 61, 62, 64, 65, 113, 114, 115, 116, 122, 127, 134, 136, 145, 151, 167, 171, 177, 180, 207, 211, 232, 233
modules, 55, 119
molecular biology, 107
Monte Carlo, 182
motivation, 47

N

Nash equilibrium, 177
National Research Council, 90
National Science Foundation, 110, 127
Nebraska, 113, 116, 123, 127
Netherlands, 183
NetSolve, 177
network(ing), vii, ix, x, 1, 4, 12, 13, 16, 34, 59, 68, 71, 93, 94, 95, 98, 100, 109, 117, 129, 133, 134, 135, 137, 138, 139, 140, 141, 142, 143, 144, 145, 146, 150, 151, 169, 172, 176, 182, 184, 206, 207, 210, 211, 213, 214, 215, 218, 221, 222, 225, 226, 227, 228, 229, 232, 233
neural network(s), viii, 93, 94, 95, 96, 98, 104, 106, 110, 111, 209
New York, 67, 90, 110, 111, 182, 183
next generation, 2
nodes, 42, 43, 44, 56, 57, 58, 59, 80, 81, 119, 120, 123, 133, 137, 139, 142, 154, 155, 159
noise, 103, 104, 206
nonlinear systems, 85
non-uniformity(ies), ix, 133, 134, 139, 145
Norway, 61
nucleotides, 106
numerical analysis, 226
numerical computations, 221

O

obligation, 18
observations, 7, 86, 87, 94, 141
one dimension, 68
OpenMP, ix, x, 166, 181, 185, 186, 187, 188, 189, 190, 191, 192, 193, 194, 195, 196, 197, 198, 199, 200, 201, 202, 203, 204
operating system, 42, 55, 63, 65, 149, 179, 180, 189, 206, 231
operations research, 68
operator, 110, 162, 217

optimal performance, 105
optimization, vii, viii, x, 1, 2, 3, 9, 11, 20, 26, 29, 34, 35, 37, 93, 94, 98, 100, 109, 111, 120, 145, 192, 213, 214, 219, 229, 232
optimization method, 37, 145
Oregon, 181, 203
organ, 205, 206
organization(s), ix, 9, 17, 27, 33, 116, 149, 150, 151, 177
orientation, 115, 206
Origin-Destination, 225
Ottawa, 39, 204
overload, 170, 176
ownership, 43

P

parallel algorithm, 91, 170, 183, 186
parallel implementation, 207, 209, 210, 211
parallel processing, ix, x, 64, 124, 133, 134, 137, 166, 181, 182, 205
parallelism, ix, x, 10, 81, 84, 86, 119, 185, 186, 187, 188, 189, 190, 191, 192, 193, 194, 195, 196, 197, 200, 201, 202, 204
parallelization, ix, 113, 115, 118, 119, 121, 123, 124, 125, 126, 127, 128, 186, 189, 190, 192, 196, 203, 204
parameter, viii, 11, 14, 23, 67, 71, 81, 94, 109, 135, 136, 138, 182
parents, 159
Pareto, 135, 138
Paris, 181
partial differential equations, 85
partition, 72, 86, 107, 196
passive, 121
password, 161
PDAs, 178
peers, 2, 4
performance, vii, viii, ix, x, 2, 3, 5, 7, 10, 11, 15, 16, 20, 22, 23, 26, 29, 30, 31, 32, 34, 35, 36, 37, 39, 40, 43, 44, 49, 50, 63, 67, 68, 69, 70, 71, 72, 74, 75, 78, 79, 80, 81, 82, 83, 84, 86, 89, 90, 91, 94, 96, 98, 100, 106, 108, 113, 115, 120, 125, 126, 127, 128, 129, 133, 134, 135, 136, 137, 138, 139, 141, 142, 145, 165, 166, 169, 170, 171, 172, 173, 174, 175, 177, 180, 181, 182, 185, 186, 189, 194, 197, 200, 202, 211, 213, 214, 215, 219, 220, 225, 226, 227, 231, 232, 233
permit, 52
personal, x, 2, 5, 34, 186, 205, 209
personal computers, 2, 5, 34
PET, 211
photons, 206
physics, ix, 165
pitch, 9, 23
Poisson distribution, 139
pools, 178
population, 187
portability, viii, 20, 54, 113, 115, 118, 120, 122, 124, 125, 126, 127
ports, 16, 17, 19, 20, 24, 25, 35
Portugal, 1
power, vii, 1, 2, 5, 34, 71, 89, 114, 120, 163, 176, 179, 180
prediction, viii, 93, 107, 108, 109, 172
prior knowledge, 108
probability, 69, 75, 76, 79, 82, 83, 94, 135, 137, 177
probability density function, 75
probability distribution, 69, 75, 79, 83, 135, 177
processor allocation strategy, viii, 67, 70, 71
production, 110, 186
prognosis, viii, 93, 108, 109, 206
program, vii, 4, 5, 7, 8, 9, 10, 11, 12, 14, 20, 22, 26, 27, 33, 34, 35, 40, 44, 45, 46, 47, 48, 51, 55, 64, 91, 120, 121, 122, 123, 185, 187, 189, 190, 191, 194
programmability, 5, 26
programming, vii, viii, ix, x, 2, 5, 7, 8, 10, 14, 23, 34, 36, 37, 39, 40, 41, 43, 44, 50, 51, 52, 57, 59, 62, 63, 94, 113, 114, 115, 116, 117, 118, 119, 121, 122, 125, 127, 130, 149, 176, 181, 185, 187, 190, 194, 205, 206, 207, 209, 214, 233
programming languages, 113, 115, 149
prokaryotes, 107
proliferation, 210
promoter, viii, 93, 106, 107, 108, 109
promoter region, 106
propagation, 50, 52, 110, 111, 209
protocol(s), vii, ix, 39, 41, 50, 52, 53, 54, 55, 56, 57, 59, 60, 61, 62, 63, 119, 123, 127, 149, 153, 176, 208
prototype, 56, 59, 63, 119, 121, 128
pruning, 106, 107, 197
psychology, 93
PVM, 116, 118, 119, 123, 166, 181

Q

QoS, 170
query, 14

R

radioactive tracer, 206
radionuclides, 206

Index

radiopharmaceuticals, 205
range, viii, 67, 70, 72, 75, 78, 79, 84, 86, 87, 88, 89, 101, 105, 135, 177, 230, 232
rash, 179
reasoning, 110, 111
recognition, viii, 93, 109, 113
reconstruction, x, 205, 206, 207, 209, 210, 211
recovery, 41, 54, 55, 61, 62, 63, 65, 137
recursion, 192
reduction, 23, 54, 106, 156, 163, 172
reflection, 114
regression, 93, 100, 101
regression analysis, 100, 101
relational database, 152
relationship(s), 137, 163, 171
relaxation, 85, 192
reliability, 127
repetitions, 85, 195
replication, 40, 59, 65, 158, 159, 163, 172, 173, 174
repressor, 110
resolution, 135, 210
resource management, 4, 184
resources, vii, ix, 1, 2, 3, 4, 5, 7, 8, 10, 11, 12, 14, 15, 19, 20, 25, 29, 34, 114, 117, 118, 121, 122, 133, 134, 137, 141, 165, 166, 167, 168, 169, 170, 171, 172, 173, 174, 175, 176, 177, 178, 180, 181, 185, 186, 207
response time, 92, 169
restructuring, 121, 128
returns, 13, 23, 24, 43, 59, 121, 177, 178
rice, 57
robustness, 215, 221
rotations, 5
routing, ix, 13, 14, 133, 134, 137, 138, 139, 140, 141, 142, 143, 144, 145, 232
rule discovery, viii, 93, 95, 109, 110
runtime libraries, 191

S

SA, 173, 174, 175, 183
safety, 119
sample, 96, 105, 106
sampling, 135
saturation, 134, 139, 216
scalability, ix, 2, 126, 128, 165, 166, 170, 186, 200, 202
scalable, x, 62, 64, 127, 181, 185
scatter, 207, 210
scheduling, vii, viii, ix, 3, 67, 68, 69, 70, 71, 72, 75, 81, 83, 84, 87, 89, 90, 91, 92, 123, 165, 166, 167, 169, 170, 171, 172, 173, 174, 175, 176, 177, 178, 179, 180, 181, 182, 184, 195, 199, 200

science, ix, 68, 165, 166, 184
scientific computing, 118
search(es), x, 85, 94, 105, 106, 109, 182, 211, 213, 215, 218, 219, 220, 221, 230
search engine, 211
searching, 230
security, ix, 2, 4, 5, 10, 13, 113, 117, 126, 127
selecting, 193
self-organization, 102
self-similarity, 134, 135, 136, 137, 139, 145
semantics, 97, 151
sensitivity, 214, 218, 226, 227
sequencing, vii, 91
series, 84, 117, 207
sharing, 52, 53, 64, 119, 167, 168, 174, 175, 179, 180, 207
signals, 28
similarity, 72, 136, 139, 180
simulation, x, 102, 110, 134, 138, 166, 182, 205
single photon emission computerized tomography (SPECT), x, 205, 206, 207, 209, 210, 212
sites, 20, 57, 151, 168, 169, 180
smoothing, 85
software, x, 1, 7, 8, 12, 40, 42, 43, 51, 57, 62, 63, 64, 65, 114, 122, 179, 180, 189, 205, 206, 207, 209, 210, 211, 231
sounds, 109
Spain, 203
SSI, 120, 124
stability, 103
stages, 19, 20, 24, 25, 26
standard deviation, 195, 196
starvation, 134
statistical analysis, 146
statistics, 43, 76, 136
Stochastic, 91, 92, 146
storage, 54, 165, 168, 174
strategies, 41, 43, 54, 61, 69, 102, 172
substitution, 155
supercomputers, ix, 165
supply, 137
Sweden, 202, 203, 204
switching, 134, 145
Switzerland, 37
synchronization, 40, 45, 49, 50, 51, 52, 55, 56, 57, 68, 85, 115, 118, 121, 191, 195, 197
systems, vii, ix, x, 2, 5, 7, 39, 40, 41, 42, 43, 44, 46, 47, 49, 50, 51, 53, 54, 55, 60, 61, 62, 63, 64, 67, 68, 69, 71, 89, 90, 108, 114, 116, 117, 118, 120, 121, 122, 123, 124, 125, 126, 127, 129, 130, 133, 134, 136, 145, 149, 153, 154, 155, 156, 163, 165, 166, 172, 177, 181, 185, 186, 187, 188, 189, 190, 191, 192, 201, 202, 206

T

Taiwan, 213, 232
targets, 14, 26, 102
task graphs, viii, 67, 71, 83, 84, 88, 89
taxonomy, ix, 165, 166, 171, 180
TCP, 123, 146, 207, 208
technology, 126, 127, 180, 184, 206, 207, 210, 211
test data, 102, 107
theory, viii, 93, 94, 96, 98, 102, 108, 109, 110
threshold, viii, 93, 105, 106, 107, 230
thymine, 106
time periods, 176
time series, 136
time use, 170, 216
timing, 91, 214, 232
titanium, 131
Tokyo, 203
topology, 68, 71
torus, 136, 137
trade, 126
trade-off, 126
traffic, ix, x, 133, 134, 135, 136, 137, 138, 139, 140, 141, 142, 143, 144, 145, 146, 200, 213, 214, 219, 222, 229, 232, 233
training, viii, 93, 96, 98, 99, 100, 102, 103, 104, 105, 106, 107, 111
transcription, 106
transformations, 5, 192
translation, 8, 192
transmission, 139
transparency, 42, 43
trees, 176
trend, vii, 1
trial, 102
triggers, 12
trust, 4
twins, 53

U

UN, 149
uncertainty, 93, 94, 103, 104
uniform, viii, 2, 7, 15, 16, 22, 23, 33, 34, 37, 45, 49, 64, 67, 78, 80, 86, 87, 88, 135, 137, 138, 139, 141, 142, 145, 177
universities, 149, 177
users, viii, x, 2, 3, 4, 57, 63, 70, 113, 117, 119, 122, 125, 126, 127, 150, 151, 167, 168, 170, 172, 176, 178, 209, 213

V

validation, 102, 107, 109
validity, 107
values, 20, 27, 40, 42, 50, 80, 85, 100, 103, 104, 105, 106, 107, 152, 173, 174, 188, 196, 215, 216, 220, 223, 225, 226, 227, 229, 230, 231, 232
variability, 135, 146
variable(s), viii, 8, 42, 51, 57, 67, 69, 70, 75, 76, 78, 79, 80, 84, 89, 97, 101, 102, 153, 154, 155, 162, 187, 188, 189, 190, 193, 197, 214, 215
variance, viii, 67, 70, 75, 76, 89, 136, 139
variation, 47, 75
vector, 56, 57, 95, 96, 98, 103, 107, 215, 216, 218, 221
vehicles, 215
Virginia, 123, 129
virtual channels, ix, 133, 134, 137, 138, 139, 141, 142
virus, 4
visualization, 5

W

Washington, 130, 204
Wavelet Transform, 31
web, 4, 178
web service, 178
websites, 150
Wisconsin, 61, 64, 183
workers, 13, 180, 209, 210, 211
workload, 167, 175
workstation, 176, 231
wormhole routing, 145
writing, 8, 43, 114, 116, 210

X

XML, 20, 22, 27, 28, 121, 184

Y

yield, 99